Refounding Democracy through Intersectional Activism

In the series *Intersectionality*, edited by Julia Jordan-Zachery, Celeste Montoya, and Anna Sampaio

WENDY SARVASY

Refounding Democracy through Intersectional Activism

How Progressive Era Feminists Redefined Who We Are, and What It Means Today

TEMPLE UNIVERSITY PRESS

Philadelphia • *Rome* • *Tokyo*

TEMPLE UNIVERSITY PRESS
Philadelphia, Pennsylvania 19122
tupress.temple.edu

Material drawn from Wendy Sarvasy, "Militarized Occupations: Evolution of Women's
International League for Peace and Freedom's 1920s Intersectional Conversation," *New
Political Science* 37, no. 4 (2015): 476–493. © 2015 Caucus for a New Political Science,
reprinted by permission of Informa UK Limited, trading as Taylor & Francis Group,
www.tandfonline.com on behalf of Caucus for a New Political Science.

Library of Congress Cataloging-in-Publication Data

Names: Sarvasy, Wendy Joy, 1948– author.
Title: Refounding democracy through intersectional activism : how
   Progressive Era feminists redefined who we are, and what it means today
   / Wendy Sarvasy.
Other titles: Intersectionality.
Description: Philadelphia : Temple University Press, 2024. | Series:
   Intersectionality | Includes bibliographical references and index. |
   Summary: "Studies turn-of-the-twentieth-century social democratic
   feminist "refounders" and the conceptual and organizing tools they offer
   for a defense of democracy"— Provided by publisher.
Identifiers: LCCN 2023042554 (print) | LCCN 2023042555 (ebook) | ISBN
   9781439924242 (cloth) | ISBN 9781439924259 (paperback) | ISBN
   9781439924266 (pdf)
Subjects: LCSH: Women—Political activity—United States—History—19th
   century. | Women—Political activity—United States—History—20th
   century. | Women social reformers—United States—History—19th century.
   | Women social reformers—United States—History—20th century. |
   Feminists—United States—History—19th century. | Feminists—United
   States—History—20th century. | Feminism—United States—History—19th
   century. | Feminism—United States—History—20th century. |
   Intersectionality (Sociology)—Political aspects—United States.
Classification: LCC HQ1419 .S378 2024 (print) | LCC HQ1419 (ebook) | DDC
   305.42097309/034—dc23/eng/20240116
LC record available at https://lccn.loc.gov/2023042554
LC ebook record available at https://lccn.loc.gov/2023042555

9 8 7 6 5 4 3 2 1

*For women and girls around the world who are
interconnecting struggles to make a socially just,
caring, and climate-friendly future.*

Contents

Preface

In 1983, during a legislative hearing on the feminization of poverty, I formulated a question that set me on a path to writing this book. As an activist in the San Francisco Bay Area, I had participated in designing the California State Assembly hearings. I attended the one in San Francisco. The speakers included recipients of various governmental social programs, as well as academics, activists, and leaders of nongovernmental organizations. They presented the case for how and why the causes of women's poverty were different from the causes of men's poverty. In short, jobs alone were not the solution for women, because they had a range of care responsibilities. As I listened to the testimony, I gained an awareness of why well-funded social programs were absolutely necessary. I also concluded that uprooting poverty and advancing social justice for a diversity of women required a larger vision.[1] So I came out of the hearing with a new question: How do we reimagine the welfare state as deeply participatory and as a space for dismantling intersecting gender, race, and class structures of power?

I soon discovered that a subset of Progressive Era women reformers, or social democratic feminists had imagined and tried to actualize what I would later call a U.S. version of social democracy. While they proposed a bundle of new social policies, they also sought a political revolution that would finally include women as full citizens. They provided me with the material I needed to answer my new question and an older one. Several years before the hearing, I had been asked to create a university course on sexual politics. I quickly realized that I would not be satisfied by merely adding women to the curriculum. Therefore, I set out to discover different approaches to this initial question: How does women's entrance into public life transform them and public life?

To gain insights from the social democratic feminists, I applied a historicist method of interpretation. The strength of this method is that it demystifies the activity of political theorizing by placing theorists in their historical context. Relying on historians and primary sources, I aimed to show how the social democratic feminists developed new ideas in the midst of their political struggles among themselves and with men. Utilizing this method, I was able to break through the standard nonfeminist interpretations of the period that marginalized them and downplayed the transformative nature of their reimagining of democracy. It also allowed me to stake out a feminist alternative to the growing consensus on a maternalist framing of their project. I defended my alternative by foregrounding the contributions of two less powerful groups—African American and immigrant Jewish social democratic feminists.

As I worked to develop satisfying answers to the two questions, I evolved my method of interpretation. Because my aim was never to confine the social democratic feminists to their own period, I moved away from a strict historicist approach. While they educated me about the feminist origins of our welfare state, I strove to make them relevant for today. I turned to deepening my conceptual presentation of their work. In this methodological turn, I had been influenced by the power of Hannah Arendt's theorizing through conceptual distinctions. The social democratic feminists utilized concepts that I interpreted, such as cosmopolitanism and social democracy. In these cases, I strove to flesh out their meanings with implications for today. Other concepts, like social citizenship and refounding, I constructed and applied to them. In those cases, I formulated the concept in such as a way as to systematize their thoughts for contemporary readers.

Throughout this adventure in excavating the social democratic feminists, I had simply assumed that their political and economic struggles had led them to rethink concepts. My historicist method supported this assumption. For example, through detailed historical research on mothers' pensions, the precursor to our narrow welfare program for needy families, I gained an insight about how their struggles produced a new understanding of equality. They exposed the necessity to play with the tension between gender difference and gender neutrality to create new synthetic notions of equality. My insight came from reinterpreting the standard narrative.

According to historians, the Progressive Era feminists were divided on how to shape public policies to advance equality between women and men. Some supported the use of gender difference; others adhered to a gender-neutral stance. While this narrative acknowledged that some on each side sought a new synthesis, ultimately an "either/or" framing submerged that observation. Applying a "both/and" mode of thinking, I uncovered examples of how they created new synthetic understandings of equality as they formulated different versions of mothers' pension programs.[2] By ignoring how the social democratic feminists reconstructed a concept—gender equality— we missed their theoretical innovations and continuing relevance. Clearly, we are still trying to figure out how to reconcile gender difference and gender neutrality in our debates over public policies and interpretations of the U.S. Constitution.

So while I strove to show that the social democratic feminists retheorized concepts in the midst of struggles, I had not delineated a method that uncovered precisely how they turned their activism into new thinking. I became aware of this missing part as a result of a comment at a professional conference, where I presented a paper on care and a social notion of work. To develop the argument, I created a conversation among social democratic feminists. I included activists who had participated in garment worker strikes as well as traditional theorists. A colleague reacted to the paper by saying spontaneously that "a strike cannot talk to a book." I think he meant that political theorists interpret texts, while historians tell the stories of past labor struggles. The strikers belonged in a history paper. Since I relish complexity, I took up the challenge of deepening my method of interpretation so that I was able to demonstrate the relationship between activism and theorizing. By adding a whole new layer to this book project, I was able to return to a question that grabbed me when I was an undergraduate: How do activists and social movements produce new ways of seeing the world? To answer this question, I began to construct what I came to call a theory-activist dynamic.

After much searching, my breakthrough came when I finally absorbed the significance of the activist roots of intersectional analysis. According to an intersectional way of thinking, race, class, and gender structures of power are mutually constitutive. There is no hierarchy of oppressions. This way of thinking developed in the midst of the struggles of social movements. Specifically, activists who worked to combine social movements were forced to interconnect categories of analysis to further their social justice aims. For example, African American women had to convince both white women and African American men that anti-racism and anti-sexism were interconnected. They had to do new thinking to persuade each audience. In the process, they showed how building coalitions could produce new transformative analyses and theories. This intersectional method of connecting activism and theorizing perfectly fit the social democratic feminists.

Using my questions to shape my interpretation of the social democratic feminists led me to formulate the purpose of this book. The answers they provided revealed the originality of the social democratic feminists in deeds and in thinking. To capture their courage, the breadth of their activism, and their lasting significance, I decided to make explicit the conceptual container I put them in from the beginning. They were refounders of U.S. democracy. The purpose of the book would be to demonstrate this claim. Ultimately, I went in this direction because we need the boldest version of them to strengthen our case for refounding democracy today.

Acknowledgments

This work was supported by the Beatrice Bain Research Group, University of California, Berkeley.

With great joy, I want to acknowledge how appreciative I am for the colleagues, friends, and family who helped me complete this book. Because most of you played more than one role, I group you together: Eileen Boris, Michael K. Brown, Molly Cochran, Elsa Dias, Shelley Feldman, Marilyn Fischer, Judith Grant, Liza Gross, Julia Jordan-Zachery, Peter Kardas, Sherry Katz, Patrizia Longo, Brenda Miller, Lin Nelson, Paul Sarvasy, Birte Siim, Kathryn Kish Sklar, and Kay Yatabe. I turned to some of you for a sense that it mattered to make these brilliant women more visible in our national narratives. Those of you who provided me with scholarly suggestions for clarifying my arguments and concepts definitely improved the book. When I disagreed, the comments provoked me to think harder to defend my position. Through stimulating conversations, adventures of all kinds, lots of walks, and our shared fierce commitment to making a better world, many of you sustained my spirit in difficult times.

I thank Aaron Javsicas and his entire team at Temple University Press for making this book possible. From our first conversation, Aaron, you provided the support, patience, and guidance that I required. I also thank Julia Jordan-Zachery, Celeste Montoya, and Anna Sampaio, the *Intersectionality* series editors, and the two anonymous reviewers.

List of Abbreviations

ACWA	Amalgamated Clothing Workers of America
AFL	American Federation of Labor
IPL	Immigrants' Protective League
ICW	International Congress of Women
ICWDR	International Council of Women of the Darker Races
ILGWU	International Ladies' Garment Workers' Union
ILO	International Labor Organization
IWSA	International Woman Suffrage Alliance
LON	League of Nations
NAWSA	National American Woman Suffrage Association
NAACP	National Association for the Advancement of Colored People
NACW	National Association of Colored Women
NCL	National Consumers' League
NWP	National Woman's Party
NYWTUL	New York Women's Trade Union League
PAC	Pan-African Congress
WPP	Woman's Peace Party
WSP	Woman Suffrage Party
WTUL	Women's Trade Union League
WILPF	Women's International League for Peace and Freedom

Refounding Democracy through
Intersectional Activism

Introduction

*Contemporary Context as a Period
of Collective Self-Reflection*

To keep a political system vital and directed at furthering the common good instead of selfish interests and ambitions, according to Niccolò Machiavelli, people periodically need to reflect on who they are. As he wrote, "It is necessary . . . that men living together under any kind of institution should often come to know themselves."[1] His insight offers an alternative way to understand our current political climate. Instead of accepting the narrative that in the early twenty-first century, we are a divided nation on the brink of civil war, we can reframe the playing out of our divisions as evidence that we are engaged in one of those necessary moments when we reexamine our guiding principles and institutions. Adopting this new narrative releases the hope that as we fiercely debate the scope of government, the value of diversity, and the role the United States should play in the world, we will forge a shared commitment to a new understanding of our common good.

Resolving our disagreements hinges in part on how we connect to past periods of collective self-reflection that I call refounding moments. The purpose of this book is to recover the neglected turn-of-the-twentieth-century social democratic feminists who shaped their refounding moment. They came from three different streams of the women's movement: African American middle and working class, immigrant Jewish middle and working class, and white Protestant native-born middle class. Together, they comprised a coalition of extraordinary women refounders that included Grace Abbott, Jane Addams, Emily Balch, Nannie Helen Burroughs, Anna Julia Cooper, Charlotte Perkins Gilman, Addie Hunton, Florence Kelley, Theresa Serber Malkiel, Pauline Newman, Rose Schneiderman, Mary Church Terrell, Lillian Wald, Ida B. Wells-Barnett, and others.[2] They offer us conceptual and organizing tools that we need today to refound democracy as a deeply just and caring project.

Because the notion of refounding violates the assumption that there is only one U.S. founding and one set of Founding Fathers,[3] I offer a concept that combines insights from Machiavelli, Hannah Arendt, and Aristotle. All three analyze the founding of new political communities. Each expands the notion beyond that of the lone founder, like Moses, who establishes the fundamental laws that give shape to a political community. In different ways, they embrace the theme of reworking the foundations. So the three theorists give legitimacy to constructing a notion of refounding, which is fundamentally about collective political agency to reshape the body politic. By formulating this concept, I aim to encourage the reexamination of our history to create a tradition of refoundings and refounders and to reveal the distinct contribution of the social democratic feminists.

From Machiavelli, I build into a notion of refounding his analysis of the need for the political community "to be reborn" through "renewal" processes that ward off or undo systemic corruption.[4] The periodic practices of collective self-reflection entail the people recommitting to a common good. New laws and institutions can guide the people toward a new understanding of the common good. Moreover, in his history of the Roman Republic, Machiavelli suggests that the people are not limited to the original founding. Consequently, political theorist Hanna Pitkin finds in Machiavelli a notion of the need for "continuous mutual co-founding,"[5] which I rename as refounding.

Turning to Arendt, I incorporate her insight about how "man's capacity for novelty" can "bring about the formation of a new body politic."[6] So she brings to the notion of refounding the centrality of newness. Studying eighteenth-century revolutions, she connects "the spirit of the revolution" to the creation of "a different form of government" that constitutes "a new beginning."[7] Arendt suggests a notion of refounding by proposing the need to institutionalize participatory spaces, such as the New England town meeting, to keep alive the revolutionary creative spirit for future innovations or new beginnings.[8]

To characterize the effects of a refounding moment on the body politic, I include Aristotle's notion of revolution as a change in the constitution. According to Aristotle, all written or unwritten constitutions answer four questions that define a political community: Who has political power? What is the end purpose? What is the concept of justice? How are the offices organized? Based on the answer to the first question, he divides constitutions into the rule of one, the rule of few, and the rule of many. Then he differentiates between healthy and corrupt forms of each. The rulers in a corrupt form equate the common good and their selfish interests; the rulers in a healthy form differentiate the common good from their partial interests.[9]

Since the revolution does not have to be violent, Aristotle suggests the possibility of peaceful refoundings. He gives the example of how abolishing the property qualification for holding public office propelled a change from rule of the few to rule of the many. Aristotle also uncovers how some revolutions were accidental, while others were not even recognized if they were caused by a series of small changes.[10] So Aristotle helps us identify a refounding moment: There is a change in the sovereign power, which brings a change in the end of the body politic, a new notion of justice, and possibly new participatory spaces.

The social democratic feminists shaped their refounding moment by interconnecting processes of collective self-reflection, new beginnings, and a revolution in the constitution. The chapters of this book show how they did this. As I reveal them as genuine refounders, it will become clear that they expanded my concept of refounding because they were part of an intentionally excluded political class. As outsiders, they were forced to innovate a method of refounding that was activist and deeply coalitional. As a result, I characterize their method as refounding from the bottom up.[11]

The social democratic feminists also faced a unique situation: The democratic rule of women and men together in U.S. history had never existed. To start a new history, they concluded that women, as a diverse grouping, could not simply add themselves to a political system that men designed based on their lived experiences and asymmetrical power. Therefore, the three streams of social democratic feminists generated analyses of the necessary changes required to create a new type of "women-friendly"[12] democracy. Out of these analyses, they produced alternative visions of democracy that allowed them to imagine their full inclusion.

I use the term "engendering democracy"[13] to refer to how they created a *new* understanding of democracy. The three streams of social democratic feminists shaped their creation by incorporating into democracy four new dimensions: a redesign of the domestic-public divide, women's economic independence, women's equal political power, and the embedding of the nation in a humanitarian transnational level. Through this radically altered vision of democracy, the social democratic feminists showed a diversity of women how to incorporate themselves into democracy. Thus, the social democratic feminists made a distinct contribution to a tradition of refoundings and refounders: They showed what it looked like *if* women refounded the body politic.

By now, it should be clear that I assume that the meaning of U.S. democracy was not settled by the Founding Fathers in the original documents, especially since the 1789 Constitution legitimized the institution of slavery.[14] Therefore, I adopt the perspective that we have experienced a number of refoundings.[15] Although we do not widely use the concept of social democracy, I introduce it to distinguish two twentieth-century refounding moments. Both illustrated refounding through lawmaking: Franklin D. Roosevelt (FDR) and the passage of the Social Security Act of 1935, the National Labor Relations Act of 1935, and the Fair Labor Standards Act of 1938, and Lyndon B. Johnson (LBJ) and the passage of the Civil Rights Act of 1964, the Voting Rights Act of 1965, and the 1965 adoption of Medicare and Medicaid. Each created a U.S. version of social democracy that combined political democracy and a welfare state.[16] Taken together, these two refounding moments expanded the functions of the state to include the regulation of the economy and the provision of social programs to alleviate substantive inequality.

Yet the evolution of U.S. social democracy has not been a story of linear progress. We are currently trying to figure out how strongly we are attached to the FDR and LBJ refounding moments and the vision of social democracy they embodied. Unfortunately, in these discussions we leave out the Progressive Era social democratic feminist refounders, who eroded the ideological hegemony of the laissez-faire interpretation of democracy as they engendered it. By not even acknowledging their refounding moment, we are unable to learn from them how to advance a parallel project: the reimagining of social democracy *after* neoliberalism.

The Challenges of Recovering the Social Democratic Feminist Refounders

Since, within our national narratives, feminists have never been embraced as refounders, who redesigned the U.S. democratic system in significant ways,[17] I use this introduction to address the three challenges I face as a theorist in recovering the full significance of the social democratic feminist refounders. First, it is imperative to interconnect the two dimensions of their refounding: the political and the social. Second, it is crucial to delineate how the social democratic feminist vision of social democracy represented, on the one hand, a rupture with turn-of-the-twentieth-century liberal democracy and, on the other hand, an engendered and diverse new beginning that contrasted with European origins of social democracy. Third, since we do not characterize the social democratic feminists as original thinkers, and since their coalitional activism drove their refounding moment, it is necessary to create a method of interpretation that reveals how their activism led them to formulate a new theory of democracy and citizenship.

Integrating the Political and the Social

When Progressive Era feminists are brought into national narratives, their political and social welfare state activism are usually separated. This approach blocks our ability to grasp how they went about creating a U.S. version of social democracy. Until recently, the political suffrage story has focused solely on the mid-nineteenth-century phase under the leadership of Elizabeth Cady Stanton and Susan B. Anthony, with a bow to Sojourner Truth. Now we are more aware of the early twentieth century's very diverse and militant period of the movement. During this phase, African American and immigrant Jewish women made crucial contributions.

Yet neither phase has garnered refounder status. According to the standard interpretation, amending the Constitution to abolish gender discrimination in voting, although it took over seventy years, merely corrected a bias in a fundamentally sound liberal democratic system. A popular generalization about the ratification of the Nineteenth Amendment has been that it constituted a big nonevent.[18] When women achieved the right to vote, it is pointed out that they did not generate the threatened bloc vote for change. They either did not vote or voted like their husbands. Also, by the time women could vote, according to some analysts, it had become a devalued activity.[19] Other scholars emphasize how state disenfranchisement laws blocked African American women from exercising their right to vote.[20]

Shifting the focus from failed political revolution to the creation of the welfare state produces a second narrative that gives social democratic feminists a visible role in the creation of preconditions for the New Deal refounding moment. Here the emphasis is on how they actively constructed ideological and some institutional foundations for the U.S. version of the welfare state. Interdisciplinary scholarship characterizes their contribution as experimenting with state and local government programs. The case of mothers' pension programs is a prime example. They provided income supplements for a selected group of low-income mothers and their children. The 1935 Social Security Act nationalized the program as Aid to Dependent Children.[21]

Historian Kathryn Sklar complicates the analysis by arguing that because male labor leaders turned to privatized collective bargaining rather than state regulation of wages and hours, it was left to the social democratic feminists to create the latter. They used sex-based labor laws as a surrogate for class-based policies to shape welfare state development.[22] For example, when Florence Kelley defended labor law protections for women workers only, she envisioned them as an entering wedge for universal or gender-neutral labor laws. In the process, as chief factory inspector for the state of Illinois from 1893 to 1897, she helped invent what we now call state feminism, whereby women act within the administrative side of the state to advance gender equality.[23] Established in 1912, the U.S. Children's Bureau innovated practices of state feminism at the national level that were imitated by other countries.

Following J. Stanley Lemons, the scholarly consensus accepts that the social democratic feminists provided key players who linked the Progressive Era and the 1930s New Deal.[24] Enfranchised feminist lobbyists, for example, achieved the passage of the first federal health services program for women and children, the Sheppard-Towner Act (1921–1929), which was administered by the Children's Bureau. The Social Security Act of 1935 included a truncated version of this program. Due to the influence of the feminist network, Frances Perkins became the first woman in a presidential cabinet when she was confirmed as FDR's secretary of labor. She brought with her the memory of witnessing the 1911 Triangle fire tragedy, where 146 mostly working-class Jewish and Italian girls and women died due to the lack of workplace safety regulations.[25]

Folding the social democratic feminists into the New Deal refounding moment is unsatisfactory because it hides from examination the distinct nature of the new beginning they set in motion. Neither just political revolutionaries nor just social welfare reformers, the social democratic feminists were both. They worked to incorporate women into political democracy and to lay the foundations for the U.S. welfare state. By interweaving the two aims, the social democratic feminists provoked a period of collective self-reflection and sparked a radical refounding of U.S. democracy as a social democracy. Therefore, I contend that they qualify as refounders.

To induct them into the Refounder Hall of Fame, I adopt the "social democratic feminist" label,[26] because the two usual labels separate the political and the social dimensions of their refounding moment. The older term, "social feminism," referred to putting social justice before absolute gender equality, defined as identical treatment of women and men. Accordingly, the social feminists pursued equal voting rights as a means for furthering social justice aims. This framing is faulty.[27] The social democratic feminists were not just seeking a list of social policies. An authoritarian regime could satisfy this end. They were engaged in refounding U.S. democracy by expanding the arenas of political participation, including within the nascent welfare state. They envisioned the new women citizens exerting their political agency by sustaining relations of interdependence between state feminist actors, elected and appointed, and a diversity of women coping with the problems of daily life.

The "maternalist" label has largely replaced the "social feminist" label. It has worsened the problem by explicitly separating women's agency in creating the welfare state from their electoral politics activism, including suffrage organizing. Comparative studies illustrate why historians adopt the separation. For example, from 1850 to 1908, German regional laws banned women from participating politically. As a result, few on the German side, who participated in a cross-border conversation on social welfare policies, supported women's suffrage.[28] Therefore, to draw comparisons between German and U.S. social reformers, the political activism, especially suffrage activism, of the latter is submerged in a narrative of how both groups pursued social justice policies. As historians Seth Koven and Sonya Michel conclude in their comparative volume on maternalist politics, "Suffrage per se was not a decisive turning point in the history of maternalist politics."[29] Yet this whole approach makes invisible how the U.S. welfare state was built from the bottom up, in part because of the quest by suffragists to show that women were capable of becoming democratic political citizens.

Addressing the U.S. context, Theda Skocpol also marginalizes the importance of suffrage activism in order to create a unity of maternalists, especially among middle-class white women, who supported state mothers' pension programs, for example, but not necessarily women's equal citizenship. Furthermore, she places social democratic feminists within her nonpolitical maternalist container. Then she argues that they were more successful at achieving their policy aims *before* they actually gained the right to vote and engaged in messy male-biased political parties and electoral politics. To make this claim, Skocpol leaves out pre-1920 women's electoral politics participation in Western states and how it paved the way for social policy gains. She also skirts over the participation of social democratic feminists, especially Addams, in the 1912 Progressive Party. Finally, while Skocpol accepts the consensus among historians that the Sheppard-Towner Act was the response of Congress to the newly enfranchised women voters, she does not draw the conclusion that women's political citizenship and the creation of the U.S. welfare state were interconnected.[30]

When scholars combine the maternalist label and political citizenship,[31] they produce a narrative of how women were incorporated into the welfare state and democracy as mothers and therefore as second-class citizens.[32] These scholars point to Supreme Court decisions and welfare policies that reinforced treating men and women differently. Certainly, the social democratic feminists were not seeking citizenship to reinforce women's subordinate position. They did not present themselves as maternalists. At most, in the period before the passage of the Nineteenth Amendment, they utilized maternalist rhetoric strategically to craft arguments that would appeal to middle-class men and women. For the three streams of social democratic feminists, the gendered incorporation of women into U.S. democracy was a positive, creative act with lasting revolutionary significance.

I have picked the label "social democratic feminism" instead of "social justice feminism," because although both terms—"social democracy" and "social justice"—were actually used in the period, only the former serves my purpose. The concept of social justice gets at how the social democratic feminists aimed to replace private charity with public sector programs,[33] but it does not necessarily include opening up political citizenship and deepening political participation of the less powerful. For this second dimension, the concept of social democracy is superior. The beauty of social democracy, understood as an expansive, fluid concept, which it was in the Progressive Era, is that it brings into relationship the two parts of the feminist refounding of U.S. democracy: the social justice side of creating the welfare state to alleviate substantive inequality and the democratic side of incorporating the diversity of women into equal citizenship with men. By interweaving the social and the democratic, the social democratic feminists created an alternative to turn-of-the-twentieth-century liberal democracy and thus theorized a U.S. version of social democracy.

Rupture with Nineteenth-Century Liberal Democracy and Alternative to European Origins

To grasp the originality of this feminist theory of social democracy, U.S. political theorizing is not helpful. Possibly as a legacy of the Cold War, the academic field does not include a political theory tradition of social democracy. Without this tradition, we cannot even acknowledge that feminists generated a new theory of democracy. They remain invisible within the field. For example, we overlook how the social democratic feminists turned care into a democratic value.[34] What political theorists do offer is a reduction of social democracy to the welfare state. Then, implicitly or explicitly, they fold the welfare state into liberal democracy, understood as a thin or minimal notion of democracy limited to elections with competitive political parties and free speech and other civil liberties.[35]

There are three distinct approaches to the relationship between the welfare state and liberal democracy. A critic of liberal democracy, Sheldon Wolin conceptualizes the welfare and warfare sides of the liberal democratic state as inextricably linked. For him, both are arenas of coercion; therefore, both are antidemocratic.[36] Theorists of liberalism, Judith Shklar and John Rawls propose the possibility of enlarging the welfare functions of the state by creating citizen social rights to health care or employment. Without an explicit discussion, both assume that liberal democracy has room for these reforms.[37] A strong advocate of social democracy, Michael Walzer explicitly states that there is no inherent incompatibility between social democracy and liberal democracy.[38]

To get at the revolutionary nature of social democracy in the U.S. context at the turn of the twentieth century, I introduce Addams's notion of "the second phase of democracy." For her, it was not an add-on or "supplement" to,[39] but a rupture with, the first phase. As she observed, "We are at the *beginning* [my emphasis] of a prolonged effort to incorporate a progressive developing life founded upon a response to the needs of all the people, into the requisite legal enactments and civic institutions."[40] To formulate this new beginning, Addams and the social democratic feminists dismantled the theoretical scaffolding that supported the liberal dimension of liberal democracy.

First, Addams called for "a definite abandonment of the eighteenth-century philosophy upon which so much of our present democratic theory . . . depends." Here she had in mind key notions of the Founding Fathers, which she characterized as static: abstract inalienable rights tied to a notion of natural man, the centrality of private property rights, government as only oppressive, and a distrust of the people. As she concluded, "the founders failed to provide the vehicle for a vital and genuinely organized expression of the popular will."[41] Thus, their version of liberal democracy depended on the liberal individualistic liberty side blocking the democratic collective self-government side.

Second, Addams uncovered how advocates of late nineteenth-century notions of laissez-faire economic *and* political logics further strengthened the liberal side against the democratic egalitarian side.[42] Supreme Court judges, for example, who accepted a theory of the strict separation of government and the market, actively prevented the enlargement of government functions in response to democratic pressure for the regulation of wages and hours. Philanthropists turned the survival-of-the-fittest version of laissez-faire into an individualistic ethical standard that judged people according to "their business capacity."[43] This market framing of human achievement reinforced old ideas of the limited role of government by leaving the responsibility of providing for human distress caused by the inequalities of capitalism in the hands of judgmental private charities.

Third, Addams showed how the late nineteenth-century imperialists further weakened democracy at home and abroad. In their defense of the U.S. annexation of the Philippines (1898), for example, they fused together militarized masculine individualism, unrestricted commercialism, and a static notion of civilization as a hierarchy with Anglo-Saxons on top. They used this combination to justify not trusting nonwhite peoples in the United States and in the world to innovate new forms of self-government and mutual aid. In place of democracy, the imperialists proposed paternalism and the denial of agency to immigrants, African Americans, and the Philippine people.

As the social democratic feminists discredited this theory and practice of U.S. liberal democracy, they established a core dimension of their refounding moment: the substitution of social for liberal, which was necessary for their recasting of democracy. In place of the Founding Fathers' notion of "inalienable" abstract rights, Addams championed a social or relational framing of rights. According to this understanding, rights were "hard-won," and they came out of struggles rooted in relations among embodied "men, women, and children." These relations could "be sustained only by daily knowledge and constant companionship."[44] The social democratic feminists also sought to replace the individualistic ethics that supported the laissez-faire economic and political logics. Their alternative was a notion of social ethics that could provide the basis for creating a welfare state directed at advancing social justice. Finally, their substitution for imperialism deepened their commitment to transforming social relationships. They proposed the development of a rooted cosmopolitan democracy that replaced hierarchies of power with egalitarian nourishing relations across a range of borders, at home and in the world.

By replacing liberal with social, the social democratic feminists generated a path to social democracy that broke with European political origins and political characteristics.[45] Gosta Esping-Andersen and Sherri Berman are especially helpful in crystallizing these origins. In his comparative analysis of welfare states, Esping-Andersen highlights the antidemocratic dimension. Pointing to France and Germany, he observes that "the first major welfare-state initiatives occurred prior to democracy and were powerfully motivated by the desire to arrest its realization." In the case of Sweden, he stresses the top-down or "ruling-class reformism" that "even preceded the birth of a labor movement."[46]

In her analysis of twentieth-century ideologies, Berman broadens the discussion of European origins beyond the welfare state to bring in the centrality of political parties and representative democracy, as utilized by revisionist Marxists. According to Berman, they crafted a distinct ideology of social democracy that broke with both liberal laissez-faire and Marxist revolutionary class struggle. Yet there is no suggestion that this new direction required a radical rethinking of the theory and practice of democracy. For the social democrats, it was sufficient to work from within "the democratic state" in order to alleviate the injustices of capitalism.[47]

Although they approach European social democratic origins differently, both Esping-Andersen and Berman agree on the centrality of political coalition building for long-term sustainability. To guarantee political support for social democracy, an organized working class with its own political party was not sufficient; coalitions that brought together the urban middle and working classes with the peasants were required. These cross-class, rural-urban alliances made possible the forging of a sense of universalistic solidarity to anchor the evolution of social democracy. Esping-Andersen and Berman assume that these coalitions form and thrive only within nation-states. For Berman, the attachment to nationalism provides the necessary glue for social democratic communitarianism, or commitment to working for the common good. Finally, both analysts insist that differences of religion, ethnicity, race, and gender are not particularly relevant for understanding social democratic political coalitions; indeed, for them, these identities, interests, and social categories primarily erode the required bonds of solidarity.[48]

The social democratic feminist origins of U.S. social democracy were quite different. A bottom-up approach, characterized by local experimentation and grassroots mobilizations, was necessary, for the very obvious reason that the social democratic feminist refounders were outsiders in the political system. To shape their version of social democracy, they released the transformative possibilities of a rich diversity with its promise of a new practice and theory of cosmopolitan democracy. As a result, they crafted a very different type of social democratic coalitional politics to refound democracy.

The social democratic feminists understood that they were not working with "a homogeneous population," which they assumed was a defining characteristic of the European version of social democracy.[49] Moreover, they rejected forced homogeneity, or a notion "of assimilation as if it were a huge digestive apparatus" spitting out uniform individuals based on an imposed Anglo-Saxon mold.[50] Stressing the creative potential of respecting differences among the peoples in the United States, the social democratic feminists rejected the European model. Specifically, Grace Abbott argued for not "blindly following Europe," with its propensity "to develop a contempt for others and to foster those national hatreds and jealousies that are necessary for aggressive nationalism."[51]

Operating within the context of U.S. diversity, Abbott defined a different approach: "Here in the US, we have the opportunity of working out a democracy founded on internationalism."[52] She called for developing "the possibilities which are ours because we are of many races and are related by the closest of human ties to all the world."[53] Reflecting her times, Abbott used race here to characterize different nationalities. She also did not fit everyone into a white/black binary. When she characterized Jews, for example, she referred to them as experiencing "the racial prejudice" and as having a "faith."[54]

Abbott explicitly interconnected U.S. internationalism at home with a new nonimperialist internationalism abroad. "If we can learn to listen to those who have suffered from a denial of self-government in Europe," she conjectured, "we may be able to avoid American imperialism and to give to the Filipino, the Porto Rican, the Negro of Santo Domingo and of the United States, the right to self-government that we have thus far denied them."[55] Addams supported this vision when she argued that the mixing of immigrants in urban settings, like Chicago, was creating the relational foundations for a new type of democracy beyond the nation-state.[56] Like Abbott, she looked to immigrants, migrant workers, and transnational families to contribute to turning the United States into a multileveled cosmopolitan social democracy.

Thus, the social democratic feminists used their refounding moment to expand the social democratic imaginary in three key ways. First, they put the full inclusion of the three streams of women at the center of their vision of social democracy. Second, they envisioned within the nation-state an international democracy built on the equalizing of power among diverse groups. Third, they sought to embed the nation-state within a new humanitarian transnationalism that supported a combination of social justice and collective self-government.

Theorizing Social Democratic Feminist Activism

Because the social democratic feminists have not been viewed as thinkers who generated a new theory of social democracy and citizenship, I adopt a method of interpretation that uncovers how their participation in movements and coalitions turned them into theorists.[57] I call my method the theory-activist dynamic. I construct it by connecting the social democratic feminists to three feminist theory traditions, each of which grapples with the problem of how to turn practice into new theories: intersectionality, pragmatist feminism, and feminist standpoint. Without the terminology, the social democratic feminists developed intersectional analyses, pragmatist experiments, and feminist standpoints. Using the terminology, I systematize their contributions to these traditions, and I further theorize their originality as theorist-activists. I do not engage with the complexities of the feminist theory traditions or apply them in any depth. My aim is only to formulate the theory-activist dynamic by combining specific insights from these traditions.

I start the construction of the theory-activist dynamic by adapting three interconnected insights on intersectionality. First, social theorist Patricia Hill Collins reminds us that social movement contexts facilitate new thinking about how gender, race, and class constitute interlocking systems of power. As she explains, "the ideas of social movements became named," as when Kimberlé Crenshaw created the term "intersectionality."[58] Since social movements seek transformation, Collins's observation reattaches intersectional critiques of mutually constitutive oppressions to the radical project of seeking social justice.

Second, through her notion of political intersectionality, legal scholar Crenshaw uncovers how movements can block or facilitate new intersectional thinking.[59] She stresses the detrimental effects of an "either/or" framing of movements. Her example is the tendency to define feminism as based on the lived experiences of white women and anti-racism as based on the lived experiences of African American men.[60] In the Progressive Era, Anna Julia Cooper articulated the problem with "either/or" for the African American woman: "She is confronted by both a woman question and a race problem, and is as yet an unknown or an unacknowledged factor in both."[61] Foregrounding African American women makes clear that adopting a "both/and" understanding of movement activism is necessary for generating intersectional thinking.

Collins supports this conclusion by pointing out that in both the Progressive Era and the 1970s, African American women activists worked to combine movements by bringing racial equality to white feminists and gender equality to African American men activists. For the latter period, she expands the pool of activists to include "Chicanas and other Latinas, native women and Asian American women" who worked across movements. As a result, Collins asserts, "women of color's analyses about intersections of race/class/gender/ sexuality were honed in the intersections of multiple social movements."[62] I utilize a "both/and" definition of political intersectionality to make visible how the three streams of social democratic feminists bridged different configurations of movements and, as a consequence, opened up possibilities for new intersectional thinking. To capture the distinctiveness of their bridging activism, I characterize it as intersectional activism, and I call them bridgers.

Third, Crenshaw's notion of "structural intersectionality"[63] establishes that a necessary condition for actualizing the potential for new thinking within contexts of interconnecting movements is that the bridgers voice their different social locations. For example, when Mary Church Terrell reminded Addams that the legacy of slavery played out on the bodies of African American women, Terrell exposed how intersectional structural inequalities of gender, race, and class shaped their different lived experiences. As a result of such exchanges among bridgers, they learned that these intersectional hierarchies of power shaped their own relationships. Therefore, as they worked to dismantle the external societal structural inequalities, they also were forced to renegotiate their own internal unequal power relations. In the process, they created new intersectional analyses and visions of refounding democracy. To put sufficient stress on how the bridgers in their coalitions took up the challenge of prefiguring new, more egalitarian relations that motivated and supported their new theorizing, I use the term "intersectional coalitions."[64]

To continue the construction of the theory-activist dynamic, I fold in two participatory spaces that were conducive to turning intersectional activism into new theorizing: pragmatist experiments and democratic conversations. The purpose of a pragmatist experiment is to create new experiences as the basis for new thinking. For my understanding of this process, I rely on philosopher Charlene Seigfried's feminist interpretation of the pragmatist tradition and on Addams's participation in that tradition. Seigfried distinguishes between "experience as origin and as the outcome of reflection, a reflection directed by the intention to change the situation so as to facilitate emancipation."[65] The purpose of feminist reflections on experience, according to Seigfried, is "to liberat[e] experience from oppressive practices."[66]

Addams turned Seigfried's insight into an activist method. Aiming to interconnect movements, Addams designed pragmatist experiments that released the emancipatory potential of women's past experiences with labor and food provisioning. Struggles over how to combine the movements evolved the experiments and the theorizing of new understandings of democracy and citizenship. I focus on how the social democratic feminists activated specific experiments in the new participatory social spaces of the feminist settlement house, the Women's Trade Union League (WTUL), and the Women's International League for Peace and Freedom (WILPF).

My notion of democratic conversation brings into the theory-activist dynamic the movement spaces where bridgers formulate new social democratic feminist standpoints. I characterize these standpoints as a type of theorizing that combines critiques of intersecting oppressions and alternative visions of social democracy. The social democratic feminists consciously shifted away from traditional women's standpoints that either assumed the moral superiority of women or were formulated as maternalist. Their new standpoints came out of struggles with men and among themselves. For their refounding moment, in their own ways, they illustrated theorist Nancy Hartsock's insights about the construction of a feminist standpoint.

Starting with the assumption that "women's experience . . . as a dominated group contains both negative and positive aspects," Hartsock defines the purpose of a feminist standpoint. It "picks out and amplifies the liberatory possibilities contained in that experience."[67] Specifically, Hartsock looks for the liberatory potential in women's traditional roles in the sexual division of labor.[68] In this way, creating a feminist standpoint is similar to designing a pragmatist experiment. Finally, Hartsock asserts that the construction of a feminist standpoint comes out of the "political struggle to change social relations."[69]

To place the creation of social democratic feminist standpoints within spaces of democratic conversations, I recast deliberative democracy as a type of struggle among bridgers. I focus on one specific problem feminist democratic theorists debate: whether or not participants in deliberative contexts can leave societal structural hierarchies of power outside the room.[70] I emphasize how the bracketing of power differentials by establishing procedural rules for deliberating is not sufficient to create equality among the participants. To release the creative/liberatory potential of unbracketing power differentials for shaping new social democratic feminist standpoints, I apply the three insights on intersectionality. The conversations go on within the context of movements. The participants are all bridgers with different bridging configurations. The bridgers speak from and renegotiate intersectional structural social locations. Because I utilize political and structural intersectionality to shape the nature of the deliberations, I call them intersectional conversations. I create an ideal type of an intersectional conversation to construct the democratic conversations and to show how they work.

There are three characteristics of the ideal type. First, since the focus is on structures, not identities,[71] I emphasize that all social democratic feminists have an intersectional structural location. In characterizing the location of immigrant Jewish women, it is important to remember that during the Progressive Era, eastern European Jews were considered a separate race, a separate nationality, or an ethnicity.[72] Therefore, I simply use "Jewish" to capture this dimension of their structural location. Following Collins, I also assume that the three streams of social democratic feminists "possess varying amounts of penalty and privilege in one historically created system" and that "[d]epending on the context, an individual may be an oppressor, a member of an oppressed group, or simultaneously oppressor and oppressed."[73] Renegotiating contradictory structural locations is a crucial part of the democratic conversation.

Second, depending on the issue, the less powerful women voice their intersectional structural locations characterized by overlapping oppressions, while the more powerful women listen and, as a result, gain new sympathetic knowledge. Here I adapt Cooper's insight that "[t]he art of 'thinking one's self imaginatively into the experiences of others' is not given to all, and it is impossible to acquire it without a background and a substratum of sympathetic knowledge."[74] My assumption is that we cannot walk in someone else's lived experience, but we can walk side by side, as Addams observed, to "see the size of one another's burdens."[75]

As a result, the second characteristic is centrally about the relational production of sympathetic knowledge through democratic conversations, a type of walking together. Both the voicing of intersectional oppressions and the willingness to experience discomfort based on listening are essential for building trust among bridgers. Third, the potentiality for crafting new social democratic feminist standpoints, characterized by new analyses and alternative visions, emerges as the intersectional activists in relationship apply their skills at bridging movements.

Applying the ideal type, I analyze examples of direct exchanges that illustrate all or parts of it. I also construct intersectional conversations either by bringing into relationship parallel conversations from the three streams of social democratic feminists or by combining direct exchanges with parallel conversations. Through these techniques, I aim to foreground the less powerful women's agency and their crucial role in formulating intersectional social democratic feminist standpoints. I adapt, for my purposes, Cooper's two-stage method of analysis. W.E.B. Du Bois described the method: "All this of woman,—but what of black women?" For both of them, while African American women shared the subordination and political exclusion of women as a class, they brought to the struggle for women's economic and political emancipation "unique" contributions, without which that emancipation was not realizable.[76] I apply this same insight to immigrant Jewish bridgers. Finally, I show that the experimental spaces facilitated intersectional conversations, and both the spaces and the conversations were necessary for coalescing an intersectional coalition suited for refounding democracy from the bottom up.

First Broad Argument

To show how the social democratic feminist refounders interconnected the political and the social, substituted social for liberal, and retheorized democracy and citizenship by practicing intersectional activism, I organize the book around two broad arguments. My first broad argument is that engendering and socializing democracy were mutually constitutive. By playing out this interdependence, the social democratic feminists illustrated what feminist democratic theorists argue: Women's full inclusion requires a radical rethinking of democracy.[77] To clarify the argument, I pull together points that have been made to define socializing democracy. Then I return to the definition of engendering democracy. Finally, I connect the argument to the theory-activist dynamic.

For the concept of socializing democracy, I draw on Addams's formulation. She stressed three meanings. The first meaning was social justice, or the pursuit of greater substantive equality through the creation of a welfare state. I add an explicit recognition that this pursuit required the exposing and dismantling of intersectional structures of unequal power. The second meaning was the mixing of diverse groups to create a new relational grounding of democracy. This aim should not be confused with assimilation, and it went far beyond validating cultural pluralism or diversity. Fundamentally, it was about actualizing democracy in daily life, including the family, the workplace, and the neighborhood. The third meaning brought attention to the need for new participatory socializing spaces where the forging of new democratic relations could occur.

Based on the activism and writings of the three streams of social democratic feminists, I delineate four aspects of engendering democracy. To innovate a new theory of democracy, all four were necessary. First, the social democratic feminists worked to transform the gendered domestic-public split that blocked women from public life. Second, they formulated notions of women's economic independence that depended on creating a women-friendly welfare state. Third, the social democratic feminists practiced an electoral politics of presence to open up public life so that the diversity of women could exercise political agency. Fourth, they embraced a new synthesis of the national and the transnational to replace U.S. militarized nationalism and economic imperialism with a new kind of multileveled social democratic nourishing politics.

To show how the social democratic feminists interconnected engendering and socializing democracy, I develop the first broad argument by applying the theory-activist dynamic. To make the case that engendering reshaped socializing democracy, I demonstrate how social democratic feminist intersectional activism took place on new participatory socializing spaces. They provided the environment for pragmatist experiments and intersectional conversations. Through these theory-activist projects, the social democratic feminists injected social democracy with the four aims of engendering democracy. To advance the argument that socializing infused engendering democracy with the aim of social justice, I theorize how the bridgers struggled among themselves through experiments and democratic conversations to undo the intrafeminist hierarchies of power that reflected the external intersectional structural inequalities. Thus, by shaping both directions of the argument, the three streams of social democratic feminists turned intersectional activism into a feminist theory of social democracy.

Second Broad Argument

When the social democratic feminists initially attempted to act in public as citizens, they proceeded without full nation-state citizenship rights. As part of the first generation of college-educated daughters, many of them became familiar with the cosmopolitan notion of citizen of the world, a standing that did not depend on nation-state citizenship. Ultimately, the strength of the notion that it included women in humanity was also its weakness. Its abstract understanding of humanity was not up to the task of showing the feminists how to actualize their citizenship. Influenced also by the late nineteenth-century socialist notion of the brotherhood of man, the social democratic feminists, through their intersectional activism, translated citizen of the world into a theory-practice of participatory multileveled social citizenship.

Their turning of world citizenship into social citizenship produced a feminist genealogy of citizenship that was radically different from the men-focused evolution T. H. Marshall captured in his very influential formulation based on English history. According to Marshall, men's citizenship began in the eighteenth century with the individualistic civil rights to property, consciousness, and (later) work. Next, in the nineteenth century, men achieved the political rights to vote and to participate in representative institutions.

Social rights to education and health care provided by the state were a product of the twentieth century. All these rights were exercised within the container of the nation-state.[78]

Using Marshall's three categories, I show how the social democratic feminists produced a feminist genealogy of social citizenship by beginning with the social dimension. My second broad argument is that to evolve from abstract citizens of the world to embodied multileveled social citizens, the social democratic feminists, through their intersectional activism, invented a participatory practice of social citizenship that socialized civil and political rights and generated a notion of the global social citizen as a synthesizer of the local, national, and transnational levels of social democracy. This argument uncovers a critical distinction between the evolution of men's and women's citizenship: The social democratic feminists interwove women's national and transnational citizenship from the beginning.

To excavate the audacity and originality of the project the bridgers set out for themselves and to strengthen my case for embracing them as refounders, I apply a genealogical method. It is inspired by Friedrich Nietzsche and Michel Foucault,[79] who utilized their versions of this method as a powerful tool to subvert by critique the dominant categories of their day. Nietzsche focused on how "those in power" shape the genealogy of values; Foucault used the method to reveal "the hazardous play of dominations."[80] In contrast to both of them, my emphasis is on how an outsider group—social democratic feminists—moved beyond critique of their intersectional oppressions. They created a genealogy that allowed them to innovate a new type of citizenship that intertwined their incorporation into public life with the creation of a U.S. version of social democracy.

So more is at stake with the second broad argument than merely describing a gendered path to citizenship. The social democratic feminists used their skills at bridging movements to evolve their multileveled citizenship in order to participate in the refounding of democracy. To show how the social democratic feminists turned themselves into citizen refounders, I construct and apply a genealogical method that highlights a surprise beginning, fresh intentions, reinterpretations, activist substitutions, historicizing of dominant concepts, the influence of contingent factors, and no teleology. I explain each where relevant in the different chapters.

The Plan of the Book

The first parts of Chapters 1–4 present one dimension of engendering democracy to support the first argument. The second parts of Chapters 1–4 present a stage in the feminist genealogy of multileveled social citizenship to demonstrate the second argument. At the end of these chapters, I discuss how each recovers the social democratic feminists as refounders. Chapter 5 distills conceptual and organizing tools for our period of collective self-reflection.

Chapter 1 puts the feminist settlement house, with its reconstruction of the gendered domestic-public divide, at the center of the social democratic feminist refounding moment. My specific argument is that by bridging movements, Addams and others turned Hull House into a socializing space for experiments that embedded the household in the public, for conversations on democratizing the family, and for practices of a new type of social citizenship. Through an exploration of interconnected Hull House experiments in cooperative housekeeping and state feminism, I show how bridging movements inspired and shaped the experiments and generated new understandings. Then I shift to how Hull House created an environment conducive to conversations on three unequal power relations within the private household. Finally, I turn to how the feminist settlement house, through its new synthesis of the household and the public, facilitated a feminist genealogy of multileveled social citizenship. I define and illustrate the two interconnected modes of participation that the social democratic feminists invented: social service and social service participatory politics.

Chapter 2 interconnects the struggle for women's economic independence with the creation of a welfare state. My specific argument is that the three groups of bridgers showed how women's economic independence required and furthered turning care into a democratic value that enlarged the purpose of the state by legitimizing earning mothers, by disconnecting care from its servile status, and by socializing the citizen civil right to work. To demonstrate the argument, I bring together parallel intersectional conversations, each focused on an interconnected aspect of economic independence: independence from men, overcoming the conflict between mothering and earning, and a public revaluing of care work. Then I turn to the second stage of the feminist genealogy of multileveled social citizenship that connected women's economic independence to the socializing of the civil right to work. I establish that the individualistic liberal notion of this right was not up to the task of facilitating women's participation in the labor market.

Chapter 3 focuses on how the social democratic feminists sought political power to actualize their visions of social democracy in daily life and through a welfare state. My specific argument is that because they bridged different movements, the three groups of social democratic feminists turned their egalitarian suffrage organizing into a space for practicing and theorizing an electoral politics of presence, capable of generating a women's bloc vote for social democracy. I construct and illustrate, with specific electoral campaigns, the notion of an electoral politics of presence. Then I apply the theory-activist dynamic to elucidate further different versions of the electoral politics of presence. For African American bridgers, I construct an intersectional conversation on anti-lynching and the racialized sexual double standard. For immigrant Jewish bridgers, I interpret the New York branch of the WTUL (NYWTUL), as a pragmatist experimental social space they shaped to actualize an electoral politics of presence for immigrant working-class women. I conclude with how egalitarian suffragists socialized the right to vote when they prefigured a bloc vote for social democracy.

Chapter 4 foregrounds how the transnational intersectional activism and theorizing of the social democratic feminists shaped both their intertwined engendering and socializing of democracy and their feminist genealogy of multileveled social citizenship. My specific argument is that before, during, and after World War I, the social democratic feminists built into their engendering and socializing of democracy the problem of how to synthesize the local, the national, and the transnational levels of participation and government, and in the process, they produced a practice and theory of social citizens as synthesizers of those levels. I reinterpret the first three chapters to show that in the prewar period, by bridging movements, the social democratic feminists produced new understandings of how to embed the nation-state within an evolving transnational level. I show how during and after the war, as bridgers, they acted directly on the transnational level by founding WILPF and by engaging with the new transnational institutions.

I approach WILPF as an experimental transnational participatory social space, and I reveal how intersectional activism defined its aim and shaped its development during the early congresses. I put particular emphasis on how, through the theory-activist dynamic, Addams drew on WILPF's protests as deeds to conceptualize a political notion of nourishing. From there, I uncover how WILPF generated two intersectional conversations: one on France's use of colonial troops for occupying the Rhineland and a second on the U.S. occupation of Haiti. Finally, I turn to how the social democratic feminists evolved their feminist genealogy of multileveled social citizenship by inventing their own distinct theory and practice of global citizenship.

Chapter 5 concludes the book by showing how the recovery of the social democratic feminist refounding moment provides us with conceptual and organizing tools for our necessary refounding moment, now shaped by our experience of the COVID-19 pandemic, the threat of an authoritarian turn, and the Dobbs decision. What is required is a resocializing of our democracy or the recreation of our social relations and the affirming of the centrality of intersectional social justice. In my concluding reflections, I make the case that to resocialize democracy, we should embrace and update, for our context, the multidimensional project of engendering democracy that characterized the social democratic feminist refounding moment. To develop this closing argument, I distill conceptual tools, one linked to each chapter, to help us reimagine social democracy and social citizenship, and I propose organizing tools to help us actualize an intersectional coalition capable of refounding our democracy.

The Feminist Settlement House
and Socializing Democracy

By putting the feminist settlement house at the center of the social democratic feminist refounding moment, this chapter establishes the reconstruction of the gendered domestic-public divide as a core component
of engendering democracy.[1] To demonstrate the book's first broad argument,
I show how the social democratic feminists fashioned this domestic-public
hybrid as a new participatory socializing space, characterized by experiments
and conversations. The conversations, in particular, revealed that the internal power dynamics of the traditional domestic sphere would have to be exposed and dismantled to advance social justice between men and women, as
well as among women. To support the book's second broad argument, I analyze how the social democratic feminists, as rebellious daughters, began their
feminist genealogy of multileveled social citizenship by utilizing the new
hybrid space to translate the notion of citizen of the world into a new type
of participatory social citizenship.

Hull House as Feminist Settlement House

In 1889, Jane Addams (1860–1935) and Ellen Gates Starr (1859–1940) located
their version of the feminist settlement house, Hull House, in a crowded Chicago working-class, immigrant neighborhood.[2] They invited other rebellious
daughters to join them in their multilayered experiment. Hull House became
a model of how activist-professional nonmarried women could live coopera-

tively and practice self-government.[3] Initially, Hull House included only single women; by 1893, seven men were residents.[4] There was a common dining area, and residents could take their meals in their rooms. It was not a collective in the sense of everyone pooling resources. Residents were expected to pay their portion of the expenses, although Addams subsidized many of them.[5] Heavy housecleaning and cooking were professionalized and when possible unionized. Residents were expected to share other chores. The majority of them worked outside the settlement house; they contributed to its projects in their spare time. In the early years, all the residents were required to take a turn at answering the front door.

To understand what characteristics made Hull House a feminist version of the settlement house, it is useful to contrast it with Toynbee Hall, the inspiration for Hull House. Located in London's East End, Toynbee Hall was a residence for men attending Cambridge and Oxford. Living among a working-class population, they tried to navigate between government aid to the poor and religious mission work. For the young men, the settlement experience was a step to pursuing a civil service job. Hull House was not a religious urban mission. The residents aimed to replace the charitable relationship by incorporating an immigrant working class, especially women, into an enlarged practice of democracy.[6] To actualize their vision, they practiced intersectional activism. In sharp contrast to the English men, Hull House women thus tied the settlement house to advancing the engendering and socializing of democracy. By 1892, Addams characterized Hull House as "An Effort Toward Social Democracy."[7]

This chapter analyzes how Hull House, as a feminist settlement house, challenged the gendered family-public divide that placed structural and ideological constraints on women's economic and political agency. This split constructed women as creatures of family relations and men as the shapers of the public. My specific argument is that by bridging movements, Addams and others turned Hull House into a socializing space for experiments that embedded the household in the public, for conversations on democratizing the family, and for practices of a new type of social citizenship. "The public" here refers to the economy, the administrative regulatory side of the state, and sometimes to Hull House itself.

To develop the argument, I begin with an interpretation of Addams's notion of civic housekeeping to explain the theme of embedding the household in the public. Next I present and illustrate Addams's pragmatist feminist method of theorizing experiments to construct a notion of social democracy that included taking democracy to daily life. Through an exploration of interconnected Hull House experiments in cooperative housekeeping and state feminism, I show how bridging movements inspired and shaped the experiments so they prefigured this new vision of democracy. Then I shift to how Hull House created an environment conducive to conversations on the unequal power relations within the private household: between household managers and domestic workers, husbands and wives, and fathers and daughters.

I construct these conversations based largely on fragments reported by Addams. To theorize them, I recover Addams's modeling of a new type of democratic conversation for the second stage of democracy. I show how her model recast democratic conversations as processes for socializing both the relational foundations and the extent of democracy. My constructions are not primarily shaped by the ideal type of an intersectional conversation, which is best suited for theorizing the interactions of bridgers. Instead, I use the conversations to uncover new issues that bridgers have to take up to propel an evolution, in Addams's terms, from a family claim supportive of the gendered domestic-public divide to a social claim. In my terms, the evolution was from a maternalist standpoint to social democratic feminist standpoints.

Finally, I turn to how the feminist settlement house, through its new household-public hybrid, supported rebellious daughters as they shaped a feminist genealogy of multileveled social citizenship. To make clear that the beginning of the genealogy was surprising, I show that a new form of public citizenship came out of a power struggle in the family and a revolt of the body. Then I establish that social democratic feminists turned to intersectional activism to develop their genealogy. Next I demonstrate how they structured the genealogy around a reinterpretation of citizenship by creating activist substitutes. To illustrate this point, I show how the rebellious daughters chose to actualize a social claim by substituting a new combination of social service and citizenship for the charity relationship. My contention is that this combination constituted a participatory version of social citizenship. I conclude the presentation of the first stage of the feminist genealogy by defining and illustrating the two interconnected modes of participation that they invented: social service and social service participatory politics.

Civic Housekeeping as Embedding the Household in the Public

According to the usual definition, "civic housekeeping" refers only to "extending domestic ideals into public life."[8] As part of the rhetoric of the late suffrage campaign, the appeal to civic housekeeping constituted a clever argument directed at middle-class men and women to assure them that if women voted, they would not alter relations within the domestic sphere. Indeed, according to the argument, women would strengthen the private family by taking an interest in public policies that directly affected it. This interpretation is inadequate for my purposes because it blocks an understanding of how Addams's concept of civic housekeeping shaped her vision of social democracy.

Specifically, there are three problems with the "extending" definition of civic housekeeping. First, it limits the analysis to two spheres, the family or household and the public. Second, it focuses only on enlargement of the purpose of politics, to include social policies and regulation of the economy, and leaves completely unexamined the undemocratic household. As a result, it never interrogates how women could extend themselves and maternal values into public life without altering the unequal power relations within the household. Third, it blocks us from analyzing the feminist settlement house as a new household-public hybrid.[9]

Addams's social democratic feminist notion of civic housekeeping rested on embedding a more democratic household within a social democratic public. This new type of public reshaped the purpose of the state to include the regulation of occupational health and safety, wages, and working hours.[10] To make her case for change, Addams presented a version of history that might have resonated with her audience. "When the family constituted the industrial organism of the day," Addams claimed, women "were able to dictate . . . the hours and . . . conditions of their work."[11] They oversaw an economy focused on use, not exchange value, since they were providing for the immediate "food and shelter" needs of their families. Then men "usurped the industrial pursuits and created wealth on a scale unknown before" by fueling an exchange-value economy.[12] This shift from use to exchange value, according to Addams, reduced women "to a state of dependency."[13] To protect their diminished position, affluent wives, in particular, adopted a style of household administration that "unnaturally isolated [it] from the rest of the community." They justified this structural arrangement by holding on to a theory that "the moral life of the family" would be "endangered by any radical change."[14]

Addams called on these women to abandon their "obsolete ideal" and regain their control over production and working conditions by consciously integrating their households within the industrial economy. Or, as she put it, "if she would secure her old place in industry, the modern woman must needs fit her labors to the present industrial" order.[15] For Addams, this meant giving up the practice of live-in servants by utilizing industrial food and joining with working-class women to support labor legislation.[16] By including both imperatives in her essay on civic housekeeping, Addams made clear that the actualization of her notion rested on changing the family and the purpose of politics through intersectional activism.

Activating the Theory-Activist Dynamic
through Nonstrategic Experiments

To achieve her aim, Addams called on women to "correct our theories by our changing experiences."[17] To begin this process, women would need to acknowledge the extent to which their lives were shaped by a "perplexity," or dysfunctional tension between old theories and changing experiences.[18] Addams pointed out perplexities when theories that had emerged under past circumstances were still holding sway under altered conditions. For example, she characterized household managers as suffering from "the perplexity of industrial transition" when they held on to an ethical conception of the family that suited a feudal, not an industrial, mode of production. The latter generated factory work as an alternative to domestic work for some young women.[19] The persistence of perplexities showed that changed conditions did not automatically produce new theories.

To show *how* to resolve the perplexities surrounding the family-public divide by constructing new theories, Addams and other Hull House residents turned to experimentation. Addams characterized the settlement as "an experimental effort."[20] The relevant kind of experiment for activating the theory-activist dynamic was *not* strategically oriented. When the residents devised models of social programs that they intended to turn over to the government to fund and execute, such as a kindergarten or an employment agency, they illustrated the strategic value of experimentation.[21] The playing out of the theory-activist dynamic required a nonstrategic kind of experimentation that put into practice the emancipatory potential of women's past experiences.

The Hull House experiments in cooperative housekeeping and state feminism illustrated the pragmatist-feminist understanding of the relationship between theorizing and nonstrategic experimentation. These experiments in embedding the household within the public created entirely new experiences that rested on extracting and replanting the emancipatory kernels of women's past experiences with economic activity. The aim was to generate new theories from these constructed emancipatory experiences. There were no guarantees that this method of theorizing would work according to plan. As Alzina Stevens (1849–1900), typesetter and journalist, noted, "experimental work . . . sometimes leads far afield from its starting-point."[22] In fact, built into this method was the understanding that the experiment and the theorizing would evolve beyond the original intentions.

The trick to designing an experiment in actualizing emancipatory potential was to start with the distillation of women's "genuine" experience.[23] By "genuine" Addams meant the emancipatory seeds of women's past common experiences in organizing matters of daily life. The extraction of these seeds rested on Seigfried's pragmatist distinction between "experience as origin and as the outcome of reflection, a reflection directed by the intention to change the situation so as to facilitate emancipation." By applying her bridging lens, Addams ably "liberate[d] aspects of the original experience that otherwise would not have been so explicitly recognized or articulated."[24]

Addams picked human labor, not the caring for small children, as the appropriate past common experience. While Hull House ran a kindergarten, provided five-cents-a-day childcare for a limited number of working mothers,[25] and held a well-baby clinic, Addams asserted that "we were very insistent that the Settlement should not be primarily for the children."[26] Moreover, Hull House did not set up an experiment to bring women together around the history of nurturing small children. Such a project would not have illustrated Addams's analysis that embedding the household within the public required women to take back control over economic activities that men had taken away from them. Women had never lost their role in the caring for small children.

Addams's choice of human labor supported her aim to shape the nonstrategic experiments by bridging the feminist settlement house movement with the labor movement. In her essay on civic housekeeping, Addams presented the logic of her choice in her description of the purposes behind the Hull House experiment called the Labor Museum. It brought the Arts and Crafts Movement, with its celebration of craft labor, to the Hull House neighborhood. On Saturday nights, there were demonstrations of the household arts. Women "representing vast differences in religion, in language, in tradition, and in nationality, exhibit[ed] practically no differences in the daily arts by which, for a thousand generations, they have clothed their families." According to Addams, "the quickest method . . . of establishing a genuine companionship" between nonimmigrant and immigrant women was "through this same industry, unless we except that still older occupation, the care of little children."[27] Addams did not develop the latter possibility further in her essay on civic housekeeping.

So Addams stressed the importance of educating women about the links between "woman's traditional work"[28] and modern industrialized production. In the process, she reinterpreted the meaning of women's primitive economic activities within an industrialized context. Then she theorized the significance of the Labor Museum experiment as having "made a genuine effort to find the basic experience upon which a cosmopolitan community may unite at least on the industrial side."[29] She envisioned a new type of bridging activism in which newly informed "American women" and experienced immigrant factory workers "could then walk together through the marvelous streets of the human city, no longer conscious whether we are natives or aliens, because we have become absorbed in a fraternal relation arising from a common experience."[30] The development of this "fraternal relation" depended on settlement house residents and their allies joining with the labor movement.

To make this bridging of movements possible, Addams defended a notion of "the labor movement" as "a general social movement concerning all members of society and not merely a class struggle."[31] Based on her experiences with the 1894 Pullman Strike and the organizing of women's unions at Hull House, in 1895, Addams distinguished between the "transient" and the "permanent" aspects of the dramatic manifestation of class struggle: the strike. The former included "the anger and opposition against the employers"; the latter referred to "the binding together of the strikers in the ties of association and brotherhood, and the attainment of a more democratic relation to the employer." Addams was particularly inspired by "the Chicago unions of Russian-Jewish cloakmakers [sic], German compositors, and Bohemian and Polish butchers," who "struck in sympathy with the cause of the American Railroad Union, whom they believed to be standing for a principle." She concluded that "it is because of a growing sense of brotherhood and of democracy in the labor movement that we see in it a growing ethical power."[32]

By aligning with those in the labor movement who folded "trades-unionism" into a broad vision whereby "industrial organization must be part of the general re-organization of society," Addams created the possibility for Hull House to join with this "growing ethical power." To support the bridging activism, she argued that "the duty of the settlement" was "to keep it [the labor movement] to its best ideal."[33] In 1906, Addams criticized "the trades union record on Chinese exclusion and negro discrimination," and she argued that this record "had been damaging" to the transformative promise of the labor movement.[34] Addams also understood that Hull House and the meaning of the feminist settlement house would be radically altered by aligning with the labor movement. As she observed, "[A] settlement must surely face the industrial problem as a test of its sincerity, as a test of the unification of its interests with the absorbing interests of its neighbors."[35] To pass this test, Hull House supported striking women workers.

To craft and theorize the Hull House experiments in redesigning the household-public split, Addams interrogated women's past economic roles in the gendered division of labor. She found two experiences with emancipatory potential: women's nonmarket-based production of the use value of daily nutritional provisions and women's humane control over working conditions. The Hull House nonstrategic experiments in cooperative housekeeping and state feminism replanted these nuggets to bring democracy to daily life. To shape the aim and the evolution of each experiment, Addams turned to the bridging of movements. When she theorized the specific meaning of each experiment, she showed how "a Settlement is led along from the concrete to the abstract."[36]

Cooperative Housekeeping: From Public
Kitchen to Coffeehouse Experiment

The evolution of this experiment illustrated the complexity of putting into practice the embedding of diverse households in the public to democratize the daily provisioning of food. The experiment began with the aim of interconnecting what urban historian Dolores Hayden calls "the grand domestic revolution," which included feminist cooperative housekeeping and the new field of feminist domestic science,[37] with the settlement house movement. As it evolved, Hull House also wove in bridging with the labor movement. The experiment centered on adapting the New England public kitchen (NEK) to the Hull House neighborhood. Ellen Richards (1842–1911), a feminist chemist from MIT, and Mary Hinman Abel (1850–1938), a nutritionist, collaborated on the design of the NEK and its menu.[38] By centralizing food production in a large standalone neighborhood kitchen, the NEK was designed to be fuel efficient and to produce low-cost, nutritious meals to be purchased by working-class families. After the Hull House residents witnessed its success at the 1893 World's Colombian Exposition in Chicago, they decided to establish one. While the NEK represented an alternative to the soup kitchen and to the saloon, which offered free lunches to those patrons who purchased alcohol,[39] the Hull House version also presented itself as a solution to the food needs of its residents.

On July 1, 1893, Hull House opened its public kitchen in the first floor of the Gymnasium Building. It outfitted the visible central kitchen with new technologies, including slow-cooking ovens designed by Edward Atkinson. The Arts and Crafts decor turned the space into an English pub. The residents hoped that the design would appeal to the immigrant neighbors with their peasant roots. The menu, based on a New England diet, included soups (tomato, vegetable, pea), beef stew, corned beef hash, and creamed cod fish and fish balls on Fridays. After a number of months struggling to keep the experiment afloat financially, the residents switched to a smaller coffeehouse operation.[40] Reflecting on its "final success," Florence Kelley (1859–1932) commented that the coffeehouse "form" was "quite different from that which filled the imagination of the residents who toiled over the beginning."[41]

Initially, Addams framed the experiment as the embedding of two types of households within an ecological and nutritious food economy. As she explained, "We hope by the sale of properly cooked foods, to make not only cooperative housekeeping but all the housekeeping in the neighborhood easier and more economical."[42] By "cooperative housekeeping," she was referring to a component of "a plan of living which may be called cooperative" that characterized Hull House and that tied it to the nineteenth-century cooperative movement.[43] Indeed, Hull House hosted a cooperative congress the same summer as the World's Fair.[44] For an understanding of "housekeeping in the neighborhood," Addams pointed to the discussions on the "economics of food and fuel" that were held by the Hull House Woman's Club, which met one afternoon a week. In fact, prior to setting up the public kitchen, Abel gave a talk there. Addams characterized the members as "the most able women of the neighborhood" who took "a most intelligent interest" in "Mr. Atkinson's inventions" and who "frankly compared" housekeeping at Hull House with their households. At this point, Addams formulated the relationship between the residents and the neighborhood women as one in which the former have acquired "a constantly increasing tendency to consult" the latter "on the advisability of each new undertaking."[45]

By interconnecting cooperative and neighborhood family provisioning of food, Addams was also confronting her gendered class privilege. During "the hard winter in Chicago" that followed the World's Fair, she gained intimate knowledge of the lack of food security in her working-class neighborhood. As she participated in relief efforts, Addams experienced severe discomfort: "I was constantly shadowed by a certain sense of shame that I should be comfortable in the midst of such distress." She began to think of Hull House as "a mere pretense and travesty of the simple impulse 'to live with the poor,' so long as the residents did not share the common lot of hard labor and scant fare."[46] To provide the relational context for her and the other residents to renegotiate their intersectional locations, Addams aimed to establish what was, in effect, a common table,[47] where the Hull House residents and their working-class neighbors would eat the exact same food. In the process, they would socialize democracy through shared daily food habits.

Aristotle's analysis of the Spartan and Cretan common tables showed how citizens eating together could be understood as a fundamental characteristic of a democratic constitution. In one treatment of the Spartan mixed constitution that combined oligarchy and democracy, Aristotle referred to how thinkers disagreed over the democratic component. Some "consider that the element of democracy appears in the Spartan system of common meals, and in the general habit of daily life at Sparta." The food served at the Spartan common table was "the same for all," establishing that there was "[n]o difference between the rich and the poor." Yet the Spartan rule that each man was expected "to bring his own contribution, in spite of the fact that some of the citizens are extremely poor and unable to bear the expense," according to Aristotle, undermined "the legislator's intent." By "legislator," Aristotle meant the founder or designer of the mixed constitution. Citizens who could not "contribute their quota are debarred from sharing in constitutional rights." To maintain the democratic purpose of the common table, Aristotle praised the Cretan practice of financing it with public funds. "This makes it possible for all alike—men, women, and children—to be fed at the public cost."[48]

Differing from Aristotle's ideal, Hull House had no access to public funds for its common table. The residents subsidized the low-cost meals, and they viewed their common table as a project of engendering democracy. To achieve this, Addams extracted the emancipatory kernels of women's past experience with food labor by linking the present and the past in her essay on civic housekeeping. Starting with an image of "dozens of young girls" entering a biscuit factory, she imagined them as part of "the long procession of women who have furnished the breadstuffs from time immemorial, from the savage woman who ground the meal and baked a flat cake, through innumerable cottage hearths, kitchens, and bake ovens," to this factory "in which they are still carrying on their traditional business." In the past, "during the ages of this unending procession," Addams claimed that women "were able to dictate . . . the hours and conditions of their work." All of this changed "since the application of steam to the process of kneading bread." Through this narrative, Addams established that women had been in charge when the use value of food was the determining factor.[49]

The Hull House public kitchen experiment reclaimed the centrality of the use value of food by adopting the new nutritional science notion of "food values."[50] As a chemist, Richards limited her notion of food values to the nutrients in the food, which were separated into protein, fat, and carbohydrates, each of which had a different caloric count based on the amount of energy it generated. Vitamins were not included because they had not yet been isolated. Richards referred to the nutritive composition as "the intrinsic value of the substance used as food for the human body."[51] She sharply contrasted food value with the cost of food, which was driven by market factors. As she insisted, "if once the public can disabuse its mind of any idea of close connection between 'food value' and cost—namely that a cheap food is a poor food, that a dear food is a good food—then a beginning in scientific dietaries can be made."[52] Richards's notion of cheap food rested on chemist Wilbur Atwater's theory of substitutions, whereby, based on equivalent nutrients, for example, within the category of protein, beans could substitute for meat.[53]

The democratizing possibilities of this notion of food values suited an experiment with a common table. Yet eating the same nutrients in unappetizing, unfamiliar food was not a sufficient draw for a diverse population with a variety of food cultures and, in some cases, strict dietary laws.[54] Richards's practical application of food values was just too constricted to support Addams's project to reclaim women's experience with producing the use value of food. While she might be able to connect, in her mind, the biscuit factory workers with the generations of women who provided food for their families, Addams's narrative left out women's valuable knowledge of the use value of food woven into the different food traditions.

Years later, to analyze why the public kitchen did not draw in sufficient numbers of working-class families, Addams did not even mention the impact of the economic depression. She stressed that the failure of the initial aims of the experiment was caused by "not reckon[ing] . . . with the wide diversity in nationality and inherited tastes."[55] She did not explore how the public kitchen might have succeeded if the manager had consulted on the recipes with "community panels," as recommended by the designers of the ideal NEK.[56] By applying the theory of substitution to the different food traditions, the manager might have created a delicious menu that furthered a new type of democratic common table.

The Hull House public kitchen experiment also demonstrated that the reclaiming of women's control over the conditions of food work was tied to professionalizing and unionizing it. This theme further demonstrated how Addams's vision contrasted sharply with Aristotle's ideal, where the food workers, including slave servants, were excluded from the democratic table. By bridging with the labor movement to build social justice for the workers into the experiment, Addams's vision was also radically different from Atkinson's reform aims. He invented the slow-cooking oven and financially supported efforts for cheap nutritious food, including the spread of the NEK, to undercut the social justice arguments for raising wages and building the labor movement. Spending less money on food, Atkinson argued, would lift the standard of living of the working class; therefore, there would be no need to regulate the labor market or legalize collective bargaining.[57]

When Addams looked back on the evolution of the Hull House experiment from public kitchen to coffeehouse in *Twenty Years at Hull-House*, she presented it as a response to investigations into the gendered exploitative working conditions of "sewing women during the busy season." They "paid little attention to the feeding of their families, for it was only by working steadily through the long day that the scanty pay of five, seven, or nine cents for finishing a dozen pairs of trousers could be made into a day's wage." As a result, these women purchased "canned goods that could be most quickly heated or gave a few pennies to the children," who bought candy.[58]

What Addams's summary of the findings of the investigations left out, but was known to the Hull House residents and others who were familiar with tenement house living conditions, was that working-class mothers were expected to carry out food work within an environment that Hayden characterizes as "kitchenless apartments from need rather than from choice." According to a 1900 survey of Chicago tenement living conditions, "cooking was done in the main room, which was provided with a stove, also used for heating." There might be a sink there or a shared sink in the hall or backyard. Ventilation might be poor or lacking entirely.[59] Moreover, there was no means to store food that could spoil, so continual shopping was required.[60] Clearly, for the Hull House residents, to make affordable healthy food available through a public kitchen was one way to help working mothers renegotiate how they combined low-paid work and family responsibilities.

While Addams did not include a discussion of the food work needs of the Hull House residents in her retrospective narrative of the evolution of the experiment, the residents were drawn to the public kitchen because they chose to live a kitchenless life. Yet they did not want to have servants prepare their meals because of their commitment to socializing democracy. So a professionalized, unionized staff was critical. Edith Abbott (1876–1957) recounted a story about the difficulty of maintaining a nonprofit, "pro-union" coffeehouse when the manager-cook was an African American man. According to Abbott, he was supported by a staff, which included a young Greek man and a Bohemian woman. When he told Addams that the Chicago cooks union would not let him join, she turned to Edith Abbott and Grace Abbott (1878–1939) to resolve the problem. Edith went to her contact in the WTUL, who refused to question the decision of the racist union. Grace found a pragmatic solution by having the manager-cook join an African American local in St. Louis.[61] The Hull House residents furthered the unionization of food work when they established a bakery that sold bread "adorned with the label of the bakers' union."[62]

Since Addams so revered food work, which she called bread labor, after a visit to Tolstoy, who castigated Addams for her class privilege and espoused the importance of bread labor, she decided that she "ought . . . to spend at least two hours every morning" baking bread in the newly added "little bakery." After all, she had grown up around the family-owned mill and had learned to bake bread as a child. She acknowledged that she "did not quite see how my activity would fit in with that of the German union baker who presided over the Hull-House bakery," but she thought that they could figure it out. The whole scheme appeared "utterly preposterous" once she returned to her Hull House life. With people waiting to see her after breakfast, letters to be responded to, and "the demands of actual and pressing human wants," she posed the question: "[W]ere these all to be pushed aside and asked to wait while I saved my soul by two hours work at baking bread?"[63] In the end, she came to understand that her schedule of socializing democracy precluded individual salvation through bread labor.

The public kitchen that was narrowed to a coffeehouse and bakery did embed some working-class households within the new food economy. Some working-class neighbors purchased nutritious take-out food. Teachers and other professionals might eat lunch at the coffee shop. According to Stevens, in 1899, "an average of 250 meals daily" were served.[64] The cooks also prepared food to be delivered to factories so working-class women would have soups and stews to fortify themselves.

Moreover, while the public kitchen failed as a neighborhood common table, the Hull House residents practiced their own version of the democratic common table, which embedded their household within the new food economy. They ate breakfast together in the coffeehouse, and its staff prepared their shared dinner meal, where they entertained guests and engaged in lively discussions. Edith Abbott described how arguments evolved over the course of a day: "Our political opinions varied widely, and our arguments not infrequently began at the breakfast table; and during the day the various participants in the current controversy seemed to have sharpened their weapons and prepared for the new arguments that were sure to be heard at the dinner table—with Miss Addams often serving as mediator and laughing as verbal shots were fired."[65]

In her evaluation of the public kitchen experiment, Addams concluded that the residents had learned an important lesson: "The experience of the coffee-shop taught us not to hold to preconceived ideas of what the neighborhood ought to have, but to keep ourselves in readiness to modify and adapt our undertakings as we discovered those things which the neighborhood was ready to accept."[66] The "preconceived ideas" pointed to the evolving science of nutrition and to sociological studies of the objective food needs of working-class mothers and their families. The phrase "ready to accept" suggested that the neighbors should play a larger role in shaping the experiment. As Addams noted, "[T]he neighborhood estimate was best summed up by the woman who frankly confessed that the food was certainly nutritious but that . . . she liked to eat 'what she'd ruther.'"[67] Her pushback indicated that consulting with the not sufficiently diverse Hull House Woman's Club was inadequate.[68] Years later, during her participation in the World War I effort to reorganize food production and consumption, Addams presented the following insight that easily fit the experiment with the public kitchen: "To make radical changes in our food habits . . . implies a struggle, none the less real, because it is concerned with domestic adjustments."[69]

Cooperative Housekeeping: The Jane Club Experiment

Initiated May 1, 1892, the Jane Club was an experiment in which unionized working-class women adopted cooperative housekeeping to embed their household within the economy. The experiment interconnected the settlement house and women's labor movements for the purpose of putting into practice the emancipatory potential of women's past control over their working conditions. Intersectional activism shaped the development of the experiment. It evolved out of Addams's relationship with Mary Kenney (1864–1943), a daughter of Irish Catholic working-class immigrants, the first American

Federation of Labor (AFL) woman labor union organizer, and the head of the women's bookbinder union.[70] Looking back, Addams reflected that this experiment was successful because "it was much more spontaneous." Also, after initial help from Hull House, "the members managed the club themselves."[71]

Both Kenney and Addams later described their first meeting, which gives us insight into how the flourishing of intersectional activism depended on the bridgers renegotiating their intersectional locations. Kenney had to complicate her class-only defined social location; Addams had to prove that she did not share the condescending attitudes of her class toward the working class. When Addams wrote to Kenney to invite her to a Hull House dinner, so she could meet some English visitors who were interested in the U.S. labor movement, Kenney's first reaction was to refuse the request. After her mother persuaded her not to be so judgmental without evidence, Kenney changed her mind. Neither of them had heard of Addams. Addams greeted her, and when she introduced Kenney to the English guests and the residents, her "first impression was that they were all rich and not friends of the workers." As she explained, "Small wages and the meager way Mother and I had been living had been making me grow more and more class conscious." She knew she came across to Addams as not "very friendly."[72]

Addams's version of their first meeting showed how she assumed Kenney would be suspicious of the intentions of the Hull House residents, who wanted to build a relationship with the president of a union, "the only one . . . composed solely of women" in Chicago. Kenney was clearly less enthusiastic. According to Addams, "She came in rather a recalcitrant mood, expecting to be patronized, and so suspicious of our motives." Kenney made Addams aware of her class privilege and forced her to think about how she could show Kenney that they could work together across gendered class lines to pursue social justice. To break through Kenney's resistance, Addams invited her to live at Hull House for "several weeks" as a guest "to find out about us for herself." It was this offer, according to Addams, that "convinced" Kenney "of our sincerity and of the ability of 'outsiders' to be of any service to working women."[73]

Kenney presented a different version of her shift in perspective. For her, the key moment was when Addams, only a few years older, asked, "Is there anything I can do to help your organization?" Kenney was skeptical, disbelieving what she heard, but Addams persisted with offers of help. When Kenney explained that the bookbinders needed a meeting place, Addams said, "The Book Binders can meet here." Then Kenney said that they needed "someone to distribute circulars," and Addams volunteered. According to Kenney, Addams paid for the circulars after consulting on how they should be worded. Kenney then described how Addams went about distributing them: "She climbed stairs, high and narrow. Many of the entrances were in back alleys. There were signs to 'Keep Out.' She managed to see the workers at their noon hour, and invited them to classes and meetings at Hull-House."[74]

This first encounter with Addams led Kenney to complicate her social location to engage in a new type of intersectional activism. As Addams reached out to her to bring women's labor organizing to the feminist settlement house, Kenney discovered "someone who cared enough to help us and to help us in our way." For Kenney, "it was like having a new world opened up." Her living at Hull House deepened these feelings. As she put it, "My whole attitude toward life changed."[75] A crucial part of her experience was taking classes, since she had left school at fourteen to support her mother and herself when her father died. Her labor activism required good writing skills; living at Hull House empowered her in this area.

For Addams and Hull House, the relationship with Kenney connected the feminist settlement house to the fledgling women's labor movement. According to Addams and Starr, "Of [the House's] standing with labor unions, which is now 'good and regular,' it owes the foundation to personal relations with the organizer of the Bindery Girls' Union, who lived for some months in the House as a guest."[76] By bringing union organizing to rooms at Hull House, Kenney created the conditions for Addams to learn about the experiences of working-class women. Addams illustrated how Hull House worked to act on what it learned in her presentation of the Jane Club experiment.

The idea for the Jane Club, according to Addams, originated at Hull House during "a meeting of working girls" in the midst of "a strike in a large shoe factory." She reported that "the discussions made it clear that the strikers who had been most easily frightened, and therefore the first to capitulate, were naturally those girls who were paying board and were afraid of being put out if they fell too far behind." In Addams's narrative, one of the working girls proposed the solution: "Wouldn't it be fine if we had a boarding club of our own, and then we could stand by each other in a time like this?"[77] In her version of the origin of the Jane Club, Addams illustrated the necessity of combining cooperative housekeeping and militant labor activism to improve working women's ability to negotiate their working conditions. According to Hayden, this interconnection of movements represented "a significant new use of the concept [of cooperative housekeeping] directed at a new constituency, single working women."[78]

Kenney recalled a different origin story. Addams approached her with the offer of a month's rent and furniture if she could find members for a "cooperative boarding club." She welcomed the project, knowing "what it would mean for working women to have a home near Hull House."[79] The initial members included two bookbinders, two shoemakers, one shirtmaker, and Kenney's mother. They employed a cook and another domestic worker. When they called themselves the Jane Club, they embedded their household within the Hull House project of redesigning the domestic-public divide. They committed themselves to showing how "any self-supporting unmarried woman, or widow without dependent children, between the ages of eighteen and forty-five" could practice democracy as a rule of living in the organization of their cooperative household.[80] Their constitution spelled out a system of collective self-government that created the conditions for striking women to feel secure in their daily living needs. They elected their officials, had regular meetings, adopted a system of arbitration to settle disputes, and taxed themselves three dollars a week to cover their room and board expenses.[81]

Their real innovation was their approach to domestic work. The domestic workers were not to be treated as if they were servants to be ordered around by members. Instead, any complaints about the food or other household matters were to be handled by a committee. Each member was responsible for cleaning her own room. By signing the constitution, she also committed to one hour a week of domestic work for the common needs, such as dishwashing. While one hour might seem very small, these women worked long hours. The housework was not supposed to "interfere with their daily occupations."[82] According to Hayden, "Their cook and 'general worker' earned about as much as the members did."[83] They would have known women—for example, Kenney's sister—who worked as domestic workers. Like Hull House, they sent out their laundry to encourage the unionization of laundry workers.[84] Most remarkably, according to their constitution, after two weeks, the domestic workers "shall be eligible for club membership," which required a vote.[85]

So the Jane Club experiment, which continued for decades, provided a rich practice in democratizing relations within the household. Or as Addams and Starr observed, "[W]hile the members are glad to procure the comforts of life at a rate within their means, the atmosphere of the club is one of comradeship rather than thrift."[86] The Jane Club showed how a cooperative household created new relations among working-class women that supported their participation in the labor movement. Thus, their two kinds of comradeship—at home and in their unions—were interdependent.

Finally, the relationship between Hull House and the Jane Club forced Hull House to clarify for itself what it meant to walk with working-class women workers and engage in intersectional activism to shape the experiment. The precipitating event occurred when Addams turned to raising money for a new Jane Club building, designed especially for cooperative living. Completed in 1899, this three-story brick structure was integrated into the Hull House complex by sharing its steam-heat and electric plants. In *Twenty Years at Hull-House*, Addams recounted how she refused $20,000 for the project from a capitalist, "a man who was notorious for underpaying the girls in his establishment and concerning whom there were even darker stories," presumably of sexual harassment. "It seemed clearly impossible," Addams explained, "to erect a clubhouse for working girls with such money." Instead, Addams turned to "an old [woman] friend of Hull-House" for the necessary funds.[87] Ultimately, the Jane Club provided Addams with a successful experiment in embedding cooperative housekeeping in the economy in such a way as to advance social justice for working-class women.

State Feminism Experiment: Participatory Enforcement of the Illinois Labor Law

Addams characterized the 1893 labor law as the "first modification of the undisturbed control of the aggressive captains of industry."[88] It banned child labor and mandated an eight-hour day or forty-eight-hour week for women and minors (ages fourteen to eighteen) in manufacture. The law also created a rigorous factory inspection system that gave the inspectors authority to prosecute violations. When Governor John Altgeld appointed Kelley the chief factory inspector, he created an opportunity for Hull House to experiment with a new form of participatory enforcement of a sex-based labor law. Because of historian Sklar's observation that Kelley's "office and Hull House were institutionally so close as to be almost indistinguishable,"[89] I suggest that Hull House became a site of an early form of state feminism, whereby feminists carve out agencies within the administrative side of the state to advance substantive gender equality.[90]

By bridging the settlement house and women's labor movements to shape the experiment, Hull House replanted seeds of the emancipatory potential of women's past experience with controlling working conditions in a participatory enforcement project. Addams confirmed that the law's "ministration was . . . centered there."[91] Providing a supportive socializing space, Hull House nurtured the bridging activism required to make the experiment a success. To undermine the potential for the deradicalization of the official factory inspectors, Hull House encouraged the development of a close relationship between intersectional activists outside and inside the state. In this way, the activist experiment showed how co-optation of the inspectors, a Chicago tradition, could be avoided.[92]

As a socializing space, Hull House fostered intersectional activism in different ways. Kelley and her chief assistant, Stevens, a labor union activist, lived at Hull House, and their official state office was just across the street. They "were usually the first customers at the Hull House Coffee Shop, arriving at 7:30 a.m. for a breakfast conference to plan their strategy for the day ahead."[93] Kelley appointed Kenney, the president of the Jane Club, as one of the ten deputy factory inspectors. Fannie Jones, another deputy factory inspector, was secretary of the Chicago Working Women's Council, which brought together unionized women from different unions. The council held its monthly open meetings at Hull House, where it gathered complaints of law violations. Addams reported that the Eight-Hour Club, made up of a range of working-class women who were affected by the law, met regularly at Hull House. The purpose of the club was to "encourag[e] women in factories and workshops to obey" the law.[94]

All of this bridging activism directed at the enforcement of the law redesigned the relationship between the family and the state by embedding a range of households within the regulatory side of the state. To bring immigrant families, who depended on the meager wages of their children for daily survival, into the experiment, Kelley turned to Addams. According to Sklar, "Addams took practical steps to limit the law's deleterious effects by becoming one of the first to investigate the need for 'widow's pensions.'" Addams brought Julia Lathrop (1858–1932), another Hull House resident who worked with the Bureau of Charities of Chicago, into the effort. She studied each case of a needy widow. Presumably, on her recommendations, the Illinois Federation of Women's Clubs provided "financial aid in the form of scholarships."[95]

Addams obliquely referred to this informal program when she pointed to the "understanding among the hard-working widows, in whose behalf the many prosperous people were so eloquent."[96] This private program illustrated strategic experimentation because it uncovered the need for a government program. Such a need reminds us that income supplements for mother-headed families originated with the aims to keep children in school and to enforce a child labor law. Thus, the Hull House state feminism experiment revealed the necessity to interconnect the social welfare and regulatory sides of a social democratic state.

When Addams turned to theorizing this experiment in state feminism, she formulated two stages of "the ideal development of the democratic state" from the bottom up. The first entailed "public agitation . . . find[ing] quiet and orderly expression in legislation enactment." The second referred to "labor measures . . . be[ing] submitted to the examination and judgment of the whole without a sense of division or of warfare."[97] The second part included participating in the actual enforcement of the law. While Addams expected Hull House to play a role in the first part under its "duties of good citizenship,"[98] the second part was unanticipated in her earliest vision of the settlement house. It took shape only because of Kelley's appointment, which led to the evolution of Hull House as a domestic-public hybrid capable of coordinating bridgers in a very innovative participatory administration of the law.

Hull House's experience with enforcing the 1893 labor law led Addams to challenge "the tendency we all have to consider a legal enactment in itself an achievement and to grow careless in regard to its administration and actual results."[99] Her conceptual innovation was to theorize the experiment in participatory enforcement of the law as a type of direct democracy.[100] As she explained, "[T]he administration of an advanced law acts somewhat as a referendum."[101] From 1893 to 1895, the period before the Illinois Supreme Court declared the sex-based eight-hour-day section of the law to be unconstitutional, Addams argued that "the people" as active enforcers of the law had become informed sufficiently on the workings of the law. As a result, in the future when it came up again for consideration, as it did in 1909, they could pass judgment on whether or not it was a valuable tool for achieving social justice.[102] Thus Addams used the experiment to theorize how community members participating in the enforcement of a labor law could advance the evolution of a deeply participatory social democratic state.

From these three nonstrategic experiments, we learn quite a bit about the complexity of activating the theory-activist dynamic. As we saw, the aim of bridging the feminist settlement house movement with other movements—the feminist food movement and the women's labor movement—inspired each experiment. The success of intersectional activism shaping the evolution of each experiment varied. In the case of the Hull House public kitchen, the failed experiment pointed to the need to expand the feminist food movement to put immigrant women with different food cultures at the center. The Jane Club experiment clearly put unionized working women in charge of playing out the bridging of movements. While the intersectional activism that actualized the state feminism experiment was quite impressive, the Illinois Supreme Court shut it down by invalidating the sex-based-labor portion of the law. Taken together, these nonstrategic experiments produced new facts on the ground that made possible new thinking about how to extend democracy to daily life. To develop this theme further, I shift to how Hull House as a socializing space facilitated democratic conversations about inequality of power within households.

Democratic Conversation: A Method of Socializing Democracy

By reembedding households in the public so women could regain a role in shaping the economy, and by presenting itself as an experimental domestic-public hybrid, Hull House evolved into a space conducive to a new type of democratic conversation. According to Wolin, "Democracy was born in transgressive acts, for the demos could not participate in power without shattering the class, status, and value systems by which it was excluded."[103] Certainly, Hull House shattered gendered hierarchies of power by transgressing the boundary between the household and the public, a necessary condition for women's inclusion in democracy.[104] Conversations on democratizing the household that took place at Hull House were transgressive acts because they opened up the household to public scrutiny by revealing the inequality of power between household managers and domestic workers, between working-class husbands and wives, and between fathers and adult daughters. As participants in these conversations, domestic workers, working-class immigrant wives and mothers, and striking daughters were transgressive actors. When they voiced their intersectional oppressions in a new women-friendly public space, they included themselves "consciously and unconsciously"[105] as actors in the refounding of democracy.

To clarify further how Hull House provided the necessary environment for a new type of democratic conversation, I draw on Addams's characterization of another domestic-public hybrid: the eighteenth-century French salon. According to Addams's interpretation, "the hostesses of the famous drawing-rooms" justified their "brilliant" hybrid by appealing to the notion that "people must come together in order to exercise justice," an Aristotelian notion. Of course, their application of Aristotle was subversive, since women were included in their conception of the people and the coming together occurred in a traditionally domestic space, not the Greek polis. Moreover, Addams claimed that the hostesses "became enormously proud of the fact that by the end of the century 'all Europe was thrown into a state of agitation if injustice were committed in any corner of it.'"[106] As the conversations on democratizing the household and family show, Hull House similarly brought women together to seek justice, with the hope that their conversations would point the way to a new combination of social justice and democracy.

By constructing three conversations based on Addams's narratives, I aim to show that she theorized a type of democratic conversation suited to the second stage of democracy. As a result, I complicate the way we understand her use of storytelling. The most popular approach argues that she aimed to create empathy for her working-class neighbors by crafting stories that translated or interpreted their experiences for her privileged social class.[107] Bringing a pragmatist feminist lens, Seigfried provides the crucial epistemological interpretation of Addams's stories by pointing out her "preference for expressing her insights as the outcome of dialogues with others."[108] From a refounding democracy perspective, I show how Addams used storytelling to create her model of a democratic conversation that was necessary for reconstituting the sovereign power.

To crystalize the defining characteristic of Addams's model, I draw on her theorizing of the charitable relationship. As she observed, "Probably there is no relation in life which our democracy is changing more rapidly than the charitable relation." Yet, she went on, "there is no point of contact in our modern experience which reveals so clearly the lack of that equality which democracy implies." Her chapter in *Democracy and Social Ethics* laid out the dilemma of a charity worker who tried to put into practice her ideal of "a larger and more satisfying democracy" within an environment of intersectional inequality.[109] This was exactly the problem Addams was addressing as she theorized a new type of democratic conversation: How was it possible to deliberate about the nature of the second stage of democracy in the context of structural inequalities?

Ultimately, the young charity worker provided an answer. She learned "humility" as "the contact with the larger experience, not only increases her sense of social obligation but at the same time recasts her social ideals." Specifically, she came to acknowledge that "her humble beneficiaries are far in advance of her . . . in self-sacrificing action." Her transformed consciousness led Addams to theorize: "She has socialized her virtues not only through a social aim but by a social process."[110] I contend that Addams translated this critical insight into her model of a new democratic conversation. It rested on the assumption that the key to formulating a new social justice ethic or purpose for democracy was to build into the deliberative process the central aim of forging a new sense of fellowship among the diverse participants.

By modeling this new type of democratic conversation, Addams directly challenged the Founding Fathers' vision and their institutional structures by arguing that they were hindering the evolution of the United States into a social democracy. The Founding Fathers relied on an abstract notion of equality found in the phrase "all men are created free and equal"; they adopted a static, nondevelopmental notion of human nature in the concept of natural man, and they did not trust the people to rule through collective self-government.[111] As a result, according to Addams, the Founding Fathers provided "no method by which to discover men" in order "to understand" and "to hold intercourse." As she explained, "A century-old abstraction [about equal rights] breaks down before the vigorous test of concrete cases and their demand for sympathetic interpretation."[112]

The specific example Addams gave to illustrate her critique of the Founding Fathers was the treatment of immigrants. While male immigrants gained the formal right to vote, Addams argued that "we have not yet admitted them into real political fellowship." To achieve the latter, she advocated shifting the focus to substantive equality. As Addams observed, "[W]e shut our eyes to the exploitation and industrial debasement of the immigrant, and say, with placid contentment, that he has been given the rights of an American citizen, and that, therefore, all our obligations have been fulfilled."[113] To discover women, Addams modeled a method of a democratic conversation in her storytelling that broke through the limitations of a formalistic notion of equality by bringing "real people" into relationship in order to "obtain a sense of participation with our fellows" by learning about their daily lives.[114]

To distill the method, I do not assume that Addams's descriptions of conversations with her neighbors at Hull House were like recorded transcripts. I think she depicted her neighbors and the words they spoke to dramatize a new type of democratic conversation that was necessary to build social democracy from the ground up. To achieve her aim, she presented herself as both a participant in the conversation and a theorist of its meaning. Ultimately, Addams's model pointed to the need for less powerful women to speak for themselves, as the rest of the book shows, and for more privileged women to learn how to listen.

In theorizing a new type of democratic conversation among differently situated women with the aim to socialize democracy, Addams grappled with how to expose and undermine the impact of the asymmetry of power among the participants. She distinguished between the roles of those who were more privileged and the less powerful participants. She posited that for the economically secure like herself, the primary role was listening. When she recounted conversations with her working-class neighbors at Hull House, she always characterized herself as listening to them. By showing how listening worked in the context of a democratic conversation shaped by unequal power, Addams filled in a gap in democratic theory.[115] For example, she went way beyond Arendt's observation that "everybody sees and hears from a different position."[116] She modeled how the ideal democratic listener was open to surprises and transformations on the part of the participants, including herself. In one conversation, not relevant to the argument of this chapter, Addams admonished herself during a pause by the speaker for "rashly anticipat[ing] the conclusion." When the speaker resumed her train of thought, Addams "found" that she "was absolutely mistaken" and had "commit[ted] a gross injustice."[117] Addams had assumed wrongly that the working-class woman speaker had not altered her consciousness as a result of her experience.

For Addams, active listening during a democratic conversation was necessary to acquire sympathetic knowledge.[118] This was her notion of relational knowledge, which depended on forging a humane relationship of trust with the differently situated speaker and not on imagining oneself inside the lived experience or consciousness of the other. The acquiring of new understandings or knowledge grew out of the listener's willingness to engage in the uncomfortable process of rethinking old ideas and values based on what she heard. As Addams explained, "[C]ontact with social experience is the surest corrective of opinions concerning the social order, and concerning efforts, however humble, for its improvement."[119] Thus, for Addams, listening, gaining new understandings, and forging a new social democratic relational foundation through a new type of democratic conversation were all interconnected.

When Addams turned to describing the role of her neighbors in the democratic conversation, she emphasized how Hull House provided a women-friendly environment for them to voice their intersecting oppressions caused by their intersectional structural locations. Yet Addams depicted her neighbors as more than suffering from oppressions. She was very attuned to the transformative effects on them of speaking in public. For example, she painted many pictures of immigrant working mothers being transformed before her eyes as they spoke. Also, in all three conversations that exposed the need to democratize the domestic sphere, Addams stressed how the working-class women asserted their agency. Thus, the experience of coming together to exercise justice at Hull House was multidimensional for the speakers.

While I incorporate Addams's insights into my formulation of the ideal type of an intersectional conversation, my three constructed democratic conversations in this chapter are not shaped strictly by applying it. The ideal type provides a framework for analyzing the struggles among social democratic feminists who were engaged in bridging movements and, as a result, in crafting new theories. Only the third conversation brings bridgers into relationship. My purpose here is to show how Addams and Hull House built socializing democracy into engendering democracy by encouraging conversations among a diversity of women, who revealed why it was necessary to extend social justice to the domestic sphere. These conversations demonstrate how Addams uncovered the range of issues bridgers would have to address to democratize the domestic sphere. By enlarging their bridging, Addams hoped that they could propel, in her terms, the shift from the family claim to the social claim and, in my terms, the shift from woman or maternal standpoints to social democratic feminist standpoints.

Democratic Conversation: Paid Domestic Work

By reporting overheard remarks from household managers and her own conversations with domestic workers, Addams zoomed in on the private family as a site of an undemocratic economic relationship. It was blocking the reembedding of the household in the public. She defined domestic work not as an art, but "as an industry, by means of which large numbers of women are earning a livelihood."[120] According to the 1900 census, more than half of employed women worked in households. Native-born white women accounted for more than two-fifths, native-born African American women were a third, and immigrant women made up about a quarter.[121] "[T]heir conditions of labor," according to Addams, were "largely in the hands of women employers."[122] Therefore, Addams suggested that any democratic conversation about paid domestic work would have to confront the unequal power relationship between the women.

By opening the Woman's Labor Bureau (WLB) in 1892, Hull House placed itself in the middle of the conflict between household managers and domestic workers. The Chicago Woman's Club (CWC) funded the WLB, most likely to provide its members with domestic workers. The WLB aimed to "train young immigrant women in domestic work . . . and then place them in well-to-do Chicago homes."[123] When Kelley took up residence at Hull House, her first job was overseeing this experiment, which she located adjacent to Hull House in a rented room in a mortuary. She intended to promote "simple justice between woman and woman" by "induc[ing] employer and employed to agree upon a standard of hours and promote self respect."[124] While there was a need for nonexploitative employment agencies, the WLB failed as a strategic experiment because, according to Kelley, women in the neighborhood were not drawn to its services.

Yet the presence of the WLB as a Hull House project and how it connected Hull House to the CWC provided Addams with material for envisioning a needed new type of democratic conversation that revealed and renegotiated the unequal power relationship. She described participating in conversations at the WLB with "women returning from the 'situations,' which they had voluntarily relinquished in Chicago households of all grades." She also characterized herself as a "listener, attentive to" conversations among household employers.[125] These conversations could have transpired in the Labor Museum, at meetings of the Hull House Woman's Club, and during interactions with the WLB members.

Taking my cue from Addams, I situate the constructed conversation at the defining moment when the domestic worker quit her job as a live-in servant. Addams groped for a language to give political meaning to the act. She suggested that it constituted a type of unconscious rebellion. Domestic workers, she declared, were "blindly fighting against conditions which limit their freedom." Their struggle connected them to "the ever recurring story of the emancipation of first one class and then another." Through many individual acts of leaving their employers, the rebellious domestic workers destabilized the labor supply. To grasp the nature of their method, Addams tried out Tolstoy's concept of "non-resistance," but it was only partially appropriate. Then she proposed a more precise term: "the non-appearance method." Her illustration was "[t]he well-known Swedish formula: 'I think I leave to-day.'"[126]

To explain her leaving to Addams, the domestic worker pointed to "loneliness" and stated that she felt "so unnatural all the time." Addams observed that after three weeks of working in a home, one young woman's voice changed so much that Addams did not recognize it. As she put it, "The alertness and *bonhomie* of the voice of the tenement-house child had totally disappeared." When a young woman quit, "her reasons [were] often incoherent and totally incomprehensible to that good lady." The employer believed that the young woman wanted "to get away from the work and back to her dances."[127] Talking with other household employers, she spoke in "a tone implying" that she "was abused and put upon; that she was struggling with the problem solely because she was serving her family . . . ; otherwise it would be a great relief to abandon the entire situation, and 'never have a servant in her house again.'"[128]

These fragments, as reported by Addams, suggested that a democratic conversation between employer and employee would expose the two intersectional social locations as the clash of two different family claims. Addams presented the household manager as embracing a family claim shaped by the overlap of gender and class that tied the well-being of her family to maintaining the last "surviving remnant of the household system which preceded the factory system": the live-in cook.[129] In contrast, the domestic worker's family claim interconnected industrial capitalism, gendered work, and religion/culture/nationality/race. One manifestation of the power struggle between employer and worker was that the household manager acknowledged only the service or "loyalty and devotion" to her family; the worker's family was of no concern to her.[130] As Addams commented, household workers "have peculiar difficulties in responding to their family claims, and are practically dependent upon their employers for opportunities of even seeing their relatives and friends."[131]

For Addams, the treatment of the two family claims by the employer was "undemocratic." It assumed that "one set of people are of so much less importance than another, that a valuable side of life pertaining to them should be sacrificed for the other."[132] Addams dramatized the sacrifice as "almost a religious devotion, in which the cook figures as a burnt offering and the kitchen range as the patriarchal altar." By speaking her intersectional location, the domestic worker revealed an important dimension of this sacrifice: sexual harassment and possible pregnancy outside of marriage. Whereas the "feudal" mistresses claimed they "carefully shielded and cared for" their servants, statistics and workers' voices exposed a different reality.[133]

Addams cited data from English hospitals "showing that seventy-eight per cent of illegitimate children born there are the children of girls working in households."[134] In discussing causes, Addams avoided the likely role of the husband or brother of the household manager. Her silence indicated her unacknowledged discomfort with raising this issue for her audience of household managers. Grace Abbott was bolder. As head of the Immigrants' Protective League (IPL), an offshoot of the WTUL, Abbott made public the voices of domestic workers. Thus, her reports help flesh out an important dimension of the constructed democratic conversation.

Abbott quoted a letter from a "Swedish girl" who asked "whether when the man in the house treats his housemaid very badly there is anything she can do when she had no witnesses." As Abbott explained, the worker was "convinced that an appeal to her employer would have resulted in her instant dismissal" and no reference. "[I]f she left without explanation," Abbott confirmed, "a reference would also be refused her." Somehow Abbott was able to help in this situation. Another example reinforced "the danger in placing girls." A "young Bohemian girl" who chose domestic work to have a "good home" was "ruined by some man in the family." She had come to the United States to get away from her own abusive family. "With a courage that humbled those of us who listened," Abbott reported, "she explained that she must have a good job so she could support her child and bring her mother to America."[135]

Addams and Abbott hoped that weaving workers' voices into a public conversation would provoke household employers into reconsidering their "selfishness"[136] and their unjust version of the family claim. To encourage them to join a new type of democratic conversation, Addams even recommended that employers read IPL reports.[137] Her aim went far beyond trying to create sympathy for the plight of the domestic worker. Addams insisted that "employers of domestic labor" would have to "become conscious of their narrow code of ethics and make a distinct effort to break through the status of mistress and servant, because it shocks their moral sense." In short, they would have to acknowledge their gendered class privilege and how unjust and undemocratic the mistress-servant relationship was.[138] Also, they would have to welcome the reorganization of their household by adopting new technologies and industrial food. Yet Addams was certain "that the mass of them would be content with the old regime if it only ran smoothly."[139]

By situating the constructed conversation at the point where the domestic worker walks away, I highlight how Addams made visible the intersectional locations of young women who chose factory work over domestic work. For many working women, except African American women, this option was part of the reason why "the old regime" was wobbling. In the case of eastern European Jews, a number of factors, including the requirement of kosher food, religious holidays, and fathers and brothers in the sewing trades, made "domestic service a rare occupation to daughters of the recent Jewish immigrants."[140] Their intersectional location, in which their Jewish dietary laws, culture, and religion shaped their gendered class position, provided daughters with a built-in resistance to domestic work. Rose Cohen's autobiographical depiction of her two-month experience in New York City illustrated this perspective.

At fourteen, in 1894, Cohen (1880–1925) had been in the United States for two years when her mother was forced, by dire economic circumstances, to hire her out as a servant. Cohen dramatized the ways the employer's family claim overshadowed her need to stay connected to her family. When she experienced shame because she had access to food while her family was starving, Cohen got up the nerve to ask for an advance on her wages. The employer did not understand that she needed the money right away so her mother could prepare the Friday night Sabbath dinner. Cohen also described her mother standing out in the street, waiting to catch a glimpse of her daughter.

At the end of the two-month experience, Cohen summarized how detrimental it had been to her sense of self: "My every hour was sold, night and day. I had to be constantly in the presence of people who looked down upon me as an inferior. I felt, though in a child's way, that . . . I was, or soon would be an inferior. I was looked upon as dull, nothing was expected from me and I would have nothing to give."[141] To illustrate how she was made to feel inferior, she recounted that her employer would put on her plate "the tail of the fish, the feet and the gizzard of the chicken, the bun to which some mishap had occurred." When she was given an apple, it would be "a spotted one." When she contemplated her future based on her growing feelings of inferiority, she declared, "My whole being shrank from this."[142] After all, her mother had insisted that she did not come to America "that my children should become servants."[143] Drawing strength from her mother and from her experience of being "a worker among other workers" in a shop, Cohen expressed the choice she would make: "'No,' I concluded, taking up the knives, and beginning to chop quickly to make up for the time lost, 'I would rather work in a shop.'"[144]

By going inside the household to expose the unequal relationship between the household manager and the domestic worker, Addams envisioned a democratic conversation between them that would lead to the reorganization of the field of domestic work, a crucial theme for Hull House from its beginning. This conversation complemented Hull House's experiments with cooperative housekeeping and the public kitchen. Both the experiments and the constructed conversation demonstrated that extending private housekeeping to civic housekeeping required radical change of the former because it was structured by intersectional inequality. The household manager did not value all family claims equally. Unreformed, she would extend an ethic of inequality to shape civic policies. The domestic worker's presence in the democratic conversation made visible the need to infuse paid domestic work with an ethic of social justice. The next chapter further develops the centrality of the domestic worker's role in refounding democracy.

Democratic Conversation: Domestic Violence

In 1913, the six-week devil baby episode began when three Italian women "burst upon the residents of Hull House . . . with an excited rush through the door." They demanded to see the baby with "cloven hoofs," "pointed ears," and "diminutive tail" who "was most shockingly profane."[145] Although no such baby existed, Hull House was deluged with thousands of visitors and inquiries. In her reporting of this affair, Addams presented herself as both participant and theorist. As a result, Addams clarified the roles of the listener and the speaker. She also revealed how both were transformed in the process of engaging in a new type of democratic conversation made possible by the hybrid nature of Hull House. Focusing on a central theme that emerged out of the incident, I construct a democratic conversation between Addams and her older immigrant working-class women visitors on the subject of the domestic tyranny of husbands over wives.[146]

Initially, Addams "confess[ed]" that she "revolted against" what she called "the empty show." Here she acknowledged her class and education privilege that blocked her from comprehending why her neighbors would insist that the devil baby lived at Hull House when the residents repeatedly assured them this claim was false. "[T]he high eager voices of old women" broke through her disgust. They enticed her to participate in a democratic conversation. She characterized herself as being "irresistibly interested" and willing to put aside whatever she was doing "in order to listen to them."[147]

Then she described herself as coming "down the stairs" from the rooms where the residents lived into the Hull House public spaces.[148] Her image harkened back to Plato's description in *The Republic* of the philosopher queen descending into the allegorical cave after having acquired knowledge of absolute justice. Her dilemma was how to communicate the truth to those who relied on their lived experiences for enlightenment. Addams may have thought that she had been acting too much like a philosopher queen, with a condescending attitude, when her epistemology was radically different from Plato's. By coming down, she opened herself up to receiving new lessons in how elderly immigrant women expanded the meaning of justice so that it applied to their experiences of domestic life.

Addams traced the roots of their conversation on domestic justice to the history of women using language through stories to gain some control over their husbands. In effect, by coming to Hull House to see the devil baby, her immigrant women neighbors demonstrated how, according to Aristotle, "language serves . . . to declare what is just and what is unjust."[149] Addams presented "the theory that woman first fashioned the fairy story . . . in an effort to tame her mate and to make him a better father to her children, until such stories finally became a crude creed for domestic conduct, softening the treatment men accorded to women."[150] Situating the devil baby story within this context, Addams described two basic versions.

The Jewish variant involved the father of six daughters. As his wife was giving birth to a seventh child, he declared that he would rather have the devil in his house than another girl. He got his wish. In the Italian telling, "a pious Italian girl" was married to an atheist. In a rage, he said that he would rather have the devil in his house than a picture of Christ on the wall. "As soon as the Devil Baby was born, he ran around the table shaking his finger in deep reproach at his father, who finally caught him and, in fear and trembling, brought him to Hull House."[151] In both accounts, by giving birth, the wives produced a punishment for the husbands who lacked respect for their wives and daughters.

The whole incident raised questions about why so many believed that the devil baby resided at Hull House. When the visitors "rush[ed] through the door,"[152] it was as if, in Jean-Jacques Rousseau's words, they were "fl[ying] to the assemblies" because they were so "interested in what happens there."[153] For Rousseau, "public affairs" went on outside of "private affairs." Hull House combined the two and thereby created expectations that it would be the ideal place for conversations on the meaning of the devil baby story "as a valuable instrument in the business of living." From the perspective of elderly immigrant women, Hull House provided a welcoming, familiar space for them to come together to exercise domestic justice. As Addams narrated, "[T]hey flocked to Hull-House from every direction; those I had known for many years, others I had never known and some whom I had supposed to be long dead." Women even came from the poor house. Addams reported that "[t]he Devil Baby seemed to occupy every room in Hull House," which meant that the assembling filled the entire house.[154]

The "hope" of being in the presence of one good case of "retribution" for "domestic derelictions" transformed Hull House into a public space for "the old women" to "come into their own."[155] The possibility of exercising justice, according to Addams, "aroused [in them] one of those active forces in human nature which does not take orders, but insists only upon giving them." In short, the devil baby incident emboldened the old women to actualize, through the democratic conversation on domestic justice that ensued, what Addams called "a living and self-assertive human quality."[156] Thus, contrary to Aristotle, who confined wives to the household, and who assumed that women were not by nature capable of ruling over men, the immigrant women were demonstrating that they "possess[ed] the knowledge and the capacity requisite for ruling as well as for being ruled," the defining characteristic of the good citizen who participated in the Greek polis.[157]

As the active listener, Addams gained a new appreciation for the women because their new self-assertiveness radically altered their presentations of themselves. As she observed, "In their talk, it was as if their long role of maternal apology and protective reticence had at last broken down, as if they could speak out freely because for once a man . . . had received his deserts."[158] They and Addams were experiencing an Arendtian moment of the "revelatory quality of speech" that "comes to the fore where people are *with* others."[159] Yet, in contrast to Arendt, Addams connected this revelatory quality to the pursuit of justice, Aristotle's understanding of the purpose of the polis.[160] For the working-class immigrant wives and mothers, the context of exercising justice in a women-friendly public space, like Hull House, was a necessary condition for them to reveal who they were.

For the "old women," according to Addams, the devil baby incident "loosened their tongues and revealed the inner life and thoughts of those who are so often inarticulate."[161] As the listener, Addams reported that their new self-assertiveness transformed their speaking style. They "talked with the new volubility." One woman told Addams, "I have never told you so much before. It's the foolish way all the women in our street are talking about the Devil Baby that's loosened my tongue, more shame to me." Addams observed that the women presented "their experiences more vividly than they had hitherto been able to do." Also, "they spoke with more confidence than they had ever done before."[162]

The women were voicing their intersectional social locations that were constituted by overlapping structures of class and gender inequality, including "much childbearing." The vivid details they provided showed how they "live under the iron tyranny of that poverty which threatens starvation, and under the dread of a brutality which may any dark night bring them or their children to extinction."[163] Addams listened attentively, "[w]ith an understanding" she characterized as "quickened, perhaps, through my own acquaintance with the mysterious child." Was she learning how to talk about domestic justice from the aged visitors to Hull House? She heard "of premature births, 'because he kicked me in the side'; of children maimed and burnt because 'I had no one to leave them with when I went to work'; women had seen the tender flesh of growing little bodies, given over to death because 'he wouldn't let me send for the doctor,' or because 'there was no money to pay for the medicine.'" Many of these testimonies of maternal anguish she had heard before. Yet within the context of the democratic conversation, Addams described how they "pierced me afresh."[164]

This conversation continued the theme of the need to politicize the family claim. By exposing in public the absence of domestic justice between husbands and wives, the conversation revealed another problem with extending private mothering into civic life. The devil baby conversation undermined any idealization of mothering. It demonstrated how extending working-class mothering into civic life amounted to providing a model of caring that was distorted by overlapping poverty, much childbearing, and a lack of protection for children. By bringing attention to these conditions through the devil baby incident, the working-class immigrant wives and mothers showed why their participation in refounding democracy was so crucial.

Democratic Conversation: Fathers and Daughters

The third democratic conversation happened during "a Garment Workers' strike." The details point to the 1910 seventeen-week strike sparked by a group of working girls. They walked out of the Hart, Schaffner, and Marx clothing factory because the "piece-rate reduction for pocket-sewing from four cents to three-and-a-half cents was unacceptable."[165] The strike grew to thirty-eight thousand first- and second-generation immigrant garment workers and led to the subsequent formation of the Amalgamated Clothing Workers of America (ACWA) in 1914. It brought into relationship middle- and working-class daughters who were dealing, in different ways, with how to break from the patriarchal imposition of the family claim so they could direct their lives according to a social claim. The backdrop to the conversation was Addams's further politicization of the family claim by reframing it as an undemocratic exertion of power over daughters.[166]

To dramatize her point, especially for her generation of college-educated daughters, Addams turned to Shakespeare's tragedy *King Lear*. Since the figure of Lear interwove the roles of political leader and father of three daughters, he suggested that the father-daughter relationship was a political one because it entailed the exercise of power. Lear and his favorite and youngest daughter, Cordelia, came into conflict when she refused to act as a dutiful daughter and left to go abroad. Addams characterized their relationship as "dictatorial," in which Lear asserted his "authority."[167] For Addams, Lear's practice of fatherhood combined "domination and indulgence."[168] Consequently, "[i]t was impossible for him to calmly watch his child developing beyond the strength of his own mind and sympathy."[169]

Addams further opened up the father-daughter relationship to political analysis when she examined the working-class immigrant family claim that obligated daughters to turn over their wages to their parents. According to one government report that Addams cited, 84 percent of them gave "all of their wages to the family fund." While she admitted that "[i]n most cases it is done voluntarily and cheerfully," Addams emphasized the cases that involved coercion. As she continued, "but in many instances it is as . . . if the tyranny established through the generations when daughters could be starved into submission to a father's will, continued even after the roles had changed, and the wages of the girl child supported a broken and dissolute father." According to Addams, this paternal tyranny led some young women to suicide, others to prostitution. Her examples were extreme to underscore the need for democratization of the working-class family claim.[170]

Addams suggested an alternative to the dutiful daughter, constrained by the patriarchal family claim, when she drew an analogy between Cordelia and the broad range of workers who supported the 1894 Pullman Strike. Or, as she put it, "a daughter's break with her father suggests the break of the employes [*sic*] with their benefactor." The analogy painted an image of the rebellious daughter characterized by the "force," "power," and "vitality" of a militant labor movement. The rebellious daughter, according to Addams, yearned to share in "this larger conception of duty" that Addams argued "surrounds and completes the individual and family life."[171]

While the analogy between college-educated daughters and striking male workers could make invisible actual working-class women and girl strikers, the democratic conversation put them at the center. Young bridgers like Bessie Abramowitz (1887–1946), a Russian Jewish immigrant button sewer who migrated to seek an alternative life to an arranged marriage, drew the Hull House residents into supporting the 1910 strike. Having taken night English classes at Hull House, she was familiar with what it offered her. She turned to Hull House as a meeting location and source of support because the male leaders of the United Garment Workers union refused to organize unskilled immigrant girls, and male skilled workers at Hart, Schaffner, and Marx initially shunned them.[172] Both groups of men seemed to be extending traditional family claim assumptions about daughters to the workplace. Even Sidney Hillman, Abramowitz's future husband and first president of the ACWA, recounted years later that "at first we made fun of it [the strike] . . . but somehow the girls managed to take out the men after awhile."[173] For three weeks, the men refused to honor the picket line. A meeting of five hundred people at Hull House increased support among the male garment workers for the spontaneous strike.[174]

Part of the democratic conversation was, of course, the strikers speaking their grievances and the middle-class daughters listening attentively so they could understand and help. This speaking and listening occurred at organizing meetings at Hull House and during a breakfast arranged by the WTUL. At the breakfast, Abramowitz recounted that employers ignored the 1909 Illinois sex-based labor law that established a ten-hour workday for women. Grace Abbott, who went to live at Hull House in 1908, had worked hard to get this legislation passed. It was a compromise, since Addams and Abbott aimed to reinstate the 1893 eight-hour day that Kelley had enforced.[175] Abramowitz told how women workers had no choice but to work twelve or thirteen hours and received no overtime pay. Apparently, one practice was to require the girls to work before and after they punched the time clock.[176]

Listening to grievances that included unfair pay, unfair fines, a lack of women's bathrooms, and workplace sexual harassment provoked listeners like the Abbott sisters to renegotiate the place of their class privilege in defining their intersectional social locations. Edith Abbott recounted how the strike affected their relationship with Julius Rosenwald, a Jewish philanthropist, personal friend, and part owner of Sears, Roebuck and Company: "We all felt very sorry . . . that he wasn't with us and that some of the girls who came to the meetings at Hull House were from" his shops.[177] In fact, almost one hundred workers from his shops joined the strike.[178] Both Edith and Grace Abbott tried to differentiate between him and his practices of exploitation. Ultimately, they lived with their personal discomfort: "[W]e had no hesitation about casting our lot with the strikers."[179] Grace, for example, participated in a range of activities, including speaking at mass meetings, building support, and even picketing. The context of the strike allowed the Abbotts to walk with a diversity of rebellious daughters.

Yet for Addams, the democratic conversation went way beyond voicing and listening to grievances. What drew her attention, as an activist-theorist of democratic conversations, was how the strikers demonstrated a shift from the family claim to the social claim. To distill this development, she designed a conversation in which the garment workers "were sitting in the very chairs occupied so recently by the visitors to the Devil Baby."[180] Since the 1910 strike happened three years before and the 1915 strike two years after the devil baby incident, clearly Addams's account of the seating arrangement was not factual. She set up the conversation this way, I contend, to theorize how the rebellious daughters broke with the elderly women's version of the family claim and through the strike forged the relational basis for a new social claim.

Addams presented herself as the democratic listener, open to new understandings of the differently situated participants. As she reported, "My conversations with these girls of modern industry continually filled me with surprise."[181] Her expectation before listening to the strikers was that working the "most monotonous" jobs under "the harshest" conditions would deaden the expectations and consciousness of the workers.[182] She discovered that for young women like Abramowitz, this was not the case. Unlike those working women who saw their real lives to be outside the workplace, in the eventual setting up of their own families, some strikers enlarged their "motives" for working to include the struggle for social justice.[183]

To theorize what she learned from listening, Addams contrasted the "endurance" of the visitors to the devil baby with that of the strikers. Maternal endurance, as in the case of caring for a very sick child, she argued, was "renewed from the vast reservoirs of maternal love and pity." The strikers were "obliged to go on without this direct and personal renewal of their powers of resistance." Instead, "their sense of comradeship in high endeavor," according to Addams, sustained them during the long strike, as they "endured all sorts of privations without flinching." These ranged from "actual hunger" and "disapprobation from their families" to lost wages. To stay out week after week, they risked permanently losing their jobs, yet they "displayed a stubborn endurance."[184]

Addams also showed how the strikers' struggle for social justice was *not* just a continuation of the "traditional" maternal struggle "against brutality, indifference, and neglect that helpless old people and little children might not be trampled in the dust." The young strikers represented an "antithesis to the visitors to the Devil Baby." As Addams observed, "[F]or the first time in the long history of woman's labor," working women were "uniting their efforts in order to obtain opportunities for a fuller and more normal living." Addams tied their development as rebellious daughters to how they were "obliged to form *new ties absolutely unlike family bonds* [my emphasis]." These new relations came out of "[o]rganizing with men and women of divers nationalities."[185] Indeed, the organizers of the 1910 strike gave speeches and distributed literature in nine different languages. Addams presented the strike as a positive context in which the participants, through their new relations of solidarity, worked through their prejudices.[186]

The significance of this third conversation is that it revealed that the social democratic feminists did not base their formulation of a social ethic on extending private household skills and private mothering into civic life. Addams's vision of embedding the household within the social democratic public required the reshaping of both by applying a new social ethic. As this conversation suggested, rebellious daughters—both the Hull House residents and the striking garment workers—played a central role in crafting the new social ethic. In addition, the first two conversations pointed to the need for expanding the subjects of their overlapping movements to include unionization of domestic workers, reproductive justice,[187] and domestic violence. Therefore, all three conversations backed up the theme that a shift from the family claim to the social claim and from a woman-maternalist standpoint to social democratic feminist standpoints rested on social democratic feminists engaging in intersectional activism.

Feminist Genealogy of Multileveled Social Citizenship: The Beginning

To recover why and how rebellious daughters took up the additional challenge to create their own feminist genealogy of multileveled social citizenship, I employ a genealogical method that interconnects Addams's theorizing with themes from Nietzsche and Foucault.[188] Foregrounding Foucault's insight about the play of contingent factors in the evolution of a genealogy, I find an answer to the why.[189] If daughters returning home after college had been treated the same as the sons, in terms of their social justice aspirations, and if they had had equal citizenship, there would have been no need for them to develop a feminist path to embodied multileveled social citizenship. But being hemmed in by the structural and cultural constraints of the family-state divide, they had no choice but to "consciously" reconstruct this divide so that they could enter public life.[190] Through their genealogy, the social democratic feminists constructed themselves as refounders, who innovated new citizen practices to evolve the new social democracy from the bottom up.

To analyze how they began this process, agreeing with Nietzsche and Foucault, I reject any notion that the end of the genealogy is present in the beginning. Following them, I distill the surprising elements in the beginning.[191] With this approach I debunk the interpretation that the unfolding of a maternalist teleology, defined as the extension of the mother-child relationship into public life, led inevitably to the new women-friendly notion of citizenship. Following Addams, who reports that the origin was provoked not by mothers but by rebellious daughters, I uncover the surprises that produced "fresh intentions,"[192] the embrace of intersectional activism, and the reinterpretations and activist substitutions that generated a new notion of participatory social citizenship.

The first element of surprise was that a power struggle within the family, between parents and their adult daughters, shaped the origin of the genealogy.[193] This struggle arose because Addams's generation of college-educated daughters was introduced in their courses to "an ever broadening range of obligations" based on "the claims of human brotherhood." When the daughter came home, she brought her awareness of "a stress of social obligation" and found herself "under an impulse to act her part as a citizen of the world." Her dilemma was to figure out how to practice citizenship of the world so that she was fulfilling her social obligation, or what Addams called "the social claim."[194] Unfortunately, her relationship with her parents, according to Addams, provided "an explicit illustration of the perplexity and maladjustment brought about by the various attempts of young women to secure a more active share in the community life."[195] This first type of perplexity captured the gap between the traditional norms for the behavior of daughters and the changing social conditions.

When the daughter tries to act on her new independence, according to Addams, "she finds herself jarring upon ideals which are so entwined with filial piety . . . that both daughter and parents are shocked and startled when they discover what is happening." Apparently, neither the parents nor the daughters were prepared to engage in the power struggle. Although her education led her to expand her expectations for her life, it had not "trained" her "in the line of action" or how to actualize the only form of public citizenship opened to her—citizenship of the world. Since the family claim was "concrete and definitely asserted," she "quietly submits, but she feels wronged whenever she allows her mind to dwell upon the situation." As a result, "she represses not only her convictions but lowers her springs of vitality."[196] This situation eventually led to a deterioration of her health.

According to historian Allen Davis, "Almost all of the first generation of college women seemed to have suffered from poor health and nervous prostration."[197] Representative of the generation of white, Protestant, middle-class, and nonimmigrant women, Charlotte Perkins Gilman (1860–1935) and Addams suffered well-documented breakdowns and were hospitalized under the supervision of Dr. S. Weir Mitchell. His treatment regime included "four to six weeks of seclusion, rest, full feeding, massage, and electric shocks." According to Mitchell, the cause of the disease was selfishness on the part of the daughter. Therefore, he lectured his patients on the need to be less selfish.[198]

I contend that recovering from these breakdowns constituted the second surprise element of the beginning of the feminist genealogy. The daughters discovered a type of resistance of the body in a positive sense of generating the "moral energy" needed to set out in a new direction, defined as "fresh intentions." After going along with Mitchell's regimen, Gilman and Addams independently rebelled. Instead of bed and milk, Addams argued, the daughter "needs . . . health-giving activity, which involves the use of all her faculties."[199] So first they repressed their desires to act as citizens of the world. Then they collapsed, because the breaking from their parents' expectations, according to historian Nancy Cott, "required an exceptional wrench from the status quo that only a minority could conceivably make."[200] For my purposes, it does not matter that some social democratic feminists did not have the experience Addams described. The crucial point is that Addams and other rebellious daughters started, in surprising ways, a genealogy of multileveled social citizenship that each stream shaped for its own purposes.

Yet to move on from the initial power struggle and from their mental breakdowns, they still had to work their way out of a second type of perplexity. As Addams explained, "The conception of life which they hold has not yet expressed itself in social changes or legal enactment but rather in a mental attitude of maladjustment, and in a sense of divergence between their consciences and their conduct."[201] This gap between their social justice ideals and social conditions and political institutions led them to experience "the strain and perplexity of the situation."[202] To lessen this gap, to turn abstract world citizenship into embodied social citizenship, Addams argued that the daughters would have to participate "in the social movements around us."[203]

While Addams turned to movement activism to evolve the genealogy, she also formulated the process of creating a new concept of citizenship. It entailed "overcoming," "substituting," and "re-creating."[204] Her choice of words echoed Nietzsche, who connected his notion of overcoming to "reinterpretation."[205] For him, the "fresh intentions" of "those in power" drove these reinterpretations and the genealogy.[206] Addams was clearly focused on reinterpretations, but in contrast to Nietzsche, she sought substitutions, especially activist ones, as the way to anchor reinterpretations. Operating as an outsider, she assumed that she had to prove the value of new thinking about citizenship by new practices.

As they embraced intersectional activism, the rebellious daughters invented a notion of social citizenship focused on its participatory dimension rather than on its social-rights-bearing status, Marshall's formulation. The core of their notion was the social service relationship as a substitute for the charitable or philanthropic relationship. According to their critique of the liberal laissez-faire version of democracy, charity complemented an unregulated market system by reinforcing the underlying individualistic market ethic and market-based intersecting hierarchies of power. Purporting to help those in need, charities judged and regulated the lives of those who were blamed for their poverty.[207]

In sharp contrast, the social democratic feminists insisted that their different versions of social service constituted practices of "citizenship." While they did not use the term "social citizenship," I justify the concept because it captures Addams's use of the notion of social claim to reinterpret citizenship of the world. I apply "social citizenship" to their new combinations of social service and citizenship. I also formulate a notion of participatory social citizenship that included two activities: interpersonal social service and social service participatory politics that incorporated engagement with the state.[208] The feminist settlement house as a new adaptable domestic-public hybrid facilitated both activities.

Citizen Social Service

Addams depicted the first type of social service relationship as between a facilitator and her working-class neighbors, who "require[d] only that their aspirations be recognized and stimulated and the means of attaining them put at their disposal." The "constant effort [by Hull House] to secure these means for its neighbors," according to Addams, constituted "the duties of good *citizenship* [my emphasis]."[209] In consultation with their neighbors, Hull House residents and others developed a range of programs, including lectures, English classes, college extension courses, and citizenship classes, and they provided meeting rooms for a broad range of cultural events. As they helped their neighbors shape their own lives, the Hull House facilitators strove to honor and support the rich diversity of the neighborhood.

To advance this aim, Grace Abbott redefined "[t]he immigration problem" as "not so much a problem in assimilation as in adjustment." Then she delineated how the facilitator could play a role: "To assist in such adjustments, we must take account, first, of those traditions and characteristics which belong to the immigrants by reason of their race [or nationality] and early environment, and, second, of the peculiar difficulties which they encounter here."[210] In 1911 she visited eastern and central Europe to understand why the young women she served at the IPL "had the courage" to leave their families and embark on an "excursion into the unknown."[211] During her four-month trip, she even visited some of their families. In her report, she emphasized the role of rigid class inequalities in peasant societies. She discovered that some women migrated because "nothing could change" economically for them in their homeland.[212] The background information she gathered deepened her understanding of the immigrants she assisted during the day at her IPL office and at Hull House in the evening. The services of the IPL included providing translators, aiding in family unification, helping with the naturalization process, and representing immigrants threatened with deportation.[213]

Lillian Wald (1867–1940), at Henry Street Settlement House on the Lower East Side of New York City, developed a second type of social service relationship between health-care professionals and their immigrant neighbors. She described her 1893 vision: "We were to live in the neighborhood as nurses, identify ourselves with it socially, and, in brief, contribute to it our *citizenship* [my emphasis]."[214] In developing a visiting nurses program, Wald, of German Jewish background, served an eastern European Jewish immigrant population. Her goal was to replace the charitable relationship with a new type of health-care service.

Wald outlined a number of characteristics of the "new" relationship between nurse and patient, "reversing the position the nurse had formerly held." Instead of stigmatizing the family by emphasizing its inadequacies, the visiting nurse should stress "the family's liberality and anxiety to do everything possible for the sufferer." The crafting of a new democratic social service relationship also depended on developing a service that was not affiliated with "a religious institution or free dispensary." While the nurse could take calls from physicians, she should not be tied to one doctor. For Wald, it was critical to develop unmediated relationships between the nurse and the family so that families could initiate the service. As she explained, "[W]e planned to create a service on terms most considerate of the dignity and independence of the patients."[215] The nurses decided to charge fees "when people could pay."[216] As the professional social service relationship evolved, Wald observed that the visiting nurse was "being socialized" as she participated in advancing "the communal health."[217]

In delineating the characteristics of the new relationship between the health-care professional and the patient, Wald was adamant "that instruction should be incidental and not the primary consideration."[218] Alice Hamilton (1869–1970), a physician, occupational health researcher, and resident of Hull House starting in 1897, recounted how she learned that "Italian women knew what a baby needed far better than [her] Ann Arbor professor did." At Hull House, she opened "a well-baby clinic" that served children up to eight years old. The main activity was bathing the children. Her Italian neighbors ignored her advice to feed babies only milk until their teeth came. Years later she observed, "So now when I see an Italian baby sucking a slice of salami I feel quite serene. Garlic, we are told, is full of most valuable vitamins and salami is full of garlic."[219]

Lugenia Burns Hope (1871–1947), at Neighborhood Union in Atlanta, Georgia, created a third type of social service relationship in which African American neighbors practiced mutual aid in the context of intraracial class differences. Four years of experience working for a Chicago charity focused on young women and for a woman who volunteered at Hull House once a week gave Hope an understanding of the distinct possibilities of feminist settlement work.[220] In 1908, Neighborhood Union was born in response to an incident where a young woman who lived with her husband and father grew seriously ill without her female neighbors knowing. By the time they checked on her, it was too late to save her life. To promote a sense of racial solidarity, the Neighborhood Union women chose as their motto, "Thy Neighbor as Thyself."[221]

Historian Dorothy Salem characterizes Hope's version of the feminist settlement house as a product of segregated Atlanta and the qualities of its African American leadership.[222] In contrast to northern settlements directed at the African American community that were initiated by white reformers and "developed as a result of black energies," Neighborhood Union was "a black-initiated, black-directed, and black-funded settlement."[223] It aimed to organize the entire African American community. Through its practice of mutual aid, Neighborhood Union linked settlement work to the legacy of another refounding moment: the post–Civil War Reconstruction period.

Both W.E.B. Du Bois (1868–1963) and Julia Anna Cooper (1858–1964) linked the African American settlement house to the overcoming of the legacy of slavery. Du Bois characterized the African American colleges created during Reconstruction as "social settlements."[224] Cooper explicitly argued that "a fitting memorial to the immortal Lincoln . . . as the great Emancipator of a much-exploited people" would be "to build and maintain at our nation's Capital a working bureau of ideals and opportunities—a 'level bridge' reaching sheer to the shores of complete emancipation."[225] Here she was characterizing her hope for an African American women-run settlement house in Washington, D.C. According to Cooper, it could "perpetuate the elemental human good for which the martyr President died" by helping "each child . . . to develop into serviceable *citizenship* [my emphasis]."[226]

Through Neighborhood Union, Hope infused their interconnecting of two refounding moments with a feminist dimension. She emphasized the aim to imbed the family within a larger public.[227] As the wife of John Hope, the president of Morehouse, a college created during Reconstruction, Lugenia Burns Hope initially utilized her own home as a center of meetings and classes. She also drew Morehouse sociologists into the training of volunteers in social science methods. As a result, they carried out various investigations, including into the conditions of the segregated African American public schools.[228]

To make possible the flourishing of relations of mutual aid, Neighborhood Union eventually established sixteen zones. Within these zones there were designated neighborhoods that were divided into districts. Chairpersons of the zones were elected. A Neighborhood Union Board of Managers included three levels of officials: zone leaders, neighborhood presidents, and district directors. The district director played the key role of organizing mutual aid. As a 1913–1914 report observed, "When families are in need, the director passes the word along and the present need is supplied." Then the report went on to list a number of examples, including helping families with food, rent, and health care.[229]

While Neighborhood Union cooperated with the Associated Charities of Atlanta, its practice of social service contrasted with the traditional charitable relationship. First, it aimed to build community among African Americans. As Neighborhood Union explained, "Our method of relief in the neighborhood is to have each neighbor feel the responsibility of his next door neighbor."[230] Second, it adopted a method of financing that depended on membership, class fees, and creative approaches to fundraising. For example, members helped finance the establishment of its first settlement house, Neighborhood House, which opened in September 1915. As the Neighborhood Union Constitution declared, it was structured "to build the sort of ethnic pride that would take delight in constructive *citizenship* [my emphasis] and happy family life."[231]

Citizen Social Service Participatory Politics

The feminist settlement house also facilitated social service participatory politics, whereby practices of citizen social service shaped the development of the public sector. The aim of social service participatory politics was to provide an alternative model to impersonal bureaucratization, or as Addams put it, the "danger of forgetting the mystery and complexity of life, or repressing the promptings that spring from growing insight."[232] The new relations of diversity forged through citizen social service provided insights about the specific social needs of different communities. When these new relations turned to addressing these needs through governmental institutions, they produced a complex, intersectional understanding of social justice. To illustrate the second women-friendly mode of citizenship, I turn to three examples.

Neighborhood Union wove together social service as mutual aid and a political campaign to improve the conditions in the segregated African American schools. Starting in 1910, Neighborhood Union moved to gain some authority over the use of school buildings by persuading the superintendent of schools to allow it to use the buildings for social service activities, especially during the summer months.[233] By 1913, Neighborhood Union administered a survey of the gross inequalities in the schools and turned to building widespread community cohesion to pressure the board of education to advance racial justice. The latter entailed visiting the homes of students who were not attending school because of the overcrowded and unhealthy conditions. These visits made visible the social needs of some families that led to the follow-up delivery of mutual aid.[234]

As a result of its organizing effort, which included reaching out to white allies, Neighborhood Union got the board of education to raise salaries for African American teachers and build one new small school. While these improvements were meager, historian Jacqueline Rouse concludes that "this was the first organized effort to investigate and confront the blatant racism of the City Council and the Board of Education" in Atlanta, "the most segregated city in Georgia."[235] So Hope, through Neighborhood Union, innovated a type of social service participatory politics appropriate for operating within a racialized public sector. It made visible how the public sector institutionalized racial injustice and how citizen social service through community organizing could open up the public sector to contestation.

Wald used an experiment in social service nursing in the New York City public schools to gain support in 1902 for what she characterized as "the first municipalized school nurses in the world."[236] She had determined the need for such a program since children were routinely sent home from overcrowded classrooms with curable conditions, like eczema and ringworm. She waited until the schools had a program of paid doctors who were responsible for sending home children with contagious diseases. Then she offered to demonstrate that visiting nurses could keep the children in school by treating their conditions. "Reluctant lest the democracy of the school should be invaded by even the most socially minded philanthropy," Wald "exacted a promise from several of the city officials" that if her experiment succeeded, they would work to have the nurses "paid from public funds" like the doctors.[237]

Wald designed the experiment so that doctors communicated their diagnoses directly to the nurses, who located themselves within the schools. They would treat the students "[w]ith the equipment of the settlement bag." If the condition was more serious, the nurse would visit the home. If the mother worked and there was no one else available, the nurse would take the student for further medical care. Wald characterized her successful effort as expanding the side of the public sector that "aim[s] at care and prevention, rather than at police power and punishment."[238]

Ida B. Wells-Barnett (1862–1931) practiced social service participatory politics through an experimental program within the punishment side of the state. In 1913 she was appointed to the position of adult probation officer within the Domestic Relations Department of the Chicago Municipal Court. She located her office at the Negro Fellowship League, the settlement house she founded in 1908 and characterized as "the Hull House for our people on the South Side."[239] Wives and female relatives would bring their grievances to her. The responsibilities of the probation officer included enforcing the court order or "sentence" for the man to provide financial support for the family, finding work for the probationer if necessary, acting as a mediator between husband and wife, and seeking charitable aid where needed.[240] Some of the cases Wells-Barnett oversaw involved domestic violence and women fearing for their lives.[241] Beyond her specific responsibilities as a probation officer, Wells-Barnett used her position to expose the racial injustices of the criminal justice system. For example, she got press coverage of the unjust use of solitary confinement for African American prisoners.[242] She also met with women in prison to discuss women's suffrage.[243] Finally, through her paid position, Wells-Barnett financed the Negro Fellowship League.

Taken together, the different practices of social service and social service participatory politics show how the three streams of social democratic feminists adapted the feminist settlement house form to suit the characteristics of their different communities. As a result, the feminist settlement house provided the necessary socializing space for each stream to turn intersectional activism into new forms of social citizenship. By labeling their community-based social service "citizenship," the three streams declared that their aims went far beyond establishing the women-friendly professions of social work, visiting nurse, and probation officer. In short, the social democratic feminists began their feminist genealogy of multileveled social citizenship by interconnecting social justice movements through citizenship practices tied to addressing the needs of daily life.

Refounding as a New Beginning from the Bottom Up

This chapter shows that to recover the social democratic feminists as refounders, we must acknowledge that they created a new beginning for democracy from the bottom up. Their unique contribution was to develop methods of socializing democracy, or of forging new democratic relational foundations. They aimed to reconstitute the people as a deeply diverse sovereign power.

To find these methods, they extended democracy to daily life. This extension was necessary to dismantle the gendered domestic-public divide that held women back from full participation in democracy.

To give structure to their purpose of engendering democracy, the social democratic feminists created new domestic-public hybrid spaces that were conducive to experimentation and difficult democratic conversations. In this way, they illustrated a key component of a new beginning: the institutionalization of new participatory spaces to keep alive the revolutionary spirit. Each stream of social democratic feminists customized the feminist settlement house participatory space to suit the needs of their different communities. They carried out their methods of socializing democracy by innovating democratic forms of social service. To make clear that they were consciously building a new stage of democracy on these new relational foundations, Addams labeled the hybrid space "social democracy" and called social service "citizenship." Clearly, the two were interdependent, because their new type of social citizenship only made sense in a social democracy. Thus, the social democratic feminists intertwined the evolution of their multileveled social citizenship with the refounding of democracy.

Women's Economic Independence and the Creation of a Feminist Welfare State

By including women's economic independence as a component of engendering democracy, this chapter further demonstrates both directions of the book's first broad argument that engendering and socializing democracy were mutually constitutive. In one direction, the social democratic feminists used women's economic independence to shape the socializing of democracy, defined as a feminist welfare state, so that it would further substantive gender equality. In the other direction, the social democratic feminists infused engendering democracy with intersectional social justice by embedding women's economic independence within the dismantling of intersecting hierarchies of power. This chapter also advances the second broad argument by showing that the second stage of the feminist genealogy of social citizenship socialized the civil right to work.

The Promise of Women's Changing Economic Position

The topic of women's economic independence did not originate in this period of refounding U.S. democracy. Mary Wollstonecraft and John Stuart Mill had tackled it earlier. Wollstonecraft asserted that women's ability "to earn their own subsistence" constituted "the true definition of independence."[1] Mill wrote, "The same reasons which make it no longer necessary that the poor should depend on the rich, make it equally unnecessary that women should depend on men."[2] Yet both recognized the cultural and structural barriers blocking women, especially married and unmarried women with children, from achieving such economic independence.

At the end of the nineteenth century, the increasing pull of the economy improved the conditions for actualizing women's economic independence. As Gilman observed in 1898, "Everywhere throughout America are women workers outside the unpaid labor of the home, the last census giving three million of them." For her, this figure provided "an undeniable proof of the radical change in the economic position of women that is advancing upon us." She praised this "increasing army of women wage-earners, who are changing the face of the world by their steady advance toward economic independence." While Gilman positioned herself as a theorist of "the spirit of the times" and not as an instigator of radical change,[3] she and other social democratic feminists, by bridging movements, created a complex notion of economic independence as one anchor of the engendering and socializing of democracy.

My specific argument is that the three groups of bridgers showed how women's economic independence required and furthered turning care into a democratic value that enlarged the purpose of the state by legitimizing earning mothers, disconnecting care from its servile status, and socializing the citizen civil right to work. This argument establishes that women could not simply add themselves as self-interested individual workers into a male-biased, laissez-faire liberal understanding of the relationship between the market and the state. The central place of care work in women's daily lives complicated the achievement of women's economic independence. The unregulated market was not suited to accommodating the integration of care and paid work. Therefore, women turned to developing state social programs and labor regulations to reshape the labor market and reconceptualize, by feminizing, the human worker.

This argument also challenges the maternalist characterization of the social democratic feminist contribution to the creation of a welfare state. According to historian Linda Gordon, they were maternalists because they operated within the framework of the male family wage, which viewed women as mothers who were financially dependent on their husbands. As a result, women adopted a "motherly role toward the poor," and they presented themselves as having the necessary maternal experiences "to lead certain kinds of reform campaigns."[4] In contrast, the argument of this chapter shows how social democratic feminists used their struggles for economic independence to extract the emancipatory potential of care from its traditionally subordinate status so that it could be utilized to shape publicly supported forms of socialized care. As this book makes clear, the inclusion of African American and immigrant Jewish bridgers strengthens the nonmaternalist interpretation. The argument of this chapter reveals how the social democratic feminists interconnected two struggles usually separated: the struggle for economic independence and the struggle for a welfare state.[5]

To demonstrate the argument, I construct intersectional conversations. In contrast to the last chapter, these conversations did not occur on the site of a new feminist participatory social space. In fact, I do not have evidence of significant back-and-forth exchanges between the participants from the three streams. This lack underscores the difficulty of engaging in intersectional activism within the intersectional structural constraints of a socioeconomic system that allowed various actors to pit the different groups of women against each other. By foregrounding the voices of African American and immigrant Jewish social democratic feminists, and by bringing them into relationship with Gilman, I establish that the three streams were pursuing similar aims. Some participants were clearly familiar with the work of social democratic feminists in other streams. Taken together, each stream produced a complex parallel intersectional conversation within what historian Evelyn Higginbotham calls "a discursive common ground."[6]

To justify my application of the ideal type of an intersectional conversation to theorize relationships between intersectional activists in parallel conversations, I establish at the outset how the three groups of social democratic feminists helped me formulate the ideal type of an intersectional conversation and how they were self-consciously bridgers. Then I turn to constructing three intersectional conversations, each focused on an interconnected aspect of economic independence: independence from men, overcoming the conflict between mothering and earning, and a public revaluing of care work. The first conversation uncovers how the social democratic feminists conceptualized the notion of independence in different ways by voicing different histories of intersectional oppression and finding seeds of emancipation in their bridging of struggles. The second conversation shows how social democratic feminists used the needs of working mothers to justify the creation of public sector programs and a new notion of socialized care. The third conversation reveals how social democratic feminists theorized the necessity to publicly revalue care work by uprooting its servile status. Finally, all three conversations clarify how the intersectional activists discredited a maternalist standpoint, based on a male family wage ideology, by crafting social democratic feminist standpoints that unfolded a complex notion of women's economic independence.

After I construct the intersectional conversations, I turn to the second stage of the feminist genealogy of multileveled social citizenship that connected women's economic independence to socializing the civil right to work. I establish that the liberal individualistic notion of this right was not up to the task of facilitating women's participation in the labor market. Then I show how Gilman's bridging of movements produced reinterpretations and substitutions. She socialized the right by turning all work directed at the common good into social service, and she feminized the human worker. I also examine how social democratic feminists responded to contingent factors by adopting a gender-difference legal strategy to justify new worker rights and to create the welfare state. All these innovations showed how the second stage of the genealogy was quite subversive of the individualistic laissez-faire version of economic citizenship.

Justifying the Application of the Ideal Type of an Intersectional Conversation

Through brief sketches, I turn to how social democratic feminists helped me formulate key dimensions of the ideal type of an intersectional conversation and why it is best suited for bridgers. First, they self-consciously voiced their intersectional structural social locations, a starting point for a conversation. Second, they advocated or practiced sympathetic understanding, a method of transforming consciousness during a conversation. Third, they utilized their skills at bridging movements to generate new intersectional analyses, a central purpose of an intersectional conversation. I illustrate the third dimension as I develop the parallel conversations.

Theresa Serber Malkiel (1874–1949), a Jewish immigrant from Russia, a former cloak maker, and a bridger of the Socialist Party and the suffrage movement, characterized the intersectional structural location of working-class women. She stressed overlapping oppressions. As she explained, "Under the present system the workingman has only one master—his employer, the workingwoman must bow to the will of husband as well. While capitalism is satisfied with the workingman's labor power, it stretches out its claws for the workingwoman's body." The first sentence established how the woman operated within two overlapping systems of unequal power. The last sentence presented a bridging of socialist and feminist movements to reinterpret Karl Marx's theory of labor power by incorporating women's vulnerability to workplace sexual harassment. Apparently, the capitalist assumed that he was buying sexual access to women's bodies when he purchased their labor power. Malkiel observed that this assumption had the potential to radicalize working-class women: "Sex debauchery on the part of the male is steadily sending woman on the war path, hastening her transition from a passive subject to a conscientious rebel."[7]

In *The Diary of a Shirtwaist Striker*, Malkiel presented a fictionalized treatment of the 1909–1910 garment workers' strike in New York City that mobilized twenty to thirty thousand "girls." Without using the term, she depicted how sympathetic understanding led a working-class woman to renegotiate her intersectional social location, or combination of privilege and oppression. Mary, the narrator of the diary, characterized herself as "a free-born American." Although she joined the strike, she began with prejudices toward the immigrant "Jew girls."[8] As she deepened her commitment to the strike, she reevaluated her attitudes and her privilege as a nonimmigrant. She came to recognize their courage, self-sacrifice for their families, loyalty to friends, and willingness to stand up for a principle.[9] After the strike was settled and on the eve of her marriage, Mary commented, "It may be foolish, but I really dislike the idea of parting with them—they have been the means of awakening me to a fuller, better life."[10] Her change in consciousness demonstrated the power of a strike to facilitate the process of walking together that was so necessary, according to Addams, for gaining sympathetic knowledge.

Anna J. Cooper presented the case for the distinctness of the African American woman's voice based on her intersectional structural location. As she asserted, "Caucasian[s] . . . cannot *quite* put themselves in the dark man's place, neither should the dark man be wholly expected fully and adequately to reproduce the exact Voice of the Black Woman."[11] Cooper further clarified her method of sympathetic understanding: "The art of 'thinking one's self imaginatively into the experiences of others' is not given to all, and it is impossible to acquire it without a background and a substratum of sympathetic knowledge."[12] To acquire this knowledge, she insisted, each intersectional activist must speak for herself.

To define the "unique position" of the African American woman "in a period itself transitional and unsettled," Cooper observed, "She is confronted by both a woman question and a race problem and is yet an unknown or unacknowledged factor in both."[13] In voicing this location, Cooper called out both white women and African American men to renegotiate their different intersectional locations. White women had to abandon their higher racial "caste" status;[14] African American men had to embrace "the woman question." Cooper called on both groups to expand their bridging activism by joining forces with African American women to actualize an interracial engendered democracy.[15]

Proud of her abolitionist Beecher family roots on her father's side, Gilman defined her intersectional location as native-born Anglo-Saxon white woman.[16] In her utopian novel *Herland*, she depicted how three men of the same group were challenged to renegotiate their male privilege by visiting a land in which Anglo-Saxon white women reproduced without men. Like Malkiel, she illustrated a type of sympathetic understanding by her choice of narrator, a sociologist named Van. Through his observations of the Herland women and how they organized daily life, Van was forced to rethink his notions of masculinity and femininity that structured his intersectional location. To make sense of his experiences at Herland, where women did not manifest his notion of femininity, Van came to realize that his former views derived from an unequal power relationship. As he explained, "[T]hose 'feminine charms' we are so fond of are not feminine at all, but mere reflected masculinity—developed to please us because they had to please us."[17] This insight led Van to dismantle his male privilege.

Historians Mary Hill and Carol Kessler argue that Gilman's two-month stay at Hull House in the winter of 1896 influenced her utopian vision.[18] Yet she did not incorporate the settlement house workers' commitment to diversity or to the creation of a new type of international democracy. Specifically, Gilman consciously opted to construct Herland so that one common woman ancestor gave birth to a pure Anglo-Saxon white lineage. The lack of diversity in Herland provided one type of evidence that Gilman resisted the need to renegotiate her own race-ethnic privilege. Her brief announcement in *The Forerunner* of the publication of Malkiel's *Diary* provided another type of evidence. She observed that "it is worth reading by those who care for this line of progress—the industrial organization of women."[19] Yet she did not engage with its critique of anti-Semitism or rethink her own intersectional location shaped by strong anti-immigrant and anti-Jewish prejudices.[20]

While Gilman presented herself as a bridger of the woman's movement and the labor movement, both of which she folded into "the twin struggle that convulses the world to-day,"[21] she limited her range of bridging. Ultimately Gilman chose not to grapple with movements directed at advancing immigrant rights and civil rights for African Americans.[22] Still, other more expansive bridgers were drawn to engage with her theories and her activism. Du Bois interacted with her work to suggest a new intersectional analysis of social service.[23] Cooper, assuming white activist-theorists to be contradictory, defended Gilman against Christian condemnation when she committed suicide due to late-stage breast cancer. As Cooper wrote to her friend Reverend Francis Grimke, "I am sure the facts in that life, leaving out its tragic end, would have been full of inspiring interest and stimulating encouragement."[24]

Gilman did not speak for all bridgers who shared her structural location. Certainly, the white Protestant settlement house workers sought to renegotiate their locations to further the forging of new diverse relations. In her autobiography, Gilman clearly separated herself from their approach.[25] On the specific topic of economic independence, Mary White Ovington (1865–1951), a settlement house resident, one of the founding members of the National Association for the Advancement of Colored People (NAACP), and a Socialist Party member, presented a stark contrast to Gilman.[26] She characterized the Anglo-Saxon as someone who avoided critical self-examination.

Ovington herself took up the challenge of unlearning racism through processes of sympathetic understanding, including conducting an empirical study of New York City African Americans with a chapter on African American women breadwinners. Ovington learned from her research and intersectional activism that a key component of sympathetic understanding was suspending the act of judging. As she explained, "[W]e must remember that when we pass judgment, we need to know whether our own standard is the best, whether we may not have something to learn from the standards of others."[27] Ovington, unlike Gilman, rejected Anglo-Saxon, white, native-born Americans as the ultimate standard for human development that all other groups were expected to emulate.[28]

These brief sketches show that the ideal type of an intersectional conversation coheres elements present in the ways representative social democratic feminists practiced thinking intersectionally. By bringing their parallel conversations into relationship, I am not imposing on them a method of analysis, but rather honoring their originality by systemizing it. The application of the ideal type in this way allows me to make visible the crucial contributions of African American and immigrant Jewish social democratic feminists. As a result, I show how Gilman's narrower range of bridging blinded her to how their contributions strengthened the possibility of achieving women's economic independence.

Economic Independence: Independence from Men

Social democratic feminists defined the first dimension of economic independence as the antithesis of financial dependency on husbands or fathers. Gilman contributed a radical critique of the ideology of the male family wage that justified the economic dependence of wives. Frances Harper (1825–1911) and Cooper showed how the racial caste system, as a legacy of slavery, constricted the pursuit of economic independence within and outside marriage for African American women. Rose Schneiderman (1882–1972), a Jewish immigrant working-class daughter, shifted the focus from marriage to the family as an economic unit. She illustrated how the death of a father could force a daughter into negotiating the role of breadwinner within an unjust gendered economic system. In different ways, they shaped their formulations by their bridging of movements.

Starting in 1890, as a speaker and writer for socialist organizations, including the Nationalist Movement and the Fabian Society, Gilman developed her understanding of women's independence. Initially, separated from her husband, Gilman was living with her daughter in California. In the midst of mobilizing women for radical change through her bridging of socialist and feminist movements, she theorized a brand of evolutionary change that was not rooted in militant class struggle.[29] Within this framework, she rejected the formulation of marriage as an equal economic partnership in which the husband earned a family wage in the marketplace and the wife received a salary from her husband/employer in exchange for her housework and maternal care.[30] According to Gilman, "[T]he salient fact in this discussion is that whatever the economic value of the domestic industry of women is, they do not get it. The women who do the most work get the least money, and the women who have the most money do the least work."[31] To explain this disparity, Gilman pointed to the unequal power between husbands and wives and how it determined the level of economic support wives received. Husbands exerted "power and will," while wives honed their skills of manipulation.[32]

Echoing arguments made by Wollstonecraft and Mill, Gilman claimed that woman's true nature was distorted by this arrangement. As she observed, "Because of the economic dependence of the human female on her mate, she is modified to sex to an excessive degree."[33] Gilman was thinking of the training of women to cultivate a posture of self-abnegation alongside their physical attractiveness in order to secure men's economic support. Instead of practicing this "excessive" femininity, Gilman insisted that women should disentangle reproductive and economic relations.

To make her case for women's economic independence from their husbands, Gilman presented her theory of the "sexuo-economic relation." Within marriage, she argued, "an entire sex lives in a relation of economic dependence upon the other sex, and the economic relation is combined with the sex-relation."[34] She acknowledged that her systemic analysis "will be so offensive to many" because the "sex relation is intensely personal." To convince her audience of the need to think on the systemic level, she drew an analogy between the institution of marriage and the institution of chattel slavery. According to Gilman, the "slaveholder" who tried to explain away "instances" of cruelty as aberrations "did not see . . . that, given the relation of chattel slavery, it inevitably" produced "evils . . . in spite of all the efforts of the individual to the contrary."[35] Similarly, the sexuo-economic structural relation inevitably misshaped the natures of men and women. Once she made her analytical point, Gilman did not take the next step of connecting the legacy of slavery to her critique of marriage and advocacy of women's economic independence. This step would have required her to listen to the voices of African American women like Harper and Cooper. Both spoke from their intersectional structural locations to an international gathering in Chicago at the 1893 World's Congress of Representative Women.[36]

In her novel *Iola Leroy or Shadows Uplifted*, Harper presented her notion of independence from the support of men by contrasting Iola and her mother, Maria, who was born a slave. Maria "had no recollection of her father, but remembered being torn from her mother while clinging to her dress. The trader who bought her mother did not wish to buy her."[37] Maria remembered playing with a brother, but she got separated from him. When her master,

Eugene Leroy, "of French and Spanish descent," decided to educate her, free her, and marry her, she embraced "the wonderful change" because her children would be born free and she would not have "the burdens and cares of maternity without the rights and privileges of a wife." Leroy requested that she not tell their children of the "negro blood in her veins," so her children grew up believing they were white.[38] They were sent to the North for their education. Maria worried constantly that if something happened to Leroy, her children would not be protected. When Leroy died suddenly, Maria's worst fear came true. Leroy's white supremacist cousin had her marriage certificate and manumission voided. Maria returned to her slave status. While Maria saw marriage to her ex-master as an advancement over slavery, Harper, by adopting a systemic approach similar to Gilman's, showed that Maria's husband, as an individual slave owner, could not alter the intertwined systems of slavery and economic dependency in marriage.

In contrast to her mother, Iola sought independence from the support of a husband by seeking to change both marriage and the racial caste system that structured the gendered labor market. After being rescued from her unscrupulous cousin, who had turned her into a slave, Iola joined the Union army as a nurse. In her depiction of Iola's transformation, Harper took her readers through a process of sympathetic understanding that rested literally on walking in someone's shoes. When Iola thought she was white, she "always defended slavery." Once she learned the truth of her mother's lineage, she embraced it and the necessity to dismantle institutionalized white supremacy. Through this narrative, Harper invited her white readers to join in a conversation on how to achieve Iola's vision.

Iola refused a proposal of marriage from white Anglo-Saxon Dr. Gresham, who promised to protect her. During one of their exchanges, he characterized the Anglo-Saxon race as "proud, domineering, aggressive, and impatient of a rival, and . . . has more capacity for dragging down a weaker race than uplifting it." In response, Iola envisioned a time when African Americans would present a "better" standard for "civilization." As she explained, "You [Anglo-Saxons] will prove unworthy of your high vantage ground if you only use your superior ability to victimize feebler races and minister to a selfish greed of gold and a love of domination."[39] Instead of Grisham, Iola chose as her husband African American Dr. Latimer, who wanted to go to the South to participate in Reconstruction. Their marriage was based on the agreement that she would work as a teacher, to "labor for those who had passed from the old oligarchy of slavery into the new commonwealth of freedom."[40]

Before marriage, while settled in the North with her mother's reunited family, Iola set out "to join the great rank of bread-winners." Uncle Robert insisted that there was no "necessity" for her "to go out to work." She justified her goal by pointing to her "theory that every woman ought to know how to earn her own living." She also asserted that "there would be less unhappy marriages if labor were more honored among women."[41] Iola, who could "pass" for white, was discriminated against at several jobs once she revealed to her fellow workers her "African blood." Nevertheless, Iola persisted with great determination to open up opportunities for African American women.

After hearing Iola's story of discrimination and witnessing her nursing care of his daughter, Mr. Cloten, a white employer, offered her a job in his store. On her first day, he informed his employees "that Miss Iola had colored blood in her veins but that he was going to employ her and give her a desk."[42] That evening he engaged in a conversation with his wife in which he pointed to the need for white residents of the North to renegotiate their intersectional locations by unlearning racism. As he put it, "In dealing with Southern prejudice against the negro, we Northerners could do it with better grace if we divested ourselves of our own."[43] By presenting this very hopeful series of events, Harper situated Iola's pursuit of economic independence within the context of the potential of the Reconstruction refounding period to advance the interconnections between movements for feminism and interracial democracy.

Addressing the post-Reconstruction era, Cooper complicated the African American women's parallel intersectional conversation on women's economic independence. She presented a two-part critique of the ideology of the male family wage. First, she recognized that higher education for African American women would undermine the economic basis of the institution of marriage. As she conceded, "I grant you that intellectual development, with the self-reliance and capacity for earning a livelihood which it gives, renders woman less dependent on the marriage relation for physical support (which, by the way, does not always accompany it)."[44] Second, with the last clause, Cooper introduced a race-sensitive critique of the family wage. African American women needed to become self-supporting, and even breadwinners, because they could not count on having the option of economic dependency in marriage. The racialized labor market segregated many African American men into a limited range of low-paying jobs, such as agricultural worker, waiter, and barber.[45]

To correct this situation, Cooper turned to a critique of the male labor movement. It was not uniting with African American men to dismantle the white supremacist economic structures. Indeed, northern immigrant workers, according to Cooper, "would boycott an employer if he hired a colored workman." While these same workers "complain of wrong and oppression," they completely ignored the exploited, hardworking African American men of the South. Cooper challenged the northern immigrant workers to "come with me" so "I can show you workingmen's wrong and workingmen's toil which, could it speak, would send up a wail that might be heard from the Potomac to the Rio Grande; and *should it unite and act*, would shake this country from Carolina to California."[46] Her depiction of the potential for African American men to strengthen the labor movement, if it organized them, illustrated how African American women bridgers, even in their defense of women's pursuit of economic independence in marriage, wove together the fates of African American men and women.[47]

Cooper also castigated, presumably, women lecturers in the North, who championed the cause of "our working girls," by which, "of course," they meant "white working girls." She reported hearing one lecturer go into "pious agonies at the thought of the future mothers of America having to stand all day at shop counters." While Cooper was "always glad to hear of" efforts to improve "the lot of any women who are toiling for bread—whether they are white women or black women," she wondered "how many have ever given a thought to the pinched and down-trodden colored woman bending over washtubs and ironing boards."[48] To make visible the intersectional structural location of this woman and her struggles for economic independence, Cooper challenged her audience to reconstruct women's labor reform efforts as welcoming to African Americans by posing this question: "Will you call it narrowness and selfishness, then, that I find it impossible to catch the fire of sympathy and enthusiasm for most of these labor movements at the North?"[49] So Cooper's analysis of women's economic independence uncovered points of tension among women that they could overcome only by bridging movements for racial equality and women's labor rights.

Schneiderman wove into her notion of women's economic independence a combination of militant labor union activism and a commitment to socialism.[50] In *All for One*, she described the series of events that led to her mother turning the breadwinner role over to her. Schneiderman's father, a tailor, died in 1892 during the first winter after her family migrated to New York City from Russia. His dream for his oldest child was to become a teacher. At the time of his death, her mother was pregnant with a fourth child. The family received food aid from United Hebrew Charities.[51]

Schneiderman's mother provided for the family by taking in sewing jobs. For a while, the family was able to rent space to a male boarder, who worked at home as a tailor. Even so, Schneiderman described "often" going to bed "hungry." Over time, Rose's two younger brothers were sent to a Jewish orphanage. She spent time in one as well, which allowed her to attend public school and learn English. When her mother brought her home, Schneiderman took over the cooking, which included delivering a prepared meal to her mother at the factory where she sewed linings in fur capes. Until they were able to reunite with Schneiderman's two brothers, she and her mother would picnic outside the orphanage and pass treats to the boys through the fence. The official policy on visiting was every three months. Before her mother lost her job, Schneiderman rushed through nine grades of school. She "loved school and studied hard." Then, at age thirteen, with no regular work for her mother, Schneiderman became the family breadwinner and had to stop her formal education.[52]

In voicing her intersectional structural location as a breadwinner, Schneiderman pointed to two crystalizing events that defined her experience of independence. United Hebrew Charities found her a job in Hearn's Department Store, where she earned $2.16 for a sixty-four-hour workweek. After several years, she went to work in a factory where she sewed the linings of caps and was paid by the piece. Working from eight to six, a good week for her was one where she earned $5.[53] Instead of behaving "as a dutiful daughter" and handing over all her wages to her mother, who wanted to decide what Schneiderman "needed for the week," she kept $1 for herself and gave the rest to her mother. According to Schneiderman, "That was my first revolt toward independence."[54]

After going through a period of radicalization involving meeting socialists and being approached to engage in organizing women cap makers into a union, Schneiderman began her development as a bridger of movements. She discovered the power of activism. As she described her awakening, "It was such an exciting time. A new life opened up for me. All of a sudden I was not lonely anymore." As she asserted her independence, Schneiderman described how her mother was not pleased with her "becoming a trade unionist. She kept saying I'd never get married because I was so busy—a prophesy which came true."[55] Like many immigrant Jewish daughters, with the absence of a father breadwinner, Schneiderman had no choice but to support her family at a very young age. In taking up this role, she folded into her intersectional location eastern European Jewish traditions of daughters providing economic support for their families, a theme this book develops further.[56]

By bringing into relationship these representative social democratic feminists who engaged in parallel conversations on the meaning of independence, I showed that it was a central focus of struggle for all them. Before Gilman wrote *Women and Economics*, Harper and Cooper were defending self-support for African American women. Presumably unfamiliar, at age thirteen, with any of the other participants and their theorizing, Schneiderman developed her own practice of independence out of necessity. In effect, the parallel conversations prepared the bridgers to engage with each other when the opportunities arose.

During the 1909–1910 New York City garment strike, some intersectional activists activated a more inclusive bridging process when they tried to build alliances between the striking immigrant women and the relatively few African American women in the garment industry. According to the 1900 census, they accounted for 813 dressmakers out of 37,514 and for 249 seamstresses out of 18,108.[57] In response to an editorial in the *New York Age*, an African American weekly, that called for African American women to continue working during the strike because the union had ignored them, Ovington turned to the integrated Cosmopolitan Club that she had helped form to put out a call for a mass meeting. At this event in an African American church in Brooklyn, according to historian Meredith Tax, "a historic if little known resolution" was passed. It called on "women of color to refrain from acting in the capacity of strikebreakers . . . because we regard their action as antagonistic to the best interests of labor." Then it urged that "organized labor exercise a proper consideration of the claims and demands of the men and women of color who desire to enter the various trades."[58]

The WTUL, an active supporter of the strikers, followed up this discussion with its own resolution at its executive board meeting at the end of the strike. According to historian Annelise Orleck, Schneiderman played a key role at this meeting when she "responded" to African American women who "asked Local 25 [of the ILGWU] to help them get jobs in the garment industry." She "prodded the League to declare its intent to reach out to African American women in large numbers."[59] This series of meetings and resolutions illustrated how struggles among social democratic feminists had the potential to advance economic independence by making intersectional activism truly inclusive.

Economic Independence: A New Synthesis of Mothering and Earning

Social democratic feminists defined the second dimension of economic independence as lessening the tension between mothering and earning through state programs that institutionalized a new notion of socialized care. To excavate their thinking, I construct three intersectional conversations. In the first one, I analyze why Gilman and Du Bois thought that working mothers led the way to women's economic independence. In the second one, I demonstrate how the pursuit of public policies to support working mothers advanced the creation of the welfare state by bringing into relationship Gilman and Mary Church Terrell (1863–1954) and others on the public policy of childcare. In the third one, I show how Gilman and Pauline Newman (1890–1986) wove a notion of a caring state into their justifications for a public policy on paid maternity leave.

Intersectional Conversation: Working Mothers at the Center

Because Gilman's theorizing focused on the unequal power dynamic between husbands and wives, she put working mothers at the center of her notion of economic independence. As she explained, "Until 'mothers' earn their living 'women' will not."[60] In making her case, she de-emphasized the importance of working widows or working daughters as agents of change. Neither group needed to undo the interconnection of reproduction and earning. Thus, Gilman's theorizing both excluded the young immigrant women and their widowed mothers *and* opened up the possibility for recognizing the critical contribution of African American working mothers.

Du Bois developed the theme of the centrality of working mothers by illustrating Cooper's method of theorizing, although he did not credit her.[61] Like Cooper, he began by discussing the situation of women in general, and then he turned to the distinct contribution of African American women.[62] His notion of the damnation of women pointed to the either-or dilemma women faced. As he observed, "The world wants healthy babies and intelligent workers. Today we refuse to allow the combination." To undo this tension, Du Bois insisted that "[t]he future woman must have a life work and economic independence," supported by her "right of motherhood at her own discretion." Then he shifted perspectives by posing the question, "All this of woman,— but what of black women?"[63]

In contrast to Gilman,[64] Du Bois did not focus on the structure of power within heterosexual marriage. In fact, he was more radical than Gilman in his defense of the right of motherhood, a term that legitimated the separation of motherhood and marriage. Instead, Du Bois exposed for analysis how white supremacist constructions of African American women hid their "combination" of mothering and earning and therefore their "revolutionary" role in the pursuit of women's economic independence.[65] As Du Bois knew, married African American women worked at higher rates than married white women. According to the 1900 census, the difference was 26 percent versus 3.2 percent.[66] By making visible their lived realities, Du Bois showed how African American women were strengthening "[t]he revolt of white women"[67] by interconnecting feminism and anti-racism movements. Or as he put it, "When, now, two of these movements—woman and color—combine in one, the combination has deep meaning."[68]

Du Bois illustrated this "deep meaning" by uncovering how African American working mothers provided a forceful intersectional critique of white supremacy and the legacy of slavery. In 1912, there was a proposal to erect a statue of "the mammy" in Washington, D.C. Du Bois joined the protest against this effort by characterizing it as a recognition "of the foster mammy, not of the mother in her home, attending to her own baby." The mammy, according to Du Bois, "existed under a false social system" of slavery.[69] For her, "there was no legal marriage, no legal family, no legal control over children." She was forced to deny the needs of her own children while she nursed the children of the master class.[70]

Du Bois made clear that a statue to the mammy reinforced the notion that African American women were meant to take care of white children. To bolster his case, he gave voice to the white mother's reflections on the African American woman: "She is thriftless and stupid . . . when she refuses to nurse my baby and stays with her own. She is bringing her daughter up beyond her station when she trains her to be a teacher instead of sending her into my home to act as nursemaid to my little boy and girl."[71] Du Bois's analysis here was similar to Addams's theorizing of the competing family claims in her treatment of domestic workers.

To dismantle this intersectional legacy of slavery, Du Bois reached back before slavery to recover the strength of the "African mother-idea,"[72] and he supported African American women in making visible their own experiences of motherhood. In her autobiography, Terrell described the circumstances of her own birth and of her great-grandmother's separation from her daughter during slavery. She also wrote movingly of her three children who died "shortly after birth" and her deep attachment to her two daughters. As she confessed, "The maternal instinct was always abnormally developed in me."[73] Wells-Barnett insisted on the acknowledgment of her motherhood role as a condition for her acceptance of various speaking tours. For example, in 1896, when she was a nursing mother with a six-month-old baby, she required white women Republican clubs throughout Illinois to provide her with a caregiver.[74]

Du Bois continued to flesh out the "deep meaning" of African American women's bridging activism by analyzing the emancipatory potential for themselves and for all women of their practices as working mothers. Here again Du Bois was building on Cooper's theorizing. Cooper, a bridger, argued that African American women led the way for the whole race. Without naming Cooper, Du Bois quoted her: "Only the black woman can say 'when and where I enter . . . and there the whole Negro race enters with me.'"[75] Then Du Bois went one step further. He argued that African American women's recovery of their maternal practice combined with their strong record of work outside the family was leading the way for all women, since they constituted "a group of workers, fighting for their daily bread like men; independent and approaching economic freedom."[76] As he concluded, "[I]n the great rank and file of our five million women we have the upworking of new revolutionary ideals, which must in time have vast influence on the thought and action of this land."[77] Thus, by making visible the critical contribution of African American working mothers, Du Bois showed how to weave a critique of white supremacy into the theorizing of economic independence for working mothers.

Intersectional Conversation: Working Mothers and Socialized Childcare

The second constructed intersectional conversation reveals parallel commitments on the theme of providing public programs for children so mothers could work outside the home. Terrell, Hope, Cooper, and others, through their national and local organizations, built community validation for working mothers by developing childcare facilities, called day nurseries, and also kindergartens, a new innovation. Gilman supported both reforms. The parallel conversations differed in their relationship to the realities of daily life. Gilman presented her notion of childcare as part of her vision of a transformed, postcapitalist "socialized economic system."[78] Terrell, Hope, and Cooper produced strategic experiments in how to accommodate working mothers, who were breadwinners, struggling within the unjust conditions of a gendered, racialized labor market that characterized the U.S. capitalist system.

Under attack from Swedish socialist Ellen Key (1849–1926)[79] and others for advocating institutionalized upbringing of babies and children, in her parallel conversation, Gilman presented her "baby-garden theory" of how childcare would work in "a transformed society." Gilman argued that she never intended to separate mothers and babies for long hours and that Key misrepresented her position.[80] Although she did not spell out the details, Gilman envisioned that the mother's "work must, of course, be adjusted to the nursing of her babies, an arrangement covering some four or five years out of a lifetime perhaps, but as to the day-long care of them, that can be performed best by those fitted for the task by nature and training."[81] Further, the new society would "so reduce the hours of labor that the mother need not be away from home more than four hours a day."[82] Therefore, "the baby shall be in the baby-garden while the mother is doing her four hours' work, and shall be at home when she is."[83] Since "the industrial activity of women" would be so crucial, her "transformed society" would also "so arrange the conditions of labor that the home and the work will not be far apart."[84] Presumably, the childcare centers would be conveniently located.

By envisioning a strong mother-child relationship made possible by the policies of an interventionist state, Gilman did not retreat from her core disagreement with Key, who assumed "that the best education of the child requires the continuous devotion of the individual mother." In contrast, Gilman insisted that "[t]he new assumption is that the interests of the child are best served by the additional love and care, teaching and example, of other persons, specialists in child culture." These specialists were necessary because Gilman believed "absolutely" that "the individual mother" could never be "all sufficient as an educator of humanity."[85] Gilman practiced her own theory by sharing the raising of her daughter with her ex-husband and his second wife.

In contrast to Gilman, Terrell, Hope, and Cooper expanded the analysis of the childcare needs of working mothers to include the discrediting of white supremacy as an ideology and as a structuring of the labor market. First, they separated day nurseries from the judgmental characteristic of charity.[86] They did not castigate mothers who worked outside their homes, and they repudiated the notion that the African American family was a failure because of the absence of the male breadwinner. As president of the National Association of Colored Women (NACW), Terrell used neutral terms in 1902: "Thousands of our wage-earning mothers with large families dependent almost entirely upon them for support are obliged to leave their children all day, entrusted to the care of small brothers and sisters, or some good-natured neighbor who promises much, but does little."[87] In 1905, Emma Greene, a graduate nurse and founder of the Hope Day Nursery for Colored Children in New York City, conveyed her sympathetic understanding of the hardships earning mothers faced: "Space is too limited to speak further of the good being done through the nursery, yet all of our hopes have not been realized. Many of our mothers complain of insufficient work. Debarred as they are from shops and factories, most of them are forced to seek employment as laundresses, house cleaners, general workers, etc. with very uncertain days of work."[88]

Second, they proposed a vision that incorporated kindergartens and day nurseries into the development of a seamless system of preschool and after-school programs. To construct this vision, they relied on sympathetic knowledge derived from Hope's survey of working mothers in a low-income neighborhood. She was acting for the Gate City Free Kindergarten Association (GCFKA) in Atlanta. Du Bois and the Atlanta Conference that he directed helped create it in 1905. The GCFKA preceded and paved the way for Neighborhood Union. Hope reported that a key finding of the survey was that earning mothers "wanted full day-care centers and safe recreational lots where the children could play."[89] Hope also "emphasiz[ed] that kindergartens could be but one of many services rendered by the centers."[90]

Third, they developed programs that produced specialized, professional teachers for early childhood education. Founded in 1892 by a group that included Terrell and Cooper, the Colored Women's League (CWL) in Washington, D.C., set up a model kindergarten with two daily sessions. Most of the forty children who attended came from families with two breadwinners. The CWL also set up a school to train kindergarten teachers for its six free programs. Through its efforts, the CWL got the attention of Congress, which led to its funding of kindergartens in the D.C. public school system and to the hiring of graduate teachers from the CWL's school.[91]

Terrell connected all these efforts to uplifting the race, the theme of the NACW. Referring to "the slaughter of the innocents" due to the lack of proper day care, Terrell argued that "by establishing day nurseries," African American women "will render one of the greatest services possible to humanity and to the race."[92] Her underlying assumption was that the "real solution of the race problem lies in the children, both so far as we who are oppressed and those who oppress us are concerned."[93] More specifically, the proper education for African Americans, starting with infancy, was crucial to undo the corrosive effects of institutionalized racism. As she explained, "Through the children of to-day, we believe we can build the foundation of the next generation upon such a rock of morality, intelligence and strength, that the floods of proscription, prejudice and persecution may descend its torrents and yet it will not be moved."[94] To advance the development of an anti-racist practice-theory of humanity, Terrell called on her white sisters to "train their children to be broad and just enough to judge men and women by their intrinsic merit rather than by the adventitious circumstances of race or color or creed."[95]

When Gilman theorized how working mothers and childcare advanced a notion of humanity, she harkened back to Plato's *Republic*, in which he argued that the private family pulled its members away from working for the common good or justice because it put the interests of the family first. According to Gilman, "the [new] human ideal" articulated "that for every one of us the main devotion of life should be to Humanity; that we should so live and *work* as to uplift and improve social conditions—and so benefit every individual, young and old." What was holding back "the growth of this higher . . . social passion," according to Gilman, was the "man-headed, woman-absorbing, child-restricting, self-serving home."[96] Therefore, getting mothers into specialized work outside the home and children into "fit places . . . to learn life in, with fit persons to teach them,"[97] were the necessary conditions for actualizing humanity.

Terrell's theorizing out of her bridging activism revealed the weakness of Gilman's notion of humanity. Without building in an explicit critique of white supremacy, Gilman's notion was inadequate for including African American working mothers, their children, and their families. Moreover, while Terrell certainly supported expert child development teachers overseeing the education of the children of earning mothers to advance humanity, unlike Gilman, she did not counterpose the private mother to the expert. Valorizing private mothering for African American women was a critical element in transforming white supremacist notions of mothering and therefore in reconstructing the notion of humanity. As Du Bois proposed, "In the midst of immense difficulties, surrounded by caste, and hemmed in by restricted economic opportunity, let the colored mother of today build her own statue, and let it be the four walls of her own unsullied home."[98] Terrell and Du Bois demonstrated that to construct a notion of embodied humanity, Gilman needed to acquire sympathetic knowledge based on listening to the historical experiences of African American mothers.

Intersectional Conversation: Paid Maternity Leave for Working Mothers

The third intersectional conversation constructs a social democratic feminist debate over a model compulsory health insurance bill. The bridgers directly raised the theme of how overcoming the tension between mothering and earning depended on turning care into a democratic public value through the development of a welfare state. The American Association for Labor Legislation (AALL) crafted the bill, which the New York state legislature considered four times between 1916 and 1919. The last time, it passed the senate but was defeated in the assembly. It covered primarily industrial workers and was funded by a combination of state tax revenue and contributions from workers and employers. Insured workers were "eligible for free medical care, sick pay, and a small death benefit."[99] The bill also included maternal medical care and sick pay two weeks before and four weeks after delivery. New York already had a law that prohibited women from working at industrial jobs during the same time frame, which deepened the tension between earning and reproducing.[100] By proposing to financially support insured earning women, according to historian Beatrix Hoffman, "the bill acknowledged women's work outside the home and the importance of their income to the household."[101]

Both Gilman and Newman, who bridged the labor and socialist movements, were on the same side, although I have no evidence that they exchanged views of their strong support for paid leave. Each put the bill within the context of social policy in other countries. The two social democratic feminists used the bill to demonstrate how a concept of the caring state was built on public policies responsive to the needs of working mothers. Yet Gilman remained focused on the future possibilities of mothers working while Newman grounded her support in the actual conditions for working mothers. Her contribution to this conversation showed how immigrant widowed mothers and their daughters were important agents of change. To make her case, she drew on the eastern European Jewish tradition that legitimized breadwinner mothers and aligned daughters and mothers to ease the tension between earning and mothering. The assimilationist framework that Gilman championed ignored this tradition, while Jewish daughters revealed the emancipatory potential of transplanting it.

In March 1916, Gilman published "Maternity Benefits and Reformers" in her monthly magazine, *The Forerunner*. While she did not name the reformers, she must have been thinking of Kelley, who headed the National Consumers' League (NCL) and had persuaded the AALL to exclude the paid maternity benefit from the 1916 version of the bill. Kelley was focused on lessening economic exploitation by institutionalizing public minimum wage boards to regulate "subnormal industries." The characteristics of such industries, according to Kelley, included no male family wage adequate enough to support a family of six, forcing the whole family to work, and the substitution of women and children for men workers.[102]

A divorced working mother, Kelley was a strong critic of encouraging the combination of mothering and earning, especially when babies and young children were part of the calculus. In 1914, she generalized, "Throughout all civilization wages in industries which employ married women tend to range so low that only when the whole family is drawn into wage earning can subsistence be earned." She viewed the combining of mothering and earning as "relatively new" to the United States.[103] Apparently, she thought it could be halted, and she therefore supported the ideology of a male family wage. Gilman characterized Kelley and her nay-saying allies: "A more pitiful misconception of the best lines of social advance by those apparently well qualified to judge has seldom been offered."[104]

Instead of engaging directly with Kelley's specific objections to the bill, Gilman presented her case for paid maternity benefits and how this priority helped build the foundations for a caring state. She placed the AALL bill within a tradition of "the best measures now advocated in so many other countries, as England, Germany, Hungary, Italy, France, Switzerland, and Russia." While the United States had not yet entered the conflict, war raged in Europe. This context probably influenced Gilman's comparison between "[t]he efforts of any army to nurse back to health its fighting units" and "the efforts of a peaceful state to preserve the health of its workers and to nurse them when disabled."[105]

With this analogy, Gilman suggested her vision of a transformed "field of politics" that covered "only the judicious caring for the people."[106] When theorizing an enlarged role for government, Gilman used both phrases: "caring for the people" and "for the service of all the people." Then she placed the latter at the center of her notion of "the democratic idea of government."[107] This was a new notion, since "[t]here has never been a democracy, so far."[108] As she explained, "To deliberately legislate for the service of all the people, to use the government as the main engine of service, is a new process."[109] Thus, Gilman suggested that the language of service was the way to translate caring into a defining characteristic of a social democracy.

Once again, Gilman defended her argument that legislating social programs for earning mothers was critical, since they could propel the United States in the required new caring or service direction because their lived experiences exposed "our worst conditions."[110] As she explained, "In their interest we shall inevitably change the brutal and foolish hardships now surrounding labor into such decent and healthful conditions as shall be no injury to any one." By embracing working mothers rather than "seek[ing] only to push them back [into the home] where they came from," reformers would have a strong ally for overturning the laissez-faire version of democracy and its necessary complement, judgmental charities. As she reported, "[I]n some 75 per cent of applications for aid, made to the New York Charity Organization Society, sickness was responsible for the distress."[111]

Like Gilman, Newman voiced a strong defense of combining earning and mothering as she argued for the paid maternity benefit before the New York legislature and in a speech to the American Nurses' Association (ANA). In contrast to Gilman, who situated herself within the white middle-class professional reform community, Newman defined herself as representing working people, especially immigrant women. Her focus was on the disagreement within the labor movement between Samuel Gompers, the head of the AFL, and its largest union, the ILGWU, the membership of which was about two-thirds women, mostly immigrants.[112] Unlike Gilman, she directly responded to Kelley's arguments. Speaking for her union and the WTUL, Newman developed an intersectional analysis. For her, the debate over a cash maternity benefit revealed how a version of assimilation or Americanization of Jewish immigrants denied legitimacy to their eastern European practice of earning mothers.

Speaking at an ANA convention in 1917, Newman described how her evolution on the issue of a government-run health insurance program came out of her participation in the labor movement. She also acknowledged that her theorizing of the need for a caring state represented a radical break with the American understanding of freedom and the state. Newman reported that when she "began to think very seriously about" the place of "social insurance, including old-age pension, sickness insurance, unemployment insurance," she was "surprise[ed]" that "men like Gompers . . . opposed the movement." When he opposed the AALL bill, Newman described her response: "I was not sure of myself." After reconsidering the disagreement on the bill, she concluded that "the conditions under which [the vast majority of people] work and live" justified her support.[113]

She traced the disagreement between herself and Gompers to the division between the 10 percent of the workforce who were organized into trade unions and "the great mass of unorganized workers." Gompers spoke for the former when he asserted that they could "take care" of themselves.[114] Indeed, in 1913 the ILGWU had opened a Union Health Center for its members.[115] Yet Newman chose to champion the unorganized. She recognized that Gompers's position that labor unions should resist interference from the state resonated with those who held to the American notion of freedom as self-reliance.[116] Newman realized that she was proposing a direction that was "new in America." Embracing this new direction, her notion of being "in the Trade Union Movement . . . for the past ten years" included supporting legislation that would provide care for the unorganized low-waged workers, men and women, who "are not in a position to look after their own sickness and their own problems."[117]

Ultimately, the AALL bill was not a panacea for social injustice, but it would provide "a step toward social responsibility." Experiencing a successful state health insurance program, Newman argued, would lead the workers to "understand that there is, after all, a connection between the state and the workers."[118] In contrast to Gompers, who viewed the state as primarily repressive of the labor movement, she supported regulatory labor legislation. Her stance was most likely influenced by her experience as a participant on the New York state commission that investigated the Triangle fire.

For Newman, the health-care law would also teach "the state" to "realize the necessity of caring for its members and caring for those who need it most," which would "make the burden of life easier for" immigrant workers, in particular.[119] Significantly, in sharp contrast to Gilman, throughout her analysis, Newman did not differentiate between immigrant working-class men and women in their need for a caring state.[120] Like African American intersectional activists who bridged feminism and racial justice movements, Newman interwove her commitment to women's economic independence with her socialist commitment to furthering class solidarity with men.

As Newman spoke for the most vulnerable workers, she countered Kelley's arguments against paid maternity benefits. In her memorandum to the AALL, Kelley made clear that she rejected "any law which provides for recognition by the state, of the practice of sending child-bearing wives out of the home into industry."[121] To bolster her position, she insisted that single working women would resent being taxed to help other women.[122] Newman pointed out that "most of the unmarried girls . . . may someday be beneficiaries themselves of that fund." Moreover, she testified, "I would be more than willing to give up more than 1.5 per cent from my own wages, knowing it would go to some woman that she might rest for a few weeks before and a few weeks after confinement."[123]

Kelley also claimed that married women would be sent to work by their African American and immigrant husbands because of the cash benefit.[124] Since she must have realized that few African American families would have been insured due to the racialized labor market that blocked their entrance into industrial jobs, Kelley was really pointing the finger at immigrant husbands, including Jewish ones. Newman embraced all working mothers but particularly took on issues connected to immigrant mothers. She translated Kelley's objection to the maternity benefit into an assertion that the proper American family did not include a mother working in industry. As Newman explained to the ANA, "People are opposed to maternity insurance because they claim that the married working woman is not an American tradition." But, she countered, "facts are facts, and there are thousands and thousands of married working women." A maternity benefit would not accelerate the number of earning mothers. According to Newman, "It is the struggle for existence that does and will drive married women into industry, not maternity benefit."[125]

By successfully defending the inclusion of the paid maternity benefit in the second iteration of the bill, Newman staked out a position that was quite different from both Gilman and Kelley. She was transplanting the eastern European Jewish "norm" of breadwinner daughters and mothers that derived from the practice of the small number of wives of religious scholars.[126] As their husbands pursued knowledge for the good of the community, the wives, along with their daughters, were expected to be the earners. According to historian Susan Glenn, "The hard-working scholar's wife acted as a legitimating symbol of the female breadwinner for the masses of east European Jews. If the scholar's wife worked, then why not the merchant's, the trader's, the watchmaker's, or the tailor's? And that was the pattern. In every stratum of Jewish society the work of women was considered both necessary and respectable."[127] Usually they engaged in commercial activities that were compatible with their maternal responsibilities.[128] In the Old Country, Jews were blocked from factory jobs.[129]

In her testimony, Newman clearly voiced an intersectional structural location shaped by her immigrant Jewish experience. In Lithuania, Newman's mother, the main breadwinner, had purchased fruit from peasant growers to sell in the market, while her two older daughters worked in a dress shop as seamstresses. After Newman's father, a Talmud scholar, died in 1901, Newman's mother migrated to New York City with her three daughters. At nine years old, Newman made hairbrushes in a factory. Her mother took in washing, and her sisters worked in the garment industry.[130] When Newman testified that single working women were aligned with earning mothers, she was presenting the eastern European Jewish norm.

One implication of Newman's theorizing was that she was seeking to substitute state legitimacy for the community support earning mothers left behind in the Old Country. The assimilation process eroded this support by presenting the ideology of the male family wage as "the model for Americanized masculinity."[131] As a result of this framing, the religious scholar who was not a breadwinner lost his standing, and Jewish women faced pressure to conform to the negligible economic role of native-born, white Protestant women.[132] According to Glenn, "While married women's economic participation had been an openly acknowledged part of Jewish family life in the Old World, over time immigrants came to think of it as a source of embarrassment."[133] Therefore, Jewish immigrant families willingly underreported the economic activities of married women to the census and other governmental empirical investigations.[134]

Yet, as Newman testified, "facts are facts."[135] Married immigrant Jewish women continued to participate in the economic support of their families. A very few mothers worked for wages and even turned to day nurseries to care for their children. By 1917, there were fourteen Jewish day nurseries that served 1,400 children in three boroughs of New York City.[136] More common economic activities were the supervision and care of boarders. According to a U.S. Immigration Commission report that gathered data from 1907 to 1908 in seven cities on women's work, Jewish married women had the highest rate, at 43 percent, of households with boarders.[137] That same report found that in Chicago, New York City, and Philadelphia, from a quarter to almost 50 percent of immigrant Jewish men were self-employed in family businesses. Glenn conjectures that "there is a strong possibility" that "their wives performed a statistically hidden economic function" as co-breadwinners.[138]

In her autobiography, *The Promised Land*, Mary Antin (1881–1949) made visible for an American audience how immigrant Jewish mothers resolved the tension between mothering and earning. Antin emphasized how her mother acquired commercial skills in Russia. She had worked in her father's business from the age of ten and had shared the breadwinning role with her husband, who gave up the vocation of religious scholar. As Antin noted, "My mother was with my father, as equal partner and laborer in everything he attempted in Polotzk."[139] When she and her children joined her husband in Boston, Antin's mother transplanted her "talent for business" to help her husband with the family-owned shop.

Antin described how her mother learned English through conversations with her customers as she weighed, measured, and computed in her head the necessary fractions. According to Antin, soon her mother was as confident as she had been "in her old store in Polotzk." Yet the setting of the Boston store was different because it was attached to the family apartment. In Polotzk, in the period when the family was well-off, the home and store had been located in separate spaces. Within that context, except on the Sabbath, the mother received help with raising her children from grandmothers and nursemaids. In Boston, under different economic circumstances, Antin's mother combined paid and unpaid work in an integrated living-working space. Antin gave a romantic hue to her mother's working conditions: "It was far more cosey than Polotzk—at least, so it seemed to me; for behind the store was the kitchen, where, in the intervals of slack trade, she did her cooking and washing. Arlington Street customers were used to waiting while the storekeeper salted the soup or rescued a loaf from the oven."[140]

In describing how her mother renegotiated the tension between earning and mothering in Boston, Antin also included discussions of the complementary roles her older sister, Frieda, played. In Polotzk, after the family's economic situation had deteriorated drastically due to a series of illnesses and the father had migrated to America to get a fresh start, Frieda, at age twelve, took over most of the responsibilities of the home as her mother peddled tea. Frieda also became a successful apprentice to a dressmaker. After arriving in Boston, she was sent to work in the garment industry because the family shop was unable to provide a satisfactory living for the growing family. Beyond paid work, Frieda, aided by the other children, also continued to organize the housework because her "mother's housekeeping was necessarily irregular, as she was pretty constantly occupied in the store."[141]

By bringing Newman, with support from Antin's portrait of her family's experience, into relationship with Gilman and Kelley, I showed how she voiced a distinct intersectional location that was shaped by a tradition of combining earning and mothering. This tradition was suppressed or hidden in the U.S. context, even among social democratic feminists. A strong advocate of assimilation, Gilman failed to recognize the emancipatory potential of the Jewish tradition of working daughters and mothers.[142] Kelley understood that Jewish immigrants brought with them traditions of earning mothers. Holding on to the ideological construct of the male family wage, which in her mind lessened the exploitation of working-class families, Kelley castigated Jewish immigrant men for exploiting their own wives. Therefore, she too discredited a tradition of earning mothers. In sharp contrast, Newman revealed the emancipatory potential of the Jewish tradition as she utilized her bridging skills to connect women's economic independence, social insurance, and the development of a democratic, caring state.

Taken together, the three constructed intersectional conversations make clear that African American and immigrant Jewish social democratic feminists discredited the male family wage in different ways. Each stream contributed a distinct subversive history of combining mothering and earning that went unacknowledged by Gilman. Yet the significance of the conversations went beyond making different histories visible. To release the emancipatory potential of each stream to envision and build a welfare state on the foundation of working mothers/caregivers, the parallel conversations foregrounded the need to uproot the legacy of slavery and reject the coercive dimensions of assimilation. Therefore, the parallel conversations produced new intersectional analyses of how to use the pursuit of women's economic independence to advance the creation of a social democratic welfare state.

Economic Independence: Revaluing Care Work by Removing Its Servile Status

The social democratic feminists defined the third component of economic independence as the uprooting of the servile status of care work,[143] so that it could be turned into a democratic value capable of shaping the welfare state. I construct two intersectional conversations. Each made a different type of contribution to this end. In the first one, I bring into relationship Gilman; Nannie Helen Burroughs (1878–1961), a student of Cooper's; and Du Bois to illustrate how bridging movements led them to retheorize service. They turned it into the needed concept to advance both women's economic independence and the socializing of care. In the second one, I continue the theme of undoing the servile status of care work by expanding its range to include the exercise of collective consumer power over the provisioning of food. I bring into relationship Gilman and militant immigrant Jewish household managers, who upended Gilman's servile framing of the wife-mother food provider.

Intersectional Conversation: Retheorizing Service

Out of her bridging of socialism and feminism, Gilman wove together a structural analysis of women as unpaid servants with a method for revaluing service work. She was not merely drawing an analogy between wives and servants.[144] When Gilman argued that woman's role was to provide "personal service—the work of a servant," she was characterizing the economic function of woman.[145] In his economic analysis of marriage under capitalism, Friedrich Engels characterized the wife as "the first domestic servant."[146] Similarly, Gilman explained, "service is no integral part of motherhood, or even of marriage; but is supposed to be the proper *industrial position* [my emphasis] of women, as such."[147] It was shaped by the unequal power dynamic within the private family. "This servant-motherhood," according to Gilman, was "the concomitant of economic dependence of woman upon man, the direct and indirect effect of the sexuo-economic relation."[148] Engels argued that the male-breadwinner model led to the husband acting like "the bourgeois" and the wife being in the position of "the proletariat."[149]

Broadening the analysis beyond Engels to pave the way for theorizing care or service as a democratic value, Gilman broke down the unpaid servant role into three kinds of "man service": "woman's service in motherhood," "woman's house-service," and woman's sex service.[150] She linked the first two to "the kind of work" required to carry out the "home industries," especially "the care of children" and "the preparation of food." To disentangle servile status from these services, Gilman insisted that these industries must be degendered, removed from the home, and turned into professionalized paid services. As she explained, "Because home industry *is* home industry, because it has been left aborted in the darkness of private life while other industries have grown so broad and high in the light of public life, we have utterly failed to recognize its true value."[151]

The "darkness of private life" had two meanings. First, the wife-mother served only her own private family. Second, how these industries were organized was hidden from public discussion, organization, and regulation. Therefore, the public had no reason to think about the value for democracy of service or care work. As Gilman explained, "Men are too busy doing other things, too blinded by their scorn for 'women's work.' Women are too busy doing these things to think about them at all; or if they think . . . they only think personally, . . . each one blindly buried in her own home."[152]

To bring home industries into "the light of public life" so that men and women together will discuss their social value, they had to be transformed into nongendered paid human work. Gilman defined "human work" as "specialized activity in some social function—any art, craft, trade or profession that serves society."[153] When she turned to "our clumsy method of housekeeping," she found "several professions": cook, manager, cleaner, and purchaser. She assumed that "many women" would be drawn to paid fields in "the very kinds of work which they are doing now," but "in the new and higher methods of execution."[154]

Clearly, Gilman was not advocating that the way to turn care into a democratic value was to have women transfer their nonspecialized private mothering and housekeeping or man service skills to welfare state programs. This approach only extended, into public, the servile status of private care work. Instead, Gilman argued that public sector programs would only advance women's economic independence if they were shaped by a revaluing of women's traditional work. By taking this approach, in her parallel conversation, Gilman showed that the theory of socialism would have to incorporate a more complicated feminist perspective than Engels's version. He advocated that all women go into the paid labor market and that "the care and education of the children becomes a public matter."[155] As Gilman's contribution to the second stage of the feminist genealogy shows, she understood that a much more fundamental rethinking of service work was required to undo women's servile status and unequal power with men.

Yet from the perspective of the parallel conversation in the African American community, Gilman did not go far enough in her analysis of servility, since she avoided thinking about the economic position of the African American servant. Burroughs showed that unless Gilman's bridging and resulting theorizing included dismantling white supremacy constructions of African American women as servants, her aim would be undermined by the labor supply of servants produced by the racialized, gendered labor market. Through her bridging activism and resulting theorizing, Burroughs put the African American woman servant at the center of the problem of undoing servility. As a result, she made a critical contribution to formulating an emancipatory notion of service both for African American women and for the race.

As a daughter of a domestic worker in a white family, Burroughs pursued a different professional path that led in 1909 to the first presidency of the National Training School for Women and Children, an institution that was created by the African American Baptist Woman's Convention. It was located in Washington, D.C., because African American women migrated from southern and western states for "job opportunities in the homes of government officials and other wealthy residents."[156] According to historian Higginbotham, "In 1900 fifty-four percent of employed black women in Washington D.C. worked as domestics."[157] A central purpose of the National Training School was to turn domestic work into a respected profession for African American women workers.

In articulating this aim, Burroughs crafted a response to Gilman, who insisted that "[s]killed labor and domestic service are incompatible."[158] Her portrait of the domestic worker was of "a young woman of the lower classes" who was "ignorant" and not committed to upgrading the quality of her work but was only interested in how quickly she could move onto marriage.[159] To "tempt really high-class labour into this field," Gilman argued that employers would have to increase significantly the "salaries."[160] Since she did not believe this would happen, she claimed that "[t]he degree of intelligence, talent, learning, and trained skill which should be devoted to feeding and cleaning the human race will never consent to domestic service."[161] Yet she granted that the hiring of a domestic worker "would be more of a step in advance if the housewife, released from her former duties, then entered the ranks of productive labour."[162] Of course, the advance here was for the affluent housewife working outside her home and not for the domestic worker carrying out her professional service inside the affluent home.

To actualize an alternative scenario, Burroughs required the support of the African American community. As she pointed out, African American "sentiment" was actively undermining the domestic worker's aim to reinvent herself and upgrade the societal valuing of her service. Burroughs exhorted members of the community to renegotiate their intersectional locations by rethinking how they were letting their class privilege lead them to "hold in contempt" domestic workers.[163] Her speaking out, according to Higginbotham, reflected how the "unprecedented migration . . . contributed to growing class cleavage in the black community."[164]

By bridging the civil rights, feminist, and labor movements, Burroughs joined together the cultivation of racial pride, training in specialized domestic work, and unionizing efforts to achieve social justice for African American domestic workers. Her bridging vision rested on the central facilitating role of autonomous African American women's institutions and organizations. Through the National Training School, its employment agency, and the

National Association of Wage Earners (NAWE), Burroughs worked to bring the domestic worker under the "broad light of public improvement,"[165] which Gilman doubted was possible. Through their own organized efforts, African American women fought for better working conditions, higher pay, and respect for their skilled domestic service. In the process, they embedded the pursuit of their economic independence within the new field of feminist domestic sciences, or "the grand domestic revolution," and within what Higginbotham calls "the politics of respectability."[166]

The motto of the National Training School was "Work. Support thyself. To thine own powers appeal." It proclaimed a strong commitment to nurturing working-class African American women's economic independence. Not all students majored in domestic service. But all students were required to take a course in African American history that was shaped by Burroughs's friendship with historian Carter G. Woodson, who helped create the field. Both a written and an oral exam were required to pass the course.[167] The crucial point for Burroughs was that the school gave its students resources and skills so that they could develop a self-image not shaped by white supremacist assumptions of gendered racial inferiority.

The professionalization of domestic skills aimed to change how the worker viewed her job and therefore herself. Recognizing the intersectional structural constraints on the opportunities for African American women, especially those in the working class, Burroughs put forward how she planned to transform the situation: "Until we realize our ideal, we are going to idealize our real."[168] As she argued, "Women will begin to look upon cooking as a profession and not as a drudgery, for cooking is no more a drudge than school teaching."[169] By reframing the status of domestic work, according to Higginbotham, the National Training School "encouraged expectation of fair treatment."[170] Yet Burroughs was not naive. She recognized that labor organizing was essential to ensure that the professionalization of domestic service produced real justice for the domestic workers. Part of the plan all along, the NAWE was formed in 1920. Its nine-point program included "to assemble the multitude of grievances of employers and employees into a set of common demands and strive, mutually to adjust them," and "to influence just legislation affecting women wage earners," since domestic workers were routinely excluded.[171]

Championing the need for migrant women to achieve self-support, Burroughs declared, "The solution of [the domestic problem] will be the prime factor in the salvation of Negro womanhood, whose salvation must be attained before the so-called race problem can be solved."[172] She did not mean that African American women should limit themselves to domestic service, but as long as it was one of their main avenues for self-support, they deserved respect. She continued, "What matters it if our women, by honest toil, make their way from the kitchen to places of respect and trust in the walks of life? Are they less honorable because they have been servants?"[173] As a force for a societal revaluing of service work, Burroughs argued, African American women "can bring dignity to service life, respect and trust to themselves and honor to the race."[174]

In his contribution to both the African American parallel conversation and the intersectional conversation I am constructing, Du Bois took up Burroughs's challenge to renegotiate his intersectional social location. He started his reflections on the servant by voicing his own experience: "I speak and speak bitterly as a servant and a servant's son, for my mother spent five or more years of her life as a menial; my father's family escaped, although grandfather as a boat steward had to fight hard to be a man and not a lackey." He also confessed, "Instinctively, I hated such work from my birth. I loathed it and shrank from it."[175]

Yet the summer before Du Bois went to graduate school at Harvard, needing "travel money and clothes and a bit to live on until the scholarship was due," he bused dirty dishes in a hotel in Minnesota. As he recalled, "I did not mind the actual work or the kind of work, but it was the dishonesty and deception, the flattery and cajolery, the unnatural assumption that worker and diner had no common humanity."[176] Du Bois ultimately "disowned menial service" for himself and his "people." In fact, he used employment as servants as "the measure of our rise." As he explained, "[T]he Negro will not approach freedom until this hated badge of slavery . . . has been reduced to less than 10 per cent."[177]

Out of his bridging of feminism and civil rights movements, Du Bois theorized the revaluing of service work by honing in on the necessity to dismantle a white supremacist construction of African Americans as servants. Specifically, he suggested that the humanistic dimension of the African American tradition of service could shape the practice of social service that social democracy required. To develop his intersectional concept of service, Du Bois began by recounting that factory work "was closed to us" and that African Americans in the South did not have enough land "to feed most of us." Then he went on to divide African American service jobs into skilled and unskilled. By the second decade of the twentieth century, according to Du Bois, there were three hundred thousand "upper servants—skilled men and women of character, like hotel waiters, Pullman porters, janitors, and cooks."[178]

So, in contrast to Burroughs, his notion of servant included men, and in contrast to Gilman, he included more types of work. If these skilled servants had been white, Du Bois asserted, they "could have called on the great labor movement to lift their work out of slavery." But this movement adopted the white supremacist assumption that *"Negroes are servants; servants are Negroes."* Enforcing the racialized labor market, trade unionists "shut the door of escape to factory and trade in their fellows' faces and battened down the hatches, lest the 300,000 should be workers equal in pay and consideration with white men."[179]

Within the category of unskilled service jobs, Du Bois placed "the bodies and souls of 700,000 washerwomen and household drudges" whose "pay was the lowest and their hours the longest of all workers." They were also cut off from an "escape to modern industrial conditions." Through sympathetic knowledge, Du Bois, like Addams, attributed agency to them. Not only did they resist sexual relations within the domestic servant context, but they "revolt[ed] against unjust labor conditions," with their subversive "sullenness, petty pilfering, unreliability, and fast and fruitless changes of masters."[180]

To transform their situation, Du Bois called for "the same revolution" in domestic work that was occurring with other kinds of work.[181] Factory workers were achieving the status of "self-respecting, well-paid men," and public service was "call[ing] for the highest types of educated and efficient thinkers."[182] To catch up, Du Bois, like Gilman and Burroughs, called for the professionalization of "the care of children, the preparation of food, the cleansing and ordering of the home."[183] Also, like Gilman, he advocated removing much of domestic work, like food preparation and laundry, from the home.[184]

Yet Du Bois deepened the theorizing when he built his notion of social service on the extraction and cultivation of the best qualities of the servant that "transcended the Menial." Here he drew on the African American tradition of providing service that "had been exalted above the Wage."[185] As Du Bois declared, "Surely, no social service, no wholesale helping of masses of men can exist which does not find its effectiveness and beauty in the personal aid of man to man."[186] To infuse democracy with the emancipatory potential of a nonservile service relation, Du Bois argued, democracy itself would have to be freed of its white supremacist structuring, or what he called "the 'manure' theory of social organization."[187]

According to this theory, a version of Aristotle's theorizing of how the polis depended on the household, Du Bois explained, "at the bottom of organized human life there are necessary duties and services which no real human being ought to be compelled to do. We push below this mudsill the derelicts and half-men, whom we hate and despise, and seek to build above it—Democracy!"[188] To reshape the necessary service foundations of democracy, Du Bois urged "black and white, rich and poor" to embrace a vision of "a world of Service without Servants."[189] In this one phrase, by foregrounding the contribution of African American women and men, Du Bois crystalized a core component of a social democratic feminist vision of refounding democracy.

Intersectional Conversation: Community Food Politics and Care Work

Immigrant, mostly noncitizen, Yiddish-speaking, Orthodox Jewish "house-wives" introduced a militant bridging method for revaluing care work direct-ed at providing nourishment. I put quotes around "housewives" because we do not know how much they were contributing to the economic support of their families. During their boycott of kosher butchers, they, like Gilman, empha-sized the economic function of the wife-mother role within the family. Yet their version of this role was quite different from Gilman's. Through their boycott, the immigrant women activated the Jewish tradition of women as proficient actors in the marketplace.

As a result, in this constructed conversation, the boycotters exposed the inadequacy of Gilman's structural analysis of gender roles and food within the private household that grew out of her bridging of socialism and femi-nism. For Gilman, "the management of the family food supply"[190] was "con-sidered a sex-function," performed by "the helpless hands of that amiable but abortive agent, the economically dependent women."[191] Furthermore, "[a]s the ultimate selecting agent in feeding humanity, the private housewife fails" because of "her position as individual purchaser."[192] Gilman also stressed that "the house-servant" lacked "technical intelligence" to evaluate the "standard of food products."[193] So, for Gilman, the household manager's inadequacies in the care area of providing food for her household were caused by and re-inforced her gendered servile status.

To improve the quality of the care work directed at fulfilling the "great function of human nutrition,"[194] Gilman insisted that "organization" was nec-essary. Unfortunately, according to Gilman, "woman, the house-servant, be-longs to the lowest grade of unorganized labor."[195] One meaning of "organi-zation" referred to "organized purchasing power" to undo the leverage of the middlemen to manipulate prices for individual purchasers.[196] Bridging fem-inism and socialism, Gilman envisioned family apartments without kitch-ens. As she explained, "[T]here would be a kitchen belonging to the house from which meals could be served to the families in their rooms or in a com-mon dining-room, as preferred."[197] This design would allow for the exercise of collective buying power. Another meaning of "organization" included a central role for government. Gilman gave an example of how the state and local governments could regulate food prices.[198] Clearly, she did not look to ethnic immigrant communities to contribute to the creation of a caring dem-ocratic food politics.

When, in 1902, the price of kosher meat increased by 50 percent, from twelve to eighteen cents a pound, it provoked a three-week boycott of kosher butchers that spread throughout New York City. At least fifty thousand Jewish families participated.[199] The organizers practiced a different notion of household food provisioning from Gilman's. Living in crowded immigrant neighborhoods, they were not isolated individual household managers. The immigrant Jewish women were part of what could be called a food community that was bound together by common dietary laws and regulations over how animals should be slaughtered. One of the leaders, Cecilia Schwartz, illustrated the close relationship between the household and the public space of the market. Standing at her apartment window, she explained the economics of meat prices to a crowd of women in the street: "If we don't buy from the butchers, they won't be able to buy from the wholesale dealers. The result will be that the wholesalers will find themselves with a lot of meat on their hands. They will sell cheap to our butchers and we will get our meat cheap."[200]

As Schwartz illustrated, immigrant Jewish women took militant action based on their knowledge of food market economics. They broke windows of kosher butcher shops, seized meat from noncompliant consumers and burned it in the streets, and tangled with the police, which resulted in their arrests and going before a judge. Initiating a new bridging between a nascent food movement and the labor movement, they described their actions in the language of strike and scabs. One of the initiators of the action was Fannie Levy, who had six children under the age of thirteen and whose husband was a cloak maker. After the retail butchers' refusal to buy meat for a week failed to pressure the wholesalers, or what was called the Meat Trust, to lower its prices, in the street among a group of women consumers, she shouted, "This is their strike? Look at the good it has brought! Now, if *we women* make a strike, then it will be a strike."[201] This was not the language of traditional household managers or servile women. It was the language of the labor movement and class struggle applied to a new food movement.

The strikers defined their gendered class struggle as one in which they, as food workers, were taking on the Meat Trust. Charged with disorderly conduct, Rosa Peskin was questioned by a judge. Apparently, she had seized a woman's meat purchase, viewing her as a scab. She responded "certainly" to the charge of throwing meat onto the street. The judge followed up with, "What do you know of a trust? It's no business of yours." Her response was, "Whose business is it, then, that our pockets are empty . . . ?"[202] Rebecca Ablowitz tied their struggle with the Meat Trust to the inadequacy of wages. She explained to the judge, "We're not rioting. Only see how thin our children are, our husbands have no more strength to work harder."[203] While Ablowitz appeared to be presenting her household as dependent on a male breadwinner's wages, in actuality, as we have seen, immigrant Jewish families depended on the combined earnings of the children, the husband-father, and the mother-wife. The women interconnected two aims in their conception of the class struggle: lowering food prices and raising wages.

In "Minimum Wage and Maximum Price," Gilman argued that minimum wage legislation was not sufficient if food prices were not regulated.[204] This 1913 article in *The Forerunner* made no mention of the militant immigrant Jewish women. Gilman never explored how they expanded the dimensions of women's economic independence to include the exercise of collective consumer power. Gilman's focus was on removing food from the responsibilities of wife-mothers so that it was no longer an unpaid gendered activity. The combination of her prejudices toward Jewish immigrants and her structural analysis, based on her version of intersectional activism, blocked her from absorbing how their nonservile militant actions led them to turn care as food provisioning into a democratic politics.

By exercising their collective consumer power, the immigrant women innovated a democratic participatory food politics that drew on their eastern European Jewish cultural support of women's participation in secular public spaces, like the marketplace.[205] Their food politics also combined strike and boycott methods. So their activism illustrated a third meaning of "organization"—community organizing. They formed the Ladies Anti-Beef Trust to coordinate the building of their strike-boycott. While women held the positions of president and treasurer, male members of the newly organized ILGWU, probably cloak makers like Levy's husband, filled the positions of vice president and secretary.[206] This structuring of the leadership interconnected women's consumer power and the labor movement. This bridging of movements also illustrated how working-class immigrant Jewish men and women struggled together.

Participation in the "strike-boycott" included going door to door, outdoor meetings, picketing, appealing to men in synagogues, drawing in supportive groups, engaging with local government officials, raising funds for bail and to reimburse consumers for seizing their meat purchases, and establishing kosher meat cooperatives.[207] Through their activism, the striking and boycotting household managers discredited Gilman's assumptions about their inability to organize around food provisioning. They not only organized consumer power but also contributed to a public discussion of the place of struggles over the cost of food care within the refounding of democracy.

Paula Hyman characterizes the boycott as "a qualified success," since it brought down the price of meat and the Brooklyn and Harlem kosher meat cooperatives continued after the activism.[208] She also suggests that it "should be seen not as an isolated incident but as a prelude to the explosion of women activists in the great garment industry strikes at the end of the decade."[209] Demonstrating that women were not servile in carrying out their household food responsibilities was inspirational for women in the waged labor market, who sought to defy the assumption that they were docile and unorganizable. Jewish immigrant daughters, like Newman and Clara Lemlich (1886–1982), while still living at home with their mothers, were leaders in 1909–1910 of "the largest strike by women workers the United States had ever seen."[210] Their activism dramatically increased the membership of the ILGWU that had supported the kosher meat strike-boycott. It also had a broader significance. Through their intersectional activism, the immigrant Jewish mothers and daughters showed that undoing the servile status of both unpaid and paid work was necessary to turn care, understood broadly, into the purpose of the social democratic state.

By bringing the intersectional activists into relationship in constructed intersectional conversations, I showed how each group worked for social policies for earning mothers. I also uncovered the distinct ways each group understood the importance of revaluing care work to turn it into a democratic public value that could reshape the purpose of the state. Both of these aims inspired the struggles that were necessary for the social democratic feminists to move from a maternalist standpoint based on the ideology of a male family wage to social democratic feminist standpoints grounded in strong commitments to women's economic independence. In the process of parallel struggles and a few examples of common struggles, the three streams of social democratic feminists revealed how a truly democratic refounding of America rested on a radical undoing of the laissez-faire version of the liberal democratic state.

Feminist Genealogy of Multileveled Social Citizenship: Second Stage

In the second stage of the feminist genealogy of multileveled social citizenship, social democratic feminists advanced the construction of themselves as refounders by interconnecting their quest for economic independence with socializing the citizen right to work. To construct this stage, I continue to unfold the genealogical method. I begin by using Marshall and Shklar to establish why the male-biased liberal individualistic framework was not sufficient to include women. Then I turn to Gilman's use of the genealogical method of reinterpretations and substitutions. To illustrate the impact of contingent factors on the genealogy, I end with an analysis of the social democratic feminist legal strategy to use sex-based labor laws as a first step to achieving universal economic social rights.

Marshall begins his genealogy of citizenship with the codification of civil rights in the British transition from feudalism to capitalism, or the "change from servile to free labor."[211] These rights included "liberty of person, freedom of speech, thought and faith, the right to own property, and to conclude valid contracts, and the right to justice."[212] Marshall also places the economic right to work within the category of civil rights. He defines it as "the right to follow the occupation of one's choice in the place of one's choice, subject only to legitimate demands for preliminary technical training."[213] Finally, Marshall observes that "civil rights were indispensable to a competitive market economy" because they constructed each male worker as "an independent unit in the economic struggle."[214]

Shklar characterizes the "duty to earn" as an essential part of citizenship standing in the United States. Earning one's livelihood was a "source of public respect" and the basis of independence, "the indelibly necessary quality of genuine, democratic citizenship." The state of economic dependence, or non-earning, demonstrated that an individual or group was "unfit for citizenship."[215] Shklar traces the origin of the duty to earn to the pre–Civil War period and the legacy of slavery. According to her interpretation, free citizens wanted to differentiate themselves from slaves living in a condition of forced "servitude." Therefore, they insisted, "We are citizens only if we 'earn.'"[216]

Both Marshall and Shklar inadvertently show why the second stage of the social democratic feminist genealogy was necessary. Marshall acknowledges that his genealogy of citizenship really applies only to "the adult male—the citizen *par excellence*," because "the status of women, or at least of married women, was in some important respects peculiar."[217] They were not entitled to the bundle of civil rights. Yet they did gain some social rights through the early British factory acts that improved working conditions and lessened their hours of work. In fact, men were excluded from these protections, according to Marshall, "out of respect" for their citizen status, "on the grounds that enforced protective measures curtailed the civil right to conclude a free contract of employment." In sharp contrast, "[w]omen were protected because they were not citizens."[218] By never figuring out how to fit the sequencing of women's social and civil rights into his genealogy of the civil right to work, Marshall legitimizes the need for a feminist genealogy of women's economic citizenship.

Shklar's individualistic understanding of the citizen duty to earn suggests a radical critique of the ideology of the male breadwinner model that assumed married women would not work outside the home. Clearly, that ideology blocked women's incorporation into civil citizenship. Shklar argues that "middle class feminists" like Gilman understood "the intimate bond between earning and citizenship."[219] Gilman, according to Shklar, embraced a "traditional individualism" when she defended women's "opportunity to participate as equals in the economic process."[220] By adopting this interpretation of Gilman, Shklar fails to come to terms with what Gilman and other social democratic feminists understood: Women could not simply add themselves as individuals to a labor market shaped by a model of the worker based on men's experiences. Thus, the limitations of Shklar's concept of earning shows why a second stage of the feminist genealogy was necessary to incorporate women earners.

For the second stage, the social democratic feminists proposed a notion of work that went beyond including unpaid work.[221] They reinterpreted work as social service because the aim of all work should be the social welfare common good. As the key reinterpreter, Gilman provided an analysis that supported Du Bois's vision of "a world of Service without Servants." She set out a hierarchy of purposes: "Work the object of which is merely to serve one's self is the lowest. Work the object of which is merely to serve one's family is the next lowest. Work the object of which is to serve more and more people, in widening range . . . is social service in the fullest sense, and the highest form of service that we can reach."[222] Through this passage, Gilman clarified that women's civil citizenship required more than becoming self-supporting individuals or joining husbands in the financial support of the family, although this would be a clear advance over the male family wage.

Echoing Mill's arguments in *The Subjection of Women*,[223] Gilman presented an analysis of the male breadwinner model as a foundation of a capitalist system driven by individualistic competition. In his defense of equal citizenship, including women's right to work, Mill emphasized "the vast amount of gain to human nature." As he asserted, "All the selfish propensities, the self-worship, the unjust self-preference, which exist among mankind, have their source and root in, and derive their principal nourishment from, the present constitution of the relation between men and women." According to Mill, men's nature "both as an individual and a social being" was "pervert[ed]" by their structural dominance over women.[224]

Gilman extended Mill's insight to show how one marker of male economic dominance, the duty to support one's family, reinforced man's "excessive individualism" by attaching him to a market economy, "full of struggling men." To maintain his position of economic power over his wife, the male breadwinner had to take the job that paid the most, instead of serving society by "his conscientious performance of the work he is best fitted for."[225] Gilman's analysis here was also reminiscent of Plato's *Republic*, in which the just ordering of the state depended on citizens doing one of three functions according to their aptitudes. By following his abilities rather than market forces, according to Gilman, the husband-father would be able to develop his social nature and his capacity for social service. Therefore, women working outside their homes was the catalyst for taking work to its highest level because it destabilized the sexuo-economic structural relation that required the continuance of a masculinized economic individualism.

In turning all work directed at the common good into social service, Gilman enlarged the notion of social service beyond the one presented in the first chapter. She called for "the capacity of individuals to feel and to think *collectively*, to grasp social values, to recognize, care for and serve social needs, to see in the common business of life, not personal expression or personal aggrandizement, but social service."[226] As she showed in *Herland*, building roads or any other kind of work that responded to social needs could be called social service. In *The Forerunner*, she characterized the food retailer as "a social servant instead of a robber, a bloodsucker on the body politic," when he operated within a system in which the state and local governments established just prices.[227]

Besides socializing the nature of work, the social democratic feminists feminized the human worker through a brilliant legal strategy.[228] It used sex-based labor laws that prescribed maximum hours and minimum wages for women as the basis for establishing legal precedents that could be used to extend socialized labor rights to male workers.[229] This payoff occurred in the late New Deal Supreme Court decisions that discredited the laissez-faire reading of the Constitution. Without going into the complexity of the legal strategy and the court decisions, I bring their broad outlines into relationship with Gilman's reinterpretation of the human worker.[230]

Gilman posited "three distinct fields of life—masculine, feminine, and human."[231] At a very basic level, the masculine was individualistic and combative, while the feminine was relational and service oriented. To construct her notion of feminine, Gilman extracted the emancipatory potential of women's roles in the sexual division of labor. The problem for Gilman was that "all human standards have been based on male characteristics."[232] Her aim was to redefine human through a liberatory feminine lens. As she argued, "[O]f the two the women are more vitally human than the men, by nature."[233]

Applying the three categories to political economy, Gilman distinguished between "the economic man" and "the economic woman" and suggested that the latter should provide the standard for reconstituting the human worker. According to Gilman, "We find existing industry almost wholly in male hands; find it done as men do it; assume that that is the way it must be done. When women suggest that it could be done differently, their proposal is waved aside—they are 'only women'—their ideas are 'womanish.'" Gilman hoped that substituting economic woman for economic man could motor a change from a masculine "survival of the fittest" to a practice of what she called "social economics" that could advance "the promotion of human life."[234] Cooper shared Gilman's aim of using women's "feminine flavor" to replace "that selfishness and rapacity" of laissez-faire economics.[235] According to Gilman, economic woman could redefine the worker *not* because she was morally superior or because man was morally inferior.[236] It was her relational self that suggested a model of the interdependent human worker with a "directly serviceable tendency,"[237] whose flourishing required the enlargement of the social welfare purpose of the state.

The legal reasoning behind sex-based labor laws provided a version of what Gilman was proposing.[238] It illustrated how the creators of the second stage of the genealogy were constrained by the contingent factor of the U.S. Supreme Court's tendency to read a nineteenth-century laissez-faire ideology into the Constitution. As Kelley explained, "[W]e have an eighteenth-century Constitution interpreted by nineteenth-century judges." What was urgently required to advance government regulation of the labor market, according to Kelley, was "a twentieth-century Constitution interpreted by twentieth-century judges."[239] To move in this direction, she played a key role in crafting a notion of economic woman that would hold up under Fourteenth Amendment "liberty of contract" jurisprudence.

As chief factory inspector of Illinois, in 1895 Kelley had witnessed how the Illinois Supreme Court could declare an eight-hour labor law for women to be unconstitutional. It reasoned that men and women were formally equal and therefore both should be unhindered by the state in their individual exercise of the liberty of contract. In 1908, when Oregon's *Muller* case was appealed to the U.S. Supreme Court, Kelley and Josephine Goldmark (1877–1950), through the NCL, jumped in to develop a legal strategy to defend Oregon's ten-hour workday for women only. An innovative approach was needed because three years earlier, in *Lochner v. New York*, the Supreme Court had declared that a ten-hour workday for bakers violated the Fourteenth Amendment's protection of the individual liberty of contract. Goldmark coordinated the research and writing of what came to be known as the Brandeis brief—after Louis Brandeis (1856–1941), who defended the law before the court. The brief aimed to subvert the laissez-faire reading of the Constitution by providing vast sociological evidence for the tangible, substantive inequality that the woman worker experienced in her family and work life.

Citing the brief in a footnote, Justice Brewer, writing for the unanimous Supreme Court, articulated a notion of economic woman that sharply differentiated her from economic man. In making his case, he explicitly dismissed the relevance of *Lochner*. According to Brewer, economic woman had a different biological function and also performed different societal roles, including the rearing of children and the maintaining of the household. Therefore, woman's "physical well-being" was "an object of public interest and care."[240] One purpose of a sex-based hours law was "to compensate for some of the burdens which rest upon her."[241] Yet her maternal function was not sufficient to justify turning care into a purpose of a democratic state.

Brewer also challenged the contention that women had achieved equal civil rights with men. His legal analysis stressed the distinction between formal and substantive equality. According to Brewer, "[W]oman has always been dependent upon man. Man established his control at the outset by superior physical strength, and this control in various forms . . . has continued to the present." While advances had been made, including in the area of married women's formal civil rights, women were fundamentally unable to achieve "an independent position in life" within the structural constraints of unequal power with men, both in the family and in the labor market. Brewer concluded that "to secure a real equality of right" for women laundry workers in Oregon, legislation was "necessary."[242]

From a social democratic feminist perspective, the landmark decision gave constitutional credence to the notion that the earning woman was vulnerable to economic and sexual exploitation because her "capacity to maintain the struggle for subsistence" differed from man's. According to Brewer, Oregon's sex-based hours law helped "protect her from the greed as well as the passion of man."[243] Yet this ten-hour limit was not sufficient to care for women workers if the fewer hours mandated by legislation resulted in employers lowering weekly wages. Such a result sparked the famous 1912 Lawrence "Bread and Roses" strike, according to Kelley, whose legal strategy expanded to include gaining constitutional support for sex-based minimum wage laws.[244]

These laws established for economic woman a publicly administered type of women-friendly collective bargaining to negotiate a living wage.[245] Male-friendly private collective bargaining, which Marshall included within the category of civil rights,[246] was not an adequate method for achieving social justice for women workers. The wage boards constituted a new type of public space where employer and worker representatives sat down together with representatives of the public to determine an industry-specific weekly minimum wage. Kelley envisioned the boards as an alternative to the "blunt weapon"[247] of spontaneous strikes to raise wages. Most of the thirteen statutes that passed between 1912 and 1919 established minimum wage boards instead of a statewide flat rate.[248] These experiments provided substitutes for a free market determination of wages. They also showed how the aim of a living wage for working women required building participatory dimensions into the construction of the welfare state.

The 1913 Oregon law, the most progressive version of the wage board concept, was challenged by a Portland manufacturer of paper boxes and one of his employees. The Oregon Industrial Welfare Commission (OIWC) had determined, through investigation and public meetings, that the weekly minimum wage in Portland for an "experienced adult woman" in manufacturing should be $8.64. This calculation was based on a weekly budget for a self-supporting woman who had to cover the costs of housing, food, clothing, transportation, and medical care. The OIWC also mandated no more than a nine-hour day within a fifty-four-hour week, as well as a noon lunch break of no less than forty-five minutes. The Oregon Supreme Court upheld the constitutionality of the law. Its decision was then appealed to the U.S. Supreme Court.

Once again, the NCL turned to Brandeis, who argued the case for the OIWC, backed up by a sociologically rich brief. When Brandeis joined the Supreme Court before it produced its decision, the NCL recruited Felix Frankfurter (1882–1965) to reargue the case. Because Brandeis had to recuse himself, a four-four court let stand the Oregon law. While no national precedent was set by the "Oregon Minimum Wage Cases," the concept of a sex-based living wage continued to gain support. In 1918, Congress passed a statute based on the Oregon model for Washington, D.C.

Frankfurter's brief reinforced the legal strategy of using economic woman to discredit the laissez-faire reading of the Constitution. As he explained, "the ends" of the sex-based labor law "are the very life of the State, namely, the health and civilized maintenance of this generation, and the healthy and civilized continuance of generations to follow."[249] To develop his point about "this generation" of workers, Frankfurter applied a concept of commodification of labor. He depicted the earning worker as one who sold her energy as a commodity to her employer, who "alone has the use of her working energy."[250] When the employer purchased it, according to Frankfurter, he owed her a wage that replenished that energy, or "the human minimum." Therefore, the "cost" of labor should be determined only by the cost of "the maintenance of the energy purchased by the employer and devoted to the industry"[251] and not by the wage bargain based on the exercise of an individualistic liberty of contract.

Frankfurter defended a new notion of "freedom of contract" that depended on "the principle of the power of the state to protect equality of bargaining."[252] He argued that "[t]he 'liberty of contract' which the present legislation would destroy is only the 'liberty' of an employer *to* abuse and the 'liberty' of an employee to *be* abused." In sharp contrast, he stated that "[t]rue freedom of contract is established, rather than impaired, by such restrictions." They create for "the parties an equal basis for bargaining," so that the employees are "not under the compulsion of a crippling necessity," such as near "starvation."[253]

Through their legal strategy, born out of necessity, the social democratic feminists reversed the male-biased historical sequencing of citizen rights by socializing the citizen right to work. According to Marshall's genealogy of citizen rights, social rights came only after the achievement of civil and political rights. Yet Marshall's conceptualization of social rights perfectly captured the social democratic feminist reinterpretation of the civil right to work. According to Marshall, social rights were created through a political process and guaranteed by the state. They provided "a modicum of economic welfare and security."[254] They "impl[ied] an absolute right to a certain standard of civilization which is conditioned only on the discharge of the general duties of citizenship." Moreover, he insisted, "[t]heir content does not depend on the economic value of the individual claimant."[255]

The Oregon wage board law assumed that women workers were carrying out their citizen duty to earn. Therefore, they were entitled to a wage not dictated by the economic laws of supply and demand, or by the unequal employer/employee relationship, but by their social right to wages that "supply the necessary cost of living" and "maintain them in health."[256] By defending this law before the Supreme Court, the NCL showed how the actualization of woman's civil right to contract depended on her first achieving a social right to a minimum wage. Yet the significance of the legal strategy went beyond evolving women's economic citizenship. Kelley and the NCL created a first step in reinterpreting the economic rights of all workers, especially the low-waged, unorganized ones.

Frankfurter explicitly acknowledged that the sociological justification for a minimum wage for low-income working women could be extended to all low-wage workers.[257] As he noted, sex-based labor laws were justified by "the fact that the mass of women employees cannot be expected to bargain on an equality with employers." For example, in Portland, prior to the law, almost 50 percent of women factory workers made less than eight dollars a week. Yet he contended that unequal bargaining power was not limited to self-supporting women. As Frankfurter observed, "[N]o individual laborer of the group working on the margin of bare living necessities can bargain *freely* with an employer under modern industrial conditions."[258] These remarks suggested that women's gendered incorporation into civil citizenship had the potential to feminize the conception of the earning citizen by substituting economic woman as the standard for legislating universal labor laws.

The significance of the second stage of the feminist genealogy of social citizenship is that it showed how the social democratic feminists attached economic social rights to citizenship. Gilman created a social democratic feminist standpoint by extracting the liberatory dimensions of women's roles in the traditional sexual division of labor. By utilizing a transformed concept of the feminine, she defended the need to feminize concepts of work and the worker. Yet her construction was not sufficient. Struggles between men and women and among women evolved the legal strategy of using sex-based labor laws to discredit the masculinized laissez-faire construction of work and the worker. As the social democratic feminists expanded their range of reforms from limiting hours of work to establishing a living wage, their formulation of gendered substantive inequalities grew more radical. Thus, forced by conservative Supreme Court justices to carve out a gendered path to economic citizenship, the social democratic feminists began the process of developing a caring state for both women and men citizen workers.

Refounding as Collective Self-Reflection by Outsiders

This chapter shows that to recover the social democratic feminists as refounders, we must recognize how, in their different streams, they developed methods of collective self-reflection. Their purpose was to radically alter the laissez-faire version of the state-economy relationship. The constructed intersectional conversations revealed these methods. Each stream centered the lives of women workers, especially working mothers, which allowed the social democratic feminists to expose how the ideology of laissez-faire assumed a male worker. As part of their project of engendering democracy, the social democratic feminists showed how including women in the economy alongside men required accommodating women's need to combine unpaid care responsibilities and paid work. The African American and immigrant Jewish streams were especially effective at revealing the subversive potential of embracing earning mothers. As outsiders, the three streams developed methods of collective self-reflection that inevitably entailed putting facts on the ground to make their points.

At the local and state levels, they engaged in debating the value of different social policies that directly affected working mothers, like maternity leave. They helped develop experiments in childcare, sex-based labor legislation, and minimum wage boards. To persuade the Supreme Court to abandon its laissez-faire interpretation of the Fourteenth Amendment, they further developed a legal strategy to use sex-based labor laws as a starting point for feminizing all workers. As a result of these efforts to redefine "what we stand for," the social democratic feminists enlarged the "who" of "who are we?" to give a diversity of working women their place in refounding democracy.

Egalitarian Suffragism and Electoral Politics of Presence

The social democratic feminists required political power to actualize their visions of social democracy in daily life and through a welfare state. As they participated in the late women's suffrage campaign, they innovated the third component of engendering democracy: an electoral politics of presence. To further develop the book's first broad argument, I show how women's political agency and socializing democracy were mutually constitutive, but only if all women gained political citizenship. Therefore, I examine how the social democratic feminists both delegitimized men's monopolization of political power and grappled with structural intersectional inequalities that divided women. Finally, to support the book's second broad argument, I uncover how the social democratic feminists evolved their feminist genealogy of social citizenship by socializing the political right to vote.

Specifically, I argue that because they bridged different movements, the three streams of social democratic feminists turned their egalitarian suffrage organizing into a space for practicing and theorizing an electoral politics of presence, capable of generating a women's bloc vote for social democracy. To develop this argument, I begin by constructing the notion of an electoral politics of presence. Next, I define egalitarian suffragism and show how it embedded the vote as a tool, or as the means for social reform, within a political revolution, defined as a change in the sovereign power. Then I analyze how the egalitarian suffragists, in different electoral campaigns, illustrated dimensions of an electoral politics of presence.

To foreground how African American and immigrant Jewish suffragists innovated the new kind of politics, I apply the theory-activist dynamic to further elucidate their different versions of an electoral politics of presence. I construct an intersectional conversation on anti-lynching and the sexual double standard to reveal how African American suffragists built into the engendering of political democracy a vision of interracial democracy. I interpret the WTUL as a pragmatist experimental social space that immigrant Jewish bridgers shaped to actualize a version of an electoral politics of presence appropriate for nonvoting immigrant working-class women. Out of their struggles, I suggest that the egalitarian suffragists replaced the traditional nonpolitical woman standpoint based on private male protection with new social democratic feminist standpoints that tied the vote to collective self-protection. Finally, I conclude with how egalitarian suffragists defended a social or relational notion of the vote, when they prefigured a bloc vote for social democracy, as an engendered, interracial, and cosmopolitan project.

Electoral Politics of Presence

Historians characterize the late suffrage campaign as a pressure group that perfected "single-issue activism"[1] or as a mass movement defined as a "platform" for a diversity of groups.[2] Both interpretations adopt a theory of democracy characterized by interest group politics, or the bargaining among narrow and specific interests. This lens reinforces the view that suffragists did not contribute to a new practice and theory of politics. Instead, they added their impressive voluntary association skills to the ongoing male-privileged system, which left women largely outside electoral party politics, including running for office.[3] Consequently, neither interpretation is adequate for recovering why and how the egalitarian suffragists practiced a new kind of women-friendly electoral politics.

To formulate a concept that reveals their contribution to engendering political democracy, I focus on how the three streams translated their bridging skills into a new type of *electoral* politics of presence. I begin with political theorist Anne Phillips's notion of the politics of presence. She explores the claim that it matters *who* presents ideas in elected assemblies. Through an examination of gender quotas and race-conscious districting, Phillips analyzes the meaning of increasing the number of women and the number of ethnic and racial minorities in legislative bodies. I shift the focus to presence in electoral politics contexts. Moreover, in her depiction of the "groups" seeking political presence, Phillips adopts an "either/or" lens when she defines them "by their gender or ethnicity or race."[4] Through "both/and" intersectional thinking, I reformulate the concept of *who* seeks presence. With these changes in mind, I build the concept of electoral politics of presence by adapting three of Phillips's insights.

First, according to Phillips, "the desire for political *inclusion* . . . is the real impetus to any politics of presence."[5] This theme directs us to uncover how the egalitarian suffragists cultivated that desire in different streams of women and thereby laid the motivational foundations for women's electoral politics of presence. Because there were local, state, and federal campaigns for women's right to vote, suffrage leaders needed to mobilize different groups of women to persuade different groups of men to support the campaigns. As a result, the three streams were forced to learn how to utilize their skills at bridging movements within political spaces shaped by electoral politics. To be effective, they subverted, in different ways, the mainstream gendered political culture that defined women as "inherently nonpartisan."[6]

Second, Phillips argues that physical presence constitutes "a major, and necessary, challenge to the social arrangements which have systematically placed women in a subordinate position."[7] African American and immigrant Jewish women played crucial roles in actualizing this dimension. Their physical presence in electoral campaigns exposed the intersectional hierarchies of power that supported both their political subordination among women and women's political subordination to men. Thus, their physical presence demonstrated what democracy would look like if the diversity of women were able to actualize their political agency.

Third, Phillips concludes that "[t]he real importance of political presence lies in the way it is thought to transform the political agenda."[8] In other words, there is a crucial "relationship between ideas and presence." She connects this assumption to her theory of deliberative democracy that "insists on . . . the capacity for formulating new positions in the course of discussions with others."[9] Through their different campaigns, the bridgers insisted on engaging in a deeply programmatic version of electoral politics because it supported widespread discussions of public policies, principles, analyses, and visions. As a result, they turned electoral politics into exercises in deliberative democracy.

Clearly, this new type of electoral politics of presence depended on taking social movements into electoral politics. In *The Second Twenty Years at Hull-House*, Addams described the characteristics of one such moment, from 1909 to 1914. During this five-year period before World War I broke out, social reform movements were widespread and settlement house workers expanded the range of their intersectional activism. Moreover, they began to believe that they could reshape the national agenda. "In such an insurgent mood," Addams observed, "men reexamine from time to time the social institutions upon which they have been relying and renew their faith in human volition as a power which may really direct and shape social conditions."[10]

To fulfill this hope, Addams joined the "insurgent" political movement represented by the 1912 Progressive Party and Theodore Roosevelt's campaign for the presidency.

Inspired by Addams's actions and reflections, I have built a concept that weaves intersectional versions of the politics of presence into an insurgent or movement-based type of electoral politics. This concept of electoral politics of presence breaks with the interest group politics interpretation of the suffrage movement by assuming that the egalitarian suffragists were acting as social movement bridgers.[11] They were seeking a refounding of democracy. Since the formulation of the vote as a tool for achieving narrow social reforms could reinforce the interest group politics framing, in the next section, I recover how egalitarian suffragists embedded the vote as tool within a vision of a peaceful political revolution.

Egalitarian Suffragism: Tool for Social Justice *and* Political Revolution

The egalitarian tendency within the late suffrage campaign, according to historian Aileen Kraditor, emerged when settlement house workers made women's suffrage a priority. She argues that they reinfused suffragism with "[t]he egalitarianism" present when suffragism first emerged in the nineteenth century out of the abolitionist movement.[12] In addition, historian Lisa Materson shows that African American suffragists kept alive the egalitarian promise when they linked women's suffrage to the Reconstruction Amendments.[13] Further, immigrant Jewish labor and socialist activists insisted on the egalitarian version of suffragism by fusing it to the politics of gendered class struggle. Taken together, the three origins of egalitarian suffragism led to an intersectional framing of "votes for women," the popular slogan of the late suffrage period. As a result, the egalitarian suffragists defined themselves in opposition to early twentieth-century mainstream suffrage leaders, who assumed that the pursuit of gender political equality could be separated from questions of white supremacy, nativism, and class inequality. Some insisted on this separation for expedient reasons; others worked for the enfranchisement of only white, native-born women.[14]

The clash of perspectives played out in the disagreement over a literacy test to qualify for voter status. It was discussed in New Orleans at the 1903 meeting of the National American Woman Suffrage Association (NAWSA), where Gilman was the sole planned speaker who presented arguments in opposition.[15] While Kraditor points out that a literacy requirement never became a core position for mainstream suffragists, the "heated debates" over it were very revealing. The racist and nativist logic of an educational test was presented by Laura Clay, a Kentucky Democrat and NAWSA leader, in a 1906 letter to Harriet Taylor Upton, an Ohio Republican and NAWSA leader. Clay claimed that the NAWSA "always recognized the usefulness of woman suffrage as a counterbalance to the foreign vote, and as a means of legally preserving white supremacy in the South." She pointed to South Carolina suffrage leaflets that presented statistics showing that adding educated white women to the electorate "would give the supremacy to the white race." She also wrote that southern suffragists "freely used the same argument in relation to the native born and the foreign born vote."[16]

In her influential defense of municipal suffrage, crafted for a 1905 Chicago city charter convention, which she presented before the 1906 NAWSA meeting in Baltimore and published as a chapter in *Newer Ideals of Peace*, Addams articulated the egalitarian suffrage position: "The statement is sometimes made that the franchise for women would be valuable only so far as the educated women exercised it. This statement totally disregards the fact that those matters in which woman's judgment is most needed are far too primitive and basic to be largely influenced by what we call education." By taking this stance, Addams expanded what constituted relevant political knowledge to include matters of daily life, and she enlarged the pool of political actors who were repositories of this knowledge. She gave the example of "thousands of workingwomen" whose "health and lives" were "intimately affect[ed]" by the "sanitary conditions of all the factories and workshops." Their unencumbered exercise of the right to vote, for Addams, was critical to advance the "effort to incorporate a progressive developing life founded upon a response to the needs of all the people, into the requisite legal enactments and civic institutions."[17]

Connecting votes for women with socializing collective self-government was the obvious next step for the social democratic feminists. They learned through their experiences that their practice of citizen social service and pursuit of women's economic independence without political power were not sufficient to bring about the founding of U.S. social democracy. As Addams declared, "Women had discovered that the unrepresented are always liable to be given what they do not want by legislators." Her examples were a child labor law that "exempts street trades, the most dangerous of all trades to a child's morals," and a mothers' pension program that provided "overburdened women" with such a small amount of financial help that they "continue to face the necessity of neglecting their young in order to feed them."[18]

Beyond the legislative branch, Addams pointed to the problem of women not controlling the administration of programs that they had incubated: "We sometimes considered it of doubtful advantage that more and more women were appointed to positions in administrative government, so long as the power of general direction [over] . . . new social experiments, was lodged altogether in the hands of men responsible only to other voting men and politi-cally free from the public opinion of the women originally concerned for the measures."[19] Addams's example was a comprehensive women-initiated Chi-cago Juvenile Court system. It kept children out of jail, provided them with education and health care while they resided in a group home, and worked to reunite them with their families by providing income supplements. Accord-ing to Addams, its integrity was threatened by male politicians who turned the government-funded civil service positions into a corrupt patronage system.[20]

With these observations, Addams appeared to fit snugly within Kradi-tor's container of "middle-class social workers for whom suffrage was never more than a tool for social regeneration."[21] Kelley and Malkiel provided fur-ther evidence for this interpretation when they pointed to how state women's suffrage successes correlated with social justice administrative and legisla-tive victories. As political scientist Kristi Andersen reminds us, "By the time the suffrage amendment was ratified in 1920, fifteen states had already given women full suffrage (a total of over 7,300,000 eligible women voters) and twelve others had legislated suffrage in presidential elections (most of the latter in 1919)."[22] In 1915, Kelley noted, "It is an interesting coincidence that Mothers' Pensions are best administered precisely in those states and cities, like Or-egon and Chicago, where women in general vote and are politically active."[23] Pointing to "Arizona, California, Colorado, Idaho, Oregon, Utah, Washing-ton, and Wyoming" and the passage of sex-based labor laws, mothers' pension laws, and laws against trafficking of women, called white slave laws, Malkiel concluded that "where women have obtained political rights they use the bal-lot conscientiously . . . for social reform."[24]

Missing in the vote-as-tool interpretation of egalitarian suffragism is the theorizing of its significance for the evolution of collective self-government. In other words, this framing really only captures one side of social democ-racy: the social policy side. Yet Addams's examples of inadequate legislation and administration of programs suggested that the problem was not a lack of social policies, but rather that they were shaped and controlled by men. So while vote as a tool appears to connect politics and social policy, it leaves unexamined the way in which, by gaining the right to vote, women aimed to delegitimize male domination of political democracy as a crucial dimen-sion of engendering and thereby refounding U.S. democracy.

In her 1914 article, "The Larger Aspects of the Woman's Movement," Ad-dams presented an interpretation of the votes for women movement as a "bloodless" political revolution that furthered the evolution of self-govern-ment within the United States and globally. To make her case, she placed the movement within the tradition of primarily eighteenth- and nineteenth-cen-tury European political revolutions. She distinguished two "complementa-ry" dimensions of these revolutions: change in the content of governmental policies and an expansion of those in power, which deepened democratization. "As the governing classes have been enlarged by the enfranchisement of one body of men after another," Addams explained, "government itself has not only been enriched through new human interests *but at the same time* [my emphasis] it has become further democratized through the accession of the new classes representing those interests."[25]

In Addams's historical overview, the enlargement of the role of government preceded the achieving of political power by the newly enfranchised class. In the eighteenth century, nobles turned "levying tariffs and embargoes" into political matters and thereby paved the way for the merchant class to insist that it should oversee "the problems of a rising commerce," rather than the "self interested nobles." In the nineteenth century, parliaments "had already begun to regulate conditions of mines," creating legitimacy for the working class to demand political inclusion so that they "could best represent" their interests. Similarly, Addams asserted, "the insistence of women for political expression, which characterizes the opening years of the twentieth century," was fueled by "the consideration by governmental bodies of the basic human interests with which women have traditionally been concerned, quite as the membership of the middle class and that of the working class each in turn followed its own interest and became a part of representative government."[26] Addams interpreted each of these political revolutions as not driven by selfish, narrow interests, but by the aim of renewing the capacity of self-government to seek the common good by addressing "new human interests."

By drawing parallels between political revolutions based on socioeconomic class and women's political revolution, Addams made clear that women were engaged in a power struggle with men. Of course, Addams knew that all women did not share the same socioeconomic class location. So she focused on the power struggle between social servants, who lobbied for sex-based labor laws and bans on child labor, and their representatives, whom she characterized as "men whose minds are fixed upon factory management from the point of view of profits." In this way, Addams suggested an economic class struggle between at least social democratic feminists, who sought to infuse relations of production with social justice, and male representatives, who viewed the world according to a market logic and sided with the owning class.[27]

By interconnecting the vote-as-tool argument with the theme that women were engaged in a nonviolent political revolution, Addams offered her understanding of the significance of egalitarian suffragism. As this book makes clear, African American and immigrant Jewish suffragists expanded the reach of the project and therefore its significance. They uncovered how structural white supremacy, class inequality, and nativism were holding back the coming to fruition of the required transformation. For the three streams of social democratic feminists, clearly much more was at stake than women embracing interest group politics.

While Addams did not theorize why women's presence in legislative bodies was essential to the evolution of self-government, she certainly implied it in her criticisms of male representatives. By the end of the 1920s, when there were eight women members of the U.S. House of Representatives, she expressed her disappointment with how they used their political presence: "Some of us feel that women in politics thus far have been too conventional, too afraid to differ with men, too ill at ease to trust their own judgments, too skeptical of the wisdom of the humble to incorporate the needs of simple women into the ordering of political life."[28] In the midst of the late suffrage campaign, social democratic feminists did demonstrate models of women using their electoral politics of presence to challenge male domination of public life.

Different Streams of Electoral Politics of Presence

I turn to Addams's participation in the 1912 Progressive Party presidential campaign of Theodore Roosevelt (TR), Wells-Barnett's organizing of African American women voters in Chicago after 1913, and Newman, Malkiel, and Wald's efforts to build support among immigrant Jewish working-class men for a 1915 New York state referendum on women's suffrage. I intentionally line up a different stream of egalitarian suffragists with a different electoral campaign. This approach allows me to make distinctions between them on how they utilized their bridging of movements to actualize aspects of an electoral politics of presence. Taken together, the examples show how they wove partisan electoral politics into the late suffrage movement.

Addams and the 1912 Progressive Party
Presidential Campaign

When Addams joined the Progressive Party in 1912, she was riding the insurgent wave of academic and movement social justice reformers who felt "the need for a new party."[29] It was the crafting of a national party platform that "expressed the social hopes so long ignored by the politicians" that drew them to a third party.[30] They had come to the conclusion that actions at the state and local levels by groups focused on single issues were inadequate. A national party that articulated a grand synthesis of social democratic aims was required "to meet that fundamental [citizen] obligation of adapting the legal order to the changed conditions of national life."[31]

As a woman citizen of Illinois, Addams could not cast a ballot for TR in 1912. She had only a very limited right to vote for a few elective school offices.

After three attempts—1905, 1907, 1908—to include women's suffrage in a revised Chicago city charter failed, Illinois suffragists returned to the state level to expand women's right to vote.[32] With the newly energized Illinois effort in the background, Addams assumed three roles in TR's campaign. At the three-day August national convention in Chicago, she was one of three women at-large members of the Provisional Committee who approved individual planks of the platform. She was also an at-large Illinois delegate who was asked to approve the entire document. After the convention, she traveled widely in the West to promote the platform.

As Addams narrated her experiences with political party politics, she theorized how creating in women of her social location the desire for political inclusion required subverting the gendered political culture. According to historian Melanie Gustafson, Addams inherited a definition of women as "inherently nonpartisan," which meant they were "motivated by issues not elections, and by principles not a search for power." Men were characterized as "inherently partisan" because they "understood ideas of patronage, rewards for loyalty, and personal and group power."[33] Addams proposed that middle-class women, engaged in philanthropic projects, scrutinize "afresh" their "role of nonpartisanship." She argued that they should abandon their practice of "standing for an impossible ideal, quite outside of the political field." Instead, they should assume a more effective insider role by "upholding moral standards within political life."[34] Through her practices and theorizing, Addams presented her audience with an inviting new synthesis of principled partisanship.

When she and other women joined the Progressive Party, according to Addams, they "deliberately" showed "that public-spirited women are ready to give up the short modern role of being good to people and to go back to the long historic role of ministration to big human needs."[35] Addams's opposition between "good" and "ministration" was her way of contrasting "motive" and "the sterner task of ascertaining the real needs" of people and "ministering to those in need in all humility of spirit." She challenged her middle-class audience to understand that "[t]he larger plans for meeting these genuine needs can only be carried out with the consent of all the people and the wisdom of such plans must be submitted to them during a political campaign." The goodness of their intentions was insufficient, because what was required was the refounding of democracy by grounding the pursuit of social justice public policies in a new democratic will. Therefore, her audience of do-gooders, according to Addams, needed to enlarge their notion of "political action" beyond the activity of turning over to government a philanthropic experiment "to increase" its "usefulness." Addams argued that their notion must now include an obligation "to enter partisan politics because there was no other way," given the nature of U.S. politics that was organized by party competition.[36]

To persuade her audience, Addams showed them how bringing principles into partisanship worked. The embrace of women's suffrage by the Progressive Party provided her with a successful example. The Provisional Committee adopted a noncontroversial women's suffrage plank: "The National Progressive party, believing that no people can justly claim to be a true democracy which denies political rights on account of sex, pledges itself to the task of securing equal suffrage to men and women alike."[37] This plank showed that the Progressive Party folded into its reimagining of political democracy a political principle of gender equality.

In describing the platform, Addams connected "equal suffrage" to three mechanisms of direct democracy—"direct primaries, the initiative and referendum." For her, this bundling indicated how the national Progressive Party aimed to spread "the political insurgency in the West" so that "the political organization of the nation might never again get so far away from the life of the people."[38] California illustrated how that insurgency worked. The 1909 adoption of the direct primary produced a 1910 Progressive Party takeover of the state legislature that led to an October 1911 special election. It resulted in a male electorate amending the state constitution to include the referendum, initiative, recall, *and* women's suffrage.[39] California also provided TR with his vice-presidential candidate: Hiram Johnson, its governor.

In sharp contrast to the smooth inclusion of women's suffrage in the platform, Addams, Du Bois, and Henry Moskowitz (1879–1936), all members of the NAACP, were unable to persuade the Provisional Committee to adopt a plank written by Du Bois. He included the following language in reference to those "who have in a generation changed from slavery to a free labor system": "The National Progressive party recognizes that distinctions of race, or class, or sex in political life, have no place in a Democracy. Especially does the party realize that [ex-slaves] . . . deserve and must have justice, opportunity, and a voice in their own government."[40] Here Du Bois broadened the reimagining of democracy to include racial justice.

The rejection of this plank, combined with a refusal to seat African American delegates from southern states, led Du Bois to leave the convention. He had been drawn to the third-party effort because of its platform and not because of TR, who during his presidency in 1906 had overseen racist treatment of African American soldiers stationed in Brownsville, Texas.[41] Du Bois flipped to the Socialist Party, whose presidential candidate was Eugene Debs (1855–1926). Eventually he joined William Monroe Trotter (1872–1934), an African American journalist and civil rights activist, in supporting Woodrow Wilson, the Democratic Party nominee. Trotter was a harsh critic of Addams for staying with TR.

Addams publicly explained why she did not follow Du Bois, who would grow disillusioned with President Wilson. She wrote of asking herself "most

searchingly whether my Abolitionist father would have remained in any political convention in which colored men had been treated slightingly." She
presented herself as trying hard to change the Progressive Party's stance on
African American delegate inclusion and the need to incorporate a principled commitment to racial equality. She described her argument before the
Provisional Committee: "I appeared ... to point out the inconsistency of pledg-
ing relief to the overburdened workingman while leaving the colored man
to struggle unaided with his difficult situation, if, indeed, the action of the
credentials committee had not given him a setback."[42] Clearly, she aimed to
persuade her audience to integrate two social justice movements through the
party platform.

Ultimately, Addams characterized "the third-party movement" as a combination of "political democracy and industrial justice—a merging of the political insurgency in the West and country districts with the social insurgency
of the cities." She insisted that "[i]mbedded in this new movement is a strong
ethical motive" and that as it grew "the rank and file" could be persuaded to
understand "the full scope and meaning of social justice" so that it included
racial justice.[43] Here Addams distilled the hope that struggles within movements could result in support for a new intersectional understanding of social justice. In the end, she delivered a seconding speech in support of the
nomination of TR, who was the ultimate arbiter of which planks made it into
the Progressive Party platform.

When it came time to vote up or down the entire platform, Addams, the
delegate, also faced a dilemma, because it called for "the building of two battleships a year, pending an international agreement for the limitation of naval
forces." It also supported the militarization of the Panama Canal, which could
facilitate future U.S. imperialist interventions. Both of these planks went
against Addams's "years" of publicly advocating a new internationalism aimed
at uprooting the causes of war. Her decision "to vote to adopt" the platform
came out of a process that she shared with other women delegates to the convention.[44]

As she explained, "We were, first and foremost, faced with the necessity
of selecting from our many righteous principles those that might be advocated at the moment, and of forcing others to wait for a more propitious season." While she justified putting at the forefront the pursuit of undoing the
damaging effects to human beings of "modern industry," she also "confess[ed]"
that she "found it very difficult to swallow those two battleships." She knew
"only too well the outrageous cost of building and maintaining them—that
fatal seventy cents out of every dollar of federal taxes which is spent indi-
rectly for war." Later she wrote, "On the whole the plank upon fortifying the
Panama Canal was really harder for me to accept than any other one."[45]
Overall, Addams chose to stay with the political party that supported wom-

en's suffrage and a range of legislation directed at achieving social justice in the workplace. She put off for the future the aims of racial justice and a new internationalism devoid of imperialism. In making public her deliberative process, she showed her audience that the pursuit of principled partisanship required significant compromises and that bridging movements to innovate new political programs was quite difficult.

Yet, as "an incorrigible democrat," Addams took solace in the fact that "[a]s a campaign speaker," who "was sent from town to town in both Dakotas, in Iowa, Nebraska, Oklahoma, Colorado, Kansas, and Missouri," she was offered "a wonderful opportunity for education not only on the social justice planks in the platform but on the history of the idealogy [sic] back of them."[46] Her speeches focused on explaining the platform, and she always celebrated the inclusion of women's suffrage.[47] To strengthen her defense of the educational possibilities of programmatic partisanship, Addams cited Aristotle, who was "reported to have said that politics is a school wherein questions are studied, not for the sake of knowledge, but for the sake of action."[48]

Addams viewed a national campaign as a unique space for linking knowledge and action. As she observed, "During the present campaign, measures of social amelioration will be discussed up and down the land, as only party politics are discussed, . . . certain economic principles will become current, and new phrases will enter permanently into popular speech."[49] Out of these conversations, Addams hoped for the coalescence of a new social democratic political will. As she explained, "We craved the understanding support which results from a widespread and sincere discussion of a given subject by thousands of our fellow citizens before any attempt should be made to secure legislative action."[50] By recounting her Progressive Party activism, which required her to utilize her bridging skills, Addams offered up for her audience of middle-class white women a demonstration of how to participate in electoral politics of presence.

Wells-Barnett, Votes for Women, Interracial Democracy, and Local Electoral Politics

Wells-Barnett crafted a different and complementary electoral politics of presence by embedding it within a past insurgent moment, defined by the abolition of slavery and the reimagining of democracy as interracial.[51] She tied her conception of principled partisanship to the history of the Republican Party. As a migrant to Chicago from Mississippi and Tennessee, she spoke for a generation who experienced the importance of the Republican Party for the southern transition from slavery to freedom. According to historian Elsa Barkley Brown, African American women in the South "reportedly initiated sanctions against men who voted Democratic."[52] Or as Cooper testified in 1892, "It is largely our women in the South to-day who keep the black men solid in the Republican party."[53] After the Republican Party abandoned its Reconstruction project, Wells-Barnett turned to African American women's physical presence in electoral campaigns to move the party back to a principled partisanship rooted in racial equality.

An opportunity emerged with the 1894 Illinois election, in which, for the first time, women exercised the right to vote for "legislatively created school offices."[54] As their separate woman's ballot indicated, they were allowed to vote for three open seats on the University of Illinois Board of Trustees. The Illinois Women's Republican Education Committee recruited Wells-Barnett. She had recently returned to Chicago from her second widely publicized visit to England, where she carried out her protest against lynching in the United States. According to Wells-Barnett, "The women insisted that, as I had been doing public speaking, and they needed public speakers, I should be one of their speaker's bureau. . . . Several dates were made for me in different parts of the state, and I joined very heartily in the movement."[55] She brought with her the support of the Ida B. Wells Club, which was formed at the end of the 1893 World's Columbian Exposition.[56] Wells-Barnett had played a key role in providing a forceful critique of the white supremacist construction of the exposition.

Through her speaking engagements, Wells-Barnett bridged civil rights and women's rights movements and pulled together an alliance of African American and white Republican women. She staked out the position that Republican women should vote straight party and not cast a vote for three women candidates across parties. To make her case, Wells-Barnett "drew attention to the Republican Party's historic commitment to racial equality and political freedom and the unfinished business of Reconstruction."[57] Of the three Republican candidates, there was one white woman, Lucy Flower (1837–1921). She pledged to work for scholarships for African American students, who would have been male until 1901, when African American women were admitted to the University of Illinois. According to Materson, "Black women's widespread canvassing enabled . . . Flower to become Illinois's first woman elected to statewide office."[58] Thus, Wells-Barnett connected African American women's desire for political inclusion to their capacity to shape the direction of the Republican Party.

A central component of her notion of Republican Party principled partisanship was a commitment to undoing racial segregation. As a result, she repudiated the strategic use of white supremacy by the mainstream suffrage movement. Wells-Barnett introduced this theme in her autobiography by describing a conversation with Susan B. Anthony (1820–1906) in 1894. Wells-

Barnett was in Rochester at the time to speak against lynching. Anthony invited her to stay at her home. According to Wells-Barnett, Anthony recounted that she had refused to help a group of African American women form a branch of the suffrage organization because she "did not want anything to get in the way of bringing the southern white women into our suffrage association." Anthony asked Wells-Barnett if the "expediency" path "was wrong." Wells-Barnett replied: "I answered uncompromisingly yes, for I felt that although she may have made gains for suffrage, she had also confirmed white women in their attitude of segregation."[59] Wells-Barnett became very adept at using her intersectional physical presence to expose and subvert the expediency case for white supremacy.

In the midst of the campaign for an Illinois suffrage law, Wells-Barnett, along with Belle Squire, a white suffragist, formed the Alpha Suffrage Club in January 1913. As president of the organization, Wells-Barnett was sent to Washington, D.C., to join the Illinois delegation to the NAWSA-sponsored suffrage parade. Scheduled for March 3, 1913, the day before President Wilson's inauguration, the NAWSA organized the march to achieve maximum political pressure. Wilson did not support votes for women. Also, the committee organizing Wilson's inauguration banned women from the traditional ritual.[60] The NAWSA aimed to bring women into the national celebration of the peaceful transfer of power. Placing the NAWSA parade in U.S. history, historian Lucy Barber characterizes the five-thousand-strong procession as the second "national political demonstration in Washington."[61]

According to an article in the *Chicago Daily Tribune*, which embedded a reporter in the Illinois delegation, there was a heated debate after the NAWSA leadership announced its Jim Crow policy to pacify the southern delegations. Wells-Barnett argued against this expedient use of white supremacy. Asked to join a segregated African American delegation at the end of the march, she declared, "If the Illinois women do not take a stand now in this great democratic parade then the colored women are lost." Supporting Wells-Barnett, Virginia Brooks, a white suffragist, spoke: "I think that we should allow Mrs. Barnett to walk in our delegation. If the women of other states lack moral courage, we should show them that we are not afraid of public opinion. We should stand by our principles. If we do not the parade will be a farce." One of the white delegates said that if she were African American, she "should be willing to march with the other women of my race." Wells-Barnett responded that "there is a difference . . . which you probably do not see." She went on to declare, "I shall not march with the colored women. Either I go with you or not at all. I am not taking this stand because I personally wish for recognition. I am doing it for the future benefit of my whole race."[62] Here Wells-Barnett used her intersectional physical presence to delegitimize racial segregation in a suffrage march because it reinforced white supremacist structures of power.

In the end, through direct action, Wells-Barnett curated an image of interracial democracy. As the march passed by, she quietly shifted from spectator to a welcomed member of the Illinois delegation. Squire and Brooks helped facilitate the transition. According to historian Wanda Hendricks, "So important was the event that a photograph of her, flanked by Squires and Brooks, appeared in *The Chicago Daily Tribune* giving the event and its participants local and national exposure."[63] Thus, through her struggles within the Illinois delegation, Wells-Barnett modeled how African American suffragists developed their own version of electoral politics of presence by bridging movements for women's political rights and interracial democracy.

A few months after the march, women finally gained the right to vote in Illinois at the local level and for president. In *Crusade for Justice*, Wells-Barnett recounted how the Alpha Suffrage Club played a crucial role in registering African American women and persuading African American men to support women's actualization of their voting power. Initially, when the club members went door to door in Chicago's Second Ward, according to Wells-Barnett, "the men jeered at them and told them they ought to be at home taking care of the babies." Wells-Barnett sent them back into the field with the message to "the women that we wanted them to register so that they could help put a colored man in the city council." The community embraced "[t]his line of argument," which produced the sixth-highest number of registrants for a ward in Chicago. According to Wells-Barnett, "Our men politicians were surprised because not one of them, not even our ministers, had said one word to influence women to take advantage of the suffrage opportunity Illinois had given to her daughters."[64]

As a result of Wells-Barnett's political skills, demonstrated through a series of chess-like moves, the Alpha Suffrage Club ably forced the white Republican men to support the nomination of Oscar De Priest for alderman in 1915. Then the club was able to turn the political presence of African American women into an effective voting bloc. As a result, De Priest became the first African American alderman in Chicago.[65] He used the crucial role women played in his election to make the case for votes for women in the 1915 forum presented in *The Crisis*. After testifying that "the women of the race seemed to realize fully what was expected of them," he went on, "I am more than thankful for their work and as electors believe they have every necessary qualification that the men possess."[66] Thus, in the midst of bridging movements, Wells-Barnett formulated and actualized a version of an electoral politics of presence that was capable of advancing engendered interracial democracy.

Jewish Egalitarian Suffragists and State
Suffrage Referenda Campaigns

During the 1915 and 1917 New York state suffrage referenda campaigns, Schneiderman, Newman, Malkiel, and other immigrant Jewish working-class egalitarian suffragists created a third version of an electoral politics of presence. Their distinct path came out of their eastern European Jewish immigrant experiences with trade unionism and Socialist Party politics.[67] Consequently, they were not burdened with having to throw off the constraints of native-born, white, middle-class, Protestant, gendered political cultures. They had only to convince their enfranchised male comrades that votes for women strengthened the class struggle.

In her autobiography, Schneiderman recalled how she was awakened to the outlook that would shape her life's work at age eighteen during an extended stay in Montreal with family friends, the Kellerts. "They were Socialists and for the first time I became interested in politics. I knew nothing about trade unionism or strikes. . . . My entire point of view was changed by the conversations I heard at their house." When she was back at work in New York City sewing linings for men's caps, "[a]n outspoken anarchist," another young woman, asked her to help form a union. "Because of the Kellerts," Schneiderman explained, "my mind was ready for Bessie's lessons."[68] A member of the Socialist Party, Schneiderman would eventually run unsuccessfully for the U.S. Senate in 1919 on the newly created New York State Labor Party.[69] According to historian Orleck, "Schneiderman and other Labor Party candidates called for a federal antilynching bill and for full civil rights for African Americans."[70]

Newman and Malkiel, a former garment worker, also embraced third-party partisanship, which was more welcoming than the mainstream parties of women running for office. They both ran unsuccessfully for office on the Socialist Party ticket. As early as 1908, even though she could not vote, Newman was the party's choice for New York secretary of state. According to Orleck, "Newman used her campaign as a platform for suffrage." The print media carried "amused commentaries" in which "writers snickered at the prospect of a 'skirted Secretary of State.'"[71] Then, in 1918, the Socialist Party nominated her for the House of Representatives from New York. By 1920, the Socialist Party supported Malkiel for a seat in the New York State Assembly.[72]

When the bridgers joined with male comrades in the labor struggles of the garment industry and in Socialist Party politics, there was no guarantee that the men would enthusiastically embrace the women's suffrage referenda. Ovington explained their reluctance to make it a priority: "[T]he majority of the men in the Socialist party recognize no division but the division of class, and no struggle but the class struggle." In contrast, Ovington observed, "many" women in the Socialist Party "recognize also a woman's struggle, the struggle of a sex for the full development of its powers and for the right to the full use of those powers."[73] Schneiderman received a letter from a male socialist who declared, "You either work for Socialism and as a result for equality of the sexes or you work for woman suffrage only and neglect Socialism."[74] The author assumed that she could not combine feminism and socialism and that gender equality would take shape somehow in the process of the socialist revolution or even after. This stance led Newman to observe about the Socialist Party program, "It is one thing to have a plank [for women's suffrage] and another thing to advocate it."[75]

Through their speeches, delivered in English and Yiddish, and their writings in radical publications, Malkiel, Newman, and Schneiderman walked their male audiences through an exercise in how to think about the interdependence of gender and class emancipation. As a result of bridging feminist and socialist movements, they produced an analysis that showed one was not possible without the other. Malkiel established a foundational assumption of the analysis when she applied the theory of historical materialism.[76] She compared the votes for women campaign to the struggle for the vote of "the propertyless workingmen."[77] Paraphrasing Marx, she wrote, "In every stage of human progress the change of economic conditions necessitates a like change in the social relation and political administration of the people. The demand for political rights by a given class was always based on the economic advance of that class." Malkiel called on her socialist male audience to acknowledge that "the millions" of paid working women were "into the market to stay." Like working men, they now "sought further development" by claiming the right to vote. Therefore, woman's "growing importance as a necessary factor in the progress of the people makes universal suffrage as great a necessity today as manhood suffrage became three-quarters of a century ago."[78]

Newman furthered the analysis for her socialist male audience by weaving in the significance of women's labor militancy and how it would shape their use of the vote to end economic exploitation. As she insisted, "Woman suffrage is at the present time a necessity for the working woman." Newman outlined a two-part process:[79] "At this time when she is first beginning to wake up to the fact that she is an industrial factor in society, and is, as a consequence, taking her place in the labor movement; when she is beginning to realize her economic power, she will, therefore, use the ballot to back up that economic power." As a result of "[u]sing both her economic and political power," Newman argued, "she will . . . do away with all present day evils," such as child labor, which Newman herself was forced to perform. Therefore, the working woman "will slowly but surely achieve the end—economic freedom."[80]

In her standard suffrage speech, delivered not just in New York, Schneiderman continued the presentation of working women's distinct need for the vote, and she went beyond Newman's theme of economic freedom to envision a long-term, radical vision of human emancipation. While men could rely solely on collective bargaining, she argued, women workers, because of their more vulnerable position in the gendered labor market, "needed the vote because they needed protection through laws." To the trade unionists in her audience, she argued, "[I]f their wives and daughters were enfranchised, labor would be able to influence legislation enormously." Otherwise, she insisted, "the lawmakers could ignore us."[81]

Then Schneiderman concluded with a vision of radical change that gave a gendered hue to Marx's distinction between the realm of necessity and the realm of freedom. Marx argued that the freedom in the first realm came about when "socialized man" regulated the conditions of the labor necessary for daily survival, including the amount of energy that was exerted. No matter how humanized the conditions became, however, this first type of freedom was still confined to the realm of necessity. What Marx called "the true realm of freedom" was dependent on the realm of necessity but could "blossom forth" only after work because it entailed the "development of human energy which [was] an end in itself." Therefore, according to Marx, "[t]he shortening of the working day [was] its basic prerequisite."[82]

Speaking as a socialist and a feminist, Schneiderman tied her case for women's suffrage to her own version of Marx's distinction: "I always said we not only wanted labor laws and bread, we wanted roses too."[83] Achieving sex-based laws regulating hours, wages, and conditions of work would create for women workers first, and eventually for all workers, the most humane realm of necessity because it would cut down on the amount of energy exerted. Turning working women into a voting power, she pointed out to her male audience, would contribute to this transformation. Yet what really inspired Schneiderman, and she hoped her audience, was the furtherance of human development as an end in itself. She picked the fragility, texture, color, and beauty of the rose, the name her father gave her upon arriving in America, to convey her vision of what was possible if women joined men as full economic and political partners in the class struggle.

Beyond gendering the class struggle, this third stream of an electoral politics of presence challenged nativism and offered a vision of a rooted cosmopolitanism.[84] These additional dimensions took shape during an exchange over the interpretation of the 1915 vote, which fell short of a victorious result. Wald, who was of German-Jewish background and not a working-class immigrant, voiced her intersectional social location in her letter to the editor of the *New York Times*. She was responding to a *New York Times* interview of Harriot Stanton Blatch (1856–1940), whose Women's Political Union (WPU) was part of the coalition that organized the referendum effort.

Blatch had been a key player in persuading state legislators like FDR and Robert Wagner, who did not support women's suffrage, to allow the male citizens to decide. According to her biographer, Ellen DuBois, "Nativism was Harriot's democratic weak spot, as it had been her mother's."[85] Her mother was Elizabeth Cady Stanton (1815–1902). Blatch's political strategy illustrated how women's suffrage could accommodate those who wanted to limit the political power of immigrants. Her compromised version of the referendum slowed down the increase of immigrant voters by setting up a five-year waiting period to vote for immigrant women who gained American citizenship through marriage.[86]

Blatch was furious when the 1915 referendum went down to defeat. She characterized her experience on election day as being "humiliated" because unlike English, French, and German women, who have only to "appeal to the men of their own nationality," American women had to address "men of twenty-six nationalities, not including the Indian." On election day, she chose as her site of poll watching "one of the most difficult places to watch" on the Lower East Side of New York City. There she "saw the young men who had been in this country but a short time, but who were citizens and whom our own men were forcing us to ask for a vote." Blatch espoused the principled position that immigrant men should be able to vote, and she conjectured that they had "improved . . . wonderfully" by being "in a free country." Yet ultimately, she characterized them as constituting a "tyranny" because they "have power to pass upon [her] and upon the native born women of America." While she castigated the "men of our country" who "force us to submit to it," she did not include them within the category of tyranny.[87]

By not acknowledging that those immigrant Jewish men on the Lower East Side actually voted for the referendum in significant numbers, Blatch left the impression that they "humiliated" her. Her language suggested that she would have preferred a homogeneous democracy. Referring to the Lower East Side as "difficult," she ended the interview with a statement that she would never again engage in direct democracy. Overall, Blatch reinforced anti-immigrant sentiments and undermined support for an emerging cosmopolitan democracy built on the political presence of immigrants.

In her public response, Wald asserted her "greater authority" than Blatch on the subject of "the support given by the foreign-born voters . . . to the suffrage amendment."[88] Through the suffrage activities at Henry Street Settlement, located on the Lower East Side, Wald bridged the feminist settlement house movement and the suffrage movement. She aligned with Carrie Chapman Catt (1859–1947), who founded the Woman Suffrage Party (WSP) to activate a new grassroots method for achieving the vote in New York.[89] Catt even tried to recruit Wald to run for office, which she refused. The WSP was more sympathetic to immigrants than the WPU; it offered an alternative version of the referendum but was forced ultimately to go with Blatch's formulation.[90]

Wald began her letter to the editor by taking up Blatch's theme of humiliation. Wald aimed "to correct any false impression that may have been created through the interview" about how poll watchers were treated in the Lower East Side. She went on to distinguish between a lack of courtesy, which did not occur, and "the general humiliation that educated adult people must feel when they are disfranchised." Then she turned to the data on voting in the Lower East Side assembly districts, which showed "a comparatively favorable acceptance of the extension of democracy and one that those who know the east side fully expected." She summarized that with the exception of one assembly district, "no other part of the city did as well." For evidence, she contrasted the lack of support from the "American-born, of Anglo-Saxon descent" or "the Anglo-Saxon naturalized citizens" with the vote for the referendum by the "foreign-born," presumably eastern European Jewish citizens. Finally, in contrast to Blatch, she characterized the election as an affirmation of the value of direct democracy: "I feel quite sure that all of the women who participated in the election have a reassurance of their faith in democracy because of their experience Tuesday."[91]

While Wald did not refer explicitly to immigrant Jewish voters, her audience would have known. Historian Elinor Lerner fills out a profile of the immigrant Jewish voters. Their youth stood out; the average age was thirty-five. Most "fled" from eastern Europe as teenagers in the late 1890s. They had been in the United States an average of nineteen years, "a shorter time than any other immigrant voter group studied." As a demographic group, according to Lerner, "Jewish voters . . . were the least 'Americanized' of all the voters sampled."[92]

In making visible their support of the referendum, Wald repudiated the negative characterizations that fueled nativism and justified its expedient use in the votes for women campaign.[93] By contrasting the votes of native-born and naturalized Anglo-Saxons with the votes of foreign-born Jews, Wald suggested that engendering democracy and building a cosmopolitan democracy were mutually constitutive. After all, young immigrant Jewish men, who had fled a repressive political context and were not constricted by native-born gendered political cultures, supported the enlarging of democracy in their new homeland. Thus, through their cross-class political presence in a statewide election, a group of Jewish bridgers practiced a version of an electoral politics of presence that put center stage a radical alteration of capitalism and an immigrant-friendly version of engendered democracy.

By analyzing the three streams separately, I have shown how each group of bridgers utilized the multileveled nature of the late suffrage campaign to actualize an electoral politics of presence. Addams and Wells-Barnett took up the project of creating a desire for political inclusion in different groups of women. Wells-Barnett showed how her physical presence exposed and challenged intersecting hierarchies of power that kept African American women in a subordinate position. Malkiel, Newman, and Schneiderman produced a new intersectional analysis in the midst of presenting their case to a skeptical immigrant Jewish male working-class audience. In all three cases, the bridgers generated intersectional visions of engendering democracy. To go into more depth on how African American and immigrant Jewish bridgers used their streams of electoral politics of presence to imbed the vote as a tool for reform within a political revolution, I apply the theory-activist dynamic to create an intersectional conversation and to analyze a pragmatist experiment.

Intersectional Conversation: Equal Suffrage, Anti-lynching, and the Sexual Double Standard

For the construction of this intersectional conversation, I begin by showing that Wells-Barnett, Terrell, and Du Bois bridged egalitarian suffragism and the struggle against disenfranchisement of African American men.[94] Then I turn to how Addams was challenged, first by Wells-Barnett and then by the evolution of her bridging activism with Terrell and Du Bois, to reveal how her white privilege affected her protest again lynching. I contend that the multileveled nature of the late suffrage campaign enhanced the ability of African American men and women bridgers to use their physical presence to voice their challenges and unbracket power dynamics. Finally, I illustrate how the bridgers demonstrated the deliberative dimensions of electoral politics as they expanded the intersectional conversation from lynching to the sexual double standard and its political implications for engendering democracy.

Anti-lynching

As Wells-Barnett asserted to the mixed-race audience at the 1909 founding of the NAACP, "[T]he lynch law regime . . . in the South . . . was wholly political, its purpose being to suppress the colored vote by intimidation and murder."[95] Her political framing justified the interweaving of the anti-lynching and egalitarian suffrage campaigns.[96] Cott explains the logic: "Black leaders and black women's organizations spoke up for woman suffrage in increasing numbers, claiming that the enfranchisement of black women would address and help to redress the forcible disenfranchisement of black men in the South."[97] In effect, the foregrounding of African American women suffragists allowed Wells-Barnett, Terrell, and Du Bois to reconnect woman's suffrage and African American male suffrage, a linking that had been severed for some suffragists by the Fifteenth Amendment.[98] Thus, by using the votes for women campaign as a force for resuscitating the Reconstruction vision of interracial democracy, the African American egalitarian suffragists bridged not only movements but also democratizing refounding moments.

In 1894, after Wells-Barnett sparked an anti-lynching campaign and while she was canvassing Illinois in the first election in which women could participate, she continued to espouse a strategy called the "new departure." It rested on the logic that women did not have to go through the amendment process; they already had the national right to vote based on an interpretation of the Fourteenth and Fifteenth Amendments.[99] While white suffragists abandoned this logic once the Supreme Court rejected it, Wells-Barnett's insistence that it was still relevant was significant because she was reasserting the lasting significance of the Reconstruction Amendments. In 1914, after Illinois women had won the right to vote for president and local officials, Fannie Barrier Williams (1855–1944) continued the narrative: "This splendid extension of the Fourteenth and Fifteenth Amendments will . . . open many avenues of progress that have been closed to colored women."[100]

In "Woman Suffrage and the 15th Amendment," Terrell's contribution to a 1915 forum on "votes for women" printed in *The Crisis*, she made explicit the connection between antisuffragism and state efforts to nullify the Fifteenth Amendment. "The reasons for repealing the Fifteenth Amendment differ but little from the arguments advanced by those who oppose the enfranchisement of women." Then she implored her audience, especially African American men, to practice "consistency" as a key component of a "sense of justice."[101] If they support African American men exercising the right to vote, then they should support women's suffrage.

Du Bois linked the two refounding moments as advancing democratization of the Constitution. In a 1912 speech delivered at the NAWSA national convention, which the organization published as pamphlet, he used Addams's unattributed theme from *Democracy and Social Ethics*: "The cure for the ills of democracy is seen to be more democracy."[102] In appealing to African American male voters to support state women's suffrage campaigns, he argued that "[a]ny extension of democracy involves a discussion of the fundamentals of democracy." This formulation suggested that egalitarian suffragism provided a public space for African Americans to question the methods, including lynching, that were used for suppressing their vote. Moreover, according to Du Bois, "If it is acknowledged to be unjust to disfranchise a sex it cannot be denied that it is absurd to disfranchise a color." Thus, he suggested that the women's suffrage movement had the potential for renewing the Reconstruction vision of interracial democracy by increasing initially, at least in the North, the number of African American voters.[103]

When Addams turned to the topic of lynching in 1901, she might very well have been responding to Wells-Barnett's appeal for white moral leaders to speak out against it.[104] Wells-Barnett's appeal, Addams's "protest," and Wells-Barnett's critique of Addams were all published in *The Independent*, a platform with abolitionist roots. In this exchange there is no direct connection to women's suffrage, but Addams would have known that lynching was a central issue for African American suffragists. As bridgers, both women were egalitarian suffragists, engaged in trying to achieve full suffrage in Illinois and nationally.

The exchange between Wells-Barnett and Addams grew out of a history of helping each other. In 1899 Addams asked Wells-Barnett to convey to the leadership of the newly formed NACW an invitation to a luncheon at Hull House. The NACW was holding its first annual meeting in Chicago.[105] The NACW strongly supported both the growing anti-lynching efforts and women's suffrage. The next reported meeting between Addams and Wells-Barnett, according to Wells-Barnett, was in 1900, when she phoned Addams to arrange a meeting of "influential white citizens of Chicago." Her aim was to inspire them to pressure the editor of the *Chicago Tribune* to stop running editorials advocating racial segregation of the schools. He had not responded to her entreaty. Therefore, Wells-Barnett determined that she needed to coalesce a group "who would be willing to do for us what we cannot do for ourselves." She described the evening meeting at Hull House and how the very supportive gathering "listened to my story." According to Wells-Barnett, Addams headed up a seven-person committee who met successfully with the editor.[106]

In Addams's initial presentation of her "protest" against substituting mob rule for the rule of law, she presented herself as a northern "outsider."[107] Like Frederick Douglass (1818–1895),[108] she put lynching within the context of a power struggle between "the former slave owner" and "his former slave." According to Addams, mob extralegal violence was used by the former to halt "a tendency toward democratic development," when the less powerful asserted "the human claim . . . to their rights rather than ask for privileges." She crossed a line with Wells-Barnett when she set out to reason with southern white men and women based on their version of the issue. As Addams delineated her method of analysis, "I have purposely treated this subject on the theory of its ablest defenders; I have said nothing of the innumerable chances of punishing the wrong man."[109] For her, the "main issue" was discrediting the theory "that crime can be prevented by cruelty."[110]

Wells-Barnett welcomed Addams's "strong protest against lynching" but then criticized Addams for building "a dispassionate and logical argument" from the basis of an "absolutely unwarrantable assumption" that the rape of white women by African American men was *the* cause of lynching. As Wells-

Barnett's investigations of lynchings showed, the empirical evidence did not support this assumption. Based on data collected by the *Chicago Tribune,* she reported that between 1896 and 1901, "four-fifths" of the victims were "not so accused" of raping a white woman, "even by the fiends who murdered them."[111] To understand the meaning of the accusation against the one-fifth, Wells-Barnett pointed out that "the Southern white man" had his own peculiar definition of rape: "any mesalliance existing between a white woman and a colored man is sufficient foundation for the charge of rape." This notion assumed that "it is impossible for a voluntary alliance to exist between a white woman and a colored man, and therefore, the fact of alliance is a proof of force."[112] According to Wells-Barnett, the rape "excuse" constituted a deception to persuade northerners of the justice of lynching so that they would feel sympathy for the lyncher, thus shifting the focus away from "the memory of thousands of victims of mob law." As she observed, "It is strange that an intelligent, law-abiding and fair minded people should so persistently shut their eyes to the facts in the discussion of what the civilized world now concedes to be America's national crime."[113]

Wells-Barnett's critique revealed the inadequacy of Addams's method of analysis, which to a large extent violated her own formulation of how to carry out sympathetic understanding.[114] Usually, she applied this method to illustrate how relationships structured understanding, but on this subject, there was no relationship. She was an outsider. She was not walking together with southerners, white or African American. Without a relational foundation, Addams attempted to reform southern lynchers by the sheer force of her logic. As she bridged movements, working with Wells-Barnett, Du Bois, and Terrell, Addams accumulated a relational foundation for her reflections on lynching. As she redirected her sympathetic understanding from southern white people to African Americans, she publicly admitted her discomfort with the place of white privilege in her intersectional location and modified her presentation of the case against lynching.

The events that led up to creating the NAACP contributed to enlarging Addams's relational understanding of how to protest lynching. In reaction to "the bloody race riot in Springfield, Illinois, on August 14, 1908," a statement went out that was signed by sixty individuals, a third of whom were women. Wells-Barnett and Terrell were the only two African American women. They were joined by Addams, Kelley, Wald, Edith and Grace Abbott, Ovington, and other white social democratic feminists,[115] who were active in the egalitarian suffragist wing of the votes for women campaign. According to Wells-Barnett, the statement called for ending "lynchings, peonage, convict labor system,[116] disfranchisement, and the jim crow cars of the South."[117] Before attending the founding meeting in New York City from May 31 to June 1, 1909, Wells-Barnett, Addams, and others planned a Chicago celebration of

Lincoln's centenary, February 12, 1909. Du Bois gave the keynote speech; through the Negro Fellowship League, Wells-Barnett organized "a chorus of one hundred voices" who sang African American spirituals.[118]

At the founding meeting, Wells-Barnett argued that anti-lynching work should be a central focus of the new organization. Two years later, according to Ovington, the NAACP adopted her suggestion.[119] In her speech "Lynching: Our National Crime," Wells-Barnett used the Springfield incident to discredit the rape "excuse." She presented the following description: "The Springfield, Illinois mob rioted for two days, the militia of the entire state was called out, two men were lynched, hundreds of people were driven from their homes, all because a white woman said a Negro had assaulted her. A mad mob went to the jail, tried to lynch the victim of her charge and, not being able to find him, proceeded to pillage and burn the town and to lynch two innocent men. Later, after the police had found that the woman's charge was false, she published a retraction, the indictment was dismissed and the intended victim was discharged. But the lynch victims were dead. Hundreds were homeless and Illinois was disgraced."[120] Left out of this narrative was the description of one of the lynched men. He "was an old citizen of Springfield who had been married to a white woman for twenty years and had reared a family of children with her."[121]

In 1911, Addams returned to the subject of lynching in *The Crisis*. This essay illustrated two dimensions to her practice of sympathetic understanding. First, she admitted that she felt uncomfortable with the subject matter. She opened the essay, "I always find it very difficult to write upon the great race problem which we have in America." She presented herself no longer as a northern outsider to the problem of lynching, since it had spread to Illinois. As she explained, "One thing, however, is clear to all of us, that not only in the South, but everywhere in America, a strong race antagonism is asserting itself, which has various modes of lawless and insolent expression." One "result of race antagonism," according to Addams, was "the readiness to irritation which in time characterizes the intercourse of the two races."[122]

Second, Addams abandoned pure logical reasoning. As she explained, when white men turn this race antagonism into a justification for lynching by combining it with sex antagonism, "they put themselves in a position where they cannot be reasoned with." Instead of trying—echoing Wells-Barnett, who was no longer active in the organization—Addams adopted an intersectional activist stance and called on the NAACP to "take up every flagrant case of lawbreaking" and "allow no withdrawal of constitutional rights to pass unchallenged." As a result, the organization "will perform a most useful service to America and for the advancement of all its citizens." Then she concluded, "Many other opportunities may be open in time to such an association, but is not this its first and most obvious obligation?"[123]

Addams continued to draw attention to her attempts to grapple with her white privilege by aligning with African Americans. In her 1912 defense of her actions as a Progressive Party delegate at large, she wrote in *The Crisis*, "I was assailed by the old familiar discomfort concerning the status of the colored man."[124] She admitted that the abolitionist tradition did not give her guidance because it seemed to offer her only the option of going to war again, which she rejected. In a 1913 article on the Emancipation Proclamation, Addams went on to chastise white people for abandoning Lincoln's vision and drew on the writings of African Americans to build her case. She repeated a standard argument Douglass, Wells-Barnett, and Terrell made to discredit the negative characterization of African American men. According to Addams, "Whenever southern men thoughtlessly brand every black man as a menace to the virtue of white women, they forget the loyal protection given by black men to white women and children during the war while they, the white men, were striving to perpetuate a system involving the continuance of Negro slavery." Addams also called for the need to study "the souls of white folks" to understand why they insisted on denying full emancipation to African Americans. She clearly had Du Bois's *Souls of Black Folk* in mind when she referred to the condition of African Americans living "behind the veil."[125] Through this series of reflections, Addams showed that perhaps her main contribution to the intersectional conversation on lynching was publicly expressing her discomfort with her white privilege and her lack of clarity on how to generate a widespread white commitment to a vision of interracial democracy.

In contrast to Addams, African American egalitarian suffragists had a very clear idea of how the votes for women campaign could propel a significant challenge to structural white supremacy. They called for using the campaign to discredit the entire system of racialized sexual politics that supported the rape "excuse." This system characterized African American men as sexual predators, African American women as by nature unchaste, and white women's purity in need of protection by white men. It justified the disfranchisement of the first two groups because they were morally depraved and of the third group because their purity was threatened by entering the public sphere.[126] When Addams referred to this sexual-political system in her 1901 protest, she directed her remarks solely to the position of the southern white woman, pointing out "that the woman who is protected by violence allows herself to be protected as the woman of the savage is, and she must still be regarded as the possession of man."[127] Tying southern white women's political disempowerment to the lawlessness of lynching and racialized sexual politics, Addams left invisible the position of those women who had no protection under the white supremacist ideal of chivalry.

When African American egalitarian suffragists spoke their intersectional social locations, they shifted the analysis from Addams's focus on white women and from Douglass's emphasis on the power struggle over manliness between white and African American men that played out on the site of white women's bodies.[128] In July 1895, their national organizational voice coalesced around the need to take action against an attack on Wells-Barnett for speaking out and writing as a journalist about lynching. She explained that a Missouri newspaper editor, in response to British protests against mob violence, "had libeled not only me, but the Negro womanhood of the country through me." He asserted that "the women are prostitutes and all are natural liars and thieves."[129]

The formation of the NACW was the response.[130] It was the second women's organization, outside of formal suffrage organizations, to support women's suffrage. The first was the Woman's Christian Temperance Union. To defend their character, African American women activists had to flesh out how the racialized sexual politics that undergirded the rape "excuse" of lynching produced a racialized sexual double standard that hid the history of sexual assault of African American women. As a result, they showed how an intersectional analysis was critical to exposing and ending the sexual double standard that was used politically to justify the disfranchisement of both African American and white women.

Sexual Double Standard

To construct an intersectional conversation on the politically charged sexual double standard, I place the participants in relationship with Wollstonecraft's theorizing in *A Vindication of the Rights of Woman*. Wollstonecraft made three relevant points. First, she "den[ied] the existence of sexual virtues, not excepting modesty."[131] Within a system of sexual virtues, individual women were judged by only one virtue—chastity. If they became unchaste, they faced "the impossibility of regaining respectability by a return to virtue." The double standard emerged because men could be unchaste, but it would not tarnish their public "respectability."[132]

Second, Wollstonecraft enlarged the notion of chastity beyond individual sexual behavior by arguing that its "effect" was to produce a type of "purity of mind." Moreover, those women "whose affections have been exercised by humane plans of usefulness," according to Wollstonecraft, "must have more purity of mind, as a natural consequence."[133] Here she suggested the possibility of acquiring a mental practice of chastity by pursuing public or socialized aims. One such aim, she argued, was the embracing of the "victims" of men's "lawless appetites." By shunning unmarried mothers, those women whose "reputations[s] may be white as the driven snow" were due "little respect." They were not practicing the "real virtue of chastity"; instead, they were perpetuating the double standard.[134]

Third, Wollstonecraft argued for turning all virtues into gender-neutral virtues that both men and women would practice. As she insisted, "Chastity, modesty, public spirit, and all the noble train of virtues, on which social virtue and happiness are built, should be understood and cultivated by all mankind, or they will be cultivated to little effect."[135] Underlying her formulation was the aim to break down the gendered wall between private and civic virtue that supported the double standard. "Let men become more chaste and modest," Wollstonecraft declared, because "[p]ublic spirit must be nurtured by private virtue."[136] As they built on and went beyond Wollstonecraft's distillation of the problem of the sexual double standard, the egalitarian suffragists worked to discredit it.

According to African American suffragists, a purely gendered analysis of chastity and the double standard was inadequate. Through their physical presence, they brought to the suffrage campaign the legacy of the racialized double standard of sexual assault and forced pregnancy under slavery. Ida Husted Harper (1851–1931), who produced edited volumes of the proceedings of NAWSA Congresses, hinted at this legacy when she characterized Terrell, who participated at the 1904 Congress, in the following terms: "Mrs. Mary Church Terrell (D.C.) a highly educated woman, showing little trace of negro blood."[137] While Terrell reported in her autobiography that she occasionally passed for white as an act of defiance, when she spoke in public, she always voiced the intersectional social location of an African American woman.[138] She clearly used her physical presence to unbracket the unequal power dynamics that structured the intrafeminist conversation. To the NAWSA participants, she pointed out, "You will never get suffrage until the sense of justice has been so developed in men that they will give fair play to the colored race." Then she presented sisterhood as an intersectional project: "My sisters of the dominant race, stand up not only for the oppressed sex but also for the oppressed race."[139]

Wells-Barnett characterized the system of racialized-gendered virtues that legitimized slavery through her critique of southern chivalry: "True chivalry respects all womanhood, and no one who reads the record, as it is written in the faces of the million mulattoes in the South, will for a minute conceive that the southern white man had a very chivalrous regard for the honor due the women of his own race or respect for the womanhood which circumstances placed in his power." While she did not challenge the notion of gendered virtues, she directly repudiated the notion of racialized-gendered virtue. As she insisted, "Virtue knows no color line and the chivalry which depends upon complexion of skin and texture of hair can command no honest respect."[140] In a 1904 piece, "Negro Womanhood Defended," Addie Hunton (1875–1943) recovered what she called "the heritage of shame." As she explained, "There is an unwritten and an almost unmentionable history of the burdens of those soul-trying times when, to bring profit to the slave trade and to satisfy the base desires of a stronger hand, the Negro woman was the subject of compulsory immorality."[141] As Wells-Barnett and Hunton made clear, within a white supremacist construction of gendered virtues beginning with slavery and continuing afterward, all African American women could never reclaim the status of moral purity by their individual life decisions.

Burroughs explicitly challenged this construct within the space of the suffrage campaign through "Black Women and Reform," her contribution to the 1915 forum on Votes for Women in *The Crisis*. As she reported, "I was asked by a southern white woman, who is an enthusiastic worker for 'votes for (white) women', 'What can the Negro woman do with the ballot?'" Burroughs responded to her that by gaining the right to vote, the African American woman would finally get public recognition for her moral "strength." She used theological language when she explained that the African American woman needed the vote "to ransom the race," or to deliver it from sin.[142] Here she implied that African American women were reclaiming their virtue after the long period of "compulsory immorality." As she noted, "The world has yet to learn that the Negro woman is quite superior in bearing moral responsibility."[143]

Burroughs pointed to two areas where the African American woman was enlarging and reclaiming her virtue. Through social service, "she has been as aggressive, progressive, and dependable as those who inspired the reform or led it."[144] This theme illustrated Wollstonecraft's notion of purity of mind fueled by engagement with humane projects. African American women also practiced traditional chastity. Here Burroughs argued that the African American woman "carries the moral destiny of two races in her hand." In her view, "Had she not been the woman of unusual moral stamina that she is, the black race would have been made a great deal whiter, and the white race a great deal blacker during the past fifty years. She has been left a prey for the men of every race, but in spite of this, she has held the enemies of Negro female chastity at bay." Burroughs argued that African American women, not afforded protection under white supremacist chivalry, needed the protection of the ballot: "The ballot wisely used, will bring to her the respect and protection that she needs. It is her weapon of moral defense."[145] Burroughs might have been thinking of how their votes would lead to changing the legal definition of rape so that it criminalized sexual assault of African American women.[146]

Terrell further illustrated "the real virtue of chastity" by addressing both southern white women and middle-class African American women. She called on the first group to "arise in the purity and power of their womanhood to implore their fathers, husbands, and sons" to stop the lynchings and sexual assaults. Here she suggested that southern white women should exercise a type of purity of mind to engage in the humane projects. In a sense, she was calling on them, "as the children of women who for generations looked upon the hardships and the degradation of their sisters of a darker hue with few if any protests," to redeem the virtue of southern white women.[147] To bolster her case that they should expose the racialized double standard that characterized slavery and persevered into the twentieth century, she declared, "For surely they must know that so long as men may despoil the women of any race with impunity, the prevailing standard of morality must necessarily be very low."[148] In effect, Terrell called on southern white women to turn purity into a public value so that both white and black women would be protected by "public sentiment" and "by law."[149]

With the second group, middle-class African American women, Terrell explicitly tied the improvement of social relations to "showing the enormity of the double standard of morals." Echoing Wollstonecraft, she explained that the double standard "teaches that we should turn the cold shoulder upon a fallen sister, but greet her destroyer with open arms and a gracious smile." Undoing this standard by embracing "the fallen woman" constituted one meaning of the NACW's motto, "Lifting as We Climb."[150] Ultimately, Terrell indicated that the way to turn chastity into a gender-neutral virtue was to abandon its racialized version and repudiate the moral judgment that a woman could never regain her virtue once it was lost.

Addams contributed to this constructed intersectional conversation on the sexual double standard through her report on the trafficking of girls and women, or the "social evil" characterized by the selling and buying of "the chastity of women."[151] In *A New Conscience and an Ancient Evil*, she drew on voluminous reports that came across her desk in her capacity as chair of the publication committee for the Juvenile Protective Association of Chicago, whose "main office adjoin[ed] Hull House."[152] She filtered this material through "her consciousness" forged during her "long residence in a crowded city quarter."[153] Addams concluded her report by describing a potential coalition of "contemporaneous social movements" that were producing the new conscience.[154]

Two movements were directly related to the trafficking of girls: The public health movement addressed sexually transmitted diseases, and the temperance movement aimed to regulate alcohol consumption. Equal suffrage, peace, and socialism were the three other movements. Addams characterized them as "mysteriously affecting all parts of the social order" and therefore they "will in time threaten the very existence of commercialized vice."[155] These movements worked for major structural changes: ending male monopolization of political power, dismantling the militarized dimension of the nation-state, and replacing capitalism with a new, socially just economic system. Together they undermined the legitimacy of the sexual double standard by combining critiques of the gendered virtues, "the history of prostitution in relation to militarism," and the economic exploitation and poverty that resulted in prostitution.

By placing equal suffrage as "first" among these three movements, Addams suggested that enfranchised women should be in charge of building this coalition.[156] She stressed that "the newly enfranchised view existing conditions more critically, more as human beings and less as politicians," who are driven to rationalize the status quo. She used the language of "newly enfranchised class" that shaped her notion of political revolution. According to Addams, "[N]ever do the sails of the ship of state push forward with such assured progress as when filled by the mighty hopes of a newly enfranchised class."[157] Yet to achieve equal political power with men, "first" women will have to uproot the sexual double standard. To show why, I turn to how Addams adapted Wollstonecraft's three themes.

Addams connected gendered virtues to the period before the political revolution when the domestic-public divide characterized the lives of those who shared her intersectional social location. In this context, the woman who "had no activity outside of domestic life" had only the virtue of "a negative chastity which had been carefully guarded by her parents." By characterizing the virtue as "negative," Addams was emphasizing that the gendered virtue was a prohibition against women's sexual activity outside of marriage. Within the gendered virtue system, according to Addams, "if a woman lost her personal virtue, she lost all." Within the same system, "a man might claim praise for his public career even when his domestic life was corrupt."[158]

Addams went on to connect egalitarian suffragism to "[t]he chastity of the modern woman of self-directed activity."[159] Echoing Wollstonecraft, Addams turned chastity into a positive virtue that directed women to shift their energy from policing their own sexual behavior to working to discredit the sexual double standard by embracing the unmarried mother and her children. She was confident that once women in the United States gained "the right to exercise political power," like enfranchised Norwegian women, they would change the laws. One unjust law mandated that "if the child dies before birth and the [unmarried] mother conceals this fact, although perfectly guiltless of its death, she can be sent to jail for a year."[160] Moreover, women with political power would be able to protect trafficked girls who must deal with the criminal justice system. Addams pointed to the example of enfranchised women in Scandinavian countries who made up "juries of women" who "sit upon such cases and offer the protection of their presence to the prisoners."[161]

Finally, for Addams, equalizing political power between women and men "will also inevitably modify the standards of men."[162] With their new status as an enfranchised class, women "will be in a position as never before to uphold the 'single standard,' demanding that men shall add the personal virtues to their performance of public duties."[163] Men must shift from gendered to gender-neutral virtues and give up their "use of a public record as a cloak for a wretched private character," according to Addams, "because society will never permit a woman to make such excuses for herself." In other words, as long as the sexual double standard persists, women will be at a severe disadvantage because, unlike men, they will have to be pure, both in their private and public behavior. Abandoning the sexual double standard will produce a "modern relationship between men and women, which the Romans called 'virtue between equals.'" This new equal relationship will "make women freer and nobler, less timid of reputation and more human."[164] Here Addams was following Wollstonecraft, who tied human to gender-neutral virtues, practiced in private and in public.

This constructed intersectional conversation shows that stopping the lynchings and the trafficking of a diversity of young girls required the egalitarian suffragists to embed the vote as a tool for social reform within their political revolution. Foregrounding African American suffragists showed how, for them, the revolution was a continuation of the Reconstruction refounding moment. To engender an interracial vision of democracy, the intersectional conversation also reveals the necessity of uprooting the racialized-gendered sexual double standard. Certainly, immigrant Jewish suffragists, such as Malkiel and Schneiderman, contributed to the critique of the sexual double standard by exposing sexual harassment in the industrial workplace.[165] Yet instead of including them in the intersectional conversation, I turn to how they shaped the political revolution through a new experimental social space, the NYWTUL.

NYWTUL as Experimental Socializing Space for Actualizing an Electoral Politics of Presence

As I have shown, Schneiderman, Malkiel, Newman, Lemlich, Wald, and other Jewish bridgers activated one version of electoral politics of presence when they built support among socialist and trade unionist immigrant Jewish male voters for the 1915 and 1917 New York state suffrage referenda. Relying on a historical materialist analysis, the bridgers argued that women's changed economic role justified a change in their political standing.[166] In these campaigns, they also enlarged the programmatic dimensions to include the replacement of a nativist view of democracy with a new international or cosmopolitan vision. Now I turn to a second version of electoral politics of presence they innovated *prior* to the referenda campaigns. It required the Jewish bridgers to direct their intersectional activism and theorizing to nonvoting immigrant working-class women.

The general strikes that led up to the first referendum campaign provided the necessary historical context. "Between 1909 and 1915," Orleck reports, "women garment workers in northeastern and Midwestern cities exploded in an unprecedented show of labor militancy."[167] Cott puts the number at "more than a hundred thousand women."[168] New York City's 1909–1910 "Uprising of the Twenty Thousand" ignited this period. Schneiderman, Newman, and Lemlich were organizers of the uprising. According to Orleck, while the Jewish bridgers were "amazed" at its "magnitude," they knew that it was "no spontaneous uprising" because "they had been organizing feverishly for almost three years."[169] The NYWTUL, as a nonstrategic experimental participatory social space, played a crucial role in facilitating their bridging activism and their theorizing of it.

Bridging Movements Shaped the Aims of the WTUL as a Socializing Space

Founded in 1903 during an AFL national convention, and the year after the militant kosher meat boycott, the national WTUL evolved into a fluid participatory social space that wove together militant labor and suffrage organizing.[170] While historians recognize the key role settlement house bridgers played in its origins, I theorize the WTUL as an example of the feminist settlement house pragmatist experimental method. I show how it allowed the Jewish working-class bridgers to create new experiences as the basis for new theorizing. According to the WTUL constitution drafted by the newly widowed Mary Kenney O'Sullivan and others, its original purpose was "to assist in the organization of women wage workers into trade unions and thereby to help secure conditions necessary for healthful and efficient work and to obtain a just return for such work."[171] This phrasing suggested an extension of the Hull House experiments with putting into practice the emancipatory potential of women's past experiences with humane control of their working conditions. In this case, it was replanted in the activity of organizing women into unions. O'Sullivan, of course, was familiar with this experimental method, since she had coordinated the Jane Club experiment and was one of Kelley's Illinois factory inspectors.

A central characteristic of the method was an openness to evolving the aim of the experiment. The original aim of the WTUL was shaped by bridging the settlement house and labor movements to organize working women into labor unions. In 1908, the WTUL extended its bridging of movements to include the votes for women campaign by establishing a suffrage department. The WTUL generally aligned with the NAWSA. As a result of its suffragist activism, historian Robin Jacoby characterizes the WTUL as "provid[ing] one of the few structures in which women's suffrage was discussed in the context of the needs and problems of female workers."[172]

Yet by 1912 the working-class bridgers decided that they were dissatisfied with the allies controlling the WTUL bridging with suffragism. Leonora O'Reilly (1870–1927), a daughter of working-class Irish immigrants, proposed that all chapters of the WTUL create a Wage Earners' League for Woman Suffrage to mobilize unionized women to support women's suffrage. O'Reilly defended the creation of a separate suffrage organization that was run by unionized women workers on the grounds that middle-class suffragists in such organizations as the NAWSA "really don't speak our language" and "rub the fur the wrong way."[173] The group chose O'Reilly for the president and Lemlich for the vice president.

During the 1915 and 1917 referenda campaigns, when Catt's WSP needed experienced organizers to mobilize working-class men, she turned to the NYWTUL working-class bridgers to coordinate the Industrial Section of the party. According to Orleck, Schneiderman and O'Reilly sent Newman "to remind" Catt "that all three of them were Socialists." Newman reported back that Catt said, "In a way, we all are."[174] The Industrial Section and the Wage Earners' League for Woman Suffrage provided the spaces in which the Jewish bridgers could speak more freely, including of their socialist perspective on votes for women.[175] In effect, the immigrant Jewish bridgers used both spaces to expand the NYWTUL bridging of movements to include the socialist movement. This expansion under the leadership of working-class egalitarian suffragists illustrated the theme of this book that the social democratic feminist refounding moment required the interconnecting of social justice and political equality.

NYWTUL as a Socializing Space for the Immigrant Jewish Bridgers

In contrast to Hull House, which was established initially as a residence for middle-class women reformers, the WTUL was from the start a new social space to bring together "allies" and working-class women. Therefore, historians focus on the theme of whether or not it was a successful cross-class organization.[176] I approach the NYWTUL solely from the perspectives of working-class bridgers. From the beginning, Newman and Schneiderman viewed the NYWTUL through their immigrant Jewish working-class perspective.[177] According to Schneiderman, she and Newman first met at "the League."[178] On its tenth anniversary, Newman declared that it had become "a working class organization" in which the allies who remained came to understand that "it must be ruled by working women and by no one else."[179] For

Schneiderman, who joined in 1906 after it played a critical role in helping her achieve "the first successful industrywide strike of capmakers" and who became president of the NYWTUL in 1918, it was "the most important influence" on her life.[180]

For Schneiderman and Newman, this new experimental social space allowed them to respond more effectively to the needs of working-class women. Speaking to the NYWTUL executive board, Schneiderman contrasted the traditional middle-class settlement house methodology with her approach. Instead of researching the working conditions, evaluating possibilities for unionization, and then reporting their findings to the chosen working women, Schneiderman advocated reaching out to waged workers and letting them guide the interventions of the NYWTUL.[181] Newman stressed that the NYWTUL organizers spread "the message of the class struggle" as they responded to women workers.[182] While they both welcomed the support of the allies, as this book makes clear, they shared the goal of creating sisterhood among waged women workers. As Schneiderman explained in her autobiography, when she joined the NYWTUL and was elected vice president, she "could give little time to the League" because her "first allegiance was to my own union."[183]

To engender the class struggle, economically and politically, Schneiderman, Newman, and others utilized the NYWTUL social space to bring into relationship the Socialist Party, the ILGWU, and the egalitarian suffrage movement. Paid organizing positions funded by the allies facilitated their bridging activism and theorizing. Male trade unionists were skeptical about channeling resources into organizing working women by hiring women organizers; therefore, the bridgers required a power base outside the male-run labor movement. The context of the state referenda campaigns with their paid positions was also a necessary condition for actualizing bridging. For example, when Schneiderman went to meet with Dr. Anna Shaw, head of the NAWSA, to get a paid position in the 1912 Ohio referendum campaign, she declared that she was "a Socialist and a trade unionist."[184]

Yet because bridging the different movements was inherently unstable, the Jewish working-class organizers were continuously renegotiating the power relations that shaped their working conditions in the WTUL and the ILGWU. They threatened to resign and occasionally followed through on their threats.[185] Because each of the movements needed them, they skillfully moved from one to the other. When Schneiderman went to work for the NAWSA in Ohio, she characterized her departure from the NYWTUL as "a leave of absence" during a period when "the White Goods [or women's underwear] Workers' strike was pending." She omitted from her autobiographical account that the suffrage opportunity arose at a moment when she was growing discontent with the NYWTUL's change in focus—away from immigrant women to native-born, more skilled women workers. When Newman found out that the ILGWU was paying male organizers more, she took a leave and worked for the WTUL in Philadelphia. When Schneiderman finally resigned from the NYWTUL and replaced Newman at the ILGWU, she experienced gender discrimination. After she laid the groundwork for a successful strike in Boston, the union brought in a male organizer to oversee it. This series of events led her back to NYWTUL organizing and to heading up the WSP's Industrial Section during the victorious 1917 referendum campaign.[186] By overlapping their participation in strikes, unionization campaigns, and statewide suffrage referenda, the immigrant Jewish bridgers produced new experiences of working-class women's economic and political agency.

Two-Stage Process

As a result, *prior* to the referenda campaigns, they developed their own distinct approach to the first dimension of an electoral politics of presence: the creation of a desire for political inclusion. To politicize immigrant working-class women, the immigrant Jewish bridgers activated and theorized a two-stage process: the development by unionized women of gendered class consciousness followed by practices of collective political agency. As Malkiel's fictionalized 1909 garment worker declared, "We must see to it that we win the strike for bread and then we can start one for the ballot."[187] Reporting back to a national WTUL audience on the white goods strikers, Schneiderman reasoned, "They have proved that if they stand firm they can beat the manufacturers. They have still to learn that if they stand firm they can beat the courts."[188] This two-stage process was necessary because the mere fact that all women were excluded as a political class from the suffrage was not an effective argument for producing the desire for political inclusion in working-class women. They required their own distinct path to shape their electoral politics of presence.

The bridgers theorized the two-stage process by drawing on their understanding of historical materialism. In outlining this theory, Marx contrasted a stable period in which "[t]he mode of production of material life conditions the social, political, and intellectual life process in general" with the period when "the material productive forces of society come in conflict with the existing relations of production." The latter, according to Marx, marked the beginning of "an epoch of social revolution." The bridgers understood that they were experiencing the disjuncture between changes in the relations of production and changes in all other aspects of life, including what Marx called "a legal and political superstructure."[189]

As Schneiderman explained, "Revolutionary changes were occurring in the economic and industrial patterns of our country. Inevitably, some institutions lagged behind in making adjustments to those changes."[190] The change she referred to here was the emergence of women breadwinners. Yet the labor movement was not organizing these workers because male trade unionists held on to old ideas appropriate for a different stage of economic development. They believed that women were not in the labor market permanently and that women could not be organized. Therefore, women trade unionists set out to reshape their working conditions and thereby to put new facts on the ground to propel the required readjustments in all other institutions. Schneiderman characterized "[t]he struggle for recognition and organization of women" as "long and bitter."[191]

First Stage: Nexus between Strikes and Union Building

The centerpiece of this struggle was the connection between strikes and union building. Schneiderman analyzed the nexus based on her successful organizing of the 1913 New York City white goods strike. "At the time," she explained, "the general strike was used as a way of organizing workers employed in mass-production industries. As a group, they would have power to ask for better working conditions and more pay but as individuals, they would be fired, one by one, for joining a union."[192] Her notion of "general strike" referred to an industrywide effort organized by the labor movement in contrast to a spontaneous, unorganized walkout of an individual shop.[193]

To activate the nexus, Schneiderman had to skillfully bridge between the NYWTUL's Strike Council and the male leaders of the ILGWU. The council was not enthusiastic about encouraging another general strike, although it was willing to support Schneiderman to focus temporarily on Local 62 of the ILGWU. The union wanted the women workers to prove their openness to unionization before it funded a second round of organizing. After three years of building support, Schneiderman pushed for both the formal authorization by the ILGWU and a public vote for strike. On the first day, "contrary to the prediction of the wise," she reported, seven thousand women workers walked off their jobs, significantly increasing the union membership.[194]

Newman and Malkiel further fleshed out the model for developing gendered class consciousness by characterizing the strike-unionization connection as constituting a time of thinking. As Newman asserted for a national WTUL audience: "To my mind a strike is **never** lost" for the workers because "[i]t has **made them think**."[195] Malkiel's fictionalized striker exclaimed, "Honestly, there's nothing that will make you think so much as a strike does. . . .

I've been thinking and thinking till my head aches."[196] Their thinking led the strikers to evolve from an individualistic to a collective understanding of their relationship to each other. Schneiderman recounted a conversation with a "young Russian woman," probably Fannia Cohn (1885–1962), who was a leader in the white goods organizing drive: "She told me how different things had been in her shop before the strike. The women looked upon each other as enemies because one might get a better bundle of work than the other. But now, since they had organized and had fought together, there was a kinship among them and she looked forward to going back to the job."[197]

Newman also theorized the emancipatory potential of the strike: "It has brought out all that is best in them. It has done away with selfishness, race hatred, foolish pride, and that well known idea of 'Each for himself' . . . and has instead developed their minds to the beauty of 'Each for all, and all for each.'"[198] Malkiel's fictionalized "more privileged" American-born striker described the impact of a mass meeting: "I felt the kinship between all the girls and myself. It seemed to me that their joy was my joy, their sorrow my own. . . . I felt as though I had been born anew and became a power. I knew that if I should happen to be hurt or abused all these thousands of men and women would stretch out their hands to lift me out of danger."[199]

To clarify further the required shift in consciousness the bridgers theorized, I turn very briefly to Rousseau's notion of the general will from *The Social Contract* and to Plato's use of the kin relationship to bond the Guardians, or leaders in *The Republic*. Rousseau turned to education through fundamental laws, as written by a lone founder, to produce in the citizens a general will that "tends to equality."[200] Like the bridgers, he sought a process of rebirth, whereby individuals would learn to act according to a collective will that advanced the common good. For Rousseau, this change amounted to "changing human nature, of transforming each individual . . . into part of a greater whole from which he in a manner receives his life and being."[201] To sustain the general will, Rousseau understood that "the force of legislation should always" reinforce relative socioeconomic equality, or "moderation" among the citizens.[202]

Even though Plato constructed an ideal just state, he still took up the practical question of how to keep the Guardians focused on the common good. He did not permit them to own private property or have private families, but these conditions were not sufficient.[203] So he insisted that they constitute themselves as a collective family in which they addressed each other as kin.[204] Through these mechanisms, he hoped to turn the Guardians into one unified body, where the hurt of one was the hurt of all.[205] In contrast to these top-down theorists, the immigrant Jewish bridgers used the strike-unionization nexus to provoke a bottom-up transformation in consciousness.

Second Stage: Development of Collective Political Agency through an Electoral Politics of Presence

To take economic class consciousness to the next stage of embracing collective political agency as an expression of the desire for political inclusion, the bridgers illustrated Malkiel's conclusion: "Our activity on the economic field trained us for self-government."[206] Speaking at the 1913 Suffrage School in Washington, D.C., Schneiderman insisted that when working women "join their union, attend their meetings, and pay their dues, they are getting their suffrage training."[207] As the bridgers reported, playing out the strike-unionization nexus required learning skills of participatory democracy. At mass meetings, working women got up and gave testimony of the abusive treatment toward them by the police and the courts. They voted on plans for action. During the 1909–1910 uprising, ten thousand strikers marched to the mayor's office to demand that he curb the physical violence toward the lawful picketers.

The unique April 22, 1912, mass meeting of the New York Wage Earners' League for Woman Suffrage demonstrated how the immigrant Jewish bridgers utilized their two-stage method to shape their stream of electoral politics of presence for working-class women. The location itself illustrated the method playing out. On November 22, 1909, in the same location—the Great Hall of the People in Cooper Union—twenty-three-year-old Lemlich had galvanized the crowd in Yiddish: "I move that we go on general strike."[208] The next day, the first, or economic, stage began with the great uprising. During the 1912 mass meeting, the unionized egalitarian suffragists illustrated the second, or political, stage. As Orleck observes, the Jewish bridgers "were talking suffrage to the same women workers they were then unionizing."[209]

The broader context for the political mass meeting was the recalcitrance of the New York state legislature to put a suffrage referendum on the ballot. In response, the WSP was organizing marches to show widespread support for letting the male citizens decide. So the meeting aimed to mobilize participation by working-class women workers for a May march.[210] As they fired up the enthusiasm of their audience for suffrage activism and the goal of a referendum, the immigrant Jewish bridgers activated their working-class women's version of the electoral politics of presence.

Unionized shirtwaist-maker Mollie Schepps took the audience of working-class women through the logic of the argument for grafting the desire for political inclusion onto gendered class consciousness. She began by establishing that while women had joined with men in the class struggle, they no longer needed "to play the silent partner."[211] They should insist on the same political rights that working-class men had. Then she contextualized votes for women within the gendered class struggle. She explained the lack of response on the part of New York City's mayor as due to the disfranchised standing of the striking women.

Finally, she evoked the memory of the 1911 Triangle fire, in which 146 mostly girls and women died either directly from the flames or because they jumped out the windows to avoid being burned to death. The exit doors had been locked to prevent union organizers from entering to talk to the workers. The owners had refused to accept the union at the end of the general strike. Of the bridgers, only Newman, starting at age twelve, had any experience of the Triangle factory. Assigned to "the kindergarten," she worked eleven-to-fourteen-hour days, depending on the season, finishing garments by trimming the threads. When the inspectors came, she was forced to climb into a box covered with rags so they would not report a child labor violation.[212]

Schepps used the tragedy to differentiate between middle-class and working-class women on the meaning of equal suffrage. As she continued the logic of her argument, "[W]e can not, and must not, wait until our sisters that live in comforts get the votes for us. We know that they have everything that their heart desires in order to make life worth while. That is no reason why they should not have the ballot, but working women must use the ballot in order to bring about conditions where all may be able to live and grow because they work. The ballot used as we mean to use it will abolish the burning and crushing of our bodies for the profit of a very few."[213] In effect, Schepps voiced for unionized working women the reasons why their gendered class struggle required them to embrace the desire for political inclusion.

Schneiderman illustrated a version of the second dimension of an electoral politics of presence: Working women's physical presence in public exposed the intersectional hierarchies of power that were keeping them in a subordinate position. She shaped her analysis as a response to an antisuffrage argument made by a New York senator who insisted that women's entrance into public life would masculinize them. First, Schneiderman showed how working women's physical presence destabilized the construct of feminine/masculine that supported male domination of public life. By pointing to the working conditions of women in foundries and laundries, she questioned how these women would lose their femininity if they voted. In foundries, they strip "to the waist, if you please, because of the heat," and in laundries, they "stand for 13 or 14 hours in the terrible steam and heat with their hands in hot starch." Schneiderman further discredited the feminine/masculine dichotomy by pointing to "women working in electric works, working all day with sleeves rolled up until they had developed the muscles of their arms as strong and hard as a strong man's; yet these women were intelligent and charming." In the end, Schneiderman conjectured, "Perhaps working women are not regarded as women."[214]

Second, Schneiderman illustrated how working women's physical presence in a legislative body made visible the gendered, exploitative capitalist system. Her example was the treatment by New York state senators of a delegation of working women who testified in favor of a fifty-four-hour-workweek bill. This bill resulted from the governmental investigation of the Triangle fire. After listening to those opposed to the bill, all but the chair of the committee left the room. According to Schneiderman, the representatives did not "care" to listen to the "evidence" that supported the need for the bill because the working women had no vote to "come back at them."[215]

Moreover, Schneiderman asserted that the state senators left the room because they could not justify their opposition to the fifty-four-hour weekly limit on women's waged work. In other words, they were cowards. As Schneiderman explained, to mask the influence of industry, the senators espoused a free market ideology, according to which "a woman is a free American citizen; you must not hinder her, let her work as many hours as she pleases."[216] Yet the senators "are not blind to the horrible conditions around them, especially among women workers." As she pointed out, some of them came "from the canning district where women and children may be working 24 hours a day," or "*from the textile district, where the whole family goes to work*," or "*from the New York district where women have to sew* 37 SEAMS FOR ONE CENT and where a woman has to IRON 70 D0ZEN SKIRTS A DAY TO EARN $1.25!"[217]

Third, Schneiderman asserted that the physical presence of working women's bodies in public showed the potential power of voting women. To explain why the senators were blocking a state referendum on suffrage, she emphasized "fear." According to Schneiderman, the politicians "know that a woman who works will use her ballot intelligently; she will make the politician do things which he may not find so profitable."[218] Here she was thinking of the financial backing of the canning industry that opposed the fifty-four-hour bill. Thus, by speaking in public at Cooper Union and by recounting her experience of going to the legislature to lobby for a sex-based labor law, Schneiderman demonstrated for her audience how working women's physical presence in public exposed the New York state senators as failed representatives.

In the end, she called on unionized women workers to embrace their political agency: "I assure you we are not going to sit down on our job; we are going to push 'Votes for Women' among working women everywhere. Those of you who want to be on the winning side . . . better join right now."[219] Yet her speech made clear that working women's political revolution went beyond achieving the formal right to vote. By becoming a segment of a newly constituted sovereign power, their presence in public life pointed to the need to enlarge the end purpose of the state to include the regulation of the economy. This change was necessary so that they could "work like human beings," who "work for the welfare of the community and not for the welfare of a few."[220]

To visualize further what their political revolution might look like, Schneiderman contributed a version of the third dimension of an electoral politics of presence: the relationship between presence and ideas in contexts of deliberation. At the mass meeting, she suggested that working-class women should be present in representative bodies to bring new ideas. "If these men [the state senators] really were representatives of the people," Schneiderman reasoned, "if they knew how the people lived, then they would think and act differently."[221] As we have seen, third parties nominated the immigrant Jewish bridgers to run for various offices so they could demonstrate, in legislative bodies, a different type of thinking and acting.

Beyond this mass meeting to mobilize immigrant working women for the suffrage cause, the Jewish bridgers used the NYWTUL participatory space to generate new thinking. By bridging the women's labor movement and the egalitarian suffrage movement, Schneiderman and others came to a new formulation of the interdependence of labor union organizing and governmental regulation of the workplace to further economic social justice.[222] Their new understanding came out of the context of the egalitarian suffrage campaign and the two new deliberative experiences it forced on them. Each required strong bridging skills. In one experience, the Jewish bridgers honed arguments to persuade immigrant women workers to take collective action by joining both unions and the suffrage campaign. In a second experience, the Jewish bridgers crafted an analysis to gain the electoral support from their skeptical male comrades for statewide suffrage referenda. A core theme the bridgers developed for both audiences was that working women, including unionized ones, needed the vote to push for labor laws that would strengthen the labor movement and lessen economic exploitation.

Looking back in her autobiography, Schneiderman distilled the new thinking. Labor organizing alone was not sufficient, and using the vote to get labor legislation passed was an incomplete end. The interconnection between the two was necessary to advance social justice.[223] Or as she put it, the NYWTUL became "an advocate of the idea of putting into law the social gains being achieved by labor through its economic struggles. It felt that labor legislation might become a powerful force for social good if it was reinforced by trade-union organizations which would see to the enforcement of the laws."[224] Here Schneiderman put working women at the center of creating and enforcing labor laws. Through her new synthetic thinking that came out of bridging movements during state suffrage campaigns, Schneiderman contributed a working-class dimension to Addams's vision of a deeply participatory regulatory social democratic state.

To put into practice her new thinking, Schneiderman required a labor movement that furthered the development of cosmopolitan democratic relations. Otherwise, the bosses would continue to use their divide-and-conquer methods effectively. As she explained, the failure to organize the Triangle Waist Company was due to "the strike-breakers' inability to understand our message of trade unionism" because of the language barrier. She argued that owners in general deliberately hired "newly arrived immigrants from several different countries who not only spoke no English, but could not communicate with each other." To illustrate the difficulty organizers faced, she pointed to how, at mass meetings, they had to provide four or five interpreters covering Yiddish, German, Polish, Italian, and Slovene.[225]

In sharp contrast to Triangle, her successful organizing of the 1913 white goods strike brought into solidarity a diverse workforce. In this case, Schneiderman had "decided that the best way to reach immigrant workers was through organizers who literally spoke their language."[226] Once diverse workers joined the picket line, they were held together by sharing "the risk of possible imprisonment or starvation." They also engaged in processes of rethinking or unlearning racism and/or prejudices against other nationalities. Newman, Malkiel, and O'Sullivan testified to the remarkable success of the latter in some of their experiences with activating the strike-unionization nexus.[227]

By interpreting the NYWTUL as an experimental participatory space for immigrant Jewish bridgers, I have shown how they used militant labor activism to shape their version of an electoral politics of presence. In the process, they revealed how women's economic independence depended on their political power at the shop floor and in the legislature. The immigrant Jewish bridgers also dramatized how the labor movement's drive for intersectional social justice was critical to forging a new cosmopolitan relational foundation for democracy. As Schneiderman explained, "the real meaning of trade unionism" was its "spirit," or "the service of fellowship, the feeling that the hurt of one is the concern of all and that the work of the individual benefits all."[228]

Shift in Standpoints: From Man Protection to Collective Self-Protection

African American and Jewish bridgers provoked a shift in consciousness from traditional nonpolitical women standpoints to political social democratic feminist standpoints. Their presence in the egalitarian suffragist movement exposed the disingenuous claim by antisuffragists that women did not need the vote because the men in their lives protected them.[229] A traditional nonpolitical woman standpoint depended on this claim.[230] Yet this private notion of protection failed both groups of bridgers. Because the African American woman had to defend her virtue within a legal system shaped by white supremacist assumptions, Burroughs argued that she "needs the ballot . . . to mould [sic] healthy public sentiment in favor of her own protection."[231] In 1914, Newman articulated a parallel viewpoint: "There is hope in all of us, that when the working woman gets the use of the ballot she will use it to protect herself and her class."[232]

Voicing their histories of "compulsory immorality" and experiences of workplace sexual harassment and exploitation, the bridgers returned again and again to the theme that they were not protected by private men. They required a new kind of social democratic state. It would provide mechanisms of collective self-protection so that they could replace the intersecting white supremacist, class, and nativist constructions of women as nonpolitical. To support this aim, the bridgers offered up a nonindividualistic theory-practice of the right to vote.

Feminist Genealogy of Multileveled Social Citizenship: Third Stage

In the third stage of the feminist genealogy of multileveled social citizenship, the social democratic feminists continued the construction of themselves as refounders by socializing the right to vote. They produced a relational notion by embedding the vote within social service relations and prefiguring new socializing spaces for actualizing the vote.[233] These spaces allowed bridgers in different contexts to craft bloc votes to interweave program and presence. To uncover this stage, I add to the genealogical method the role of historicizing the origins of the dominant ideology in order to debunk it.[234] I begin with how Marshall's analysis points to the need for a social democratic feminist genealogy and how the scholarly interpretation of the late suffrage movement blocks a recognition of it. Then I turn to how Addams applied the historicist method to the Founding Fathers and formulated a substitution suited to the second stage of democracy. Finally, I theorize the bloc vote by looking at three specific examples.

In his brief overview of the evolution of manhood suffrage in England, Marshall emphasizes the shift from viewing "political rights as a secondary product of civil rights" to enacting the "principle" of "attach[ing] political rights directly and independently to citizenship" status. Prior to 1918, citizenship did not include the right to vote. This right was a privilege of "a group monopoly" who met the economic requirements. Marshall argues that basing voting rights on success in exercising civil economic rights suited "nineteenth-century capitalist society." In celebrating "the granting of old rights

to new sections of the population" in 1918, Marshall separates manhood suffrage from the first stage in the enfranchisement of women that was included
in the same reform: "I say 'manhood' deliberately in order to emphasize the
great significance of this reform quite apart from the second, and no less important, reform introduced at the same time—namely the enfranchisement
of women."[235] He puts the two achievements on separate tracks because only
the former illustrated his ordering of the evolution of citizenship rights. Thus,
Marshall's analysis of the right to vote points to the need for uncovering how
it fit within a genealogy of women's citizenship.

Scholars recognize that during the late suffrage movement, suffragists
pulled away from appeals to abstract inalienable or natural rights because
they were not effective in persuading men to extend the vote to women. The
suffragists crafted a new justification: Women as a group would bring something different to politics. To characterize this new gendered defense, scholars use a variety of terms, including "expedient," "essentialist," "maternalist," "the ideology of domesticity," and "gender difference."[236] While the new
group justification suggested a fundamental critique of individualistic liberal democracy, scholars characterize the achievement of the vote as the
incorporation of women into liberal democracy. Reflecting the consensus,
Shklar observes that while gaining the vote for women was not "easy or even
inevitable," in the end "the inherent political logic of American representative democracy, based on political equality, did prevail." This logic derived
from the Enlightenment notion of "citizenship perceived as a natural right
that bears a promise of equal political standing in a democracy."[237] The implication of this approach is that there is no need to explore how the new
nonindividualistic justification of women's suffrage contributed to the evolution of the social democratic feminist genealogy.

Kraditor's very influential analysis illustrates the problem with the consensus for interpreting the egalitarian suffragists. Echoing Addams, she argues that "[w]hen the state ceased being regarded as a mere restrainer of men's
interference with one another's rights and became a social welfare agency,"
the suffragists moved away from stressing "the ways in which women were
the same as men and therefore had the *right* to vote" to emphasizing "the ways
in which they differed from men, and therefore had the *duty* to contribute
their special skills and experience to government." But Kraditor does not take
the next step to explore how this shift from individualistic right to socialized
duty marked a break with liberal democracy. Instead, she concludes that the
suffragists were "seeking to realize and further the ideals of the Founding
Founders," and certainly "not to replace those ideals."[238] Thus, Kraditor limits the contribution of the egalitarian suffragists to reinterpreting the Founding
Fathers so that a genealogy of liberal democratic political citizenship that
they began included women.

Yet Addams explicitly rejected the option of reinterpreting the Founding Fathers' genealogy. She contextualized "the founders of the Republic" as "strongly under the influence of the historians and doctrinaires of the eighteenth century." Rather than building on their ideas, she boldly argued for "a definite abandonment of the eighteenth-century philosophy upon which so much of our present democratic theory and philanthropic activity depends."[239] Applying the genealogical tool of historicizing origins in order to debunk dominant ideas, Addams stressed that the founders' ideas reflected their context. To justify their revolution against an oppressive government, they appealed to abstract inalienable rights. Her critique was that their negative view of government and their notion of rights based on natural man did not suit the new conditions.[240] As she declared, "[R]ights are not 'inalienable,' but hard-won." This observation certainly applied to the more than seventy-two-year struggle for women's suffrage, but it also suggested the possibility that the meaning of the right to vote changed along with the struggle.[241]

Addams defended the substitution of a relational formulation for the abstract individualistic one. She argued for building a notion of rights based on "deal[ing] with real people and obtain[ing] a sense of participation with our fellows."[242] She criticized the notion that it was sufficient to grant "the franchise to the varied immigrants among us" because "we have not yet admitted them into real political fellowship."[243] She tied her critique of an abstract individualistic framing of rights to a call for an embodied notion of common humanity, which she argued the founders lacked because they "did not really trust the people at all." Such a notion involved "dissolv[ing] 'humanity' into its component parts of men, women, and children and to serve their humblest needs with an enthusiasm which . . . can be sustained only by daily knowledge and constant companionship."[244]

Her relational substitution complemented Gilman's analysis of putting social service at the center. Addams suggested how social service turned voting into another dimension of actualizing the social welfare common good. In her early justification for incorporating women as voters, she wrote, "[W]oman, if she takes a citizen's place in the modern industrial city, will have to earn it . . . in the service of its complex needs."[245] Later, in the midst of her analysis of political revolution, after citing "an able man long ago," Addams posited that "the qualities most valuable in an electorate are social sympathies and a sense of justice, then openness and plainness of character, lastly habits of action and a practical knowledge of social misery." As we have seen, the egalitarian suffragists cultivated these qualities in their capacities as social servants. Yet Addams went beyond voting to envisioning social service as a prerequisite for presence in legislative bodies: "Woman's value to the modern states, which constantly are forced to consider social reforms, lies in the fact that statesmen at the present moment are attempting to translate the new social sympathies into political action."[246] So voting as an extension of social service supported Addams's vision of political revolution that depended on social democratic feminists combining program and presence.

To advance this combination, social servants needed a new socializing space that combined movements and electoral politics. I am calling this space a bloc vote, not of all women, but of social democratic feminists who aimed to refound U.S. democracy.[247] It is a participatory space, and not just a number of votes, because the practice of this type of intersectional activism depended on bridgers coming into relationship to listen to each other and craft a common policy program.[248] This formulation of the bloc vote showed that voting was not an isolated individualistic act and that a women's bloc vote was not just the expression of narrow group interests. Instead, the prefigurations of the social democratic feminist bloc vote showed how egalitarian suffragists translated their political revolution into a new type of interracial, cosmopolitan, socially just democracy by increasing women's presence electorally and in representative institutions.

As we have seen, in 1915 Chicago, Wells-Barnett showed that a bloc vote of African American women could elect the first African American alderman, thereby advancing interracial democracy. In 1918, Schneiderman led the effort to actualize a bloc vote to unseat four incumbents in the New York state legislature who were impeding social democratic policy goals. According to Orleck, Schneiderman was excited about "tapping the power" of the newly enfranchised working women voters.[249] She rallied the voters "from the back of a horse-drawn truck as it moved slowly down the streets of each legislator's district." Banners on the sides of the truck backed up her message. According to one, "Working women ask you to defeat Albert Ottinger [a Republican state senator]. He voted against giving working women in industry a way that would give them a chance to live in decency and health." Two of the four replacements were women, increasing women's presence in legislative bodies.[250]

A core of social democratic feminists envisioned the third example of a bloc vote when they tried to turn the 1921 National Woman's Party (NWP) convention into a space for bridgers to deliberate about a postsuffrage program. As Crystal Eastman (1881–1928), a bridger of socialism and feminism, argued in her vision for the convention, attended by five hundred delegates, "We need a program in order to understand each other." For her, this understanding would come through listening to each other during "deliberations." She also pointed out that the resolutions had to be broad ranging, including birth control, protecting African American women's right to vote, and disarmament.[251]

The importance of bridging as the method for crafting this bloc vote was brought out when Ovington, Kelley, Hunton, Mary Talbert (1866–1923), and

Terrell worked to persuade Alice Paul (1885–1977), the head of the NWP, to make the enforcement of African American voting rights a centerpiece of its program and to allow Talbert to make the case for this priority by speaking from the podium.[252] Historian Paula Giddings describes how Hunton, the NAACP's field secretary, strategized to achieve this aim. She not only drew on the white women who bridged the NAACP with egalitarian suffragism to pressure Paul, but she also took a delegation of sixty African American women bridgers to confront Paul. Terrell, who had picketed the White House to demand the right to vote and had received an NWP pin for her courage, was the speaker at this meeting.[253] No doubt she presented her intersectional analysis and policy proposals necessary for the founding of engendered interracial democracy. Talbert reported, "Miss Paul, although thoroughly hostile to the delegation, said it was the most intelligent group of women who ever attacked her."[254] Clearly the bridgers were unable to get Paul to reexamine her white privilege, acknowledge her intersectional location, or consider an intersectional approach to advancing women's equality.

Rejecting that the NWP should go forward by turning itself into a socializing space for building a bloc vote based on bridging movements, Paul maintained the continuing relevance of her pre-suffrage strategy. She believed fervently that the only way to unify women was to insist on a strict gender-neutral formal equality approach to undoing women's subjection.[255] Therefore, she blocked the flourishing of an intersectional conversation that interconnected structural race and gender oppressions and formulated new syntheses of gender-neutral and gender-difference notions of equality.[256] The minority resolution suggested such an orientation, which built on the power of bringing together different streams of bridgers during the suffrage struggle. The assumption of the defeated resolution was that unity in the form of a bloc vote would be built by acknowledging and addressing substantive differences among women. While the bridgers did not succeed in turning the NWP into a new socializing space for crafting a social democratic feminist bloc vote, they demonstrated that they sought ways to shape their new political presence through bridging skills. The next chapter shows how they embedded this aim in a new transnationalism.

The significance of the third stage of the feminist genealogy is that it showed how the meaning of a citizen right was reconstituted through the struggle to achieve that right. In the case of the right to vote, women could not persuade men to include them in a universal, disembodied, abstract right. As a result, especially during the last two decades of the campaign, the egalitarian suffragists presented themselves in all their diversity. To make their case for suffrage to their distinct communities, they recast political equality. A formal standing was not sufficient. Instead, they argued for a notion of the right to vote that rested on dismantling the intersectional structures of power.

In the process, they made clear their understanding of a social democratic bloc vote: It would continue the struggle for substantive political equality.

Refounding as a Political Revolution

This chapter shows that to recover the social democratic feminists as major league refounders,[257] we must acknowledge that their imbedding of the vote as a tool for social policy within their political revolution provided a radical interpretation of the Nineteenth Amendment. They did not intend to merely activate "the inclusionary potential" of the liberal democratic system.[258] Through their intersectional conversations on anti-lynching and the sexual double standard and their experiments with expanding women's participation in the labor movement, they made clear that democratizing the right to vote constituted a political revolution. Applying Aristotle's concept of revolution in the constitution allows us to see their expansive vision of refounding by enfranchising women.

Through their intersectional coalitions, they recreated the sovereign power. African American egalitarian suffragists explicitly connected votes for women with the Fifteenth Amendment to guarantee that both African American women and men were included in the sovereign power. Immigrant Jewish egalitarians suffragists tied the vote to including in the sovereign power a rich diversity of immigrant working-class women and men who were fighting to end economic exploitation. By reimagining the sovereign power in these very specific ways, the egalitarian suffragists defined their revolution as a change in the constitution from an oligarchic form shaped by a white male sovereign power to a democratic form characterized by an interracial and cosmopolitan sovereign power.

This new democratic sovereign defined a new end of the body politic: engendered, interracial, cosmopolitan social democracy. It went way beyond any maternalist form to a vision of women's equal power with men as the basis for shaping an expansive government that regulated the economy and provided social programs. This new end furthered and required a notion of intersectional social justice. Thus, the social democratic feminists, through their arguments for women's suffrage, provided an interpretation of the Nineteenth Amendment as a democratizing political revolution in the constitution.

4

The Transnational

Surrounding and Completing the National

The purpose of this chapter is to foreground how the transnational intersectional activism and theorizing of the social democratic feminists shaped both their intertwined engendering and socializing of democracy and their feminist genealogy of multileveled social citizenship. Although they used the term "international," they meant more than relations between nation-states, and therefore they innovated a new understanding of going beyond the nation-state to a level of engagement that we call transnationalism. In her report back from the 1915 International Congress of Women (ICW) in The Hague, where over a thousand women met, some from warring nations, Addams suggested the core assumption of their notion: "[T]hey came together to declare the validity of *the* [my emphasis] internationalism which surrounds and completes national life, even as national life itself surrounds and completes family life."[1] They specifically sought to surround and complete nationalism by a tangible humanity or new humanitarianism, which they translated into cosmopolitan relations, global norms, human rights, and new mechanisms of global government like the League of Nations (LON) and the International Labor Organization (ILO). By strengthening the transnational level, they built into their refounding moment the aspiration to uproot the causes of war and imperialism and further a global humane common good.

The framing of the social democratic feminists as maternalist pacifists hides the breadth and depth of their multileveled political project.[2] Therefore, this chapter adds another dimension to my critique of the maternalist interpretation. As World War I made clear, appeals to mothers could rally them to both oppose militarism and send their sons into battle.[3] Even before the United States entered the war, Addams declared, "The belief that a woman is against war simply because she is a woman and not a man cannot of course be substantiated."[4] Ellen Key, who did not attend the 1915 ICW but sent a message of support from Sweden, articulated the central political problem transnational feminists faced: They would have to teach women how to resist militarized nationalistic urges. According to Key, "Woman's sympathy is nothing to be depended upon so long as it subjects itself to the teaching of nationalism that force is right, and that the ends justify the means."[5]

Pacifism alone also was not an adequate container because social democrats divided over whether or not "militarism might be used as an instrument for advanced social ends."[6] For example, John Dewey (1859–1952) and Blatch defended the war effort because they hoped it would accelerate the socialization of the economy and the common welfare. They changed their minds only after they became aware of the postwar devastation.[7] They then joined Addams in her firm commitment to democratic means. As she explained, "But some of us had suspected that social advance depends as much upon the process through which it is secured as upon the result itself."[8]

African American social democratic feminists further complicated the means-ends debate among pacifists by bringing in the problem of how best to achieve racial justice. In their report back on their experiences of serving African American soldiers during the war, Hunton and Kathryn Johnson (1878–1955) situated their "afterthought" within "that consistent adherence in the teachings of the Prince of Peace . . . although it must be accompanied by righteous and indignant protest against injustices." They laid out two opposing positions within the African American community. Some doubted that serving would improve race relations and therefore "would be a needless sacrifice"; others felt that by demonstrating a willingness to die for one's country, the African American soldier would contribute to the undoing of the legacy of slavery. Hunton and Johnson concluded that both stances were unsatisfying.[9]

The "transnational" label allows us to put center stage one of the defining characteristics of the social democratic feminists: They excelled at crossing borders. Historian Alan Dawley places them within the "most cosmopolitan" generation of American reformers.[10] They went abroad for education. The immigrants among them migrated from one country to another. Attendance at international conferences was a regular activity for some of them. Delegations traveled around the world to meet with women in other nations. Wells-Barnett went to England to rally support for her anti-lynching campaign. Others engaged in cross-border social policy networks in which they shared the results of their experiments. They hosted visitors from abroad and arranged the logistics of their speaking engagements. Most traveled back and forth through the levels: local, state, national, and transnational. Along the way, they became multilingual.

Fundamentally, the social democratic feminists shaped their intersectional activism with an understanding that crossing borders was essential for them since they lacked full nation-state citizenship. According to their feminist genealogy of social citizenship, they began as abstract citizens of the world. In their different streams, they turned this status into new practices of embodied social citizenship within the United States. This chapter completes their genealogy by uncovering how they brought the transnational level in to create multileveled practices and theorizing.

My argument is that before, during, and after World War I, the social democratic feminists built into their engendering and socializing of democracy the problem of how to synthesize the local, the national, and the transnational levels of participation and government, and in the process, they produced a practice and theory of social citizens as synthesizers of those levels. To develop this argument, I begin by reinterpreting the first three chapters to show that in the prewar period, by bridging movements, the social democratic feminists produced new understandings of how to embed a nonmilitarized nation-state within an evolving humanitarian transnational level. Then I turn to how, during and after the war, as bridgers, they acted directly on the transnational level by founding WILPF and engaging with the new transnational institutions. I approach WILPF as a transnational experimental participatory social space, and I reveal how intersectional activism defined its aim and drove its development during the early congresses. I put particular emphasis on how, through the theory-activist dynamic, Addams drew on WILPF's protests as deeds to conceptualize a political notion of nourishing. From there, I uncover how WILPF generated two intersectional conversations: one on France's use of colonial troops for occupying the Rhineland and a second on the U.S. occupation of Haiti. Finally, I complete the picture of how the social democratic feminists evolved their feminist genealogy of multileveled social citizenship by inventing their own distinct theory and practice of embodied global citizenship.

Interconnecting Cosmopolitan Neighborhoods and Anti-imperialism

In returning to the feminist settlement house neighborhood, I now use it to illustrate historian Dawley's understanding of how the social democratic feminists engaged in "the dual quest for improvement at home and abroad" and how their "thinking took shape in response to events overseas."[11] For Addams, her relevant dual quest was to redesign relations within the nation-state and have the United States go out into the world based on these new relations of trust. This aim required validating the development of the United States as a new type of international democracy that was capable of applying a new cosmopolitan ethic to its relations with other peoples and nations.[12] As an opponent of the U.S. annexation of the Philippines, in 1899, Addams introduced her goal before the Central Anti-Imperialist League of Chicago: "Unless the present situation extends our nationalism into internationalism, unless it has thrust forward our patriotism into humanitarianism we cannot meet it."[13] To support her anti-imperialist stance, Addams theorized the emancipatory potential of her diverse neighborhood to generate the required practices of a new rooted cosmopolitanism and the possibility of "cosmic patriotism."[14]

The gendered terms of the national debate influenced her theorizing. While the pursuit of a multifaceted national self-interest might have caused the Philippine-American War,[15] Theodore Roosevelt (TR) argued that imperialism was necessary to keep American men manly. With the closing of the frontier, he insisted that American men needed to engage with "savage virtues" in foreign lands to hone their Anglo-Saxon manly virtues.[16] As an anti-imperialist, philosopher William James (1842–1910) took up the challenge to achieve the same qualities of masculinity without war: "The war-party is assuredly right in affirming and reaffirming that the martial virtues, although originally gained by the race through war, are absolute and permanent human goods." He characterized these virtues as "intrepidity, contempt of softness, surrender of private interests, obedience to command."[17] He proposed to cultivate them through "the immemorial human warfare against nature."[18] All young men, including "our gilded youth," would be drafted into a system of national service. They would "get the childishness knocked out of them" by being sent to "coal and iron mines, to freight trains, to fishing fleets in December, to dishwashing, clothes-washing, and window-washing, to road-building and tunnel-making, to foundries and stoke-holes and to the frames of skyscrapers."[19] As a result of their "service to the state," James insisted, "the women would value them more highly, they would be better fathers and teachers of the following generation."[20]

Addams built her anti-imperialist case against TR by theorizing a non-militarized masculinity grounded in labor as an activity that nourished life. In broad terms, she insisted that "it is the workers, who year after year nourish and bring up the bulk of the nation."[21] In sharp contrast to James, she sought not a moral *equivalent* to war but a moral *substitute* for war. If the imperialists took from Darwin the notion of struggle, which James sought to redirect, she built her substitute on Darwin's assumption that we were also wired for mutual aid.[22] The challenge she posed for herself was "to discover a moral substitute for war, something that will appeal to the courage, the capacity of men, something which will develop their finest powers without deteriorating their moral nature, as war constantly does."[23] She found this substitute in "the spirit of adventure to be found in the nourishing of human life, in the bringing of all the world into some sort of general order and decent relationship one with another."[24]

By characterizing men workers as laboring nourishers, Addams constructed them as carrying out the function of women in the tribal division of labor. When she went searching for her substitute, Addams turned to "the long history of industrial progress," which included the tribal stage. In this stage, according to Addams, the men "secure[d] the raw material for food and shelter" by hunting, and the women transformed "the flesh of the wild creature into proper food and the pelt into clothing." According to this gendered division of labor, "[w]omen's part in this life, broadly speaking, was industrial, as man's was military."[25] Building on this version of gendered history, Addams crafted a theoretical framework that lined up industrialism with nurture and militarism with conquest. As she explained in proposing a notion of patriotism that went beyond the nation-state, "We continue to found our patriotism upon war and to contrast conquest with nurture, militarism with industrialism, calling the latter passive and inert and the former active and aggressive, without really facing the situation as it exits."[26]

Addams explicitly grounded her theorizing of a feminized substitute in the bridging of labor and anti-imperialist movements. She brought the history of working men organizing to the Central Anti-Imperialist League: "The first international organization founded not to promote a colorless peace, but to advance and develop the common life of all nations was founded in London in 1864 by workingmen and called simply 'The International Association of Workingmen.' They recognized that a supreme interest raised all workingmen above the prejudice of race, and united them by wider and deeper principles than those by which they were separated into nations." As a result, the working men took the position that "in case of war a universal strike be declared."[27] The opposition of the AFL to the annexation of the Philippines provided further evidence.

Addams hypothesized that organized workers opposed imperialist wars because, as the producers and nourishers, they were called on to pay taxes and provide sustenance for standing or occupying armies. She did not analyze how workers were turned into soldiers. Clearly, her point was that working-class men engaged in two distinct types of practices: feminized producing or nourishing and masculinized fighting. She applauded the organized efforts to tie the former to a vision of transnational solidarity, while she avoided the issue of how the fear of competition from an influx of new immigrant Asian workers might have fueled the AFL's anti-imperialist stance.

To theorize her own vision of a substitute for war that would reconfigure nationalism through what she labeled a "new internationalism," Addams turned to the emancipatory potential of "the unencumbered proletarian."[28] In their daily lives, members of that class crossed borders, including those between intersectional locations. For example, she pointed to "the indications of an internationalism as sturdy and virile as it is unprecedented . . . in our cosmopolitan neighborhood: when a South Italian Catholic is forced by the very exigencies of the situation to make friends with an Austrian Jew representing another nationality and another religion, both of which cut into all his most cherished prejudices, he finds it harder to utilize them a second time and gradually loses them."[29] Addams also theorized the significance of the sojourner migrant worker. An Italian neighbor went back and forth from Naples to Chicago. Economic globalization of labor created the conditions for him to engage in "a network of personal acquaintance and kindly relationship on an international basis." His experience led Addams to conceptualize a type of rooted cosmopolitanism: "So far as labor is mobilized and annually crosses from one side of the world to the other, there is doubtless forming at the very base of society a new conception of international relations."[30]

In *Newer Ideals of Peace*, Addams gave her richest depiction of her multinational neighborhood as practicing a new type of rooted cosmopolitan relationship that could potentially resist the pull of militarized nationalism. As she explained, "It is possible that we shall be saved from warfare . . . by the 'quarrelsome mob' turned into kindly citizens of the world through the pressure of a cosmopolitan neighborhood. It is not that they are shouting for peace . . . but that they are really attaining cosmopolitan relations through daily experience." Addams theorized that her neighbors were "laying the simple and inevitable foundations for an international order as the foundations of tribal and national morality have already been laid."[31] She was not arguing that neighbors and coworkers acted like nation-states.[32] Her point was that through their helping relations and their labor struggles, her diverse working-class neighbors were constructing a transnational ethic from the ground up. In sharp contrast to an abstract notion of humanity, Addams posited that her neighbors were engaged in processes of synthesizing their different nationalities into a new "cosmopolitan humanitarianism."[33] This outcome was made possible by the fact that "all the peoples of the world have become part of the American tribunal."[34]

Her hope that cosmopolitan cities could provide models for how the United States should go out into the world rested on rejecting the Anglo-Saxon model of how to engage with a diverse working class within the United States and with peoples in other countries.[35] This model rested on a hierarchical notion of civilization with Anglo-Saxons on top. Within the United States, she charged that "we have persistently ignored the political ideals of the Celtic, Germanic, Latin, and Slavic immigrants who have successfully come to us," and "in our overwhelming ambition to remain Anglo-Saxon, . . . [w]e have failed to work out a democratic government which should include the experiences and hopes of all the varied peoples among us."[36] Outside the United States, she accused imperialists, like TR, of adopting the English "methods of the conquest and government of remote and alien peoples." She contested their adoption of a notion of civilization as "the opening of gold mines, the establishment of garrisons, the controlling of the weaker men by brute force." Instead, she argued that "civilization is an idea, a method of living, an attitude of respect toward all men."[37]

Turning this notion of civilization into a cosmopolitan ethic that embedded nationalism within transnationalism required putting nourishing and trust of the people at home and abroad at the center of the U.S. practice of self-government. Clearly, Addams was not proposing isolationism. "For the sake of its own development," she argued, "democracy needs to get out of national lines. It seems at this moment to be struggling and drowning in a narrow nationalism."[38] When she turned to how the United States should go out into the world, she clarified that her notion of the feminized nourishing of transnational relations included growing a variety of forms of self-government.

Addams argued that the United States was suppressing the "social energy" required to evolve self-government because of its interconnected distrust of "our own people" and "other peoples."[39] By calling for trusting democracy as the method for evolving relations at home and abroad, she proposed that the United States approach "the people . . . of a different color, . . . of a different tradition from ours," and "nourish them into another type of government, not Anglo-Saxon even."[40] Instead of adopting an imperialist posture, the United States should understand that "all progress must come from the native soil"[41] and that "mingling in an absolute equality"[42] was a necessary condition to "nourish it." In this way, the United States would contribute to the development of "the most wonderful thing in the world, a new combination of people coming together in the line of self-government."[43]

Taking this analysis back to Chapter 1's presentation of the feminist settlement house as a new domestic-public hybrid produces two further insights. First, we gain another level of significance as to why Addams chose to emphasize labor rather than maternal care of children in her concept of civic housekeeping. Significantly, she included this concept as a chapter in *Newer Ideals of Peace*. In this chapter, she linked civic housekeeping to the hope that the Hull House Labor Museum could raise consciousness about labor as a substitute for militarism by turning middle-class women into its champion. After advocating that they needed to study the history of industrialism and come out of their domestic space to "walk" with immigrant working-class women, Addams stressed that "this attitude of understanding and respect for the worker is necessary, not only to appreciate what he produces, but to preserve his power of production, again showing the necessity for making that substitute for war—human labor—more aggressive and democratic."[44] Second, the Hull House public kitchen now emerges as an early experiment with tying together the two meanings of nourishing as a feminized substitute for militarism: the provision of food and the growth of self-government. After World War I, Addams further develops her political notion of nourishing by theorizing a transnational common table supportive of different forms of collective self-determination.

Economic Independence and Evolving Transnational Norms

In returning to the theme of Chapter 2, women's economic independence, I now place it within the context that historian Daniel Rodgers characterizes as "a largely forgotten world of transnational borrowings and imitation, adaptation and transformation," in the area of social politics and that historians Kathryn Sklar, Anja Schuler, and Susan Strasser call "a transatlantic dialogue" between U.S. and German women reformers.[45] Rodgers applies the label "social maternalists" to the women participants because he assumes a liberal, individualistic notion of feminism. According to his notion, women who stressed their "social duties—not for self but for the elevation, protection, and education of others" de-emphasized notions of gender-neutral "equal rights and equal justice."[46] In sharp contrast, Sklar, Schuler, and Strasser reject the maternalist framing and the either/or framework that Rodgers accepts when they insist that the pursuit of feminist social justice was at the heart of the transnational dialogue.[47] To reinforce their critique of social maternalism, I stress how reformulating gender equality by engaging with the tension between gender-difference and gender-neutral sameness shaped the pursuit of economic independence as a cross-border project.

As historians of the international women's movement, Ulla Wikander and Leila Rupp document how participants at international conferences disagreed over sex-based labor laws and how to achieve women's economic independence. The 1906 Bern meeting of the International Association for Protective Labor Legislation sparked the controversy. Male representatives from sixteen nations, not including the United States, agreed to the "first two international conventions on labor protection." One prohibited "the use of white phosphorus in the match production industry"; the other prohibited "women's night work in industry." To enact each, a national government had to ratify it and turn it into law.[48]

The following year, Addams used Bern to support her argument for the need to substitute industrialism for militarism. She characterized Bern as shifting international relations from "warfare and statecraft" to "the affairs of industry." According to her, "In doing this they entered into the realm which has traditionally and historically belonged to women." In effect, the men were feminizing international relations by "considering the human side of indus-try," but without women's presence, which Addams noted.[49] Their absence made a difference, according to Wikander, because unlike the men who sought the regulation of labor to create uniformity in international trade, women raised the question of the effect of sex-based labor laws on the achievement of substantive gender equality.[50]

Wikander traces how seventeen international women's congresses held between 1889 and 1914 in Europe, the United States, and Canada allowed women to voice their disagreements. According to her, they "never resolved" their conflict over the ban on women's night work.[51] Rupp argues that they were actually debating whether or not sex-based labor laws were the correct means for furthering the ends of gender equality.[52] As I have shown in the postsuffrage context in the United States, exposing and working to resolve the tension between gender-difference and gender-neutral equality constituted a distinct feminist contribution to social democratic policy discussions.[53] Among social democratic feminists, both exposing and resolving were di-rected at advancing the evolution of an alternative system to the liberal, lais-sez-faire one. When this debate crossed borders, it produced an additional payoff: the possibility of creating transnational norms or conventions on labor standards and mechanisms for enforcement that could support the advance of women's economic independence within nation-states.

To illustrate how this transnational level was taking shape in the prewar period, I further theorize the significance of the interconnection between sex-based labor laws and women factory inspectors for advancing women's eco-nomic independence.[54] Because she had been a chief factory inspector and had operated within a cross-border environment, Florence Kelley embraced the challenge to dissect the interconnection for a German audience. Along with Addams, Kelley played a central role in the German-U.S. dialogue on social policy. Both "were fascinated by the powerful state structures of Ger-man government."[55] Through articles written in German for a publication that provided "investigation of social conditions in all lands,"[56] Kelley knew that her analysis of a state-centered reform would travel easily across borders. In her presentation of the U.S. practice of women factory inspectors, espe-cially her Illinois version, Kelley provided a multilayered account of the ten-sion between gender-neutral and gender-difference equality.

On its face, a law that combined an eight-hour workday and forty-eight-hour workweek for women in certain industries and the requirement of wom-en factory inspectors appeared to be a reform based solely on the logic of dif-ferences between women and men. This logic shaped the early English and German practices of hiring women factory inspectors, although each system interpreted it differently. The English inspectorate was actually gender seg-regated until 1921, with the women operating out of the London headquarters. Yet they had the same authority as men factory inspectors to prosecute cases in court at a time when women could not practice the law. In Germany, the women were contingent workers, with narrow duties. They were denied the retirement benefits of the office and the authority to prosecute violations of the law. Some state systems in the United States also were structured by the gender-difference argument, according to Kelley, with different responsibilities for women and men inspectors.[57]

In very strong terms, Kelley defended a gender-neutral understanding of the factory inspector. "Those who advocate appointing women as factory inspectors," she asserted, "support the general principle that all professions and occupations should be open to those who want to pursue them." Based on her "past experience," she concluded, "women possess the qualities necessary for the job just as much as men."[58] Among those qualities, Kelley included "good health," "a clear mind," and "a certain cunning."[59] Since reformers used the issue of women's health to justify the need for sex-based labor laws, Kelley examined this problem for women factory inspectors. After proposing that they dress in practical clothes, like those worn by women bicyclists, to be better equipped to deal with inclement weather and to avoid accidents caused by long, bulky skirts getting caught in the machinery, she claimed that there was nothing to stop women from adapting to the physical pressures of the job. Plus, there were opportunities for rest when they filled out paperwork. Pointing to the longevity of female inspectors in Pennsylvania and New York, Kelley declared, "[T]heir health has in no way been affected, thus decisively disproving the argument that women's health cannot withstand the demands of the profession."[60]

To further justify her gender-neutral version of the factory inspector, Kelley addressed the claim that girls and women workers would not "tell men about the impropriety and harassment they suffer." Drawing on her experience backed up by other states, she insisted that the gender of the inspector made "no difference with respect to workers' bringing complaints." They mailed complaints directly to the office, and many were unsigned or signed by a fake name. Once the office received the complaint, Kelley noted, the inspector "usually" got "to the root of the problem." Instead of finding the gender of the inspector to be an important factor in the receiving and resolving of complaints, Kelley pointed to the worker's fear of antagonizing the boss. Moreover, Kelley suggested that "workers do not entrust us with their personal concerns" or with "moral lapses" because they do not fall within "decreed regulations of the factory law." In effect, Kelley did not expect workers to raise issues that today would fall within Title VII workplace sexual harassment law. As she explained, "Complaints about moral offenses of employers, supervisors, or other employees are directed neither to male nor to female inspectors. We are hired to inspect and to prosecute violations of the law; we are not a counseling but rather an executive authority."[61]

Yet while the job itself might have required gender-neutral skills, Kelley had to acknowledge that the path to the job for women was gendered. Surveying seven years of experience with factory inspectors in seven U.S. states, Kelley noted that "the appointment of women did not keep up with the growth" of the field. For example, in 1897, women held only 20 percent of the positions in New York. As political appointees, Kelley argued, women faced discrimination because they were not voters or connected to a powerful political figure. Governor John Altgeld, a reformist Democrat, appointed Kelley, but when he left office, she lost her position. She championed putting the inspectorate within a civil service system so that presumably the most qualified would be chosen. But Kelley also admitted that "women are usually only appointed when the law unconditionally demands it." The 1893 Illinois law, which she helped shape, stipulated a gender quota of five women factory inspectors.[62] Therefore, to prove they could do a gender-neutral job, Kelley suggested, women required differential treatment in the recruitment process.

Committed to achieving the goal of gender-neutral labor laws that protected women and men, Kelley found herself enforcing a law that assumed men and women were different. She explained to her German audience why gender-neutral labor laws were so hard to pass in the United States: "It is much easier to find approval by appealing to the sympathy of the masses for the welfare of helpless working women and children than to find it by suggesting absolutely necessary measures to protect the lives, bodies, and health of men, who are fathers, husbands, and breadwinners of the same women and children." In a laissez-faire, liberal democratic system, according to Kelley, the people assumed that men were capable of protecting themselves in the labor market and through the use of their voting power.[63] Therefore, Kelley conveyed to her German audience that she saw gender difference in the form of sex-based labor laws as her main tool for building support to overturn this system.

In effect, Kelley's analysis illustrated the prewar social democratic feminist climate in which gender-difference and gender-neutral arguments coexisted.[64] Operating within an unequal power dynamic, Kelley was unable to resolve the tension. As a result, she revealed the complexity of formulating a new concept of gender equality that reflected the necessary bridging of feminism and the women's labor movement. Yet she experimented with how to advance a new synthetic notion through two interconnected public policies: sex-based labor laws in female-crowded fields and gender quotas in hiring in male-dominated fields. Both policies indicated that the pursuit of women's economic independence inevitably brought forward the need to enlarge the state's regulatory role in the economy as a necessary condition for overcoming the tension between difference and equality.

Kelley further complicated her analysis by going beyond a pure focus on gender equality when she foregrounded the intersectional locations of her crew of factory inspectors. In sharp contrast to both the English and German models, Kelley chose working-class women to be her deputies, and she gave them a glowing recommendation: "Women of the working class have proven to be the best and most active factory inspectors, particularly those nominated by the unions." They excelled at the job because they were "used to hard work" and had "a particular interest in protecting their fellow workers." They also infused the job with a radical edge, which led employers to complain that the inspectors were advancing the class struggle and "not the interest of the whole society." Kelley responded that the employers, like those who successfully persuaded the Illinois Supreme Court to overturn the eight-hour workday, did not place a value on "prevent[ing] the exploitation of the working class and keep[ing] them from being destroyed totally, body and soul."[65] According to Sklar, under Kelley's leadership, the men and women factory inspectors did engage in "vigorously promoting union organizing."[66]

Characterizing her factory inspectors as "representative of the population of Illinois," Kelley further fleshed out their intersectional social locations by acknowledging their nationalities and languages: "Three are American-born with American parents, five have Irish parents, and one has German parents, while one has immigrated from Ireland, one from Sweden, and one from Russia, the last a Jew." Among them they had proficiency in "four languages that are widely used among the working class in Illinois, namely English, German, and Swedish and the dialect of Russian Jews." Unfortunately, none of them spoke "Bohemian, Polish, or Italian, although a large part of the working class is only accessible with the help of these languages."[67] By assembling a diverse group of factory inspectors, Kelley brought them into the refounding moment. As Kelley's portrait showed, they were actualizing Addams's vision of the United States as an evolving cosmopolitan democracy.

Chapter 2 explored how the NCL, under Kelley's leadership, pursued a strategy of using sex-based labor laws to discredit the laissez-faire ideology that justified the absence of U.S. regulation of labor relations. Now I emphasize how Kelley's championing of factory inspectors as a cross-border development revealed a whole new dimension of that strategy. Its success rested, in part, on the effective use of the evolving transnational level, defined here as the cross-border production of knowledge by factory inspectors and other actors, who documented the industrial working conditions that made government regulation imperative. Those other actors included two central figures in the cross-border networks that Kelley participated in: Beatrice Webb

(1859–1947), an English Fabian socialist, and Alice Salomon (1872–1948), a German Jewish feminist social worker.

In effect, the 113-page Brandeis brief submitted for *Muller v. Oregon* (1908) was a compilation of the evolving transnational knowledge. The brief assumed a borderless world in which the problems faced by industrial workers were the same in U.S. states and in industrialized Europe. It documented how twenty states and seven nations in Europe adopted sex-based labor laws as the remedy. Noting that no labor laws abroad or in U.S. states had been repealed, except for the Illinois eight-hour day when Kelley was chief factory inspector, the brief argued that "there has been a general movement to strengthen and to extend the operations of these laws." The title of its second part was "The World's Experience upon which the Legislation limiting the Hours of Labor for Women is Based." Interweaving over ninety reports from factory inspectors and other governmental and nongovernmental sources from the states and Europe that covered "a period of more than sixty years," the brief demonstrated the importance of factory inspector reports and provided evidence of an evolving transnational standard of limiting paid working hours, at least for women.[68]

To illustrate how the production of transnational knowledge worked, I foreground the brief's analysis of the laundry industry. While the 1903 Oregon ten-hours law applied to "any mechanical establishment or factory or laundry," Muller was an owner of a laundry. Therefore, laundresses took center stage in the brief. Specifically, the brief placed the situation of the Oregon laundresses within the context of the campaign by factory inspectors in England to have Parliament extend its factory acts to include the regulation of laundry work. While the role of women factory inspectors was not explicitly acknowledged in the brief, they carried out the crucial investigations. In England, they drew on the support of the laundresses, who publicly demonstrated in favor of their inclusion.[69] To illustrate the political campaign, the brief included excerpts from an 1891 debate in the House of Lords. England started regulating laundry workplaces in 1895 but did not limit working hours to a sixty-hour week until 1907.[70] Germany did not regulate the laundry industry.[71]

By situating the Oregon law within the context of the knowledge generated by the English campaign, the brief argued that Oregon was only responding to a development that crossed borders: the industrialization of laundry work. According to one of the reports, the necessary condition for this change was the production of new types of laundry machinery. England imported many of them from the United States.[72] So reports on the dangers of laundry work included in the brief reflected the impact of cross-border economic trade relations as well as the sharing of versions of sex-based labor laws.

The brief's presentation of the laundry industry also confirmed its role in the feminization of the industrial worker, which I argued in Chapter 2 was crucial for making economic woman the standard for the paid worker. The brief adds a new cross-border dimension to the feminization process. The reports from England gave a new status to laundry work by conceptualizing it as part of the industrialized economic system, even when it was performed in small home shops. In a 1900 annual report, the English chief inspector of factories characterized the change: "With this advent of machinery and sub-division of labour, the whole character of the industry has changed. It is becoming more and more evident that, from the smallest to the largest laun-dry, the industry is passing—has indeed in some respects already passed—out of the peculiar position which it has hitherto occupied, and is taking its place alongside ordinary trades." Presumably "peculiar" referred to how the industrial nature of laundry work had been hidden by the characterization of it as "a simple home occupation."[73]

Along with this revised understanding of the work came a new framing of the laundress. She should no longer be viewed as a "casual laborer," whose work due to English custom was "carried on in spurts," with "shamefully long [fourteen to fifteen] hours" per day over a period of three or four days a week, to be followed by "days of idleness."[74] Instead, the passages quoted in the brief pointed to the need to restructure the laundry industry through the enforce-ment of a uniform day with reasonable hours and the adoption of health and safety measures. In short, although she was a woman doing traditional wom-an's work, the laundress should be given her rights as a protected industrial worker. While the laundress represented a new type of feminized industrial worker, the NCL's goal was to feminize, defined as in need of labor protec-tions, the entire industrial labor force.

Felix Frankfurter characterized the 1908 *Muller* Supreme Court decision as "[t]he turning point"[75] because it gave the NCL its first entering-wedge legal victory, which successfully used a sex-based labor law to advance the goal of universal labor laws. The decision provided "an epitome," or synopsis, of the Brandeis brief "in the margin." In this way, the Supreme Court conveyed le-gitimacy on the NCL's use of transnational knowledge to interpret the Four-teenth Amendment. Justice Brewer, writing for the court, distinguished ju-risprudence from the bulk of the material in the brief, and he acknowledged, "We take judicial cognizance of all matters of general knowledge."[76]

The epitome characterized a quoted statement by a German factory in-spector as providing an overall summary of the key points in the brief. He provided a four-part justification for a ten-hour workday: "the physical or-ganization of woman," "her maternal functions," "the rearing and education of children," and "the maintenance of the home." In the decision, Brewer ap-peared to draw on the statement when he wrote that the "legislation and opinions" in the brief "are significant of a widespread belief that woman's physical structure, and the functions she performs in consequence thereof, justify special legislation restricting or qualifying the conditions under which she should be permitted to toil."[77] He put particular emphasis on the long hours of standing that were required for laundry work, a theme that was stressed in the brief. Brewer's use of the material in the brief showed that he was persuaded that support for limiting the hours of work *for women* was only growing. In the unanimous decision, Brewer indicated that the U.S. Supreme Court placed the U.S. Constitution within the evolving cross-border consensus.

While the brief and the court decision hide the contributions of women factory inspectors, both strengthened the justification for the profession. In analyzing the transnational dimension of the brief and the decision, I emphasized the profession's role in the production of transnational knowledge culled from common workplace conditions. Kelley's support for the profession also pointed to the need to have an enforcement mechanism once a labor law was passed. Ultimately, her chief factory inspector experience and her defense of sex-based labor laws, which included quotas for women factory inspectors, helped build the cross-border network of women activists. This network ably influenced the content of the ILO charter so that it established a transnational norm in support of "a system of inspection in which women should take part."[78]

Evolving Human Rights by Engendering Them from the Bottom Up

In returning to the late U.S. women's suffrage movement, I now place it within the context of the activism of the International Woman Suffrage Alliance (IWSA) that was founded between 1899 and 1904 by Susan B. Anthony; Anita Augsburg (1857–1943), a German lawyer and suffragist; and Carrie Chapman Catt, its first president. International relations theorists Margaret Keck and Kathryn Sikkink depict the IWSA as one of the forgotten "historical precursors" of "advocacy networks" that coordinate activists to act "beyond borders" in international politics. Historian DuBois characterizes the IWSA as "a self-consciously transnational popular movement." She and historian Rupp stress how the IWSA provided suffragists with strategic "resources" to fight their national battles. According to Rupp, the IWSA's efforts illustrated "the privileging of nationalism" by an international organization.[79] Certainly, U.S. suffragists organized transnationally to generate new momentum because they were frustrated with their lack of progress beyond four western states—Wyoming (1889), Colorado (1893), Utah (1895), and Idaho (1896). Yet the significance of the IWSA went beyond developing strategic tools. Through their organizing, transnational suffragists embedded women's multileveled suffrage campaigns within the evolution of a truly transnational product: a feminist origin for the human right to vote.

To understand this evolution, it is necessary to examine how the IWSA utilized the language of rights. According to Keck and Sikkink, it engaged in symbolic politics through its appeals to the Enlightenment notions of equal rights. They assume that the IWSA's aim was to extend this notion to women by granting them the right to vote.[80] The charter of the organization, crafted by the three founders, certainly illustrated this symbolic politics when it appealed to the language of inalienable rights from the U.S. Declaration of Independence, evoking the spirit of the American Revolution.

Yet as we have seen, women claiming the right to vote as an inalienable right had not persuaded enough men in power to expand the electorate. According to historian Alexander Keyssar, the Founding Fathers did not adopt the notion of the right to vote as a natural right "because they feared the universalist implications of natural rights." As he shows, their fear shadowed the efforts of movements to expand voting rights.[81] By 1912, Terrell would suggest that the symbol had become completely ineffective because "[t]o argue the inalienability and the equality of human rights in the twentieth century . . . seems like laying one's self open to the charge of anachronism."[82]

Clearly a refreshing of the human rights tradition was required. The IWSA founders started by engendering the abstract notion of inalienable rights presented in the Declaration of Independence. They explicitly included women and expanded the range of inalienable rights to include the right to self-government "in the home and the state."[83] As the IWSA grew with more auxiliaries from different parts of the world, it revitalized the whole notion of human rights for the twentieth century by going to its roots through a bottom-up cross-border method. The IWSA was in a unique position to pursue this path because, as historian DuBois observes, no other voting rights movement built such "links between national experiences."[84] Thus the IWSA produced a new understanding of the human right to vote that grew out of its bridging movements across borders, with special emphasis on bridging movements in the East with movements in the West.

In her 1909 presidential address during the Fifth IWSA Congress in London, Catt distinguished the notion of strategic resources from a notion of a new twentieth-century stage in the evolution of human rights. As she observed, for "practical minds," the IWSA "has furnished a much needed medium of exchange for news and reports." Specifically, the IWSA had widely publicized the details of each national movement and how it was working to discredit antisuffrage forces. Members had traveled "to give strength to the weak, courage to the timid, confidence to the doubting." As a result, Catt claimed, "the suffragists of no land work isolated and alone." While she celebrated these practical achievements, Catt characterized them as acting on the level of "the sordid struggle of each nation."[85]

Then she went on to distill how, out of their new cross-border relations, "many of us" had learned what was only hinted at before: that there was a greater "significance . . . magnitude . . . grandeur" to "our movement." Fundamentally, the transnational suffragists were riding "the onward swelling tide of human rights," and "the tide of woman's enfranchisement" was "coming in." So as they "[d]iligently and persistently" worked in their "own land," Catt argued, they "work[ed] with the consciousness that behind" them was "that mysterious, omnipotent, divine law of evolution which . . . has compelled human society continually to accept new rights and new liberties."[86] Certainly Catt was creating here a sense of inevitability as a type of strategic resource that could be used to strengthen the resolve of the suffragists. Yet, she was also suggesting that a cross-border relational method for creating embodied human rights could counter the resistance to the evolution of human rights.

"Society," she noted, "has ever shrunk back in terror from each new experiment and has clung tenaciously to that environment with which it has been most familiar." So Catt called on the IWSA to support the suffragists around the world to contest the customs and laws in their separate nations that were holding back their freedom and the evolution of human rights. What a transnational organization offered them, according to Catt, was an infusion of the energizing "spirit of the 20th century which the world calls Internationalism" and which had "to be experienced rather than defined in words." According to Catt, it provided the suffragists with "a motive more impelling than any we have experienced before." It required them to embrace "the task of emancipating" all women. "Under the influence of this new spirit," Catt claimed, "we realize that we are not enlisted for the work of our own countries alone." Instead, she declared, "our task will not be fulfilled until the women of the whole world have been rescued from those discriminations and injustices which in every land are visited upon them by law and custom."[87]

To work toward this end, the IWSA anchored the human right to vote in "the fraternity and the co-operation of our International connection." By making visible, in a 1913 comprehensive report, all the ways women around the world were pursuing their right to vote, the IWSA provided "proof" of "the growth and universality of the movement."[88] To make the linking of different countries possible, the IWSA required only that its auxiliaries seek to "secure the suffrage for the women of that land upon the same terms the suffrage is now, or may be, granted to men." Moreover, as Catt explained, "we do not interfere with the campaigns, nor the rights, nor the methods of any one of our auxiliaries."[89] According to the report, thirty-nine states or countries allowed women to vote for members of town councils, and eighteen made them eligible to run for town council seats. At the level of state or province or national legislature, nineteen gave women the right to vote for representatives, and thirteen made them eligible to run for the office of representative. From these findings, the report concluded that "the advance is worldwide" because Eastern and Western women were working for the same end.[90] Breaking through the East-West ideological construct was crucial for establishing that the right to vote was indeed a universal goal.

At the 1913 Seventh IWSA Congress in Budapest, Aletta Jacobs (1854–1929)—Dutch medical doctor, assimilated Jew, and birth control advocate—and Catt discredited the construct based on their 1911–1912 trip around the world, especially their experiences in China after the 1911 revolution led by Sun Yet-Sen and the Revolutionary Alliance. His republican vision for China included women's suffrage, although he did not support universal suffrage.[91] According to historian Rebecca Mead, those Chinese men in San Francisco who supported the 1911 California women's suffrage constitutional referendum "were usually supporters" of Sun Yet-Sen. Mead cites one analysis of the popular vote that showed "half of the approximately eight hundred voting Chinese in San Francisco approved the referendum." Since the measure lost in San Francisco and won statewide by only 3,587 votes, this voting bloc was significant. One of Catt's California correspondents, who reported to her on the support from younger Chinese men, suggested that Catt might find women voting in China.[92] When Jacobs and Catt reached China, they went in search of voting women. Arriving during the two-year period of heightened women's activism as revolutionaries and suffragists,[93] Catt and Jacobs succeeded in experiencing the excitement and potentiality of a revolutionary movement in the East to advance women's emancipation. They drew on their new consciousness of Eastern women to alter the IWSA's understanding of its role.[94]

A central theme of Catt's presidential address was that there was "no evidence of a sudden awakening" among Asian women. Indeed, it was Catt who "awakened"[95] to the inaccuracy of the orientalist construction of the Asian woman as "the satisfied, contented sex" with her subordinate position. As Catt observed, Western and Eastern "[m]en said so, and we believed them. It was never true." Speaking of Asian women broadly understood, she argued, "there has been rebellion in the hearts of women all down the centuries."[96] Absent was her 1909 use of the categories of civilized and uncivilized.[97]

After speaking with "many women all over the East who had never heard of a woman's movement," she concluded that "isolated and alone they had thought out the entire programme of woman's emancipation, not excluding the vote." They understood what was required of them: "to arise, to burst the shackles of tradition, and to demand the freedom which is the just heritage of every human being." Therefore, while it was "in an unorganized, incipient stage," Catt insisted, "there *is* a serious woman's movement in Asia." She included in this movement "women physicians in many countries, a woman lawyer in India, women's papers in India, Burmah, and China; many well-educated women in all lands, and a greater demand for girls' schools than any authority is able to provide." She also pointed to equal suffrage in cities like Rangoon and Bombay and reminded her audience not to "forget that nine Chinese women have served a term in the Assembly of the great Province of Kwantung [Guangdong], of which Canton [Guangzhou] is the capital."[98]

Then she described how she and Jacobs "had the privilege of seeing these women sitting in the Assembly and of talking, by means of interpreters, with several of them." Catt explained that the province had been a center of the revolution. When the provinces were permitted to set up provisional assemblies, the leaders in Kwantung [Guangdong] "decided to reserve ten seats . . . for women, and to permit women to elect them." In effect, Catt noted, "[u]niversal suffrage was temporarily established, men voting for the men members, and women for the women members." One of the elected women resigned under pressure from her family. While Catt characterized the remaining nine as "women of mature years and educated," she left out that two of them—Zhuang Hanqiao and Deng Huifang—had been in the Revolutionary Alliance's Explosives Section. Overall, Catt presented a glowing impression. The Chinese women representatives were "dignified, self-respecting, intelligent women, with an abiding faith in the new China and the coming emancipation of Chinese women."[99]

While Catt went to great lengths to stress the independence of the Asian woman's movement, she concluded her speech by describing the type of relationship she envisioned growing between Eastern and Western women. Very aware of the "suspicion" in the East "towards everything Western," she explicitly rejected the imperialist construct of the East and West. Clearly, it was undermining the building of bonds across borders. Instead of embracing Rudyard Kipling's "familiar verse" that "The East is East and West is West, And ne'ev shall this twain meet," Catt proposed that "the women of East and West have a common cause, a solidarity of interest," because they shared a common enemy—traditions that held back their "common liberation." After musing that she wished "we could put a protecting arm around these heroic women and save them from the cruel blows they are certain to receive," she recognized that this was not possible: "We can only help them to help themselves." They must fight their own struggles and "follow the vision in their souls," Catt remarked, "as we have done and as other women before us have done."[100]

Jacobs's role in Budapest was to introduce the Chinese suffragists, who were unable to attend but sought to become an auxiliary of the IWSA. She conveyed her discomfort in substituting her voice for theirs. It was "not an easy task." "Till the last moment," Jacobs "hoped that that some of the Chinese women themselves would be present here to tell . . . what nowadays is going on in the minds of the new women of new China." Unfortunately, according to Jacobs, "political troubles . . . probably prevent them from being here." So she turned to give her audience a vivid sense of what it was like to "know the Chinese women in their own country." She described the scenes that she and Catt witnessed: "Chinese women sitting in Parliament," and speaking "in crowded meetings to a mixed, enthusiastic audience with an eloquence none of us can surpass, about the miserable social position of the Chinese women." While Jacobs pointed to inequalities that shaped the lives of Chinese women, including the inadequate educational opportunities, especially higher education, and polygamy, she stressed their bravery and commitment to change. "And, still in every town we visited," Jacobs narrated, "we found young, bright, intelligent women with the same love for freedom as inspires us, who hunger after righteousness just as we do, and who devote not only all their money, but their entire life to the struggle for the improvement of the position of the women of their country."[101]

To bring the unfiltered voices of the Chinese suffragists to the Budapest audience, Jacobs presented the banner that they had given to Catt and herself. By "translating the words, which they embroidered upon this bright red satin," Jacobs said, "you will learn perhaps better what is going on in the minds of the new Chinese women than can be expressed by my words." Her translation was "The Mutual Helping Society to the International Alliance—Helping each other, all of one mind." The society was part of the coalition of groups that made up the Women's Suffrage Alliance (WSA) in China, initially started by the Chinese Socialist Party in November 1911. Jacobs interpreted the meaning to convey that the Chinese women wanted the IWSA's help and that the IWSA had gained "new sisters."[102] This interpretation was supported by the fifth original goal of the WSA: "make contacts with comrades in other countries for mutual support."[103] The phrasing also suggested the embedding of different national suffrage campaigns within an evolving transnational unity directed at achieving women's emancipation around the world.

By the time Jacobs and Catt presented their remarks in Budapest, they were filtering their descriptions of their enlightenment and joy at being present during a revolutionary moment through their knowledge that the repression of women's voices was occurring. Catt pointed to the provisional constitution of the national Chinese government and how it did not include equal rights, including women's suffrage. This constitution overturned women's suffrage and eligibility for office in the province the two had visited. Catt noted that "women appeared in considerable numbers to present their claim for a share in the new Republic."[104] She left out of her account how the women used force when they were denied presence during the writing of the provisional constitution.

According to historian Ono Kazuko, "The women protested and broke the glass windows, drenching their hands in fresh blood. The guards who tried to keep them from entering were kicked and knocked to the ground."[105] The Chinese suffragists closely followed the international suffrage movement, especially the militant English methods.[106] While Jacobs also left out their militancy, she reported, "[A]ll the leaders of the woman-movement know that their life is uncertain, and that any day the men may find a reason to silence them when their eloquence and their enthusiasm make too many converts."[107] By November, the national government would dissolve the WSA with its eleven branches; the following March, women's political activism in groups and campaigns would be forbidden.[108]

To accommodate the membership of the Chinese suffragists, the IWSA changed its requirements for admission. A new section of the constitution established that where it was not possible to sustain a suffrage organization, becoming an auxiliary could rest on having a committee of at least ten who were "forwarding the women's movement."[109] To place, in the historical record, "the first time an Eastern nation had been admitted into the Alliance," the congress enthusiastically adopted a resolution. It included the following sentiment: "A movement which can thus unite Eastern and Western women in one aspiration may be truly said to go to the roots of humanity."[110] This phrasing suggested the promise of a transnational organization like the IWSA. At its best, it could recast the notion and experience of humanity by bringing into relationship different contextualized and mutually supportive women's movements and thereby break through the ideological construct of East and West that justified Western hegemony. In the process, it could universalize the right to vote from the bottom up and thus further the embedding of the nation within a transnational aim to evolve human rights through the pursuit of women's rights.

Because the IWSA preceded the eruption of the late U.S. suffrage campaign, Catt was in a position to infuse it with transnational significance by seizing on the state-by-state victories to finesse the place of the United States within transnational suffragism. In Budapest, she made the case that "the largest gains" had been in the United States because five new states had enfranchised women—Arizona (1910), Washington (1910), California (1911), Kansas (1912), and Oregon (1912)—bringing the total to nine states. Catt measured the magnitude of "the victory" not by population but by territory covered, which was one-third of the nation. She claimed that "France, Germany, Great Britain, Austria, Hungary," and "the kingdom of Italy" would all fit within this land mass. Along with size, she stressed that the nine states were rich in "resources." Therefore, she concluded that "this vast section," with a current population of about eight million, including two million women, was "bound to take a conspicuous place in history."[111] In fact, Catt had helped create this history. Indeed, her path to leadership in both the NAWSA and IWSA began in the West in 1893 during the successful first state popular suffrage referendum in Colorado.[112]

The western state victories, according to Catt, were "a guarantee of ultimate woman suffrage for all the North American Continent." As suffrage spread to adjoining states, she argued that "[e]ach new victory had been an endorsement of the experiment already tested and proved." By demonstrating widespread support in the country, the nine states "will now exert the same influence on the remainder of the United States." If she needed further proof of the spread beyond the West, news came during the congress of the victory in the Illinois legislature. Yet Catt did not stop with her vision of a complete U.S. victory; she also claimed that the nine states "will now collectively exert the same influence . . . upon their neighbouring nations."[113] In this way, Catt demonstrated how the United States was contributing to universalizing the right to vote from the bottom up.

Representing the western United States, specifically California, Maud Younger (1870–1936) brought to Budapest the tangible results of women voting. She prefaced her remarks by commenting that enfranchised women "had been able to achieve more in 20 months of voting than in the past 20 years of influence." For examples, she pointed to the passage of a mothers' pension bill, a law that "raised the age of consent from 16 to 18," and "humane laws for the treatment of prisoners and the insane." She concluded by suggesting that exercising the vote was also transforming women.[114]

Yet the anti-Asian racist dimension of Younger's suffragism complicated the bottom-up model of evolving transnational human rights. Her California experience exposed the tensions between the subnational, national, and transnational levels. In contrast to Catt and Jacobs, who awakened to the damaging effects of the East-West ideological construct for universalizing women's voting rights, Younger had participated in California's 1911 state suffrage campaign to mobilize trade unionist men and women in San Francisco, based partially on the denigration and persecution of Asian workers.[115] Thus, Younger's political evolution revealed the complexity of creating a new transnationalism based on the metaphor of concentric circles, according to which the transnational surrounds and completes the national.

Born to affluence in San Francisco, Younger became a trade unionist and a defender of the vote for working-class women. Her radicalization began in New York City, where, starting in 1901, she experienced settlement house life at College Settlement, located in the Lower East Side. She also joined the NYWTUL and became an organizer of waitresses, working as one herself to understand the working conditions. Returning to San Francisco after the 1906 earthquake, she was elected president of Waitresses' Local 48 in 1908. In 1911, after the California legislature agreed to let the men of the state vote on women's suffrage but before the election, Younger worked to pass an eight-hour workday for women. The California sex-based labor law built on the successful NCL legal strategy in *Muller*.[116] So Younger appeared to fit within the egalitarian suffrage tradition as a bridger of labor and feminist movements to advance social justice.

Yet in one fundamental area—race relations—Younger did not represent the aspirations of the egalitarian suffragist bridgers presented in Chapter 2. She operated within San Francisco labor union politics, which was built on a strong defense of the national Chinese Exclusion Act of 1882 and the stigmatization of Asian workers. Her bridging of movements reflected this politics of intolerance and prejudice, revealing that bridging was not inherently emancipatory unless it was explicitly anti-racist. At the 1909 national WTUL convention in Chicago, the conflict between the western U.S. version of social justice without Asian workers and the eastern U.S. understanding of brotherhood emerged. Louise LaRue, secretary of Local 48 and a close ally of Younger's, presented a resolution in support of extending the federal exclusion law to include all Asians. She said the resolution came from the laundry workers' union with the support of the San Francisco Labor Council. Schneiderman, according to Orleck, "rose to deliver a blistering denunciation of racism." She declared, "The movement we stand for is the brotherhood of man, and we are not going to exclude certain people from that brotherhood on the account of color, degree, or caste." The WTUL convention voted down the resolution.[117]

In Budapest, Addams's presence symbolized the embedding of her local, state, and national stream of egalitarian suffragism within the evolution of a transnational human right to vote. She came away from Budapest with the impression that "the movement for equal suffrage was growing, pushing and developing in all the countries upon the face of the earth, that the coming together of its representatives was no perfunctory matter, but the free exchange of genuine experiences and untrammeled hopes." She characterized the movement as "both amorphous and sporadic, or carefully organized and consciously directed, but it was always vital and constantly becoming more widespread."[118] The IWSA illustrated Addams's call for embodying humanity by forging new relationships across differences and for approaching rights not as natural but as coming out of struggles.[119] The transnational feminists continued the struggle for human rights as women's rights when Jacobs took the initiative to replace the cancelled 1915 Berlin IWSA Congress, due to the war, with a meeting in The Hague. It wove together the pursuit of a transnational commitment to women's political rights with the aim of devising "methods of bringing about the peace."[120]

By re-viewing the earlier chapters through a transnational lens, I showed that the social democratic feminists had a multileveled understanding of their refounding moment from the beginning. Taken together, the three prewar cases showed them working to shape a new humanitarian transnational level that could surround and complete their version of social democracy at the national level. To find a substitute for U.S. militarism, for example, Addams theorized how the practices of mutual aid and labor solidarity by her diverse immigrant working-class neighbors constituted a new type of feminized nourishing internationalism that the United States should extend into the world. Kelley generated transnational knowledge of working conditions and labor legislation to strengthen the case for such legislation within the United States. By explicitly including women in their concept of human rights, the IWSA initiated "a new stage in the history of human rights" that would come to full fruition with the Universal Declaration of Human Rights.[121] Ultimately, their prewar intersectional activism and their theorizing of it prepared the social democratic feminists to take on the challenge, during and after the war, to interweave their refounding moment with the reconstruction of the postwar world.

Acting on the Transnational Level during War

When Jacobs got a positive response from individual suffragists who, in the midst of war, agreed to attend the ICW, she initiated an experiment with a new type of feminist transnational participatory socializing space that could support a new practice of women's transnational political agency. Meeting from April 28 to May 1, 1915, in The Hague, the transnational feminists came from twelve different nations. At their 1919 congress in Zurich, they adopted the name Women's International League for Peace and Freedom. I cannot do justice to the 1915 meeting, its courageous participants, or WILPF's evolution.[122] Instead, I foreground the role of intersectional activism in shaping the early WILPF congresses. By applying the theory-activist dynamic, I interpret them as pragmatist nonstrategic experiments in a new type of transnational relations that put into practice the emancipatory potential of women's past experiences. To make the case for this interpretation, I draw on Addams's reflections.

As in her theorizing of Hull House's nonstrategic experiments, Addams began her analysis of the ICW with a search for a past experience of women from which she could extract an emancipatory potential. The war context made it clear to her that any essentialist notion of women as maternal pacifists would not work. As she asserted, after traveling in war zones, "the majority of women as well as men in the nations at war doubtless" believed that the "war is inevitable and righteous." The most Addams was willing to claim for "women, who brought men into the world and nurtured them until they reach the age for fighting," was that they "must experience a peculiar revulsion when they see them destroyed, irrespective of the country" in which they were born. For evidence, she recounted conversations with a small subset of women "who sent their sons and husbands into the war, having themselves ceased to believe in it."[123] Clearly, revulsion provided a tenuous basis for generating an emancipatory potential.

Instead, by weaving evolutionary theory into her pragmatist method,[124] Addams turned to "deep-set racial impulses," such as "those primitive human urgings to foster life and to protect the helpless of which women were the earliest custodians and even those social and gregarious instincts that we share with the animals themselves." So modern women, socialized to accept a militarized version of nationalism, could not be counted on to oppose war or embrace solidarity across borders. Instead, uprooting and replanting kernels of those primitive urgings in receptive environments held out the promise of actualizing a new experience of embodied humanity. Indeed, Addams proposed that "[t]hese universal desires must be given opportunities to expand and to have a recognized place in the formal organization of international relations which up to this moment have rested so exclusively upon purely legal foundations in spite of the fact that international law is comparatively undeveloped."[125] By 1921, as she walked through the rose garden of WILPF's international office in Geneva, "a charming old house," Addams conjectured "that we might be profoundly grateful if our organization was able in any degree to push forward the purposes of the League of Nations and to make its meaning clearer."[126]

To understand how WILPF evolved into an organization that could play such a role, it is critical to understand how intersectional activism shaped WILPF's original aim of creating an experimental transnational socializing space. All participants at The Hague were required to accept two "fundamental planks": "international disputes should be settled by pacific means," and "the Parliamentary franchise should be extended to women."[127] In her address of welcome, Jacobs defended this aim of bridging movements because some peace activists did not think suffrage belonged on the program. Jacobs insisted that the organizers "never called it a *peace* congress." Instead, they proposed "an international Congress of women to protest against the war, and to discuss ways and means whereby war shall become an impossibility in the future."[128]

Then Jacobs went on to interconnect equal political power for women and the uprooting of the causes of war by making explicit the underlying assumption of the ICW: "[T]he introduction of woman suffrage in all countries is one of the most powerful means to prevent war in the future." As Jacobs insisted, "Not until women can bring direct influence to bear upon Governments, not until in the parliaments the voice of the women is heard mingling with that of men, shall we have the power to prevent recurrence of such catastro-phes."[129] Here Jacobs went beyond the right to vote to the necessity of wom-en's equal presence in legislative bodies.

In making her case, Jacobs asserted that "women judge war differently from men."[130] Resolution two passed by the ICW elaborated on why this might be the case: "This International Congress of Women opposes the assumption that women can be protected under the conditions of modern warfare. It pro-tests vehemently against the odious wrongs of which women are the victims in time of war, and especially against the horrible violation of women which attends all war."[131] The imperative to give voice to women's different experi-ence of war, including sexual assault, certainly supported Jacob's conclusion that "[t]herefore on a programme of the conditions whereby wars in future may be avoided, the question of woman suffrage should not be lacking, on the contrary, it should have the foremost place."[132] Resolution nine turned Jacobs's reasoning for foregrounding women's "political enfranchisement" into one of the five principles of justice on which ICW's notion of permanent peace was based.[133]

By declaring themselves bridgers, the women who met at The Hague cre-ated an audacious political act intended to prove the power of the deed. In proposing the 1915 ICW, Jacobs stressed the importance of physically meet-ing in public: "[J]ust because there is this terrible war the women *must* come together somewhere, some way, just to show that women of all countries can work together even in the face of the greatest war in the world. Women must show that when all Europe seems full of hatred, they remain united."[134] An-other formulator of the ICW, Lida Gustava Heymann (1868–1943), a German suffragist and an advocate for decriminalizing prostitution, explicitly used the language of deed: "To protest not only with words, but with deeds; and this Congress was a deed."[135]

After the war, Addams reflected on WILPF's use of deeds to change think-ing: "The members of the Woman's International League for Peace and Free-dom had certainly learned from their experience during the war that widely accepted ideas can be both dominating and all powerful. But we still believed it possible to modify, to direct and ultimately to change current ideas, not only through discussion and careful presentation of facts, but also through pro-paganda of the deed."[136] Addams used "propaganda" here to refer to propa-gating new ideas.

Emily Balch (1867–1961), professor of economics and sociology at Welles-ley College, resident of Denison House Settlement in Boston, an WTUL activist, and living in a neutral country, captured the heady excitement their coming together produced. As she wrote, "What stands out most strongly among all my impressions of those thrilling and strained days at The Hague is the sense of the wonder of the beautiful spirit of the brave, self-controlled women who dared ridicule and every sort of difficulty to express a passionate human sympathy, not inconsistent with patriotism, but transcending it." All the participants, according to Balch, shared "the same moving consciousness of the development of a new spirit which is growing in the midst of the war as the roots of the wheat grow under the drifts and tempests of winter."[137] Writing from Munich, Heymann offered her reflections on the meaning of the ICW for the participants: "The Hague gave fresh courage for new activity."[138]

The ICW as deed actualized the emancipatory potential of women's primitive urgings by channeling them into a new experience of embodied humanity. It provided the basis for an intersectional rethinking of the method for reconstituting international relations. The construction of the twenty abstract resolutions adopted in 1915 showed how the bridgers wove women's equal political presence into rethinking international relations. For example, under "Principles of a Permanent Peace," the ICW adopted and provided its intersectional reinterpretation of the very influential phrase, "democratic control of foreign policy." Formed in England at the start of the war, the Union of Democratic Control (UDC) initially defined this notion as calling for the replacement of "secret diplomacy" with "parliamentary control over foreign policy."[139] Helena Swanwick (1864–1939), the first woman on the UDC's executive board, brought the concept to the ICW. In its resolution, the ICW "urges that Foreign Politics shall be subject to Democratic Control; and declares that it can only recognize as democratic a system which includes the equal representation of men and women."[140] Sophonisba Breckinridge (1866–1948), Hull House resident and professor at the University of Chicago, inserted this clause.[141] Her use of "equal representation" suggested that the aim was to have equal numbers of women and men participating in parliamentary debates over foreign policy.

Under the theme of "International Cooperation," the ICW provided another example of intersectional rethinking. The ICW called for "a permanent International Conference, holding regular meetings in which women should take part, to deal not with the rules of warfare but with *practical proposals* [my emphasis] for further International Cooperation among the States."[142] This phrasing is significant because it suggested a shift away from a purely legalistic and masculine method of carrying out international relations to a new feminized social service orientation. The ICW went further by proposing a multileveled vision of women's political agency in resolution fifteen: "[I]t to be essential both nationally and internationally to put into practice the principle that women should share all civil and political rights and responsibilities on the same terms as men."[143] Clearly, those responsibilities included playing a significant role in shaping a postwar association of nations to evolve a new humanitarian transnationalism.

While intersectional activism shaped the aim of the 1915 ICW and guided its rethinking of democracy and international relations, its impact would not have been possible without the bridgers adopting a procedural rule.[144] Scottish suffragist Chrystal MacMillan (1872–1937) defined the necessary "general rule of debate" as "discussion on the relative national responsibility for or conduct of the present war should be outside the scope of the Congress."[145] So the ongoing war was to be left outside the meeting rooms. The French suffragists did not attend the ICW. They protested the rule and sent their own manifesto, which was not read at the ICW but was published in the formal report alongside Addams's response.

In contrast, two Belgian suffragists, who helped to conceptualize the ICW, attended. They had to get permission from the occupying German officials to participate and arrived late, to a warm welcome. "A moment of great interest," Addams recounted, "was the entrance of the two Belgian delegates, who shook hands with the German delegation before they took their places beside them on the platform, dedicated to 'a passionate human sympathy, not inconsistent with patriotism, but transcending it.'"[146] Here Addams was quoting, without attribution, Balch's words. Addams's image of delegates from warring countries sitting side by side followed her description of the rule of debate. The juxtaposition suggested that the rule was absolutely necessary because it clarified the purpose of the deed: By coming together, women from neutral and warring nations could construct a program on how to rebuild the postwar world.

To further demonstrate women's transnational political agency, the ICW put in motion a second deed by adopting an "action to be taken" resolution proposed by Rosika Schwimmer (1877–1948), a Jewish Hungarian suffragist who was active in the IWSA and had traveled to the United States to mobilize women to protest the war. Her intersectional activism helped motivate the formation of the Woman's Peace Party (WPP), which was well represented at the ICW. The resolution "delegate[d] envoys to carry the message expressed in the Congress of Women to the rulers of the belligerent and neutral nations of Europe and to the President of the United States."[147] Addams and Jacobs, accompanied by Hamilton, were dispatched to the countries at war; Balch, Schwimmer, and MacMillan were sent to the neutral countries. "As women," Addams argued, "it was possible for us, from belligerent and neutral nations alike, to carry forward an interchange of question and answer between capitals which were barred to each other."[148] During May and June, the prime ministers, foreign ministers, and presidents of fourteen countries received the envoys.

Both deeds created new experiences of women acting during war to keep alive the hope of the transnational that surrounds and completes the national. Addams drew out the precise meaning of the new experiences. On one level, their deeds subverted the wartime reinforcement of "the obsolete division between the lives of men and women." As Addams characterized this division, "The man bold, combative, conquering; woman sympathetic, healing the wounds that war has made."[149] Clearly, the ICW was not a nursing brigade or a charity. Through the delegations, ICW members modeled new roles as public diplomats in the midst of war. Addams reported that after Wilson "studied the resolutions," he "consider[ed] them by far the best formulation which up to the moment has been put out by any body." While Addams admitted there was no way of knowing "how much influence [on Wilson] they may have had upon the 'Fourteen Points,'" clearly she used this example to show that the ICW was a transnational political actor.[150]

On a second level, their deeds prefigured the role women could play in the postwar peacemaking negotiations. According to Addams, women's "organized and formal" presence in the reconstruction process would provide a force for uprooting the causes of war so that the new transnational governmental bodies could actualize a new humanitarianism. Women would play this role because their political revolution, as Addams had shown, was tied to the changing understanding of the purpose of government.[151] To strengthen the case for including "women's voice in the peace settlement," the ICW included, in its resolutions, a second "action to be taken": The ICW will convene a conference at the same time and the same place as the formal Peace Conference "for the purpose of presenting practical proposals."[152]

Acting on the Transnational Level during the Armistice and Peacemaking

WILPF's 1919 Zurich Congress continued its tradition of utilizing propaganda of the deed. It met in Zurich because initially the official Paris Peace Conference did not invite the Central Powers to participate. As in 1915, during the 1919 armistice and peacemaking phases, WILPF planned to bring together women from neutral and warring countries. Although the transnational feminists received criticism, according to Addams, for "holding an international Congress so soon after the war," they persisted because they knew that a deed was necessary to provoke a new way of thinking about cross-border relations. Otherwise, the old diplomacy, focused on underdeveloped international law and treaties, would dominate.[153]

By adopting the new name, Women's International League for Peace and Freedom, the transnational bridgers reaffirmed their commitment to intersectional activism by stating that their purpose was to interconnect women's freedom and permanent peace. Heymann, who became WILPF's international vice president, offered her interpretation: "Our name alone is a program."[154] WILPF defined this program by shifting from the wartime formulation of abstract principles to the peacemaking period of crafting practical proposals. I show how this shift required WILPF to evolve its experimental transnational participatory social space by adding a new procedural rule and embracing a new type of postwar fellowship. Specifically, I focus on WILPF's protests of the militarized use of food—or "bread," to use Addams's term. By applying the theory-activist dynamic, I interpret how Addams theorized the protests to support her political concept of nourishing, first introduced in her anti-imperialist writings.

The Zurich Congress formulated a new procedural rule to make deliberation during the peacemaking phase possible among bridgers from belligerent nations. The English summary reported that a "tradition" began in WILPF "that if a wrong has been done, it should be the section belonging to the country which does the wrong that should appeal for right." Following this rule, the German delegates "denounced the invasion of Belgium," while the delegates from Allied nations "denounced the blockade and the injustices of the Peace Treaty." Historian Jo Vellacott uses these quotes to illustrate "the determination to move beyond national interest"[155] by achieving a consensus on this rule. In her 1924 brief history of WILPF, Heymann presented a multileveled interpretation: "[E]ach member felt responsible not only for her own nation, but for the whole world. Those who feel such responsibility never say, 'My country, right or wrong,' but are always ready to criticize their own country or their own government when it is wrong."[156] From the perspective of deliberative democracy, I interpret this rule as giving the bridgers a way to talk about the injustices of the war to build bonds of trust within WILPF. As a result of this rule, WILPF modeled a type of deliberation that built truth telling into intersectional activism.[157]

Yet even this new procedure was not sufficient during the armistice without the flourishing of what Addams characterized as "a new fellowship."[158] In her Zurich presidential addresses, she theorized how it was rooted in a common experience. Significantly, the experience was not of physical depravation or personal loss of loved ones. While Addams's oldest nephew died fighting, clearly the U.S. delegation had not suffered to the same extent as their European sisters. Yet I think there is another reason Addams went in a different direction. She wanted to characterize WILPF women as courageous political actors. Therefore, Addams argued that their new fellowship came out of their experiences of being public or political pacifists in a time of war. Because the delegates held "to their principles," and went against public opinion and their governments, which was not easy, according to Addams, they had "similar experiences with governmental espionage and control as to demonstrate without doubt that the war methods are identical in all nations."[159]

As delegate testimonials revealed, these methods included imprisonment and being followed by the police.[160]

Addams explicitly connected the common experience of wartime political repression to WILPF's capacity to provide a vibrant transnational participatory social space conducive to deliberation. As a result of the shared experience, the 1919 delegations were "like-minded" across borders. They proposed similar resolutions to be discussed.[161] "[S]ecure in their sense of good-will and mutual understanding," the participants "spoke freely."[162] Out of the resulting "sisterhood and comradeship,"[163] the delegates protested to reshape the peace treaty and the purpose of the LON.

Toward a Political Notion of Nourishing

In her second presidential address, Addams viewed these protests as deeds through her pragmatist experimental method. She began with women's basic primitive experience of "the desire to feed their children." Then she conjectured about the possibility of transplanting the emancipatory potential of this experience in new transnational relations and institutions that could bring the world together to tackle the problem of postwar hunger. Success at this effort, Addams argued, depended on both "adequate international transportation of food" and "the feeling that the value of the life of one child is as great as the value of the life of another child." For WILPF to hasten this humanitarian turn in international relations, Addams threw out a challenge: "Is this Conference of Women willing to begin with these primitive obligations and needs?"[164]

To clarify that she viewed WILPF's purpose as an effort to redirect transnational politics to achieve a lasting peace, she turned to discrediting the depiction of women's gendered postwar role. "Your Swiss papers have said, as many others have said, that women must keep close to these human obligations, and allow politics to be attended to, they all imply, by men." Addams responded, "And yet women, I think, can well retort that the present situation of the world is not altogether to the credit of men."[165] Here she illustrated how Zurich was building on the 1915 intersectional aim of interconnecting feminist and peace movements. In her history of WILPF, Heymann asserted that the delegates to The Hague "did not ask for political rights, for participation in political life, merely in order to continue the style of politics which men had introduced into the world." Instead, "[t]hey wished to change politics" by demonstrating a new understanding of how to imbed nationalism within a new humanitarian transnationalism.[166]

WILPF's protest put alleviating the postwar famine at the center of the new direction. In her narrative, Addams introduced the theme by utilizing her Hull House understanding of fellowship as a walking together through the streets of a city. In this case, the walk brought into relationship two women who had lived in warring nations. Addams admitted to the potential discomfort of meeting up with a WILPF member from an enemy country. As she explained, "[I]nevitably we felt a certain restraint—self-consciousness." When she "turned a corner and suddenly met" an obviously very ill Austrian comrade, probably Leopoldine Kulka (1872–1920), a Jewish writer, all of Addams's anticipated awkwardness fell away. They "spoke of the coming Congress" and how it would give "a demonstration that a few women were to be found in each country who could not brook that such a state of affairs should go unchallenged." Addams here was referring to "the subject of procuring food" for the hungry during the armistice period.[167]

The impact of food depravation and other hardships was present in the faces of the delegates to the Zurich Congress. Therefore, this second congress's deed continued the tradition of using the physical presence of the women to provoke new thinking about how to rebuild the world. As one journalist reported, "Thus nearly all the delegates from the Central Powers showed the strain of under feeding. On the one hand they were nervous and excitable, on the other dull and slow to keep abreast of events."[168] Clearly, WILPF's protest as deed sent a compelling message: Women who experienced starvation should be present at the formal peacemaking table to make the case for the urgency of solving the hunger problem to heal cross-border relations after the war. Not only were they not present, but according to a "close observer" of Paris 1919, as reported by Addams, "it was an extraordinary fact that starving Europe was the one subject upon which it had been impossible to engage the attention of the 'big four' throughout their long deliberations."[169]

According to Addams, the first resolution of the 1919 Zurich Congress was on famine and the blockade of German ports. The Allies continued the blockade on trade until July 1919 to pressure the Germans into agreeing to the terms of the peace treaty. Emmeline Pethick Lawrence (1867–1954) from the English delegation introduced the resolution. It called on the key actors in Paris "to develop" the structures of inter-Allied cooperation created for "the purposes of war into an international organization for the purposes of peace, so that the resources of the world—food, raw materials, finance, transport—shall be made available for the relief of the peoples of all countries from famine and pestilence."[170] Thus, WILPF's vision for postwar rebuilding went beyond private charity to the formation of a new transnational governmental structure that would regulate the global provisioning for basic human needs.

To encourage this development, WILPF urged a number of "immediate" actions, starting with an end to the blockade. "If there is insufficiency of food or transport," WILPF called for "prohibit[ing] the use of transport" across borders for "the conveyance of luxuries until the necessaries of life are supplied to all peoples." To achieve this end, WILPF proposed a system of rationing "the people of every country so that the starving may be fed." In short, WILPF repudiated the use of food as a tool for coercing agreement to the terms of the peace treaty. Instead, WILPF advocated the "immediate" provisioning of food to those in need by "international action" as the "only" way to "save humanity and bring about the permanent reconciliation and union of the peoples."[171] There was an exchange of telegrams with Paris on the subject of WILPF's resolution. Wilson's "prompt reply" was shared with the WILPF Congress. According to Addams, he "expressed sympathy with our famine resolution, and regret that the Paris Conference could not act upon its suggestions."[172]

When the food blockade was extended to Russia and a very short-lived "soviet regime in Hungary," Addams reported that WILPF "made a first protest against this unfair use of the newly formulated knowledge of the world's food supply and of a centralized method for distribution." WILPF held out the hope that the LON would utilize this knowledge to support the spread of self-government. Instead, the official Paris Peace Conference tied food provisioning to the "sinister" aim of provoking regime change. According to Addams, the two Hungarian delegates to the Zurich Congress had opposing views of the Hungarian soviet regime, "but they both felt hotly against the blockade which had been instituted against Hungary as an attempt to settle the question of form of government through the starvation of the people."[173] Taken together, the two protests as deeds demonstrated, for Addams, "the inevitability of the relationship" between "peace and bread."[174]

This pairing was at the heart of Addams's theorizing what I am calling a political notion of nourishing. I view this concept as her effort to create a substitute for "the political concepts of the 18th century." They might have been "abstractly noble," she reasoned, but they were not up to the task of addressing "the social conditions" of the postwar world. According to Addams, they did not "evoke a human motive transcending and yet embracing all particular nationalisms."[175] To correct this inadequacy, Addams turned to the "need to feed the hungry" to provide "a great controlling motive in the world at the present moment, as political democracy, as religious freedom, had moved the world at other times."[176]

In her early anti-imperialist writings, Addams had argued for substituting labor that nourished life for militarized imperialist actions. She had gendered the distinction based on her interpretation of history: Women created the food; men hunted. Addams rooted her substitute in the bridging of anti-imperialist and labor movements. At the time, she had no women's movement to weave into the mix. During the war, she tried to enlarge the bridging to include the white women's club movement by narrowing her focus to food, or "bread," labor.

Once the United States got into the war and established the Department of Food Administration (DFA), Addams became a speaker for the public effort to conserve food. The campaign popularized the public kitchen, feminist domestic sciences, and even the term "common table," all of which had played a part in the Hull House experiment with neighborhood food provisioning.[177] The DFA provided food for the inter-Allied program to feed soldiers and civilians in war zones. Addams theorized this unique transnational program as an experiment in the feminization of international relations. For her, it embodied, in a governmental program, the emancipatory potential of women's primitive bread labor.

Interpreting women's gendered role through history and traditional myths, Addams linked feminine to the "human use" value of food and masculine to the exchange or "moneymaking value" of food. As she narrated, "We are told that when the crops of grain and roots so painstakingly produced by primitive women began to have a commercial value their production and exchange were taken over by men."[178] In effect, the Allied food program feminized cross-border relations because "the motive for producing and shipping food . . . was no longer a commercial one but had for the moment shifted to a desire to feed hungry people." As she explained, "Commercial competition had been suppressed, not in response to any theory, but because it could not be trusted to feed the feeble and helpless."[179]

Addams's presentation of this new transnational governmental program stressed its humanitarian dimensions. She also linked it to the changing nature of the purpose of government and how women's political agency was required if the purpose of government was to feed the hungry. Therefore, she sought out women's groups for her DFA talks so she could challenge them to interconnect their daily bread labor with the goal of providing for the world's need for food. She envisioned them building support for a postwar permanent transnational governmental regulation of this basic human need.[180]

Looking back at her attempt to persuade the General Federation of Women's Clubs to embrace her vision, Addams admitted being "disappointed."[181] She had hoped she could use women's gendered history with bread labor to "break through into more primitive and compelling motives than those inducing so many women to increase their war spirit."[182] Clearly, Addams was hoping to persuade middle-class white women to embrace the contradiction between food provisioning and war. The audience that was receptive to Addams's argument that the "obligation to feed the world . . . was incompatible with warfare" was, of course, WILPF.[183]

WILPF's receptivity illustrated how intersectional activism unfolded in a transnational participatory socializing space to support new intersectional thinking. WILPF's protests as deeds created new experiences of women exerting their political agency to establish a clear demarcation between the militarized use of food and the transnational coordination of food provisioning to feed the hungry. Addams saw the latter as a first step to creating a new postwar humanitarian transnational level that could surround and complete the demilitarization of the national level. Moreover, WILPF's protest on the militarized use of food for regime change in Hungary provided Addams with a specific example of her early double use of nourishing. WILPF's discussion among Hungarian delegates on different political sides revealed that nourishing as providing food and nourishing as growing different varieties of self-government were interconnected. Thus, WILPF's protests as deeds provided the experiential grounding that Addams had lacked to theorize a political notion of nourishing that interconnected peace and bread.

In her closing presidential address at Zurich, Addams emphasized both the centrality of feeding the hungry across enemy lines and the importance of the 1919 WILPF Congress as a deed. She praised the capacity of the delegates to create the transnational socializing space that facilitated their deliberations, shaped by "genuine friendship and understanding." Inspired, Addams declared, "If it can be done in small groups, then it can be done on a larger scale."[184] By the 1921 Vienna Congress, Addams reported that the delegations of women were "sorely disillusioned by their experiences during the two years of peace." Yet according to Addams, they shared one conclusion: "They all alike had come to realize that every crusade, every beginning of social change, must start from small numbers of people convinced of the righteousness of a cause; that the coming together of convinced groups is a natural process of growth."[185] I would add that both intentional intersectional activism and thinking were essential to realizing this hopeful potentiality.

Intersectional Conversation: Use of Colonial Soldiers in Military Occupations

At the Zurich Congress, Terrell reshaped WILPF's intersectional aims to include the movement for racial justice. As part of the U.S. delegation, Terrell guided WILPF in this direction with a resolution: "We believe no human being should be deprived of an education, prevented from earning a living, debarred from any legitimate pursuit in which he wishes to engage or to be subjected to humiliation of various kinds on account of race, color or creed."[186] In her speech, delivered in German, Terrell "expressed regret" that the Paris Peace Conference refused to adopt an antidiscrimination resolution proposed by the Japanese to protect foreign nationals. It read, "The equality of nations being a basic principle of the League of Nations, the High Contracting Parties agree to accord, as soon as possible, to all alien nationals of States members of the League equal and just treatment in every respect, making no distinction, either in law or in fact, on account of their race or nationality."[187] To her WILPF audience, as the only woman of color present, Terrell "appealed for justice and fair play for all the dark races of the earth." Specifically, she bridged racial justice and peace movements by declaring, "You may talk about permanent peace till dooms-day, but the world will never have it till the dark races are given a square deal."[188]

Terrell set the stage for WILFP members to model a type of deliberation appropriate for crossing racial borders to develop the transnational that surrounds and completes the national. To make visible their model, I construct two intersectional conversations. The theoretical and interpretive challenges differ from earlier chapters because each transpired within one organization, WILPF. Both foreground the role of African American bridgers and demonstrate clearly how their presence and unbracketing of power dynamics within WILPF was necessary to complicate the conversation so that the participates could shape new intersectional analyses of permanent peace with racial justice. Therefore, these intersectional conversations come closest to illustrating the dynamics of the ideal type. The evolution from the first to the second conversation also provides evidence for historian Joyce Blackwell's characterization of WILPF as being "in the vanguard in race relations" because "some of its black and white members were determined to work together despite pervasive racism and racial indifference in America."[189]

Without Terrell's determination to reframe the issue for her white-privileged sisters in the U.S. section of WILPF, there would have been no intersectional conversation on where WILPF stood on the issue of the military use of colonized men.[190] To get their attention, she unbracketed the power dynamics within WILPF by using the tool of the less powerful in an organization. Like Schneiderman, when she was discontented with the anti-immigrant direction of the NYWTUL, in a March 18, 1921, letter to Addams, Terrell volunteered to resign from the executive board where she was "the only colored member." She had been asked to make it unanimous that the section would protest the French use of its colonial troops in the occupation of the Rhineland. Germany had claimed that the black troops were sexually assaulting white women. As Terrell explained in her autobiography, her grievance was not that the members were acting out of "race prejudice." She "knew" that her white-privileged sisters were motivated by wanting to end the occupation, which was created by the peace agreement.[191] As a result, they were focused only on the cross-border tension between France and Germany and its implications for undermining permanent peace.

To get them to see the white supremacist implications of the petition, Terrell stressed to Addams that the claims of the propaganda campaign directed at a U.S. audience were untrue. She reported on Catt's investigations through German members of the IWSA. "The propaganda against the black troops,"

Terrell argued, "is simply another violent and plausible appeal to race prejudice."[192] Addams would have known that Terrell here was making the connection between the false rape excuse to justify the lynching of African American men in the United States and the claims of Germany about the French African occupiers. Terrell's point was that if WILPF gave legitimacy to the German campaign, it could lead to more racially motivated violence in the United States.

Moreover, the Germans were using the assumptions of racialized sexual politics to get WILPF to put pressure on the French government. As Terrell reminded Addams, "Charges are usually preferred against soldiers of all races who are quartered in the land they have conquered."[193] The German campaign was relying on the "race prejudice" of the American people. Terrell's reflections suggested that the actualization of Addams's vision of embodied humanity required the expunging of the racial caste system supported by racialized sexual politics from both the national and the transnational levels.

To achieve this end, Terrell's reflections called for WILPF to enlarge its notion of violence against women by developing an intersectional analysis. In 1915, the ICW had issued a protest against "the horrible violation of women which attends all war."[194] Then the German campaign expanded WILPF's understanding to include the lack of protection for women under military occupations once the fighting ends. For women who were suffering sexual assault under either condition, Terrell expressed deep sympathy. To explain why sexual assault was a painful topic for her, she pointed to the history of African American women: "I belong to a race whose women have been the victims of assaults committed upon them by men of all races. As a rule, these men have ruined and wrecked the women of my race with impunity."[195]

Placing herself within the context of the history of slavery and its legacy allowed Terrell to make the connection for Addams between the practices of racialized sexual politics within and outside the United States. She pointed to reports on the behavior of soldiers during the U.S. occupation of Haiti, which Terrell knew Addams and WILPF opposed. As Terrell noted, "[I]t is not at all difficult for me to believe that white Americans would treat colored women as brutally as our soldiers are said to have treated Haitian women."[196] By linking behavior in Haiti to behavior within the United States, Terrell was encouraging Addams and WILPF to interconnect the contexts of wars and occupations with the daily lives of African American women. Otherwise, WILPF would not be able to fully understand how racialized sexual violence undermined the goal of permanent peace.

Terrell achieved her aim to squash the petition. In a short letter dated March 29, 1921, Addams declared, "I . . . came to exactly the same conclusion which you have reached—that we should protest against the occupation of enemy territory—not against any special troops."[197] By shifting the focus to the creation of a transnational norm that delegitimized militarized occupations, Addams bypassed the topic of racialized sexual politics. Presumably, if there were no occupations, sexual assaults perpetrated by the occupiers would cease. Yet the intersectional conversation did not end with this exchange of letters.

At the July 10–17, 1921, Vienna Congress, Balch continued the conversation in her defense of the following resolution: "Resolved that this League make every possible effort to oppose the military use of 'native' populations."[198] Germany's propaganda campaign and Terrell's intervention had forced WILPF to deepen its understanding of the relationship between colonial imperialism and war. Balch asserted that imperialists sought political and military control of foreign territory because a colonized people represented a supply of soldiers. Therefore, imperialists went to war over territory because of their need for more and more fighters.

In sharp contrast to the German propaganda campaign, Balch opened her analysis by engaging in some reflections on the domestic dimensions of empire. She characterized the practice of using colonized men in European wars as "the outrageous wrong done to the soldiers and their families." The men were torn "from their homes and from all women of their own race."[199] She went on to compare their forced conscription to chattel slavery. With these brief remarks, Balch built her defense of the resolution on a critique of the exploitation of colonized men, which included destabilizing their domestic lives.

In a "subsequent note," Balch returned to the controversy that provoked Terrell's letter of resignation. Balch declared that she had "purposely avoided other questions involved in the use of coloured troops in occupied districts." Her reasoning was that "these questions are of quite a different order and complicate the issue." Echoing Terrell, she expressed sympathy for women in the occupied territory who had been "actually" assaulted. Balch also expressed sympathy for Terrell and others who felt the campaign to remove French colonial troops was "a studied insult." Yet Balch did not unmask the propaganda campaign as untrue. She also did not point to the history of sexual assault by *all* occupying forces. Instead, she concluded that the whole incident had undermined "the path of friendship and mutual respect between the races."[200] Presumably, she was referring to the tension that emerged within WILPF as well as between races outside of WILPF. Thus, while Balch was unable or unwilling to complicate her economic and political analysis of the military use of colonized men by weaving in racialized sexual politics, she did reaffirm WILPF's commitment to pursuing interracial fellowship.

As if to reinforce this theme and show how interracial fellowship rested on foregrounding African American women's intersectional analyses, Addams followed up Balch's remarks by introducing Helen Curtis into the intersectional conversation. She was a widow whose husband had been the U.S. minister to Liberia from 1915 to 1917. Since Liberia was not a French colony, it is unclear how much experience she had with African colonial soldiers. She definitely had experience with the racially segregated U.S. military. Curtis was the first African American woman allowed to sail from New York City in 1918 to provide social services through the YMCA for African American soldiers in France. Prior to her appearance in Vienna, Curtis had also participated in the postwar African American women's crusade against lynching.[201] After the WILPF Congress, she would attend the Pan-African Congress (PAC), where she was one of the few women to deliver a speech.

As summarized in the WILPF Congress report, her brief remarks make sense only if she was describing the treatment of African American soldiers by the U.S. military. Her observations extended Terrell's theme of racialized sexual politics and how it played out in militarized zones. Curtis reported that the men complained "that they were not allowed to speak to a white woman." According to Hunton and Johnson, both of whom joined Curtis in France, this was an explicit policy of the United States, not France.[202] With only the option of "visiting public houses," the soldiers were exposed to sexually transmitted diseases. Finally, Curtis assured her WILPF audience that "there would be no end to the conflict between the different races until all use of force was stopped and until all nations disarmed."[203] Like Terrell, Curtis suggested the interconnection between U.S. racialized sexual politics and U.S. militarism, a theme that was further developed in the second intersectional conversation.

Intersectional Conversation: Domesticating Empire and an Imperialist Care Ethic

This intersectional conversation shaped WILPF's 1926 protest against the expansion of U.S. imperialism through its protracted (1915–1934) military occupation of Haiti.[204] Addams narrated how in early 1916, the WPP, as the U.S. branch of the ICW, actively opposed the Wilson administration's actions in Haiti. The U.S. military supposedly went into the sovereign black republic to put down an insurrection. Yet instead of leaving once order was restored, the United States installed a puppet president and took over the administration of Haiti's finances. Breckinridge was dispatched to Washington to present the case for leaving Haiti. According to historian Mary Renda, the WPP and Du Bois "were among the very few" voices of dissent until 1920.[205] Ultimately, the WPP had to accept that Wilson's actions in the Caribbean showed that he was not committed "to reduce the theory [of self-determination for all peoples] to action." According to Addams, the WPP "dreaded" that "the hunt for naval bases as an excuse to subdue one revolution after another and to set up military government" portended that "such a line of action" represented how the United States would conduct its future "international relationships."[206] So for the WPP, the invasion of Haiti clearly illustrated the conflict between imperialism and self-government.

While WILPF provided a transnational participatory space for championing anti-imperialist campaigns, its initial analysis of economic imperialism was not adequate for understanding how exactly the United States was undermining Haitian self-determination. The conditions for complicating the analysis emerged in 1926. With pressure from WILPF's Haitian and African American women members, Balch organized the 1926 fact-finding mission that produced the book *Occupied Haiti*. The composition and purpose of the delegation continued WILPF's tradition of generating deeds to alter understandings by modeling, in this case, interracial cooperation and transnational solidarity. The six-member delegation included African American bridgers Charlotte Atwood and Hunton, as well as Balch. Atwood bridged WILPF with African American women's social service activism in Washington, D.C.; Hunton bridged WILPF with the International Council of Women of the Darker Races (ICWDR) and the PAC.[207] As they evolved their intersectional conversation, the interracial delegation demonstrated the potential for new intersectional theorizing when bridgers came into relationship to achieve a very specific common goal: building support for ending the U.S. occupation of Haiti.

NAACP executive secretary James Weldon Johnson (1871–1938), who had been a U.S. diplomat to Venezuela and Nicaragua, played a crucial role in reshaping WILPF's analysis of U.S. imperialism. Initially, he viewed the U.S. invasion of Haiti through the lens of U.S. strategic interests. After all, he had been "part of the [U.S.] military and diplomatic machinations" in 1912, when the U.S. marines landed in Nicaragua to install a pro-U.S. regime.[208] By 1918, Johnson was a critic. He went to Haiti in 1920 to investigate the situation for the NAACP.

His resulting influential articles in *The Nation* and *The Crisis* included and went beyond an economic analysis of imperialism and "individual cases of cruelty" to posit that the occupiers operated from a white supremacist perspective.[209] "The modern imperial policy," according to Johnson, "had been based" on the "idea of racial inferiority of the black peoples of the world."[210] In the specific case of Haiti, Johnson explained, "Americans have carried American hatred to Haiti. They have planted the feeling of caste and color prejudice where it never before existed."[211] At the summer school following the 1924 WILPF Congress in Washington, D.C., Johnson argued that "the idea of race inferiority, which for so long has been made the excuse for acts of hypocrisy, injustice, and violence," was at the root of "the lynchings in this country" and "our treatment of Haiti."[212] Thus Johnson made clear to his

WILPF audience that the successful dismantling of U.S. imperialism in Haiti rested on eradicating "the conscious or unconscious" white supremacist ideology that shaped U.S. domestic life.[213]

To construct how the 1926 WILPF delegation to Haiti evolved the intersectional conversation, I do not have direct exchanges among Atwood, Hunton, and Balch. Instead, I utilize chapters in *Occupied Haiti* that were attributed to different authors and the last chapter, "Conclusions and Recommendations," a collaborative effort. As with the first intersectional conversation, I foreground the crucial contributions of the African American bridgers. Certainly, Hunton and Atwood reinforced for Balch the point that complicating an economic analysis of imperialism by weaving in race and sexuality was imperative. The occupation of Haiti, of course, provided the perfect context for making this point. To show how Hunton, Atwood, and Balch crafted an intersectional analysis that included Johnson's emphasis on white supremacist ideology and went beyond it, I organize the 1926 conversation around the themes of domesticating imperialism and an imperialist care ethic. According to the delegation, both undermined Haitian self-government.

In their coauthored chapter, "Racial Relations," Hunton and Balch pulled together a number of Johnson's disjointed points to conceptualize how racialized sexual politics structured U.S. control of Haiti by reshaping domestic life. As they outlined the stages, they illustrated anthropologist Ann Stoler's analysis of how settler colonialism was structured by sexual politics.[214] At the beginning, social relations were fluid. When American wives arrived, "Haitians felt that the color line was drawn much as it is in the southern part of the United States."[215] In contrast to Johnson, who emphasized the detrimental role of individual male occupiers who came from the South, Hunton and Balch put the U.S. military as a "caste system" at the center of their analysis.[216]

Hunton brought firsthand knowledge to this theme from her experience in France serving soldiers, especially African American soldiers, at the YMCA canteens. She and Kathryn Johnson, educator and NAACP organizer, described how the YMCA and the U.S. military enforced social segregation among the soldiers. They also reported that the military went further by carrying out a propaganda campaign intended to persuade the French to adopt U.S. white supremacist constructions of the African American male.[217] According to Hunton and Johnson, the French resisted this effort and treated African Americans as their social equals.

In the Haitian case, Hunton would have observed that the U.S. military continued to model a caste system and spread practices of racial segregation to the civilian population by regulating sexual relations. As she and Balch reported, the military not only excluded African American soldiers but instituted a practice of anti-miscegenation. They gave an example of a man who was discharged from U.S. military service after marrying a Haitian woman. They also pointed to claims that prostitution and the transmission of sexually transmitted diseases had increased, a development "inseparable from any military occupation."[218] In a different chapter, Balch drew out the consequences of the military's practice of racialized sexual politics: "[I]t is obvious that illegitimate children of soldiers and native women are being added to the population in Haiti, as in the Philippines."[219] Thus, Hunton and Balch suggested that in practicing racialized sexual politics, the U.S. military was undermining the self-determination of the Haitian people by aiming to remake their domestic-family relations.

Through the second theme—the imperialist care ethic—the WILPF delegation explicitly theorized the opposition between imperialism and self-government. This theme exposed how, according to philosopher Uma Narayan, a "care discourse can sometimes function ideologically, to justify or conceal relationships of power and domination."[220] In 1924, James Weldon Johnson illustrated Narayan's critique and implicitly challenged WILPF members to clarify how Addams's cosmopolitan vision of nourishing other peoples into their own forms of self-government avoided this outcome. Johnson debunked the "material improvements" justification for the occupation. He showed that in the areas of the roads, sanitary regulations, and health care, the gains were exaggerated and bought at too great a price: the loss of self-government for the Haitians.[221] As he explained to his WILPF audience, the U.S. occupiers saw themselves as carrying out what Kipling called "The White Man's Burden," with its assumption of white supremacy. Through this idea, Johnson argued, the occupiers "condone and justify acts of treachery and cruelty and metamorphose them into acts of beneficence and Christianity."[222]

Recasting Johnson's analysis through the lens of the social democratic feminist social service tradition, Atwood, in her chapter, "Health and Sanitation," responded to Johnson's challenge. She examined how the occupying forces used the unequal charity relationship to impose a racial hierarchy in Haiti. They took over the health-care system and denigrated the role of Haitian health professionals. Atwood proposed an alternative social service model that constituted a practice of empowerment by "working shoulder to shoulder to a common end." Distilling the core characteristic of the alternative to imperialist care, Atwood wrote, "When Americans learn to work *with* and not merely *for* Haitians, and not until then will their efforts be truly fruitful."[223] According to her vision, this type of cross-border helping strengthened habits of self-government.

Reinforcing Atwood's theorizing, the conclusion to *Occupied Haiti* laid out the case for why helping through imperialist relations does not work. Even if the occupiers "have tried to benefit the people of Haiti," the delegation argued, "the occupation has cared for the American financial interests . . . at the expense of our poor and weak neighbors," and "[t]he determining element in the situation . . . is the fact that it rests on force."[224] By shutting down the legislature and a free press, the U.S. established a political "despotism—benevolent in the opinion of the despots, but not in the minds of all those who are supposed to enjoy it."[225] Therefore, "Haitians . . . complain . . . a generation is growing up without any political experience or habit of political responsibility or initiative, and that the government was never so militarized."[226] Consequently, the WILPF delegation concluded that the purported "object" for continuing the occupation "to help Haitians in the fundamental matter of self-government" was actually having the opposite effect. "We are training them," the delegation explained, "to subordinate themselves, and work under others who take responsibility."[227] Finally, the conclusion returned to Atwood's theme by bringing into it the detrimental effects of imposing a racial caste system: "It is obviously impossible to have normal relations or fruitful cooperation with a population which is treated as of an inferior caste."[228]

Taken together, these examples of protest as propaganda of the deed and intersectional conversations showed how WILPF practiced intentional intersectional activism and intersectional thinking. Based on the deeds as experiments, Addams theorized WILPF's contribution to formulating a new political notion of nourishing that was required for reconstructing the postwar world. Through their participation in WILPF's intersectional conversations, African American social democratic feminists shaped new intersectional analyses by provoking their white sisters into complicating their understanding of how domestic and cross-border relations were inextricably linked. Terrell, Curtis, Hunton, and Atwood uncovered why eradicating the U.S. racialized caste system rooted in its racialized sexual politics was necessary to further WILPF's aims of delegitimizing colonialism and economic imperialism in order to create a world of socially just relations among peoples. Finally, WILPF's intersectional activism contributed to the social democratic feminists completing their genealogy of social citizenship as a multileveled practice.

Feminist Genealogy of Multileveled Social Citizenship: The Last Stage

In the last stage of their genealogy, the social democratic feminists presented themselves as multileveled refounders. Their path challenged both Marshall's depiction of the evolution of citizenship within the container of the nation-state and the political theory debate that counterposes nation-state and cosmopolitan notions of citizenship.[229] As the social democratic feminists evolved from abstract citizens of the world to embodied multileveled global social citizens, they shaped a feminist genealogy that wove together women's nation-state citizenship and world citizenship.[230] Therefore, they demonstrated how the quest for women's full citizenship required a cosmopolitan reinterpretation of nation-state citizenship.[231]

Yet the end product was not built into the beginning. Following Nietzsche and Foucault, my genealogical method eschews any teleology. Instead, I stress the centrality of contingent factors and how the social democratic feminists responded with fresh intentions and reinterpretations of an abstract or legalistic notion of global citizenship by providing activist substitutions. They extended social service to the transnational level and suggested a new women-friendly notion of global social citizenship that rested on synthesizing local, national, and transnational levels.

Once the war broke out, the mosaic of contingent factors, including the war itself, the peacemaking, and the new transnational institutions that followed, radically altered the context in which the social democratic feminists acted to embody humanity by interconnecting the national and transnational. After 1914, they embraced a type of world citizenship that was not possible before the war. At the 1919 Zurich Congress, Kelley presented a resolution on the LON that included the language of world citizenship: "In order to win whole-hearted support from all men and women who to-day realize their world citizenship, the fundamental principle of a League of Nations must be that it is open on the same conditions to all nations who wish to unite with it." WILPF advocated a democratic vision of the LON where world citizens would be represented "by elected delegates of *all* nations."[232] Yet WILPF did not limit its notion to participation in a new form of world government. Balch presented a resolution that directed national chapters to work on shaping their educational systems so that "[i]nstruction in civics should develop a world consciousness and give an introduction to the duties of world-citizenship."[233] She did not enumerate those duties, but the actions of WILPF members suggested that these duties had enlarged beyond acting in cosmopolitan urban settings, Addams's prewar formulation.

To clarify further how the feminist genealogy generated a reinterpretation of global citizenship, I stress three dimensions. First, I conceptualize it as global *social* citizenship to underscore the centrality for the social democratic feminists of citizen social service. In different ways, they wove into their constructions of global citizenship all aspects of social service. I include here social service, social service participatory politics, paid work as social service supported by a welfare state, and the vote as an extension of social service into electoral politics.

Second, I characterize global social citizenship as multileveled to theorize how it was constituted by the path of the social democratic feminists, which was characterized by moving back and forth through the levels. In 1932, Addams recounted that "[i]t was quite as natural" for Grace Abbott and Hamilton "to go to Geneva," to serve on LON committees, "as they had already gone from Chicago to Washington," where they had various governmental appointments.[234] Yet it is important to note that such fluidity between levels was not available for all social democratic feminists. Because the U.S. government did not want civil rights activists to voice their critiques of U.S. racial politics in Paris during the peacemaking process, it denied Wells-Barnett a passport to go abroad. Schneiderman was able to travel to Paris, but she was refused a visa to Zurich to attend the 1919 WILPF Congress. So "soon after the Russian revolution," she was considered "suspect" because she was born in Russia-controlled Poland.[235]

Third, I distill their method of actualizing their global social citizenship as an intentional synthesizing of local, state, national, and transnational levels. In developing this dimension, I am guided by Addams's use of "synthesis" in her theorizing of the "challenge" women faced during the war to "so enlarge their conception of duty that the consciousness of the world's need for food should become the actual impulse of their daily activities."[236] The first part of this chapter showed how, prior to 1914, the social democratic feminists engaged in synthesizing when they worked to embed the national within the evolving transnational they were helping create. The second part of this chapter uncovered how, once the war started, they faced a much more complicated context for synthesizing levels. Confronting a militarized version of nationalism, Addams began to use the metaphor of concentric circles to help WILPF members visualize their evolving citizenship.

In her opening address to the 1924 WILPF Congress in Washington, D.C., she began by enumerating governmental and nongovernmental examples of efforts "to live according to the principles of a New International Order." She included how "Gandhi has shown that a national movement for self-determination may be successfully conducted by moral energy ignoring brute force." Then Addams defined her "dual capacity" as an "international officer and servant" and "American citizen."[237] Avoiding the term "world citizen," possibly because of the hostile political climate, Addams's use of "servant" suggested a practice of "world service." In 1917, Grace Abbott had characterized new transnational relations as world service.[238] Following these reflections, Addams turned to her metaphor: "I am not of those who believe that devotion to international aims interferes with love of country, any more than devotion to family detracts from good citizenship; rather as Mazzini pointed out the duties of family, nation, and humanity are but concentric circles." Finally, she apologized for the hostile reception the WILPF delegates received in the United States and even suggested that perhaps they should have held the congress in Europe.[239] Thus, Addams voiced both the difficulty of synthesizing the levels during the postwar U.S. context, shaped by a Red Scare, racial violence, and xenophobic policies, and the necessity for WILPF members to persist in practicing multileveled social citizenship.

Addams grounded her vision for WILPF's practices of citizenship in the assumption that the war had redirected women's evolution as citizens by attaching a new robust transnational dimension. Reflecting on the timing of her state's successful 1917 suffrage referendum, Eastman supported this point: "We women of New York State politically speaking, have just been born. We have been born into a world at war, and this fact cannot fail to color greatly the whole field of our political thinking and to determine largely the emphasis of our political action."[240] Addams herself explicitly downplayed the argument that women were rewarded with the vote because of their service to militarized nationalism. Instead, she argued that the new women citizens were captivated by the possibility of influencing the reconstruction of international relations. "That so many of the voting women have exhibited an intelligent and sustained interest in world affairs," Addams postulated, "may be due to the fact that women received the vote in so many countries immediately after the war, when the relations between nations were of necessity widely discussed."[241]

Speaking before the NAACP in 1922, Hunton backed up Addams's analysis by explaining how African American women viewed their new political citizenship within a growing international consciousness. Hunton declared that "colored women are more than colored women today; they are American citizens." They planned to actualize their citizenship by reaching across borders. According to Hunton, African American women were filled with "bigger thought" or multileveled "thinking in terms national and in terms international."[242] Her remarks reflected the founding of the ICWDR following the 1922 national meeting of the NACW. Terrell, Hunton, Burroughs, and Hope were among its first officers.[243]

As the three streams of social democratic feminists extended their newly achieved nation-state political citizenship to the transnational level, they synthesized the levels in ways that reflected their different opportunities based on their power differentials. Specifically, Hunton and Schneiderman expanded the presence of social democratic feminists in transnational civil society, while Abbott and Hamilton adapted social democratic feminist methods and policy priorities for their participation on LON committees. They were also connected to WILPF in different ways. Abbott and Hamilton attended the 1915 Hague Congress; Hunton was active in the U.S. branch and participated in the WILPF fact-finding mission to Haiti; Schneiderman had WTUL representation at WILPF congresses but missed her opportunity to attend in 1919. Taken together, the social democratic feminists crafted four models of how to extend their bridging of movements to the transnational level. In the process, they demonstrated a new notion of global social citizenship as the synthesizing of levels.

When Hunton successfully organized the 1927 PAC in New York City, she modeled one type of synthesizing levels that was open to African American bridgers. They folded women's feminist social service and civil rights organizations within cross-border relations among peoples of African descent in order to strengthen their presence in transnational civil society. In 1919, with financial backing from the NAACP, Du Bois had revived the PAC to coincide with the Paris peacemaking process. He hoped to use it as a vehicle for making the case that self-determination should be extended to colonized peoples.[244] As one of the few women present, Hunton reminded the audience of the "importance of women in the world's reconstruction and regeneration." The 1927 PAC demonstrated their crucial role in growing participation in the Pan-African movement. Overall, five thousand people attended, including delegates from ten foreign nations. The majority of the 208 paid delegates, from twenty-two U.S. states, represented African American women's organizations. The PAC passed a resolution of support for the recommendations of the 1927 WILPF report for ending U.S. imperialism in Haiti.[245]

Through this congress, Hunton showed how African American women bridgers synthesized levels and thereby advanced Du Bois's vision of embodying humanity. As he wrote in 1920, "A belief in humanity is a belief in colored men." He argued that the white supremacist notion of humanity had to be toppled and reconstructed by the incorporation of people of color. Building their solidarity across borders, with particular emphasis on people of African descent, was a crucial step in this reconstruction. Du Bois included in his vision "the future world-citizen," who would recognize no gendered or racialized hierarchies of power.[246]

In the WILPF report on Haiti, Hunton discussed the need to create Pan-African solidarity between Haitians and African Americans. Their common origins in Africa did not prevent the Haitians from "look[ing] down on American Negroes." Hunton advocated that "there should be more intercourse" between the two groups.[247] Since four Haitian women were members of the ICWDR, it provided one space for nurturing cross-border solidarity.[248] Thus, in different ways, African American social democratic feminists experimented with how to synthesize levels of organizational life.

When Schneiderman proposed an International Congress of Working Women (ICWW) to coincide with the first meeting of the International Labor Conference (ILC), the policymaking arm of the ILO, to be held in Washington, D.C., in the fall of 1919, she initiated the modeling of a second type of synthesizing of levels. It depended on organized working women activating, on the transnational level, a productive external-internal tension between civil society and the state. As the two official WTUL representatives to the Paris Peace Conference, Schneiderman and Swedish American immigrant Mary Anderson (1872–1964), who had been a unionized boot maker and labor organizer, symbolized the required nexus. Schneiderman's activist bridging location was outside the state in her NYWTUL leadership role; Anderson, as assistant director of Women in Industry Service, practiced state feminism inside the U.S. Labor Department. Through the ICWW resolutions, unionized working women presented a vision of how they intended to participate in the postwar reconstruction by bringing an inside-outside nexus to the ILO and the LON.[249]

Supported by French and British trade union women, the WTUL put out a call for the conference that emphasized its historic and democratizing significance: "[F]or the first time in history of the world the elected representatives of the organized working women of all countries . . . will endeavor to bring their influence to bear upon the determinations of the international labor conference . . . in which . . . no direct vote or representation is provided for women." Over ten days, nearly two hundred women from nineteen nations, including Japan, "assume[d] their new responsibilities" by taking "joint action . . . for universal industrial justice."[250] *Life and Labor*, the WTUL's publication, concluded that the ICWW had successfully "strengthened the hands of the women technical advisers" inside the ILC meeting. The ILO constitution called for each national delegation to include a woman adviser when issues affecting women were to be considered. The majority of these twenty-three advisers attended the ICWW. They succeeded in persuading the ILC to adopt the ICWW's proposal on paid maternity leave (six weeks before and six weeks after birth).[251]

To ensure the direct representation of women within the ILC, the ICWW called for amending the ILO constitution. It established four voting delegates for each nation: two from government, one from labor, and one from employers. The ICWW proposed adding a labor and an employer representative for a total of six voting delegates. It also called for instituting a fifty-fifty gender quota for government and labor representation. The result would be that each delegation would have at minimum two voting women, one representing government and one representing labor.[252] Under this system, if the United States had been a member, which it was not until 1934, Schneiderman could have been a labor representative and Anderson could have been a government representative. When they still hoped that the United States would join, both had asked President Wilson to appoint women as delegates to the 1919 ILC.[253]

The ICWW also passed a series of resolutions that supported the institutionalization of multileveled state feminism. For example, it endorsed the creation of "a bureau" in the ILO "to collect and pass on information of best methods of infant and maternity care." Since the U.S. Children's Bureau already collected such information, the resolution suggested that it provided a state feminism model that was appropriate for the transnational level. To address the multidimensional problem of unemployment, the ICWW advocated setting up a system of multileveled women-run labor bureaus: "That in the International Labor Office and in the national and local labor offices there must be a woman as director of the departments specifically relating to women." The following year, Anderson would be appointed the first head of the U.S. Women's Bureau. To tackle "hazardous occupations," the ICWW proposed "[t]he appointment of a committee including women under the League of Nations, international in personnel, to coordinate the work of national research in the dangerous trades."[254]

By passing these proposals, the ICWW clarified how to set up a productive tension for intersectional activists between transnational civil society and transnational governmental bodies. First, a multileveled system of governmental agencies was required to coordinate activities. Second, mandated appointments of women to head various agencies were necessary to allow intersectional activists to act inside the state. Third, gender-based quotas for membership in state delegations to the ILO were needed to turn the ILO into a space of negotiation between women state representatives and members of women's labor unions. Although the ICWW did not survive beyond 1924, it provided an experimental social space for organized working-class women to fill in the dimensions of their version of multileveled social citizenship.

When, in 1922, Grace Abbott, chief of the U.S. Children's Bureau, was appointed by the State Department to be the first American to participate on any LON committee, she practiced a third model of synthesizing levels. It brought local, state, and national social service methods, issues, and analyses into the structuring of the social welfare side of the transnational governmental body. Coming from a nonmember nation, Abbott served in an "unofficial advisory and consultative capacity" at the 1923 meeting of the LON's Advisory Committee on Traffic in Women and Children. She persuaded the delegates to appoint an international group of experts, who would utilize a scientific method to generate new transnational knowledge on causes and solutions. Pointing to the cross-border nature of trafficking, she dismissed the value of limiting the research to the collecting of national reports.[255] Her recommendations reflected her expertise in an empirical method of inquiry and with the subject of trafficking. She had been superintendent of the Chicago IPL and had spent four years as head of the Illinois Immigration Bureau.

As a result of her citizen social service, Abbott evolved a social democratic feminist analysis of trafficking that put the protection and support of immigrant women and girls at the center. She rejected the moralizing formulation that society had to be protected against them. "The immigrant girl," she wrote in 1917, "suffers from industrial and legal discrimination which are the common lot of working women. In addition, she must overcome the stupid race prejudice which leads many Americans to conclude that she suffers less from shame and humiliation than do other women and girls."[256] Abbott called on her readers to confront the unfairness of the double standard. As she explained, "These laws applied the double standard of morality in the tests for exclusion and deportation." While the male trafficker might be punished, "the man who is himself immoral is not regarded as an 'undesirable' immigrant."[257] Therefore, she reasoned that "severity in dealing with the immigrant girl" would not improve "the moral health of the country."[258] Instead, she emphasized that the aim should be to uproot the economic and social causes of trafficking. Her participation at the LON gave her the opportunity to take this aim to the transnational level.

Addams placed Abbott's effort to synthesize levels on the subject of trafficking within the context of the social democratic feminist project to embody their world citizenship or membership in humanity. She refined this theme by developing the concept of "efforts to humanize justice," which at its core was about "that marvelous longing for juster relations."[259] One dimension of "the humanizing of justice," according to Addams, was "an enlargement of the field of justice" so that those who had been excluded from the category of humanity were now entitled to the status "of human being," which brought with it a "measure of justice."[260] Since the prostitute "tests advancing moral standards more piercingly" than any other group or situation, Addams praised the 1927 LON report for producing a complex, fact-based picture of cross-border causes and solutions for problems faced by a very vulnerable group of women.[261]

In 1927, Abbott further synthesized levels by bringing her experience with state feminism at the U.S. Children's Bureau to advance the develop of transnational knowledge, and eventually transnational standards, on a range of issues affecting children, including infant health and child labor.[262] In both of these areas, she administered national laws within the U.S. multileveled federal system. Abbott played a critical role in Geneva by persuading the delegates to establish two subcommittees and change the name of the commission to Advisory Commission for the Protection and Welfare of Children and Young People. One committee continued with the trafficking focus; one committee produced transnational knowledge on "the present conditions of children and what has been found possible and practical under given conditions in different countries."[263] To carry out the "scientific" research in the new area, Abbott requested and got the expansion of the number of assessors or experts.[264] Lathrop, who had lived at Hull House and was the first head of the U.S. Children's Bureau, got one of the positions. Her presence linked the Child Welfare Committee to U.S. state feminism.

In her memorandum on the reorganization of the commission, Abbott laid out a vision that honored both national differences and the project of evolving transnational standards. Perhaps envisioning future transnational conventions, Abbott argued that "the experience of each country should be a part of the common experience which we should all take into consideration in our decisions as to what is in the interest of children." She also suggested that the new committee could "make recommendations as to international action that from time to time may be needed."[265] When she reflected back on the significance of her early work for the LON commission, Abbott characterized its accomplishments as developing cooperation and generating useful, fact-based reports. Yet ultimately, she concluded, "more important" was "that a foundation has been laid for what should be a world center for research, consultation and education as soon as the nations are ready to build upon it."[266] So Abbott drew on her synthesizing skills to begin the process of evolving a transnational governmental institution that had the capacity to fold nations into a new global multileveled project that advanced the welfare of children.

When Hamilton, an expert in occupational health, decided in 1919 to carry out an ILO resolution through her U.S. Labor Department job, she practiced a fourth model of synthesizing levels. It depended on her individual bridging efforts through governmental appointments to bring transnationalism to a hostile national context. In her autobiography, *Exploring the Dangerous Trades*, Hamilton, trained as a medical doctor and bacteriologist, traced her "interest in industrial diseases" to her Hull House citizen social service experience. "Living in a working-class quarter, coming in contact with laborers and their wives," she explained, "I could not fail to hear tales of the dangers that workingmen faced, of cases of carbon-monoxide gassing in the great steel mills, of painters disabled by lead palsy, of pneumonia and rheumatism among men in the stockyards."[267] Appointed to the Illinois Occupational Disease Commission in 1910, Hamilton was assigned the role of "managing director" of the first statewide survey of "occupational poisons," which included "lead, arsenic, brass, carbon monoxide, the cyanides, and turpentine."[268] Then, in 1912, she became a federal agent in the new U.S. Labor Department to carry out a national survey, starting with "the lead trades." The position was not salaried. According to her contract, the government would pay her only for the report she produced. As a result, she felt free to design her job.[269]

Hamilton was ending her relationship with the government, on her way to teaching at Harvard Medical School, when she made the decision to fulfill the ILO resolution that called on industrialized nations to investigate the presence of and ways to control carbon monoxide. "The resolution . . . was not incumbent on Americans," she explained, "since we refused to join the

I.L.O., but I had always been given a free hand in the choice of fields to investigate." She consciously seized the opportunity to counter the hostility of key actors in the United States. As she noted, "[O]ur State Department did not even dare to answer official letters from the League Secretariat, and, as far as the I.L.O. was concerned, neither trade-unions' nor employers' organizations were in favor of any kind of internationalism."[270] Hamilton personally investigated steel mills in Illinois, focusing on "the question of permanent damage following acute gassing."[271] Through her findings, she synthesized the levels by linking the U.S. Labor Department and the ILO in the production of transnational knowledge on an occupational poison.

In 1924, Hamilton expanded her individual efforts at synthesizing levels when she was appointed by the Council of the LON to join its Health Committee. Due to pressure from "some good feminists," the Council was committed to including "at least one woman."[272] Hamilton was both the sole woman and the sole expert in industrial medicine. In characterizing the Health Committee, she stressed how it practiced a type of internationalism that was "devoted to the welfare of all." On other committees Hamilton observed, "the delegates from certain countries had the interests of their country in mind far more than the welfare of the whole." These delegates "could not forget that they represented their countries and must defend national interests." In sharp contrast, on the Health Committee, Hamilton noted, "nobody represented his government, all had been chosen on the basis of their scientific standing, and all were working for the control of disease no matter where."[273]

To illustrate how the Health Committee pursued transnational aims, she pointed to its breakthrough in getting countries to share news about epidemics. As she observed, "Never had it been possible to make governments exchange this sort of information; on the contrary, every effort had always been made to conceal an outbreak of cholera, plague, typhus, smallpox."[274] Hamilton also gave an example of how the Health Committee solved the methodological problem of how to study infant mortality across borders when "it was decided to adopt the method originated by our Children's Bureau." A study of six European nations revealed that poverty was "the most important factor but a close second was bottle feeding."[275]

Hamilton's efforts to connect the United States to the evolving transnational understandings of the world's health took the form of speaking in public about the Health Committee's work. At a time when the U.S. government "severely ignored" the LON, she aimed to build support from the bottom up by informing her audience of how LON's activities affected their lives. "I always felt that the very words 'League of Nations' made my hearers' minds close with a snap," she reported, "so skillfully had they been conditioned against it." So she started her talks by remarking that she was only discussing the Health Committee. To break through "the black mantle of anti-Wilson hatred and of resolute isolationism and xenophobia which descended on us after the war," Hamilton turned to stories about the activities and findings of the Health Committee. "[I]n a short time," she reported, "they were listening eagerly."[276]

Ultimately, Hamilton viewed the Health Committee as paving the way for the necessary transnational health organization that she assumed would take shape after World War II. "And surely among the first tasks that will face such an organization," Hamilton insisted, "will be the control of epidemics and the restoration of public health service." Thus, through her model of synthesizing levels, she showed how one individual could keep alive the promise of transnational government so that when the United States moved away from "narrow nationalism," it could build on the work of transnational committees like the LON's Health Committee.[277]

Taken together, these four models of synthesizing levels reveal that the social democratic feminists extended their bridging activism through social service to the postwar transnational level. In the process they invented a practice and theory of global social citizenship that was deeply political and participatory.[278] They explicitly rejected the narrowing of their new political agency to the providing of private charity to humanity, one understanding of cosmopolitan citizenship.[279] They embraced the political project of shaping new transnational relations and institutions to uproot the causes of discord. They also worked to embed the local and the national within the purview of these new institutions. Thus, the social democratic feminists advanced the evolution of social democracy as a multileveled project as they evolved their skills as synthesizers of those levels.

Refounding as Multileveled

This chapter shows that to recover the social democratic feminists as refounders, we must acknowledge that they conceptualized refounding as a multileveled project that required a new humanitarian transnational that surrounded and completed a new social democratic demilitarized national. Their distinct contribution was to develop a range of methods. Before the war, they activated methods of building a new transnational level from the ground up. Living in an immigrant neighborhood, Addams foregrounded the role transnational families, migrant workers, and cosmopolitan urban neighborhoods played in modeling a new relational foundation for shifting from imperialism to social welfare. Drawing on her experience as a factory inspector, Kelley showed how factory inspectors across borders generated transnational knowledge to evolve transnational norms of socially just labor standards. Seeking fresh momentum, Catt embedded the U.S. suffrage struggle within a new transnational organization that sought to universalize women's right to vote as a human right by building support at the local, state, and national levels around the world.

During and after the war, the social democratic feminists expanded their methods. They acted directly on the transnational level with the purpose of strengthening a humanitarian emphasis in the reconstruction of the post-war world. Some enlarged transnational civil society. A few embedded the United States within the LON and the ILO. Thus, the social democratic feminists actively embraced their insight: To refound U.S. democracy, they had to change *both* the national level and the transnational level.

Refounding Democracy through Intersectional Activism

Conceptual and Organizing Tools for Today

M y purpose in writing this book has been to recover and validate the social democratic feminists as refounders. I constructed a notion of refounding appropriate for the task of analyzing political outsiders who engaged in refounding from the bottom up. I brought together Machiavelli's argument for periodic processes of collective self-reflection, Arendt's theme of a new beginning, and Aristotle's concept of political revolution in the constitution. Through this combination that is rooted in political theory, I created a substitute for legal scholar Bruce Ackerman's influential legal model of constitutional moments.

While Ackerman creates legitimacy for developing a concept of refounding by focusing on three constitutional moments—the founding, the Reconstruction period, and the New Deal—his model is inadequate for my purposes for two reasons. First, it privileges "higher lawmaking," or a new understanding of the Constitution outside of the formal Article V amendment process. As we have seen, the social democratic feminists were part of the movement to get Congress to propose and the states to ratify the Nineteenth Amendment. Ackerman downplays the significance of this amendment because it does not fit his model, which relies heavily on the New Deal period. Second, Ackerman separates the role of movements, which he recognizes are necessary for amending the Constitution, from his preferred version of higher lawmaking or refounding. The latter depends on a political dance in which the president, the Supreme Court, and Congress are the key participants. The people come in through their electoral validation of the new direction for the country.[1] Since the social democratic feminists utilized the method of bridging social movements for their refounding moment, Ackerman's model is not up to the task of illuminating their originality. At best, his model relegates their method to the role of stage hands who prepare the way for the refounding show, which is performed by the political elites.

In these closing reflections, I turn to the advantages of my conceptual container of refounding. First, my refounding interpretation of the Nineteenth Amendment strengthens the case for a reconsideration of its meaning for a post-Dobbs world. As Aristotle observes, reforms of electoral rules transform the constitution by reconstituting the sovereign power. A new sovereign power brings change in the purpose of the body politic and a different notion of justice. The social democratic feminists envisioned women voters reconstituting the body politic as a social democracy and enacting a new notion of intersectional social justice. They infused their egalitarian suffragism with this understanding of the meaning of the Nineteenth Amendment. Therefore, I contend that they provide us with a movement-based thick interpretation of the Nineteenth Amendment that we need at a time when women are losing their citizenship rights under the Constitution.[2]

Second, I want to stress that as outsiders, the social democratic feminists had to invent a bottom-up method for their refounding moment. In a context in which we cannot look to our elite political leaders, especially the Supreme Court justices, to protect democracy against an authoritarian patriarchal turn, the social democratic feminist bottom-up method of refounding has become even more important. They shaped this method by releasing the transformative potential of intersectional acting and thinking. At the core of their refounding method was their ability to bridge movements. They practiced bridging in new experimental socializing spaces, including transnational ones, that facilitated difficult democratic conversations. By working to coalesce the intersectional coalitions that were necessary for refounding, the three streams of social democratic feminists prefigured the relational foundations of an engendered, interracial, and cosmopolitan social democracy.

My assumption has been that this recovery and validation project would provide conceptual and organizing tools for our current moment of collective self-reflection, now shaped by our experience of the COVID-19 pandemic, the threat of an authoritarian turn, and the Dobbs decision.[3] For those of us committed to a robust, socially just democracy, we face the task of replacing a corrupt system that has legitimized the significant weakening of the socializing dimensions of our democracy. What is required is a resocializing of our democracy, or the recreation of our social relations and the affirming of the centrality of intersectional social justice. I have demonstrated that for the social democratic feminists, engendering and socializing democracy were interdependent. In these concluding reflections, I make the case that to resocialize democracy, we should embrace and update, for our context, the multidimensional project of engendering democracy that characterized the social democratic feminist refounding moment. This argument illustrates Addams's dictum that Du Bois repeated: "[T]he cure for the ills of Democracy is more Democracy."[4] To develop this closing argument, I distill conceptual tools to help us reimagine social democracy and social citizenship, and I propose organizing tools to help us actualize intersectional coalitions capable of refounding our democracy.

Conceptual Tool #1: The Feminist Settlement House and Expanding the Democratic Imaginary

By proposing the feminist settlement house as a conceptual tool worthy of study for our context, I suggest that it was not just a formation to transition us to a welfare state or a necessary environment that supported educated women as they created professional fields that they could enter.[5] My claim is that it constituted an unacknowledged feminist contribution to our participatory democracy imaginary. This imaginary includes the Greek polis, the New England town meeting, the Paris Commune,[6] workplace democracy,[7] and cooperatives. To understand how it both shared some elements with these forms and constituted an entirely new form, I place it within the context of Addams's call for the reinvention of self-government.

Because Addams attributed the "difficulties" of her day to "the lack of connection between" the "industrial organization" and "our inherited democratic form of government," she discredited the continuing relevance of that political system by historicizing it. "If self-government were to be inaugurated by the advanced men of the present moment," she conjectured, they would not turn to inspiration from "the Greek city and the Roman Forum," as the Founding Fathers did. Instead, they would carefully study early types of villages and preindustrial workplace organizations, or "primary cells of both industrial and political organizations, where the people knew no difference between the two, but, quite simply, met to consider in common discussion all that concerned their common life."[8] While Addams did not explicitly point to the feminist settlement house as a new form of self-government, Hull House fit because it reconnected the industrial and the political through its hybrid form, its experimental method, and its cosmopolitan ethic.

As I have shown, Hull House put the undoing of the gendered domestic-public divide at the center of the refounding moment because it was a necessary condition for engendering democracy. Addams and other social democratic feminists created domestic-public hybrids that allowed them and their neighbors to embed their households in the public. This central characteristic showed how Hull House combined the aim to produce new syntheses of daily life, the economy, and politics with the imperative to incorporate a diversity of women into self-government. The evolution of Hull House also demonstrated that the need to reshape the domestic-public relationship was never ending because as women increased their presence in public, they exposed new, unexpected dimensions of this relationship that required change. In effect, the feminist settlement house provided a hybrid location that demonstrated the necessity of building into the new understanding of self-government a commitment to a permanent revolution of the domestic-public relationship.

To sustain this permanent revolution, the feminist settlement house practiced democracy as an open-ended experiment. As I have shown, Hull House engaged in both nonstrategic and strategic experiments to interconnect daily life, the economy, and government. The nonstrategic experiment showed how redesigning the gendered public-domestic divide opened up possibilities for prefiguring different ways of taking democracy to daily life, including the provisioning of food and cooperative living arrangements, and for modeling new transgressive family formations. The strategic experiment provided a method both for enlarging the purpose of the state by incubating new social programs that could be turned over to it and for keeping those government programs accountable to those affected and to social movement actors. Clearly, the interdependence of the two types of experiments turned the feminist settlement house into a dynamic form of self-government appropriate for a diverse population with varied needs.

With homelike qualities, the feminist settlement house welcomed a diversity of newcomers to join in the creation of an enlarged democracy. In the process, social democratic feminists reinterpreted the cosmopolitan right to hospitality. Immanuel Kant distinguished from philanthropy this "right of the stranger not to be treated with hostility when he arrives on someone else's territory." For Kant, this limited right did not include "the right of the guest" or the right to citizenship. Also, the stranger "can indeed be turned away, if this can be done without causing his death."[9] To democratize hospitality, Hull House rejected a negative, temporary relationship between hostess and stranger and substituted practices of walking together—the white-privileged native born, the immigrant, and the descendant of slaves—to refound democracy. Thus, the feminist settlement house, in its various forms, ably recreated over and over again the relational foundations of democracy.

In the midst of our period of collective self-reflection, I would argue that we need to study the feminist settlement house for its relevance to resocializing democracy. To access its lessons, Hamilton's organic metaphor should guide us. In her 1943 defense of the continuing need for the settlement, Hamilton wrote of it as "a growing plant." She insisted that Addams assumed that "each generation should approach the problems of its day with fresh ideas, perhaps building on the foundations of the past, but following the lines of its own inspiration."[10]

To take up Hamilton's challenge, I propose three steps. First, we formulate a political theory tradition of social democracy that acknowledges the theoretical contributions of the social democratic feminists who created feminist settlement houses. Second, we create a record of how various actors in different contexts, addressing different problems, actualized the promise of the feminist settlement house. Some examples are community organizations during the 1960s War on Poverty,[11] local food movements, worker centers, and feminist institutions such as battered women's shelters and bookstores. Third, we encourage new generations to make their own unique contribution to the theory and practice of the feminist settlement house legacy by embracing the openness of its theory and the adaptability of its form.

Conceptual Tool #2: Women's Economic Independence and Discrediting Neoliberal Ideology

By advancing economic independence for women as a conceptual tool for our period of collective self-reflection, I focus on how the social democratic feminists used this tool to discredit and build a substitute for the laissez-faire liberal worldview that dominated their times. To resocialize democracy, we face a parallel challenge to delegitimize and replace our contemporary neoliberal worldview.[12] To underscore the connection between the two periods, I define the "neo" aspect to capture how advocates today are reclaiming, *after* the institutionalization of the welfare state, the worldview that preceded it.[13] The defenders of the turn-of-the-twentieth-century version not only justified a limited role for government in the regulation of the economy, but they also reconceptualized human existence as fundamentally individualistic, competitive, and self-caring. Karl Polanyi's characterization of their project is especially relevant for formulating this conceptual tool: "To separate labor from other activities of life and to subject it to the laws of the market was to annihilate all organic forms of existence and to replace them with a different type of organization, an atomistic and individualistic one."[14] For their substitute, the social democratic feminists connected women's economic independence to the reclaiming of the centrality of human interdependence through the decommodification of labor infused with social ethics.

The formulation of their substitute evolved out of their recognition that the market-based worldview interwove a theory of commodification of labor and an ethical system that justified an exploitative version. Without using the term, the NCL's brief on minimum wage boards explained commodification.

The worker sells her energy, or labor power, to the employer, turning it into a commodity like a bag of sugar. The employer purchases the worker's energy and pays wages determined only by market forces. Yet the problem was not the commodification of labor but that the exploitative version, according to Kelley, "sacrificed . . . human welfare" to the pursuit of profits.[15] Addams analyzed the supportive market-based ethical system and how charities enforced it. They provided meager palliatives for workers in what Kelley labeled "socially subnormal industries."[16] These industries did not pay a living wage and therefore increased poverty in the community. According to Addams, charities reinforced an individualistic ethic when they judged "poor people solely upon the industrial side," or their "money-earning capacity."[17] As Schneiderman's family history illustrated, wedded to an ethics of self-sufficiency and self-care, charities removed children from their low-waged widowed mothers and found jobs for children to perform the breadwinner role.

The social democratic feminists understood that they had to delegitimize both dimensions of the market-based worldview. To construct their substitute worldview, they offered two new combinations of decommodification and social ethics. Decommodification foregrounded the relational, interdependent aspects of labor but did not require the end of commodification or paid work.[18] Social ethics replaced individualistic ethics by infusing waged labor with social justice and a commitment to the social welfare common good. The social democratic feminists linked each new melding of decommodification and social ethics to women's roles in social reproduction. I include in the notion of social reproduction the daily maintaining of the waged woman worker, the reproduction of her family in its various forms, and societal reproduction.

For the first new combination, the social democratic feminists proposed a type of decommodification that built a social ethic into all paid work by reconceptualizing it as social service. Gilman created a hierarchy of the purposes of labor: "Work the object of which is merely to serve one's self is the lowest. Work the object of which is merely to serve one's family is the next lowest. Work the object of which is to serve more and more people . . . is social service."[19] Du Bois expanded Gilman's theorizing by formulating a notion of paid work as social service that was based on the emancipatory potential of the African American tradition of personal service. As he insisted, "Surely no social service, no wholesale helping of masses of men can exist which does not find its effectiveness and beauty in the personal aid of man to man."[20] The latter he differentiated from the cash nexus of the market. Then he called for the eradicating of the servile status of service work. Fundamentally, Du Bois's notion of work as social service rested on both dismantling a legacy of slavery and honoring a distinct undervalued and underappreciated African American tradition of work. By turning all work into social service, Gilman and Du Bois emphasized the relational context of labor and how important it was for social reproduction. Du Bois's phrase "a world of Service without Servants" wove intersectional social justice into societal reproduction.

For the second new combination, the social democratic feminists presented a type of decommodification that infused work with social ethics through the state's regulation of the employer/worker relationship. To achieve this aim, the social democratic feminists turned the purpose of the state into service. Gilman theorized how governmental protections of waged workers advanced "the democratic idea of government as service." Her example was paid maternity leave. As she explained, "To deliberately legislate for the service of all the people, to use the government as the main engine of service, is a new process."[21] Kelley innovated sex-based labor laws to establish constitutional support for the state's interest in caring for the well-being of women workers. For example, by supporting public sector wage boards, she created a new public space for women workers and their employers to negotiate living wages.[22] All these examples pointed to the state addressing the daily needs of the working woman and her family for the purposes of social reproduction.

In the midst of our moment of collective self-reflection, I would argue that the women's economic independence tool has become especially relevant because the pandemic experience created an opening for debating a social democratic feminist substitute for the neoliberal worldview. The early stages of the pandemic made us conscious that we are interdependent beings, reliant on a range of low-waged agrifood and care workers for our daily survival. The state had to expand it service in the area of public health because privatized solutions were not up to the task. Women, and especially women of color, constituted the majority of essential workers.[23] For this reason, I am focusing on women workers. Applying the women's economic independence tool to the label "essential" provides a specific way to capture the emancipatory potential of our pandemic experience.

The two combinations of decommodification and social ethics allow us to create a critical standard for proposing a socially just conception of essential work and essential worker. Clearly, essential women workers modeled paid work as social service directed at carrying out the social welfare common good. We learned how they negotiated the pulls of the three purposes of labor as outlined by Gilman. Before mask mandates, public health measures, and vaccines, by going to work at a grocery store or commercial farm, they put social service ahead of the health of their families and themselves. Yet they did not necessarily choose to serve the common good. The state and corporations used the designation of essential work for coercive purposes. Meatpackers, for example, had no choice but to work without adequate protections to carry out their social service.

To release the potential of "essential" to protect women workers, we obviously need to expand and make permanent state service. We learned yet again that women are especially vulnerable economically because of their multiple roles in social reproduction. A national childcare program and reinventing such social democratic feminist innovations as wage boards would demonstrate that we value the workers who allow us to reproduce ourselves on a daily basis.[24] In fact, California has established a ten-person council to set wages and working conditions for fast-food workers. Thus, this tool helps us strengthen the social justice potential of the label "essential"[25] and, in the process, advance the resocializing of democracy by engendering it.

Conceptual Tool #3: Egalitarian Suffragism and Retheorizing the Gender Gap

By turning egalitarian suffragism into a conceptual tool, my claim is that the egalitarian suffragists provide a new understanding of our gender gap in voting as constituting a bloc vote for resocializing our democracy. To access their insights, we need to retire the metaphor of waves to analyze the women's movement,[26] as well as the standard interpretation of the absence of a postsuffrage women's bloc vote.[27] The wave metaphor places the egalitarian suffragists within a phase of the women's movement that ended in 1920 with the ratification of the Nineteenth Amendment. This narrative discourages an investigation of the continuing relevance of their new type of electoral politics. Interpreters of the significance of achieving women's right to vote emphasize *only* that in the 1920s, women failed to vote as a bloc to change the outcome of elections. This dismissal halts the search for how the egalitarian suffragists began the process of coalescing a bloc vote for intersectional social democracy. In effect, both framings deter us from recovering the beginning of an evolving social democratic feminist bloc vote that persists today in our gender gap.

As I have shown, the egalitarian suffragists created a new type of electoral politics of presence. They were bridgers of movements who actively participated in electoral politics. Because of the multileveled nature of the votes for women campaign, *during* the fight for a federal constitutional amendment, they learned how to use spaces of electoral politics to advance the bridging of movements. Through their electoral activism, they brought into the national conversations such social justice topics as economic class inequality, structural white supremacy, and the need for substantive gender equality of power. As a result, they suggested three insights about how to retheorize the gender gap as a bloc vote for intersectional social democracy.

First, the egalitarian suffragists showed how movements and electoral politics were not necessarily antithetical, especially in the context of insurgent electoral politics or refounding moments. To distill this insight, I stress the programmatic dimension of movements instead of their mass tactics. Both Addams and Du Bois approached electoral politics as providing arenas to build momentum for radical programs based on bridging movements. As Addams showed in her participation in the 1912 Progressive Party campaign of TR, a third-party presidential race provided a space for expanding the democratic conversation. As a campaign speaker in the West, she reported having "a wonderful opportunity for education not only on the social justice planks in the platform but on the history of the idealogy [*sic*] back of them."[28] In November 1915, Du Bois urged "everyone" of the "200,000 Negro voters" who could participate to vote "Yes" for statewide women's suffrage referenda.[29] Du Bois infused these campaigns with the theme of the need to protect the right to vote for all African American men. Thus, along with Wells-Barnett and Terrell, he utilized an electoral space, where some African American men could have an impact on the outcome, to revive the Reconstruction vision of interracial democracy.

Second, the egalitarian suffragists showed how a bloc vote for social democracy would come out of mobilizing women voters based on different streams of bridging movements. Before the adoption of the Nineteenth Amendment, Wells-Barnett and Schneiderman mobilized women's voting blocs. In 1915, Wells-Barnett bridged civil rights and feminism to marshal an African American women's bloc vote to elect the first African American man to the Chicago City Council. By bridging feminism and the immigrant women's labor movement, in 1918, Schneiderman inspired working-class women to vote as a bloc to defeat four state representatives who opposed sex-based labor laws and to elect two women representatives who supported these laws. While each bloc vote could be interpreted as merely the playing out of a narrow group interest, I emphasize the larger refounding significance. Taken together, African American and immigrant Jewish social democratic feminists organized bloc votes to advance a radical rethinking of democracy as an interracial and social justice experiment.

Third, the egalitarian suffragists pointed to the need to conceptualize a bloc vote for social democracy as a dynamic participatory space, where bridgers from different streams met to generate new programs. This insight was suggested by one side of the 1921 conflict over the direction of the postsuffrage NWP. Unfortunately, Alice Paul was able to assert her control over the NWP to block the actualization of turning it into a participatory space for bridgers. African American social democratic feminists tried to shake her confidence in a strict formal equal rights approach for unifying women as a political force but were unsuccessful. Clearly, from the perspective of coalescing a bloc vote for interracial social democracy, welcoming and working with African American bridgers to ensure the actualization of their voting rights was crucial. So while they did not succeed in the context of the NWP, Eastman, Kelley, Hunton, Terrell, and others began a postsuffrage history of bridgers, working together, to craft a social democratic feminist program that could energize the voting power of diverse groups of women.

In the midst of our period of collective self-reflection, when movements such as the Women's March and Black Lives Matter are channeling energy into insurgent electoral politics, resulting in a diversity of women entering elected office, I would argue that we should utilize this tool to retheorize the gender gap as a bloc vote of a diversity of women for resocializing democracy. We usually mark the beginning of the gender gap from the 1980 election of Ronald Reagan to the presidency. According to exit polls, 55 percent of men versus 47 percent of women voted for him, producing an 8 percent gender gap.[30] This voting pattern fueled the 1980s conservative revolution.

The consensus now is that this divergence was produced by white men pulling away from the New Deal Democratic coalition.[31] They were called the Reagan Democrats. A significant bloc of women voters persisted in supporting an activist state and a range of social justice policies.[32] They were fulfilling the promise of egalitarian suffragism. To retheorize the gender gap based on the continuing support for social democracy of some groups of women voters, we need to shift our focus of analysis. Instead of emphasizing the differences between genders, we should turn to uncovering the evolution of this women's bloc vote from the Progressive Era to today. The egalitarian suffragism tool can guide us.

To adapt the first insight about the interconnections of movements and electoral politics, I turn to the relationship between egalitarian suffragism and the New Deal realignment. I suggest, based on new research of women's votes,[33] that the efforts of egalitarian suffragists to link women voters to social democracy produced important results starting in 1928. Because historians and political scientists have made class the salient factor to interpret the origin and evolution of the New Deal coalition,[34] they have blocked our exploring this lineage. In 1928, for example, Schneiderman actualized this lineage when she voted for Al Smith, the Democratic Party candidate for president.[35]

This reinterpretation illustrates a central argument of this book: The social democratic feminists combined the creation of the welfare state with engendering democracy, a dimension of which was electoral partisan politics. The linkage here between movements and electoral politics was that new women voters joined with men to form a bloc vote for social democracy, a version of which was FDR's New Deal. From a sample of ten states, J. Kevin Corder and Christina Wolbrecht estimate that the three million additional Democratic votes from 1928 to 1936 were evenly divided between men and women.[36] When men pulled away from the New Deal coalition, women remained and thereby produced the type of bloc vote that was anticipated right after the Nineteenth Amendment.

To apply the second insight about disaggregating women voters according to different currents of bridging movements, we must uncover how our gender gap came out of the evolution of smaller blocs of diverse women voters from suffrage to the present.[37] A good example is the 1960 mobilization of unionized women, who made up one-quarter of union members, to elect John Fitzgerald Kennedy (JFK). Esther Peterson (1906–1997) coordinated the Committee of Labor Women for Kennedy and Johnson, which drew in three hundred members. The daughter of Danish immigrants, Peterson advanced the Schneiderman-Newman stream of bridging. She entered the labor movement by working for the ACWA's Education Department. She got to know JFK when the AFL-CIO assigned her to lobby him when he was a U.S. senator. Once president, JFK appointed Peterson to two positions: director of the Women's Bureau and assistant secretary of labor.[38] These roles allowed her to advance the social democratic feminist program, especially in the area of women's economic independence.

To further illustrate the second insight, I turn to the contribution of African American Addie Wyatt (1924–2012), who joined Peterson in her efforts to elect JFK. Wyatt developed the stream of labor union women to expand the presence of African American women workers. She bridged the labor and civil rights movements at a time when African American women were able to expand their workplace opportunities beyond domestic work. They shared with white women workers the gender segregation in the labor market. And they were constrained by racial segregation within women's paid work, including within Wyatt's own meatpacking industry.

When, in 1953, Wyatt became president of the Chicago local of the United Packinghouse Workers of America (UPWA), a progressive union, she worked to align it with the campaign to uproot Jim Crow inside the workplace. By 1954, in meatpacking, the integration of African American and white women workers was the rule on the line. Wyatt also succeeded at desegregating the bathrooms, the locker rooms, and the cafeteria. All women workers had the same rights and benefits in the union. In 1964 Wyatt pressed the UPWA at its convention to include sex in its civil rights plank.[39] Taken together, Peterson and Wyatt show the necessity of looking inside the labor movement,[40] usually interpreted to be a crucial interest group for electoral victories of the Democratic Party. By foregrounding labor union women, we can make visible how their intersectional activism within the context of the labor movement contributed to the coalescing of a diverse working women's bloc vote for social democracy.

To utilize the third insight about the gender gap as a participatory space for bridgers to formulate new social democratic feminist policies, we must go in search of those spaces from suffrage to today. I offer three examples. First, in 1961 the President's Commission on the Status of Women (PCSW) brought together different generations within the three streams under Peterson's guidance. On the protective labor legislation subcommittee, for example, Wyatt argued for listening to the voices of working-class women, especially elderly women and women of color, to conceptualize policy.[41] The PCSW produced an influential report that pulled together the evolving social democratic feminist program, most of which we have not yet achieved, including equal pay for comparable worth and a national childcare program.[42]

Second, in the early 1980s, in the San Francisco Bay Area, the Women's Economic Agenda Project (WEAP) helped organize the first national legislative hearings on the feminization of poverty.[43] Women from different organizations testified and ultimately generated a discussion of the intersectional causes of women's poverty. WEAP connected the new gender gap in voting with the feminization of poverty, carrying forward the tradition of tying a women's bloc vote to a social democratic feminist program of policies.[44] Third, for at least the last fifty years, conferences that shaped the reproductive justice movement brought bridgers together to place the fundamental right to abortion within a broader context of intersectional social justice.[45]

Inspired by the egalitarian suffragists, I am proposing a reformulation of the gender gap as a participatory space for bridgers to interact. In that space, they would utilize intersectional thinking to craft a social democratic policy agenda. I am attempting to counter the ways that pundits present the gender gap in voting. They focus only on the right to abortion or make up characterizations of crucial women swing voters as soccer or security moms. Neither assertion is backed up by data.[46] I am not making a claim about all women. I suggest only that the social democratic feminist women who support an activist state and social justice policies could become an independent force for resocializing democracy. By embracing the legacy of the egalitarian suffragists, who tried to turn the NWP into a participatory space for formulating a bloc vote for social democracy, we gain a conceptual tool for making visible the continuing social democratic feminist project of socializing democracy by engendering it.

Conceptual Tool #4: Feminist Cosmopolitan Recasting of Social Democracy

To recommend the feminist cosmopolitan recasting of social democracy as a conceptual tool for our period of collective self-reflection, I assume that it will bolster our case for defining democracy as an experiment in which people from vastly different intersectional locations join together to shape and advance a multileveled, socially just common good. To defend this vision, we have much to learn from the key insight of the feminist genealogy of multileveled social citizenship: Women's full incorporation into democracy depended on their developing national and transnational citizenship *at the same time.* The social democratic feminists wove together the levels by forging new social relations that crossed a wide range of differences or borders at home and abroad. As they evolved their multileveled social citizenship by bridging movements, they expanded the European social democratic imaginary. It was shaped by nation-state boundaries and a notion of solidarity dependent on *not* recognizing diversity beyond class and the rural-urban divide. To resocialize our democracy, my claim is that we need to adapt, for our context, three insights the social democratic feminists produced as they engendered multileveled cosmopolitan democracy.

First, the social democratic feminists asserted that evolving self-government within the United States was interdependent with supporting, through noncoercive means, the development of self-government abroad. Addams showed how a new internationalism, or rooted cosmopolitanism, domestically and abroad, was possible once we embraced and trusted the rich diversity of peoples in the world. She put immigrants, migrant workers, and transnational families at the center of her reimagining democracy. They were creating a relational foundation for connecting peoples across borders and within the United States. Du Bois expanded this vision by putting peoples of African descent at the center. For example, after the war, he linked the NAACP to the PAC, interconnecting the pursuit of interracial democracy at home and the decolonization movements abroad. The IWSA provided a specific example of how building cross-border relations from the bottom up could advance democracy as a multileveled project: the right to vote within a nation-state and as a transnational human right.

Second, the social democratic feminists demonstrated that enlarging the social welfare side of the state within the United States depended on codifying new transnational knowledge and constructing transnational governmental institutions. The latter provided participatory spaces where representatives of different peoples could address cross-border humanitarian problems. This "newer humanitarianism,"[47] or feminization of politics that the social democratic feminists embraced required a nonmilitarized world: the substitute of nurture and nourish for masculinized militarism. As I have shown, Addams theorized the potentiality of global food politics to substitute "a new set of motives"[48] for the old militarized international relations. Her vision put women's daily life activities with food at the center of this new type of multileveled politics and social citizenship.

To introduce her theorizing of "A Food Challenge to the League of Nations," Addams justified the necessity for a new social welfare direction for international relations by pointing to the example of epidemics and what happened when they did not receive an adequate transnational coordinated response. Although the world had just experienced the 1918 influenza pandemic, Addams did not draw on this experience. Instead, she returned to a series of European cholera epidemics that occurred between 1851 and 1892. Because of the constraints of national sovereignty and an unwillingness of leaders to put aside their traditional language of diplomacy, according to Addams, "even when under the pressure of great human needs," the diplomats at international conferences failed to respond effectively.[49] In sharp contrast, Hamilton reported that the LON's Health Commission created a new type of transnational space. It generated transnational knowledge on epidemics and worked to expand public health services globally. Like Addams, Hamilton emphasized women's agency, especially the role visiting nurses could play around the world.[50]

Third, African American social democratic feminists emphasized that the actualization of the first two insights depended on acknowledging and dismantling intersectional hierarchies of power. Specifically, they uncovered how a white supremacist theory and practice shaped *both* the U.S. nation and its imperialist and colonialist activities. While Addams and Balch were anti-imperialist, they did not explicitly interconnect white supremacy at home and abroad. As I have shown, Terrell, Hunton, James Wilson Johnson, Du Bois, and others illustrated their insight through their analyses of how the United States, through its military, extended domestic policies of racial segregation to France during World War I and to Haiti under U.S. occupation. For example, Terrell and Hunton uncovered how the military, in both examples, practiced racialized sexual politics, which justified lynchings of African Americans in the United States. By exposing the truth of U.S. history, domestically and internationally, the African American social democratic feminists expanded the feminist cosmopolitan recasting of social democracy to include truth telling in order to build the necessary social relations of trust.

In the midst of our period of collective self-reflection, I would argue that rediscovering the social democratic feminist cosmopolitan vision can help us think about how to put healthy relations of diversity at the center of our understanding of who we are. The three insights take us back to the two meanings of socializing democracy: the relational foundation of democracy and the social justice aims of democracy. For the social democratic feminists, working together to address daily life issues tied to advancing social justice was their method of how to socialize democracy. As global food insecurity, climate change, and the pandemic—three urgent multileveled crises—have shown us, we live in a deeply unequal world. The vision reminds us that rebuilding our relations across all kinds of intersectional locations and borders is the only way to bring the world together to save itself. Yet to have a chance of advancing this aim, like WILPF after World War I, conflicting sides have to be at the table. We have to tell the truth of what our nation has done, and we have to work to make amends. Ultimately, what is required is a complicated discussion of multidimensional reparations for both our domestic and our international history.

Organizing Tool #1: Recovering Women Refounders as a Resource for Intersectional Activists Today

By interpreting the three streams of social democratic feminists as refounders, my intention has been to create a tradition of refounders that could inspire intersectional activists today to believe in the possibility of multileveled change. The social democratic feminists persevered through difficult times, and they acted with great courage. Out of necessity and commitment, they devised bottom-up methods to carry out their refounding. As a result, they expanded greatly the range of women who became refounders. Ultimately, the acknowledgment of their refounding moment provides legitimacy for today's intersectional activists to create their own new beginning with their own methods of refounding.

Organizing Tool #2: Lessons on How to Become an Intersectional Activist

The recovery of the three streams of social democratic feminists provides lessons in how to acquire skills at bridging movements to become an intersectional activist. Lesson number one is to adopt a both/and perspective on movements. Lesson number two is to combine movements during struggles. The social democratic feminists bridged movements as they engaged in a range of struggles that included labor strikes, state voting rights referenda campaigns, anti-imperialist movements, anti-lynching campaigns, and protests of World War I. Lesson number three is to combine movements by creating experimental socializing spaces that prefigure alternative practices of socially just forms of democracy.

Organizing Tool #3: Forming Intersectional Coalitions by Intentional Bridgers

By characterizing the social democratic feminists as coming from three different streams of bridging movements, I showed how each stream created its own type of intersectional coalition. I also showed how the social democratic feminists crafted intersectional coalitions together. The latter was illustrated by the egalitarian suffrage movement. What made their coalitions intersectional was that they were shaped by intentional bridgers who were skilled at renegotiating unequal power within and among the streams. The bridgers engaged in uncomfortable conversations to create trust across intersectional social locations. As they deliberated, the bridgers generated new intersectional thinking as the basis for crafting new intersectional policies and programs. Thus, the social democratic feminists provided some guidance of what is required today to form intersectional coalitions.

By my construction of the social democratic feminists as refounders and my distillation of conceptual and organizing tools, I hope that I have made them useful for our current challenges. The need for a refounding is even more pressing today than when I began writing this book. Certainly, this time the leadership and the range of participants will be much more diverse. Yet there are indications of continuity with the social democratic feminist refounding moment. Voting rights are center stage. We are more aware than ever that we are globally interdependent based on our experiences of climate change, the pandemic, immigration, and the agrifood system. To take on these and other challenges, including reproductive justice, young women of many different intersectional locations are speaking and acting. Their fierceness and courage give me hope that we are already engaged in refounding democracy through intersectional activism.

Notes

PREFACE

1. See Sarvasy and Van Allen 1984.
2. See Sarvasy 1992.

INTRODUCTION

1. Machiavelli 1979, 352. See Pitkin (1987, 273–280). I rely on her interpretation of Machiavelli.

2. Starting in chap. 1, I provide birth and death years for each social democratic feminist.

3. While Foner (2019, xx) uses the term "second founding" to refer to the post–Civil War Thirteenth, Fourteenth, and Fifteenth Amendments to the Constitution, he does not develop a concept. Cf. Bernal (2017, 2) on "founding beyond origins."

4. Machiavelli 1979, 351–353.

5. Pitkin 1987, 279.

6. Arendt 1965, 34–35.

7. Arendt 1965, 280, 35.

8. See Pitkin 1998, 217–219.

9. Aristotle 1967, books III and IV. Aristotle also analyzed and advocated the benefits of mixed constitutions.

10. Aristotle 1967, 210, 209–210.

11. Cf. Ackerman (1991, 136), who explicitly rejects a bottom-up method for his three constitutional moments that could be called refounding moments. I return to his model in the concluding chapter.

12. I use "women-friendly" as shorthand for a welcoming environment for a diversity of women to create a transformed democracy or welfare state. Cf. Hernes (1987, 15–16), who developed the term within the Nordic welfare state context.

13. My use of "engendering democracy" plays with two ways of defining engender. The first definition is "to cause something to come into existence." So engendering democracy refers to bringing a feminist version of democracy into existence. The second definition separates "en," which means "put into," and "gender," which means, for my purposes, feminine and women. So engendering democracy refers to putting women into a feminized or women-friendly version of democracy.

14. See Bernal (2017, 2) on "founding beyond origins." See Ackerman (1991) for his analysis of three constitutional moments.

15. For example, I would argue that the Reconstruction period after the Civil War was a refounding moment that introduced elements of social democracy. As I show, African Americans linked it to their formulation of the social democratic feminist refounding moment.

16. Within the complex debate among feminists over how to characterize the welfare state, I have always theorized it as a contradictory space that women can utilize to pursue their emancipation. See Sarvasy and Van Allen 1984; Sarvasy 1988, 1992. See Gordon (1990) for different feminist approaches to the characterization of the welfare state. See W. Brown (1992) and Mink (1995) for interpretations of the welfare state as repressive.

17. For an exception, see Vetter 2017.

18. Shklar 1991.

19. Ritter 2006.

20. Terborg-Penn 1983, 1998; Jones 2021.

21. On the postsuffrage feminist politics of mothers' pensions, see Sarvasy 1992; for an analysis of the impact of the legacy of the programs on the welfare reform debates in the 1980s, see Sarvasy 1988.

22. Sklar 1993.

23. See Hernes 1987; Alvarez 1990.

24. Lemons 1973.

25. According to the Triangle fire archive at Cornell's Kheel Center, the 146 victims included 16 Jewish men.

26. See Cobble (2021, 2–3) for why she also chose the label "social democratic feminist."

27. For a comprehensive discussion of the term, see Cott 1989.

28. Sklar, Schuler, and Strasser 1998, 4–5, 33.

29. Koven and Michel 1993, 3.

30. Skocpol 1992.

31. For how the recovering of the social democratic feminists moves us beyond the either/or debate among political theorists who theorize women's citizenship, see Sarvasy 1997, 64–70.

32. Mettler 1998, 40; Ritter 2006.

33. Sklar, Schuler, and Strasser 1998, 6.

34. Tronto 1993, 2013; J. White 2000.

35. For a more nuanced treatment of the four political theorists, see Sarvasy 2000.

36. Wolin 1989.

37. Rawls 1971; Shklar 1991.

38. Walzer 1990.

39. Addams (1893b) 1970, 4; Kloppenberg 1986, 7. See Nackenoff (1999, 2009) on how Addams did not fit within the liberal tradition.

40. Addams (1906) 2007, 104.

41. Addams (1906) 2007, 18, 22.

42. In her analysis of neoliberalism, Wendy Brown (2005) argues that laissez-faire liberalism did not have a political rationality, only a bundle of economic policies. I excavate both economic and political logics to offer an alternative interpretation.

43. Addams (1902) 2002, 12.

44. Addams (1906) 2007, 21, 19.

45. For a different interpretation, see Kloppenberg 1986.

46. Esping-Andersen 1990, 15, 108.

47. Berman 2009, 569, 565.

48. Berman 2009, 568, 574; Esping-Andersen 1990, 17–18.

49. Addams (1906) 2007, 84.

50. Addams (1906) 2007, 52–53.

51. G. Abbott 1917, 277–278.

52. G. Abbott 1917, 277.

53. G. Abbott 1917, 281.

54. G. Abbott 1917, 270. For analyses of how racial categories were fluid and imprecise during the Progressive Era, see Barrett and Roediger 1997, and specifically for the case of how Jewish immigrants were categorized, see Goldstein 2006.

55. G. Abbott 1917, 281.

56. Addams (1906) 2007.

57. For other approaches to theorizing activism, see Sparks 1997; Ackelsberg 2010.

58. Collins 2011, 92.

59. See Cho, Crenshaw, and McCall (2013, 795), who conceptualize intersectionality as "a way of thinking about and conducting analyses."

60. Crenshaw 1995, 357, 360, 376–377.

61. Cooper (1892) 1988, 135.

62. Collins 2011, 91.

63. Crenshaw 1995, 358–360, 367.

64. For different approaches to utilizing a notion of intersectional activism and intersectional framings of coalition, see Murib and Taylor 2018; B. Roth 2004, 219–224; Heaney 2021; S. Roth 2021; Ishkanian and Pena Saavedra 2019; Taylor 2022.

65. Seigfried 1996, 154.

66. Seigfried 1996, 105.

67. Hartsock 1985, 232.

68. Hartsock 1985, 232.

69. Hartsock 1998, 236. See Grant (1993), who also ties standpoint to feminist politics.

70. See Sarvasy (2015, 477–481) for an extensive discussion of the bracketing problem in feminist treatments of a proceduralist version of deliberative democracy. Cf. Benhabib 1996; Fraser 1997; Young 1997.

71. This is a critical distinction for Crenshaw 1995.

72. It is striking that historians have no uniform way of characterizing immigrant Jewish working-class women. See Kessler-Harris 1976; Glenn 1990; Orleck 1995.

73. Collins 1991, 225.

74. Cooper (1892) 1988, 185.

75. Addams (1902) 2002, 7.

76. Cooper (1892) 1988, 144; Du Bois (1920) 2004, 128.

77. Pateman 1989; Phillips 1991; Mansbridge 1993; Gould 1993.

78. Marshall 1965.

79. Nietzsche 1956; Foucault 1984. For my understanding of the genealogical method, I drew on Ansell-Pearson 1999 and Prinz 2016.

80. Nietzsche (1956, 209) attributed to "those in power" the capacity to shape the genealogy through "fresh intentions" and "processes" in "reinterpretation." Foucault (1984, 83) stressed domination: "Genealogy, however, seeks to reestablish the various systems of subjection: not the anticipatory power of meaning, but the hazardous play of dominations."

CHAPTER 1

1. Addams ([1902] 2002, 38) pointed to "periods of reconstruction" of the family and the state. She also insisted that "[t]here is no doubt that many women, consciously and unconsciously, are struggling with this task."
2. For a very imaginative interpretation of Hull House that captures its dynamic qualities, see Jackson 2001.
3. Hayden 1982; Sklar 1985; Muncy 1991.
4. Knight 2005, 275.
5. Sklar 1990.
6. Sklar 1995, 200–205, 369n9. See also Sklar 1985.
7. Addams 1892.
8. Skocpol 1992, 36.
9. For a different critique of the extending formulation, see Jackson 2009, 155.
10. Addams (1906) 2007, 105.
11. Addams (1906) 2007, 109, 105.
12. Addams (1906) 2007, 111, 113.
13. Addams (1906) 2007, 113.
14. Addams (1906) 2007, 111.
15. Addams (1906) 2007, 103, 113.
16. Addams (1906) 2007, 109.
17. Addams (1906) 2007, 103.
18. Seigfried 2002a, xxii–xxxi.
19. Addams (1902) 2002, 48.
20. Addams (1893b) 1970, 22.
21. While Addams linked the strategic experiment to individual philanthropists, it also applied to Hull House experiments that were adopted as government programs. She contrasted the strategic with "a line of social experiment involving social righteousness in its more advanced form." This second type got at the roots of social injustices, particularly in wage labor. Her distinction inspires my notion of nonstrategic experiments. See Addams (1902) 2002, 73–74.
22. Stevens 1899, 45.
23. Addams (1902) 2002, 7.
24. Seigfried 1996, 154–155.
25. Jackson 2001, 61.
26. Addams (1910) 1961, 86.
27. Addams (1906) 2007, 112.
28. Addams (1906) 2007, 113.
29. Addams (1906) 2007, 112.
30. Addams (1906) 2007, 111–112.
31. Addams (1910) 1961, 158.
32. Addams 1895, 202, 200–201.
33. Addams 1895, 191, 188.

34. Addams (1906) 2007, 53.

35. Addams 1895, 193.

36. Addams (1910) 1961, 215.

37. Hayden 1982, esp. chap. 8.

38. Hayden 1982, 157.

39. Hayden 1982, 157.

40. Jackson 2001, 124–135.

41. Kelley 1898, 553.

42. Addams (1893a) 1970, 49.

43. Addams (1910) 1961, 309 and chap. 7. See Hayden 1982, chap. 8; Knight 2009. For John Stuart Mill's linking of cooperation and socialism, see Sarvasy 1985.

44. Addams (1910) 1961, 109.

45. Addams (1893a) 1970, 49.

46. Addams (1910) 1961, 186–187.

47. Addams drew on a notion of "a common table," and the "comradeship" that it "expressed," in her theorizing of food rationing during World War I. See Addams (1922) 2002, 117.

48. Aristotle 1967, 60, 178, 79, 81–82.

49. Addams (1906) 2007, 104–105.

50. Addams (1910) 1961, 101.

51. Richards 1904, 126.

52. Levine 2008, 20.

53. Levine 2008, 15–16.

54. In *I Came a Stranger: The Story of a Hull-House Girl*, Hilda Satt Polacheck (1989, 124, 126), an immigrant eastern European Jew, recounted the story of when Addams hosted a dinner to celebrate Polacheck's wedding. Addams told Polacheck to inform her mother that the chicken salad was made from kosher chicken. After praising Addams for her "tolerant, generous, understanding heart," Polacheck commented, "But what she did not know was that the dishes, the butter, the cream in the coffee, the ice cream, and the small cakes baked with butter made everything not kosher."

55. Addams (1910) 1961, 102.

56. Levenstein 1980, 385.

57. Levenstein 1980, 371–372.

58. Addams (1910) 1961, 101.

59. Hayden 1982, 153.

60. Ewen 1985, 172.

61. E. Abbott 1950b, 394.

62. Stevens 1899, 43.

63. Addams (1910) 1961, 192, 196–197.

64. Stevens 1899, 43; Moore 1897, 634.

65. E. Abbott 1950a, 377.

66. Addams (1910) 1961, 103.

67. Addams (1910) 1961, 102.

68. Jackson 2001, 84–86.

69. Addams (1918) 1976, 157.

70. Nutter 2000.

71. Addams (1910) 1961, 105.

72. Kenney 1969, 34–35.

73. Addams (1910) 1961, 157.

74. Kenney 1969, 35.

75. Kenney 1969, 35.

76. Residents of Hull House 1895, 214. The term "girls" was applied to working-class women of all ages. It reinforced the societal norm that married women should not work for wages. Except in quotes, I use "women" for adult women.

77. Addams (1910) 1961, 105.

78. Hayden 1982, 167.

79. Addams (1910) 1961, 105; Kenney 1969, 35.

80. Marks 1901, 482.

81. Marks 1901; Hayden 1982, 167–168; Jackson 2001, 135–141.

82. Residents of Hull House 1895, 214.

83. Hayden 1982, 219.

84. Jackson 2001, 189; Marks 1901, 483.

85. Marks 1901, 483.

86. Residents of Hull House 1895, 214.

87. Addams (1910) 1961, 106–107.

88. Addams (1910) 1961, 154.

89. Sklar 1985, 671.

90. Hernes 1987; Alvarez 1990.

91. Addams (1910) 1961, 154.

92. Tax 1980, 73–74.

93. Sklar 1985, 671.

94. Residents of Hull House 1895, 216.

95. Sklar 1995, 240.

96. Addams (1910) 1961, 153.

97. Addams (1902) 2002, 76.

98. Addams (1910) 1961, 100.

99. Addams (1910) 1961, 163.

100. See Stivers (2009) on Addams's philosophy of public administration.

101. Addams (1910) 1961, 152.

102. Addams (1910) 1961, 152.

103. Wolin 1996, 37.

104. See Jackson (2009) for a different interpretation of Hull House as transgressive, based on her notion of "queer domesticity."

105. Addams (1902) 2002, 38.

106. Addams (1916) 2002, 55. According to Aristotle (1967, 7), "justice belongs to the polis." On the French salon, see Landes 1988, 21–28; on Arendt and the salon of Rahel Varnhagen, see Benhabib 1995. Addams ([1916] 2002, 48) quotes "the gifted" Varnhagen in her setup to the third conversation.

107. Knight 2005, 273; Elshtain 2002, 30–31.

108. Seigfried 2002b, xxiii–xxiv.

109. Addams (1902) 2002, 11.

110. Addams (1902) 2002, 33.

111. Addams (1906) 2007, 20–21.

112. Addams (1906) 2007, 25.

113. Addams (1906) 2007, 24, 26.

114. Addams (1906) 2007, 25, 20, 18.

115. Bickford (1996) is the exception.

116. Arendt 1989, 57.

117. Addams (1916) 2002, 32–33. With her understanding of the importance of listening in conversations shaped by asymmetrical relations, Young (1997) comes the closest to Addams.

118. For a different interpretation of sympathetic knowledge that connects it to feminist care ethics, see Hamington 2009, chap. 4.

119. Addams (1902) 2002, 7.

120. Addams 1896, 536.

121. Hayden 1982, 170.

122. Addams (1906) 2007, 109.

123. Sklar 1995, 177.

124. Sklar 1995, 178.

125. Addams 1896, 536n1; (1902) 2002, 51.

126. Addams 1903, 239.

127. Addams (1902) 2002, 58.

128. Addams (1902) 2002, 51.

129. Addams 1896, 536.

130. Addams 1903, 240; (1902) 2002, 51, 58–59.

131. Addams (1902) 2002, 57.

132. Addams (1902) 2002, 57.

133. Addams 1894, 629; (1902) 2002, 57.

134. Addams (1902) 2002, 57.

135. G. Abbott 1917, 51, 73–74.

136. Addams (1902) 2002, 51.

137. Addams 1903, 239.

138. Addams (1902) 2002, 58.

139. Addams 1903, 230.

140. Addams (1902) 2002, 57; (1906) 2007, 110.

141. Cohen (1918) 1995, 181.

142. Cohen (1918) 1995, 176, 181.

143. Cohen (1918) 1995, 159.

144. Cohen (1918) 1995, 180–181.

145. Addams (1916) 2002, 7.

146. See Fischer (2010) for a complementary, more complete interpretation of the devil baby incident that connects it to Greek tragedy.

147. Addams (1916) 2002, 9.

148. Addams (1916) 2002, 9.

149. Aristotle 1967, 6.

150. Addams (1916) 2002, 18.

151. Addams (1916) 2002, 8.

152. Addams (1916) 2002, 7.

153. Rousseau 1992, 266.

154. Addams (1916) 2002, 17, 9, 17.

155. Addams (1916) 2002, 25, 17, 10.

156. Addams (1916) 2002, 9–10.

157. Aristotle 1967, 32, 105.

158. Addams (1916) 2002, 20–21.

159. Arendt 1989, 180.

160. See Pitkin (1981) on how Arendt leaves out justice in her treatment of Aristotle.

161. Addams (1916) 2002, 10.

162. Addams (1916) 2002, 10, 24, 25.

163. Addams (1916) 2002, 12, 23.

164. Addams (1916) 2002, 21, 25.

165. Breitzer 2010, 50. For details on the 1910 strike, see Weiler 1979–1980 and Buhle 1976.

166. Addams (1902) 2002, 36.

167. Addams (1894) 1982, 111.

168. Addams (1902) 2002, 46.

169. Addams (1894) 1982, 114.

170. Addams 1913c, 81–82; (1910) 1961, 149, 179.

171. Addams (1894) 1982, 109, 115, 114.

172. Pastorello 2009, 107.

173. Pastorello 2008, 25.

174. Breitzer 2010, 51.

175. E. Abbott 1950a, 390–392.

176. Pastorello 2008, 29; Amalgamated Clothing Workers of America Research Department 1922, 24.

177. E. Abbott 1950b, 499.

178. Breitzer 2010, 59.

179. E. Abbott 1950b, 499.

180. Addams (1916) 2002, 48.

181. Addams (1916) 2002, 49.

182. Addams (1916) 2002, 43.

183. Addams (1916) 2002, 49.

184. Addams (1916) 2002, 48–49.

185. Addams (1916) 2002, 49–50.

186. Addams (1916) 2002, 52, 54.

187. Alice Hamilton ([1943] 1985, 109–113) described how she joined the birth control movement. At Hull House she had conversations with working-class Italian women, who discussed their methods of abortion. Hamilton clarified that she did not support eugenics arguments for birth control. Her aim was to bring safe forms of birth control to a population that was already using methods, like falling down stairs when pregnant, to limit their family size.

188. Nietzsche 1956; Foucault 1984.

189. I agree with Foucault (1984, 80) on his emphasis on the play of contingent factors, or "the vicissitudes of history," in the unfolding of a genealogy.

190. Addams (1902) 2002, 38.

191. Following Nietzsche, Foucault (1984, 80) wrote of the "surprises" and "accidents that accompany every beginning."

192. Nietzsche 1956, 209.

193. Nietzsche (1956, 153, 160–161, 195) situated the origins of genealogies of moral concepts in specific historical power struggles between "the ruling class and the slave class" and between debtors and creditors.

194. Addams (1902) 2002, 42, 40.

195. Addams (1902) 2002, 36.

196. Addams (1902) 2002, 40–41.

197. Davis 1973, 25.

198. Knight 2005, 120.

199. Addams (1902) 2002, 35, 39–41. I am adapting Foucault's (1984, 87) insight that while "the body" is "poisoned by food or values, through eating habits or moral laws; it constructs resistances."

200. Cott 1987, 40.

201. Addams (1902) 2002, 6.

202. Addams (1902) 2002, 9.

203. Addams (1902) 2002, 39.

204. Addams (1906) 2007, 7. Addams demonstrated her method in her creation of a new understanding of peace.

205. Nietzsche 1956, 209.

206. In my application of a genealogical method, I agree with Nietzsche (1956, 209) on the point that actors can create and shape a genealogy through "fresh intentions" and "processes" in "reinterpretation."

207. Addams (1902) 2002, 12.

208. Sarvasy 1997.

209. Addams (1893a) 1970, 55–56. For an interpretation of Addams's concept of citizenship that links it to the ethic of care, see Nackenoff 2009.

210. G. Abbott 1917, 296–297.

211. G. Abbott 1917, 57–58.

212. G. Abbott 1917, 58–60.

213. E. Abbott 1950a, 384; Costin 1983, 71–73. On how the IPL contributed to building the U.S. welfare state from the bottom up, see Nackenoff 2014.

214. Wald 1915a, 8–9.

215. Wald 1915a, 27–28.

216. Wald 1915a, 28–29.

217. Wald 1915a, 60.

218. Wald 1915a, 27.

219. Hamilton (1943) 1985, 70.

220. Rouse 1989, 16–17.

221. Rouse 1989, 65–66.

222. Salem 1990, 97.

223. Salem 1990, 94, 97.

224. Du Bois (1903) 1989, 70.

225. Cooper 1913, 14–15.

226. Cooper 1913, 14. See Hutchinson 1981.

227. Neverdon-Morton 1989, 163.

228. Salem 1990, 191.

229. Neverdon-Morton 1989, 152.

230. Neverdon-Morton 1989, 152.

231. Rouse 1989, 89.

232. Addams (1893a) 1970, 45–46.

233. Neverdon-Morton 1989, 150; Rouse 1989, 79.

234. Neverdon-Morton 1989, 157.

235. Rouse 1989, 78–79, 57.

236. Wald 1915a, 53.

237. Wald 1915a, 51.

238. Wald 1915a, 60.

239. Duster 1970, 333, 356.

240. Schechter 2001, 194–195.

241. Schechter 2001, 197.

242. Schechter 2001, 197.

243. M. Thompson 1990, 102.

CHAPTER 2

1. Wollstonecraft (1792) 1992, 185.

2. Mill 1965, 765.

3. Gilman (1898) 1966, 153, 63, 137–138.

4. L. Gordon 1994, 53–59.

5. See L. Gordon (1994, 54, 126–143) on how immigrant Jewish and African American creators of the welfare state do not quite fit into her maternalist framework. See also Boris 1993.

6. Higginbotham 1993, 198. See also Fraser's (1997, 81) discussion of "parallel discursive arenas" in her formulation of "subaltern counterpublics." I prefer "intersectional conversation" to "subaltern counterpublic" because it foregrounds tensions within the counterpublic, a theme that Fraser (1997, 82) acknowledges but puts aside.

7. Malkiel, n.d., 11.

8. Malkiel (1910) 1990, 81.

9. Malkiel (1910) 1990, 81–88, 94, 109, 130.

10. Malkiel (1910) 1990, 211.

11. Cooper (1892) 1988, III.

12. Cooper (1892) 1988, 185.

13. Cooper (1892) 1988, 134.

14. Cooper (1892) 1988, 87.

15. Cooper (1892) 1988, 75, 134–135.

16. Gilman (1935) 1990, 3–4. Gilman ([1898] 1966, 147–148) explicitly praised the innovative qualities of those with "Anglo-Saxon blood."

17. Gilman (1915) 1979, 59.

18. Hill 1980, 277. Kessler (1995, 90–93) reprints Gilman's letters to her young daughter that describe her days at Hull House.

19. Gilman 1911b, 86.

20. Lane 1990, xvii–xviii.

21. Gilman (1935) 1990, 319; (1898) 1966, 138.

22. Contrast this approach with a vast literature that divides between bracketing her prejudices and arguing that her theory is fundamentally racist and anti-Semitic. In the first category, see Lane 1979; Hill 1980; P. Allen 1988; Kimmel and Aronson 1998; J. Allen 2009. In the second category, see Bederman 1995; Ganobcsik-Williams 1999; Weinbaum 2001; Mattis 2010.

23. Du Bois (1920) 2004, 140.

24. Washington 1988, xlii–xliii.

25. Gilman (1935) 1990, 184.

26. Ovington (1947) 1970.

27. Ovington (1911) 1969, 224–225.

28. For Gilman's theory of social evolution, see Ganobcsik-Williams 1999.

29. Buhle 1981, 74–79; Van Wienen 2003.

30. Gilman 1903, 52.

31. Gilman (1898) 1966, 14–15.

32. Gilman (1898) 1966, 21–22, 7.

33. Gilman (1898) 1966, 38–39.

34. Gilman (1898) 1966, 5.

35. Gilman (1898) 1966, 81, 83, 84.

36. See Carby (1987, 3–6) for a discussion of the African American women's campaign to be included as speakers. Cooper (1894) and Frances Harper (1894) were speakers.

37. F. Harper (1893) 1987, 69.

38. F. Harper (1893) 1987, 61, 74, 77, 65.

39. F. Harper (1893) 1987, 97, 116.

40. F. Harper (1893) 1987, 271.

41. F. Harper (1893) 1987, 205, 210.

42. F. Harper (1893) 1987, 208, 211.

43. F. Harper (1893) 1987, 212.

44. Cooper (1892) 1988, 68. See Alexander 1995; May 2004.

45. Cooper (1892) 1988, 252, 256.

46. Cooper (1892) 1988, 255.

47. D. White 1993, 252.

48. Cooper (1892) 1988, 254.

49. Cooper (1892) 1988, 255.

50. Glenn 1990, 4.

51. Schneiderman with Goldthwaite 1967, 13, 27–28.

52. Schneiderman with Goldthwaite 1967, 29, 28, 33–34.

53. Schneiderman with Goldthwaite 1967, 34, 43; Schneiderman 1905.

54. Schneiderman with Goldthwaite 1967, 44. See Glenn 1990, 163. According to Glenn, daughters received a weekly allowance that averaged 11 percent of their wages.

55. Schneiderman with Goldthwaite 1967, 50.

56. Glenn 1990, 79, 189; Ewen 1985, 105.

57. Ovington (1911) 1969, 150.

58. Tax 1980, 224–225.

59. Orleck 1995, 90–91.

60. Gilman 1916, 66.

61. For critiques of Du Bois for not making explicit the contribution of African American women intellectuals, see Carby 2007; J. James 1996. See Balfour (2005) for an interpretation that shows how Du Bois was further developing Cooper's analysis. See Gilkes (1996) for Du Bois's gender analysis.

62. Cooper (1892) 1988.

63. Du Bois (1920) 2004, 128.

64. For Du Bois's reference to Gilman, see Du Bois (1920) 2004, 140. For discussions of Du Bois and Gilman, see Aptheker 1982; Oliver 2015.

65. Du Bois (1920) 2004, 143.

66. Pleck 1990, 367.

67. Du Bois (1920) 2004, 140.

68. Du Bois (1920) 2004. For an argument against interpreting Du Bois as an intersectional theorist, see Gillman and Weinbaum 2007, 3–5.

69. Du Bois (1912) 1995, 294.

70. Du Bois (1920) 2004, 131, 133.

71. Du Bois (1912) 1995, 294.

72. Du Bois (1920) 2004, 129–131. See Rabaka (2003) for a discussion of Du Bois's treatment of African American motherhood.

73. Terrell 1940, 1, 5, 106–107.

74. Duster 1970, 243–244.

75. Du Bois (1920) 2004, 134.

76. Du Bois (1920) 2004, 139.

77. Du Bois (1920) 2004, 143.

78. Gilman 1913c, 149.

79. For her arguments for the right to motherhood outside of marriage, a plan for educating mothers, and a system of government-funded education stipends for mothers to self-support as they raised children to the age of seven, see Key 1909, 1911, 1913a, 1913b, (1914) 1970.

80. Gilman 1913a, 259, 262.

81. Gilman 1914b, 8.

82. Gilman 1913a, 259.

83. Gilman 1913a, 262.

84. Gilman 1913a, 259.

85. Gilman 1913d, 37.

86. See Michel (1993, 290), who contrasts the views of the National Federation of Day Nurseries, founded in 1898, with the views of African American women activists. The latter "accepted maternal employment as a fact of life, and simply wanted to free working mothers from anxiety by keeping their children safe."

87. Terrell 1902, 174.

88. Durst 2005, 144.

89. Rouse 1991, 12–13.

90. Rouse 1991, 12–13.

91. Harley 1982, 261; Salem 1990, 79–80.

92. Terrell 1902, 174.

93. Terrell 1902, 175.

94. Terrell 1902, 175.

95. Terrell 1902, 176.

96. Gilman 1913d, 38.

97. Gilman 1913d, 37.

98. Du Bois (1912) 1995, 294.

99. Hoffman 2001, 2.

100. Hoffman 2001, 138, 149. Gilman (1916, 65) quotes a version of the bill that established eight weeks of sick benefit.

101. Hoffman 2001, 149, 147.

102. Kelley 1911, 304.

103. Kelley 1914, 17.

104. Gilman 1916, 66.

105. Gilman 1916, 65–66.

106. Gilman 1913c, 148.

107. Gilman 1911a, 187, 188.

108. Gilman 1911a, 222.

109. Gilman 1911a, 188.

110. Gilman 1916, 66.

111. Gilman 1916, 66.

112. Glenn 1990, 171; Hoffman 2001, 121.

113. Newman 1917, 943.

114. Newman 1917, 943.

115. Hoffman 2001, 121.
116. Hoffman 200l, 129, 135.
117. Newman 1917, 942, 943.
118. Newman 1917, 944.
119. Newman 1917, 944.
120. Hoffman 200l, 122.
121. Hoffman 200l, 141.
122. Hoffman 200l, 140.
123. Hoffman 200l, 142, 143.
124. Hoffman 200l, 141.
125. Newman 1917, 945; Hoffman 200l, 143.
126. Glenn 1990, 14.
127. Glenn 1990, 12.
128. Glenn 1990, 66–67, 74–75; P. Hyman 1980, 98.
129. Glenn 1990, 69.
130. Orleck 1995, 19, 25.
131. Glenn 1990, 116–117.
132. Glenn 1990, 77–78.
133. Glenn 1990, 66.
134. Glenn 1990, 76.
135. Newman 1917, 945.
136. Glenn 1990, 71.
137. Glenn 1990, 67.
138. Glenn 1990, 76.
139. Antin (1912) 1969, 52, 65.
140. Antin (1912) 1969, 68, 196.
141. Antin (1912) 1969, 144, 254–255.
142. Gilman 1914a.
143. See Tronto (1987, 649) for the argument that the ethic of care should be understood not as the result of gender difference but as the result of the subordinate position of the caregiver.
144. See Mattis 2010.
145. Gilman 1911a, 36.
146. Engels 1978, 744. See Van Wienen (2003, 616, 620–621), who presents the case for interpreting Gilman within the Marxist socialist tradition. In 1896, as a delegate, Gilman attended the International Labor and Socialist Congress in London.
147. Gilman 1911a, 36.
148. Gilman (1898) 1966, 279–280.
149. Engels 1978, 744.
150. Gilman 1913c, 146.
151. Gilman 1903, 113.
152. Gilman 1903, 116.
153. Gilman 1913d, 36.
154. Gilman (1898) 1966, 245, 246.
155. Engels 1978, 746.
156. Higginbotham 1993, 212. The women who came to Washington, D.C., were part of "the hundreds of thousands of blacks" who, according to Higginbotham (1993, 189) "abandoned the Jim Crow South between 1900 and 1920."
157. Higginbotham 1993, 217.

158. Gilman 1903, 121–122.

159. Gilman 1903, 110–111.

160. Gilman 1903, 121.

161. Gilman 1903, 122.

162. Gilman 1903, 119.

163. Burroughs 1902, 324, 326.

164. Higginbotham 1993, 205.

165. Higginbotham 1993, 112.

166. Hayden 1982. Higginbotham (1993, 214–215) links the National Training School to the new field of domestic science.

167. Wolcott 1997, 95–96.

168. Higginbotham 1993, 212.

169. Higginbotham 1993, 215.

170. Higginbotham 1993, 221.

171. Higginbotham 1993, 219.

172. Burroughs 1902, 325.

173. Burroughs 1902, 327.

174. Burroughs 1902, 329. This interpretation adds another subversive dimension to what Higginbotham (1993) calls the politics of respectability.

175. Du Bois (1920) 2004, 85, 86.

176. Du Bois (1920) 2004, 86–87.

177. Du Bois (1920) 2004, 87, 89.

178. Du Bois (1920) 2004, 86, 89.

179. Du Bois (1920) 2004, 89.

180. Du Bois (1920) 2004, 90.

181. Du Bois (1920) 2004, 90.

182. Du Bois (1920) 2004, 90.

183. Du Bois (1920) 2004, 91.

184. Du Bois (1920) 2004, 93.

185. Du Bois (1920) 2004, 90.

186. Du Bois (1920) 2004, 91.

187. Du Bois (1920) 2004, 92.

188. Du Bois (1920) 2004, 92–93.

189. Du Bois (1920) 2004, 93.

190. Gilman 1903, 129.

191. Gilman (1898) 1966, 227.

192. Gilman (1898) 1966, 229–230.

193. Gilman (1898) 1966, 228–229.

194. Gilman (1898) 1966, 226.

195. Gilman (1898) 1966, 230.

196. Gilman 1903, 132.

197. Gilman (1898) 1966, 242.

198. Gilman (1898) 1966, 228; 1913b, 270.

199. P. Hyman 1980.

200. Orleck 1995, 27.

201. P. Hyman 1980, 93.

202. P. Hyman 1980, 100.

203. P. Hyman 1980, 100.

204. Gilman 1913b.

205. P. Hyman 1980, 103; Orleck 1995, 26–27.

206. P. Hyman 1980, 102.

207. P. Hyman 1980, 102.

208. P. Hyman 1980, 96.

209. P. Hyman 1980, 105.

210. Orleck 1995, 57.

211. Marshall 1965, 77.

212. Marshall 1965, 71.

213. Marshall 1965, 75.

214. Marshall 1965, 87.

215. Shklar 1991, 92, 2, 92, 8.

216. Shklar 1991, 1, 67.

217. Marshall 1965, 81, 76. See Ritter (2006) for how married women's peculiar status affected their citizenship.

218. Marshall 1965, 81.

219. Shklar 1991, 84.

220. Shklar 1991, 88.

221. See Pateman (1989, chap. 8) for a critique of Marshall and a defense of revaluing unpaid care work.

222. Gilman (1898) 1966, 279.

223. I interpret Mill within the socialist tradition (Sarvasy 1985) and interconnect his feminism and socialism (Sarvasy 1991).

224. Mill 1993, 196, 197.

225. Gilman (1898) 1966, 107; 1903, 319–321.

226. Gilman 1913d, 36.

227. Gilman 1913b, 270.

228. It should be placed in the context of two other successful incremental legal strategies: Thurgood Marshall's leadership of the NAACP Legal Defense Fund to overturn the constitutional protection for legal segregation, and Pauli Murray's and Ruth Bader Ginsburg's efforts through the ACLU Women's Rights Project to include sex in interpretations of the Fourteenth Amendment's equal protection clause.

229. See J. Zimmerman 1991; Novkov 2001; Ritter 2006. For different interpretations, see Erickson 1989; Lipschultz 1989, 1996.

230. I bypass the extensive debate on whether or not sex-based labor laws were the best approach and focus only on the role they played in the social democratic feminist genealogy of social citizenship. For critiques of sex-based labor laws, see Baer 1978; Kessler-Harris 1982. Lipschultz (1989, 135n8) points out that the critics do not sufficiently differentiate between "hours restrictions and night work elimination" and "minimum wage laws."

231. Gilman 1911a, 24.

232. Gilman 1911a, 21.

233. Gilman 1911a, 237.

234. Gilman 1911a, 236–237.

235. Cooper (1892) 1988, 57–58.

236. Gilman 1911a, 255.

237. Gilman 1911a, 256.

238. By bringing Gilman and Kelley into relationship, I show how the maternalist labeling of Kelley and other social democratic feminists hides their project. They combined, in very sophisticated ways, the feminist aim of women's economic independence and the creation of the welfare state to achieve social justice.

239. Kelley 1911, 313.

240. Brandeis and Goldmark ([1908] 1969) reprint the unanimous decision for the U.S. Supreme Court after the brief, 6.

241. Brandeis and Goldmark (1908) 1969, 7.

242. Brandeis and Goldmark (1908) 1969, 6.

243. Brandeis and Goldmark (1908) 1969, 7.

244. Kelley 1912, 1005.

245. See Dorothy Douglas (1919) for framing the wage negotiations carried out by minimum wage boards as a type of collective bargaining. Although Hart (1992) does not use the concept of state feminism, her treatment of the Washington, D.C., minimum wage board suggests that it constituted a type of state feminism.

246. Marshall 1965, 93–94.

247. Kelley 1912, 1010.

248. Douglas 1919.

249. Frankfurter and Goldmark 1917, A13.

250. Frankfurter and Goldmark 1917, A29.

251. Frankfurter and Goldmark 1917, A36, A30. Compare Frankfurter's analysis with Marx's (1978d) theory of labor power.

252. Frankfurter and Goldmark 1917, A45.

253. Frankfurter and Goldmark 1917, A47.

254. Marshall 1965, 72.

255. Marshall 1965, 94.

256. Frankfurter and Goldmark 1917, A3.

257. See Novkov 2001, 146, 174.

258. Frankfurter and Goldmark 1917, A44.

CHAPTER 3

1. Graham 1996, introduction, 153.

2. Cott 1987, 29.

3. For analyses of women's partisan activism before and after the Nineteenth Amendment, see Gustafson, Miller, and Perry 1999; Andersen 1996.

4. Phillips 1998, 5.

5. Phillips 1998, 114.

6. Gustafason 1997, 11.

7. Phillips 1998, 82.

8. Phillips 1998, 176.

9. Phillips 1998, 25, 149.

10. Addams 1930, 12–13.

11. For an interpretation of suffragism itself as a social movement, see DuBois 1989.

12. Kraditor 1981, 143–144.

13. Materson 2009b, 8–11, 44–45.

14. Kraditor 1981; Terborg-Penn 1983, 1998.

15. Kraditor 1981, 136.

16. Kraditor 1981, 132, 138.

17. Addams (1906) 2007, 104.

18. Addams 1914, 6.

19. Addams 1930, 90–91.

20. Addams 1913b, 25.

21. Kraditor 1981, 150.

22. Andersen 1996, 50.

23. Kelley 1915, 16.

24. Malkiel, n.d., 12.

25. Addams 1914, 2, 1.

26. Addams 1914, 2–3.

27. Addams 1914, 6.

28. Addams 1930, 109–110.

29. Addams 1930, 23.

30. Addams 1930, 31.

31. Addams 1930, 29–30.

32. Buechler 1986, 149–153. Addams ([1910] 1961, 236–238) described the 1908 campaign in which she "acted as chairman of the federation of a hundred women's organizations."

33. Gustafson 1997, 11.

34. Addams 1913b, 25.

35. Addams 1912, 13.

36. Addams 1913b, 25.

37. Gustafson 2014, 117.

38. Addams 1930, 30; (1912) 1982, 174.

39. On the California women's suffrage movement, see Mead 2004, chap. 7; Katz 1995.

40. Gustafson 2014, 128.

41. Terrell (1940, chap. 27) describes the incident and her role in protesting it at the highest levels of power.

42. Addams (1912) 1982, 172, 170.

43. Addams (1912) 1982, 174.

44. Addams 1912, 14.

45. Addams 1930, 37.

46. Addams 1930, 29, 38–39.

47. Gustafson 2014, 137.

48. Addams 1930, 39.

49. Addams 1930, 39.

50. Addams 1930, 40.

51. Materson 2009b, 8, 21.

52. E. Brown 1997, 82.

53. Cooper (1892) 1988, 139.

54. Buechler 1986, 149. I rely on Materson (2009b, chap. 10) for details on the 1894 election.

55. Duster 1970, 234.

56. Materson 2009b, 27–28.

57. Materson 2009b, 39.

58. Materson 2009b, 20.

59. Duster 1970, 230.

60. Barber 2004, 51.

61. Barber 2004, 12. According to Barber, the first national demonstration in Washington was Coxey's Army, May 1, 1894. The aim of this march was to enact national legislation that would provide men with jobs building public roads. Barber (2004, 44) also argues that the NAWSA procession "set a precedent that decisively shaped the possibility for other activists seeking to march on Washington."

62. Hendricks 1995, 269.

63. Hendricks 1995, 269.

64. Duster 1970, 346.

65. Duster 1970, 345–348. See Hendricks 1999.

66. De Priest 1915, 179.

67. See Orleck 1995, 41–43; Lerner 1981.

68. Schneiderman with Goldthwaite 1967, 47, 48–49.

69. Orleck 1995, 111–112.

70. Orleck 1995, 112.

71. Orleck 1995, 42.

72. Orleck 1995, 94, 110; Miller 1978, 204.

73. Ovington 1914, 145. See Buhle (1981) on the Socialist Party and women's suffrage.

74. Orleck 1995, 99.

75. Tax 1980, 313n65.

76. By foregrounding their utilization of the theory of historical materialism, I aim to strengthen the case that they were engaged in producing new theory through their activism. Cf. Orleck 1995, 88.

77. See Keyssar (2000, 67–70) for a different version of the history of the working-class male vote.

78. Malkiel, n.d., 9–10.

79. I develop further how the bridgers theorized and actualized this two-part process to produce a desire for political inclusion in working-class women.

80. Newman 1914b; Orleck 1995, 107.

81. Schneiderman with Goldthwaite 1967, 121–122.

82. Marx 1978c, 441.

83. Schneiderman with Goldthwaite 1967, 122; cf. Orleck 1995, chap. 3.

84. For a discussion of democratizing the notion of cosmopolitanism, see Sarvasy 2009.

85. DuBois 1997, 134.

86. Blatch and Lutz 1940, 188–189.

87. *New York Times* 1915, 3.

88. Wald 1915b.

89. Daniels 1979; Graham 1996, 55–58.

90. Blatch and Lutz 1940, 139–140.

91. Wald 1915b.

92. Lerner 1986, 225–226.

93. See Kraditor (1981, chap. 6) for a discussion of nativism in the mainstream suffrage movement.

94. See Aptheker 1982.

95. Wells-Barnett (1909) 1990, 261.

96. For an explicit connection between enfranchisement and the passing of an Illinois law "for the suppression of mob violence," see Wells-Barnett (1910) 1990, 270.

97. Cott 1987, 31.

98. DuBois (1989, 200–202) argues that the severing provided the necessary condition for the development of an independent feminist movement.

99. DuBois 1987, 853–860.

100. F. Williams 1914, 566.

101. Terrell 1915, 14.

102. Du Bois (1912) 1970, 237.

103. Du Bois 1914, 180.
104. Wells-Barnett (1900) 1990, 246.
105. Duster 1970, 258–259.
106. Duster 1970, 274–278.
107. Addams (1901) 1977, 23.
108. Douglass 1892; (1893) 1991.
109. Addams (1901) 1977, 27.
110. Addams (1901) 1977, 23.
111. Wells-Barnett (1901) 1977, 29.
112. Wells-Barnett (1895) 1991, 145.
113. Wells-Barnett (1901) 1977, 29–30.
114. Cf. Hamington 2005.
115. Salem 1990, 148.
116. See Terrell 1907; Haley 2016.
117. Duster 1970, 321.
118. Duster 1970, 322.
119. Ovington 1924, 112.
120. Wells-Barnett (1909) 1990, 262.
121. Duster 1970, 299.
122. Addams 1911, 22.
123. Addams 1911, 23.
124. Addams (1912) 1982, 173.
125. Addams 1913a, 566.
126. Aptheker 1982; Carby 1985.
127. Addams (1901) 1977, 27.
128. Douglass 1892; (1893) 1991.
129. Duster 1970, 242; Schechter 2001, 115.
130. See Feimster 2009, chap. 4.
131. Wollstonecraft (1792) 1992, 140.
132. Wollstonecraft (1792) 1992, 247–248.
133. Wollstonecraft (1792) 1992, 231, 234.
134. Wollstonecraft (1792) 1992, 255.
135. Wollstonecraft (1792) 1992, 256.
136. Wollstonecraft (1792) 1992, 84, 256.
137. I. Harper (1922) 1969, 105.
138. Terrell 1940, 239, 259, 373.
139. I. Harper (1922) 1969, 106.
140. Wells-Barnett (1895) 1991, 147.
141. Hunton 1904, 281.
142. Burroughs 1915, 10.
143. Burroughs 1915, 10.
144. Burroughs 1915, 10.
145. Burroughs 1915, 10.
146. Higginbotham 1993, 190; Freedman 2013, chap. 4.
147. Terrell 1904, 862.
148. Terrell 1905, 23.
149. Terrell 1905, 19.
150. Terrell 1902, 178, 175.
151. Addams 1913c, 9.

152. Addams 1913c, ix. For a different interpretation of *A New Conscience and an Ancient Evil*, see V. Brown 2010.

153. Addams 1913c, 10.

154. Addams 1913c, 181.

155. Addams 1913c, 191.

156. Addams 1913c, 191.

157. Addams 1913c., 191, 198.

158. Addams 1913c, 211.

159. Addams 1913c, 211.

160. Addams 1913c, 192–193.

161. Addams 1913c, 194.

162. Addams 1913c, 212.

163. Addams 1913c, 211–212.

164. Addams 1913c, 212.

165. Malkiel, n.d., 11, 13; Schneiderman with Goldthwaite 1967, 86–87; Orleck 1995, 72–74.

166. Malkiel, n.d.

167. Orleck 1995, 53.

168. Cott 1987, 23.

169. Orleck 1995, 57.

170. For fuller treatments of the WTUL, see Davis 1964; Jacoby 1975; Dye 1975, 1980; Tax 1980; C. Hyman 1985; Lehrer 1987; Nutter 2000; Vapnek 2009.

171. Davis 1964, 11.

172. Jacoby 1975, 133.

173. Vapnek 2009, 145.

174. Orleck 1995, 106.

175. For more details on the Wage Earners' League for Woman Suffrage and the Industrial Section of WSP, see Jacoby 1975; Orleck 1995; Vapnek 2009.

176. See Dye 1975, 1980; Jacoby 1975.

177. For a discussion of WTUL prejudice against or misunderstanding of immigrant Jewish women workers, see Orleck 1995, 67–68; Kessler-Harris 1976, 13.

178. Schneiderman with Goldthwaite 1967, 113.

179. Newman 1914a.

180. Kessler-Harris 1987, 164; Schneiderman with Goldthwaite 1967, 76.

181. Orleck 1995, 46.

182. Newman 1914a.

183. Schneiderman with Goldthwaite 1967, 80.

184. Schneiderman with Goldthwaite 1967, 121.

185. Orleck 1995, 71.

186. Orleck 1995, 71; Schneiderman with Goldthwaite 1967, 121; Kessler-Harris 1987, 168.

187. Malkiel (1910) 1990, 104.

188. Schneiderman 1913, 136.

189. Marx 1978b, 4–5.

190. Schneiderman with Goldthwaite 1967, 5.

191. Schneiderman with Goldthwaite 1967, 6.

192. Schneiderman with Goldthwaite 1967, 105; Schneiderman 1913.

193. Schneiderman with Goldthwaite 1967, 89–90.

194. Schneiderman 1913.

195. Newman 1911, 296, emphasis in original.
196. Malkiel (1910) 1990, 85.
197. Schneiderman with Goldthwaite 1967, 86.
198. Newman 1911, 296.
199. Malkiel (1910) 1990, 106.
200. Rousseau 1992, 203.
201. Rousseau 1992, 214.
202. Rousseau 1992, 225.
203. Plato 1967, 156.
204. Plato 1967, 162.
205. Plato 1967, 163–164.
206. Malkiel, n.d., 8.
207. Lehrer 1987, 122.
208. Orleck 1995, 60. Because she had been a leader of the strike, Lemlich (1912) was able to address a middle-class audience to make the case for the necessity of the vote for working women. She described in detail their working conditions and their inability to get the bosses to listen to them because they did not have the political power of the vote.
209. Orleck 1995, 97.
210. Vapnek 2009, 150.
211. Glenn 1990, 207.
212. Orleck 1995, 35; Schofield 1997, 85.
213. Schepps (1912) 1976, 217–218.
214. Schneiderman (1912) 1998, 3, 4, 2.
215. Schneiderman (1912) 1998, 3–4.
216. Schneiderman (1912) 1998, 4.
217. Schneiderman (1912) 1998, 5, emphasis in original.
218. Schneiderman (1912) 1998, 5.
219. Schneiderman (1912) 1998, 5.
220. Schneiderman (1912) 1998, 2.
221. Schneiderman (1912) 1998, 5.
222. For the debate over the meaning of the WTUL's support for protective labor legislation, see Dye 1975; Kirkby 1987.
223. Cf. McGuire 2009.
224. Schneiderman with Goldthwaite 1967, 6.
225. Schneiderman with Goldthwaite 1967, 97–98.
226. Orleck 1995, 47.
227. Schneiderman with Goldthwaite 1967, 8; Newman 1911, 296; Malkiel (1910) 1990; O'Sullivan 1912.
228. Schneiderman with Goldthwaite 1967, 67–68.
229. Wheeler 1995, 35.
230. Pateman 1994, 340–341.
231. Burroughs 1915, 10.
232. Newman 1914b.
233. For my understanding of a relational notion of rights, I draw on Nedelsky 2001 and Minow 1990.
234. According to Nietzsche (1956, 159, 155), who criticized philosophers for not adopting a historicist methodology, "we need a critique of all moral values; the intrinsic worth of these values must, first of all, be called into question. To this end we need to know the conditions from which those values have sprung."

235. Marshall 1965, 77–78. Women who met a property qualification and the age requirement of thirty got the right to vote. In contrast, all men over the age of twenty-one with no property qualification gained the right to vote. For a comparison of the women's suffrage movements in the U.K. and the United States, see Banks 1986, chap. 8.

236. In order: Kraditor 1981; Keyssar 2000; Marilley 1996; Ritter 2000; Cott 1987.

237. Shklar 1991, 38, 57. See also Marilley 1996, 3; Ritter 2000.

238. Kraditor 1981, 66, 252.

239. Addams (1906) 2007, 21, 20, 18.

240. Addams (1906) 2007, 28.

241. Addams (1906) 2007, 21, 22.

242. Addams (1906) 2007, 19.

243. Addams (1906) 2007, 24.

244. Addams (1906) 2007, 21, 19.

245. Addams (1906) 2007, 114.

246. Addams 1914, 4.

247. See Cott (1990) for an analysis of the nonappearance of a women's bloc vote after the ratification of the Nineteenth Amendment.

248. In theorizing the meaning of the bloc vote, I have been influenced by critical legal studies, critical race studies, and critical feminist studies, all of which approach rights as a space for renegotiating power dynamics. See Crenshaw et al. 1995; Unger 1983; P. Williams 1987; Schneider 2000.

249. Orleck 1995, 110.

250. Orleck 1995, 110.

251. Cook 1978, 62, 61, 60.

252. See Cott 1987, chap. 2, for a treatment of the NWP and Alice Paul.

253. Terrell (1940, 316–317) reprints the letter that awards her the pin and that describes the public ceremony to be held at the national convention. She and her daughter Phyllis received pins. Terrell does not recount the meeting with Paul.

254. Giddings 1985, 168. For the whole effort, see Giddings 1985, 166–169; Cott 1987, 68–70; Terborg-Penn 1998, 156.

255. Cott 1987, 307n25.

256. Cook 1978, 62–63. The difference/equality debate broke out in the 1920s over sex-based labor laws and the ERA, but there was no common socializing space to build unity or a bloc vote among social democratic feminists. See Sarvasy (1992) for how social democratic feminists pursued new syntheses of equality and difference through the policy of mothers' pensions.

257. Ackerman (1991, 196) places "the women's suffrage movement" within "constitutional movements that have had an important but somewhat less sweeping, impact on constitutional values and structures."

258. Ackerman 1991, 316.

CHAPTER 4

1. Addams, Balch, and Hamilton (1915) 2003, 60. The passage comes from the chapter entitled "Women and Internationalism," written by Addams.

2. Elshtain 1987, 235–236; Goss and Heaney 2010, 29.

3. See Steinson 1980; Zeiger 1996.

4. Addams, Balch, and Hamilton (1915) 2003, 60.

5. Key 1916, 104.

6. Addams (1922) 2002, 76.

7. For during the war, see Dewey (1918) 1982 and Blatch 1918; for after the war, see Dewey 1945 and Blatch 1920.

8. Addams (1922) 2002, 76.

9. Hunton and Johnson (1920) 1971, 253. See Scheiber and Scheiber (1969) for the evolution from hope for racial justice to disillusionment with the Wilson administration.

10. Dawley 2003, 54.

11. Dawley 2003, 2, 5.

12. See Sarvasy (2009) for a discussion of Addams's distinct contributions to contemporary cosmopolitan theorizing.

13. Addams (1899) 2003, 1. At the beginning of 1899, the Senate debated and ratified the Treaty of Paris to end the Spanish-American War. Then it voted to annex the Philippines when a tie vote was broken by the vice president. Under the leadership of Emilio Aguinaldo, the Filipinos resisted the United States. The Philippine-American War lasted officially until 1902.

14. Addams (1906) 2007, 115. For discussions of how Addams's cosmopolitan or international theorizing was different from her contemporaries, see Herman 1969; Hoganson 2001; Hansen 2003; Fischer 2009.

15. See Hoganson (1998, 210–214n14) for the scholarly debate over the factors that led to the Spanish-American War.

16. Hoganson 1998, 150–151. See also Bederman 1995; Jacobson 2000; Kramer 2002.

17. W. James (1910) 1970, 11.

18. W. James (1910) 1970, 13.

19. W. James (1910) 1970, 12.

20. W. James (1910) 1970, 13.

21. Addams (1904b) 1976, 47.

22. Addams (1902) 1976, 20.

23. Addams (1904b) 1976, 47.

24. Addams (1904c) 1976, 49.

25. Addams (1907a) 1976.

26. Addams (1906) 2007, 120.

27. Addams (1899) 2003, 1–2.

28. Addams (1906) 2007, 19.

29. Addams (1910) 1961, 217.

30. Addams (1917) 2003, 166. This passage fleshed out a prewar example (Addams (1907b) 1976, 56).

31. Addams (1906) 2007, 13.

32. Elshtain 2002, 220–221.

33. Addams (1906) 2007, 43, 57.

34. Addams (1906) 2007, 130.

35. See Kramer (2002) for an analysis of how appeals to Anglo-Saxonism, understood as blood or culture, justified U.S. colonial imperialism in the Philippines.

36. Addams (1906) 2007, 28.

37. Addams (1900) 1976, 16.

38. Addams (1901) 2003, 11.

39. Addams (1901) 2003, 10.

40. Addams (1904a) 1976, 46.

41. Addams (1904a) 1976, 45.

42. Addams (1901) 2003, 11.

43. Addams (1904a) 1976, 45.

44. Addams (1906) 2007, 111–112.

45. Rodgers 1998, 7; Sklar, Schuler, and Strasser 1998, 1.

46. Rodgers 1998, 19.

47. Sklar, Schuler, and Strasser 1998, 4–6. They acknowledge that "social democrat" fits the U.S. women but does not work for the cross-border conversation because in Germany, it had the meaning of belonging to the Social Democratic Party.

48. Wikander 1995, 51.

49. Addams (1907a) 1976, 54.

50. Wikander 1995, 53.

51. Wikander 1995, 32–33, 30.

52. Rupp 1997, 140.

53. See Sarvasy 1992.

54. I dealt with factory inspectors as part of a pragmatist experiment to present a model of state feminism. Here I bring them into relationship with the theme of women's economic independence.

55. Sklar, Schuler, and Strasser 1998, 4.

56. Sklar, Schuler, and Strasser 1998, 18.

57. McFeely 1988, 16–17; Quataert 1983, 104–105; Kelley (1897) 1998, 100–101.

58. Kelley (1897) 1998, 97, 99.

59. Kelley (1897) 1998, 99.

60. Kelley (1897) 1998, 101–102.

61. Kelley (1897) 1998, 102–103.

62. Kelley (1897) 1998, 96–99.

63. Kelley (1897) 1998, 103–104.

64. See Sarvasy 1992, 334–339.

65. Kelley (1897) 1998, 100.

66. Sklar 1995, 249.

67. Kelley (1894) 1998, 92.

68. Brandeis and Goldmark (1908) 1969, 17, 18, 113.

69. McFeely 1988, 9, 36–41.

70. McFeely 1988, 36–40.

71. Quataert 1993, 176, 169.

72. Brandeis and Goldmark (1908) 1969, 105.

73. Brandeis and Goldmark (1908) 1969, 105, 104.

74. Brandeis and Goldmark (1908) 1969, 112.

75. Frankfurter 1916, 362.

76. *Muller v. Oregon* (1908) 1969, 4.

77. *Muller v. Oregon* (1908) 1969, 4–5.

78. Lubin and Winslow 1990, 1.

79. Keck and Sikkink 1998, 51–58; DuBois 1991, 20; 1994, 254; Rupp 1997, 111.

80. Keck and Sikkink 1998, 51–58.

81. Keyssar 2000, 13.

82. Terrell (1912) 1995, 154.

83. Whittick 1979, 31–32.

84. DuBois 1991, 20.

85. IWSA 1909, 62.

86. IWSA 1909, 62–63.

87. IWSA 1909, 65, 62–63.

88. MacMillan, Stritt, and Verone 1913, vii.

89. IWSA 1909, 63–64.

90. MacMillan, Stritt, and Verone 1913, xi.

91. Edwards 2008, 68.

92. Mead 2004, 138, 147, 218n90.

93. See Kazuko 1978; Edwards 2008.

94. Bosch with Kloosterman 1990, 98–99.

95. Catt (Marilley 1996, 196) referred to her "sad awakening" after her visit to China. She no longer believed that "America had a monopoly on all that stands for progress."

96. IWSA 1913, 89, 88.

97. IWSA 1909, 63.

98. IWSA 1913, 89, 90.

99. IWSA 1913, 95; Edwards 2008, 88; Kazuko 1978, 90.

100. IWSA 1913, 97–98.

101. IWSA 1913, 32–33.

102. IWSA 1913, 33; Kazuko (1978, 80–81, 85–86) lists "the Women's Assistance Society" as part of the WSA coalition.

103. Kazuko 1978, 81.

104. IWSA 1913, 96.

105. Kazuko 1978, 83.

106. On the relationship between Chinese and English suffragists, see Edwards 2008, 81, 71, 89; Kazuko 1978, 89.

107. IWSA 1913, 33.

108. Kazuko 1978, 89, 91.

109. IWSA 1913, 64.

110. IWSA 1913, 62.

111. IWSA 1913, 87.

112. Mead 2004, 53, 65.

113. IWSA 1913, 87.

114. IWSA 1913, 59.

115. Englander 1992, 49–50; Mead 2004, 137–138.

116. Englander 1992, 110–118, 128–129; Mead 2004, 13, 122–124.

117. Englander 1992, 50; Orleck 1995, 90.

118. Addams 1930, 87–88.

119. Addams (1906) 2007, 19, 21.

120. Cook 1978, 238–239.

121. As Glendon (2001, 177) wrote, "By expressly including women . . . the Preamble signals that the Declaration is not just a universalizing of the eighteenth-century 'rights of man,' but part of a new stage in the history of human rights."

122. See Bussey and Tims 1965; Costin 1982; Vellacott 1993; Alonso 1993; Rupp 1997; Schott 1997; Blackwell 2004; Plastas 2011; Confortini 2012; Cochran 2017.

123. Addams, Balch, and Hamilton (1915) 2003, 60–61.

124. See Fischer 2019.

125. Addams, Balch, and Hamilton (1915) 2003, 61.

126. Addams (1922) 2002, 139.

127. Addams, Balch, and Hamilton (1915) 2003, 6.

128. ICW 1915, 7.

129. ICW 1915, 7.

130. ICW 1915, 6.

131. Addams, Balch, and Hamilton (1915) 2003, 72.

132. ICW 1915, 8.

133. Addams, Balch, and Hamilton (1915) 2003, 74.

134. Cook 1978, 238.

135. Addams, Balch, and Hamilton (1915) 2003, 68.

136. Addams (1922) 2002, 138.

137. Addams, Balch, and Hamilton (1915) 2003, 9.

138. Addams, Balch, and Hamilton (1915) 2003, 68.

139. Swartz 1971, 25.

140. Addams, Balch, and Hamilton (1915) 2003, 74.

141. ICW 1915, 100.

142. Addams, Balch, and Hamilton (1915) 2003, 74–75.

143. Addams, Balch, and Hamilton (1915) 2003, 76.

144. I would argue that this rule brought into the deliberations an explicit recognition of unequal power in the midst of war.

145. ICW 1915, xxxix.

146. Addams (1922) 2002, 10.

147. Addams, Balch, and Hamilton (1915) 2003, 77.

148. Addams (1922) 2002, 11.

149. Addams, Balch, and Hamilton (1915) 2003, 65.

150. Addams (1919) 2003, 199–200.

151. Addams, Balch, and Hamilton (1915) 2003, 65.

152. Addams, Balch, and Hamilton (1915) 2003, 76.

153. Addams (1922) 2002, 87, 90. For a lively history of the official conference, see MacMillan 2003.

154. WILPF 1924, 42.

155. Vellacott 1993, 33.

156. WILPF 1924, 43.

157. I would argue that this rule provided one model of how to unbracket power inequalities during deliberations.

158. Addams (1919) 2003, 201.

159. Addams (1919) 2003, 200; (1922) 2002, 90.

160. Addams (1919) 2003, 200. For Addams's description of her own experience with political repression, see Addams (1922) 2002, chap. 6.

161. Addams (1919) 2003, 200.

162. Addams (1922) 2002, 94.

163. Addams (1919) 2003, 202.

164. Addams (1919) 2003, 199.

165. Addams (1919) 2003, 199–200.

166. WILPF 1924, 42.

167. Addams (1922) 2002, 90–91.

168. Sklar, Schuler, and Strasser 1998, 235.

169. Addams (1922) 2002, 122–123.

170. Addams (1922) 2002, 92.

171. Addams (1922) 2002, 92.

172. Addams (1922) 2002, 92.

173. Addams (1922) 2002, 95.

174. Addams (1922) 2002, 2.

175. Addams (1922) 2002, 115.

176. Addams (1922) 2002, 121.

177. For the context, see Veit 2013 and Kingsbury 2010.

178. Addams (1922) 2002, 48.

179. Addams (1922) 2002, 48–49, 51.

180. See Sarvasy (2009), where I develop a notion of Addams's feminist multileveled bread politics, derived from her wartime experiences, to illustrate her notion of rooted cosmopolitanism. See Fischer (2007) for an interpretation that places her wartime efforts within the context of care ethics.

181. Addams 1930, 146.

182. Addams (1922) 2002, 44.

183. Addams 1930, 146.

184. Addams (1919) 2003, 202.

185. Addams (1922) 2002, 127.

186. Terrell 1940, 333.

187. MacMillan 2003, 317–318.

188. Terrell 1940, 335. In her autobiography, Terrell (1940, 330) defined herself as a bridger by noting that both Addams, as WILPF's president, and Moorfield Storey, the NAACP's president, urged her to attend the 1919 Zurich Congress. On African American women bringing race to the peace movement, see Blackwell 2004; Plastas 2011.

189. Blackwell 2004, 12.

190. See Sarvasy (2015) for a more detailed presentation of the intersectional conversation, including the historical context.

191. Terrell 1940, 360. See Nelson (1970) for a complex treatment of the French occupation of the Rhineland.

192. Terrell 1940, 363.

193. Terrell 1940, 362.

194. Addams, Balch, and Hamilton (1915) 2003, 72.

195. Terrell 1940, 361.

196. Terrell 1940, 361.

197. Terrell 1940, 363.

198. WILPF 1921, 76.

199. WILPF 1921, 76.

200. WILPF 1921, 78.

201. Plastas 2011, 52.

202. Hunton and Johnson (1920) 1971, 186. See Chandler (1995) on African American women providing social service in France.

203. WILPF 1921, 78.

204. See Renda (2001) for a broad-ranging treatment of the meaning of the U.S. occupation of Haiti.

205. Renda 2001, 19.

206. Addams (1922) 2002, 33–34.

207. On Hunton, see Chandler 2005; Plastas 2011, 40–57. For the ICWDR, see Rief 2004, 214–218; Materson 2009a.

208. Renda 2001, 188.

209. Johnson (1920a) 1995, 217.

210. Johnson (1924) 1995, 65, 63.

211. Johnson (1920a) 1995, 217.

212. Johnson (1924) 1995, 64.

213. Johnson (1924) 1995, 65.

214. Stoler 2002, chaps. 2, 3.

215. Balch 1927, 115.

216. Johnson (1920b) 1995, 251; Balch 1927, 116.

217. Hunton and Johnson (1920) 1971, 183–184.

218. Balch 1927, 119.

219. Balch 1927, 135.

220. Narayan 1995, 135.

221. Johnson (1920a) 1995, 213.

222. Johnson (1924) 1995, 64. See Renda (2001) for an in-depth analysis of how paternalism shaped the U.S. occupiers.

223. Balch 1927, 156.

224. Balch 1927, 150, 152.

225. Balch 1927, 129.

226. Balch 1927, 153.

227. Balch 1927, 152, 153.

228. Balch 1927, 155.

229. See Hutchings and Dannreuther (1999) for the debate.

230. I use interchangeably "citizen of the world," "world citizenship," "global citizen," and "cosmopolitan citizenship." For recent debates among theorists of this concept, see Held 1995, 1998; Archibugi 1998; Linklater 1998, 1999; Hutchings 1999; Yuval-Davis 1999; Carter 2001; Bosniak 2001; Sarvasy and Longo 2004.

231. Cf. Hutchings 1999; Yuval-Davis 1999; Carter 2001. In her study of comparative feminisms, Katharine Anthony (1915, 3) attributed to women "an unconscious internationalism," because of their exclusion from nation-state citizenship, and she argued that their enfranchisement "has come too late to inculcate in them the narrow [nation-state] views of citizenship."

232. WILPF 1919, 69–70.

233. WILPF 1919, 132.

234. Addams (1932) 1976, 214–215.

235. Salem 1990, 227; Schneiderman with Goldthwaite 1967, 130–136.

236. Addams (1922) 2002, 47.

237. Addams (1924) 1976, 184–185.

238. G. Abbott 1917, 277.

239. Addams (1924) 1976, 185.

240. Cook 1978, 267.

241. Addams 1930, 103–104, 111.

242. Plastas 2011, 49–50.

243. Rief 2004, 215.

244. Contee 1972.

245. Plastas 2011, 53–54; Materson 2009a, 38–39; Chandler 2005, 278.

246. Du Bois (1920) 2004, 35, 119. See Balfour (2010) on Du Bois's notion of humanity.

247. Balch 1927, 113, 126.

248. Materson 2009a, 39.

249. For Schneiderman's experiences with and hopes for the ICWW, see Schneiderman with Goldthwaite 1967, 130–138, 170–171. See Cobble (2014) and Vapnek (2014) for complex interpretations of the ICWW, its significance, and the historical conditions that

undermined its ability to sustain itself. See Boris (2019) for evolution of the ILO beyond the early period.

250. *New York Times*, 1919.

251. Cobble 2014, 1069–1070.

252. "With the First International Congress of Working Women," 1919, 311–312.

253. Cobble 2014, 1063.

254. "With the First International Congress of Working Women," 1919, 314.

255. E. Abbott 1947, 5–6.

256. G. Abbott 1917, 79.

257. G. Abbott 1917, 76.

258. G. Abbott 1917, 78.

259. Addams 1930, 340.

260. Addams 1930, 319, 305, 320.

261. Addams 1930, 328, 325.

262. Costin 1983, 95.

263. E. Abbott 1947, 6.

264. Costin 1983, 94.

265. E. Abbott 1947, 6.

266. E. Abbott 1947, 36.

267. Hamilton (1943) 1985, 114.

268. Hamilton (1943) 1985, 118–119.

269. Hamilton (1943) 1985, 128.

270. Hamilton (1943) 1985, 255, 254.

271. Hamilton (1943) 1985, 257.

272. Hamilton (1943) 1985, 302.

273. Hamilton (1943) 1985, 316.

274. Hamilton (1943) 1985, 309.

275. Hamilton (1943) 1985, 314–315.

276. Hamilton (1943) 1985, 299.

277. Hamilton (1943) 1985, 299–300, 317.

278. For discussions of cosmopolitan citizenship and the need to create participatory models, see Linklater 1998; Thompson 1998.

279. Heater 1990, 272–276.

CHAPTER 5

1. Ackerman 1991.

2. For other thick interpretations of the Nineteenth Amendment, see J. Brown 1993; Siegel 2002, 2019; Hasen and Litman 2020. For a notion of movement-driven jurisprudence, see Guinier and Torres 2014.

3. For a preliminary interpretation of the significance of the Dobbs decision, see Sarvasy 2022.

4. Addams (1902) 2002, 9.

5. Muncy 1991.

6. Marx 1978a.

7. Pateman 1970.

8. Addams (1906) 2007, 67.

9. Sarvasy 2009, 188–189. See also Sarvasy and Longo 2004.

10. Hamilton (1943) 1985, 108.

11. Naples 1998.

12. For a different approach to this challenge that de-emphasizes the potential of women's economic independence to discredit a neoliberal understanding of capitalism, see Fraser 2009.

13. Harvey 2007. Cf. Wendy Brown (2005), who adopts a narrow economistic interpretation of laissez-faire and then draws a sharp contrast between nineteenth-century thinking and contemporary neoliberalism.

14. Polanyi 1957, 163.

15. Kelley 1911, 311.

16. Kelley 1911, 304.

17. Addams (1902) 2002, 12.

18. Esping-Andersen 1990, 37. For a feminist critique of Esping-Andersen's notion of decommodification, see Orloff 1993.

19. Gilman (1898) 1966, 279.

20. Du Bois (1920) 2004, 91, 93.

21. Gilman 1911a, 187, 188.

22. Kelley 1911, 311.

23. Robertson and Gebeloff 2020.

24. See Andrias (2016), who argues for bringing back wage boards.

25. For how the pandemic experience created an opening for adopting a concept of essential citizenship for women agrifood workers, see Sarvasy (forthcoming).

26. Cobble, Gordon, and Henry 2014; Laughlin et al. 2010.

27. Corder and Wolbrecht 2016.

28. Addams 1930, 39.

29. Du Bois 1915, 29.

30. Carroll 2018, 125–126.

31. Carroll 2018; Whitaker 2008.

32. Greenberg (2000, 5–6) shows that while southern white women joined white men in shifting their party identification away from the Democratic Party in the 1960s, many of them returned after Reagan to produce an 11 percent gender gap in party identification in 1992.

33. Corder and Wolbrecht 2016.

34. Freeman 2002, 17.

35. Cobble 2021, 158.

36. Corder and Wolbrecht 2016, 219.

37. This analysis builds on Smooth's (2006) intersectional reframing of the gender gap and her analysis of the crucial role of African American women voters.

38. Cobble, Gordon, and Henry 2014, 19, 48–49.

39. Cobble, Gordon, and Henry 2014, 9, 44–45; Cobble 2004, 78–79, 82, 89.

40. As Cobble, Gordon, and Henry (2014, xiii) explain, "Feminism was integral to larger progressive changes, with the result that it has sometimes blended so entirely into larger movements that historians have not noticed it."

41. Walker-McWilliams 2016, 109.

42. Harrison 1989, chap. 8.

43. On the feminization of poverty and how an intersectional analysis of women's poverty was necessary, see Sarvasy and Van Allen 1984.

44. E. Zimmerman 1984. The concept of the feminization of poverty made visible how a range of care responsibilities played a major role in causing women's poverty.

45. See Silliman et al. (2004) for the different streams of women of color and the ways they defined the reproductive justice movement.

46. Carroll 2018, 2006.

47. Addams (1906) 2007, 17.

48. Addams (1922) 2002, 114.

49. Addams (1922) 2002, 115.

50. Hamilton (1943) 1985, 311.

References

Abbott, Edith. 1947. "Three American Pioneers in International Social Welfare." *The Compass* 28 (4): 3–7, 36.

———. 1950a. "Grace Abbott and Hull House, 1908–21: Part I." *Social Science Review* 24 (3): 374–394.

———. 1950b. "Grace Abbott and Hull House, 1908–21: Part II." *Social Science Review* 24 (4): 493–518.

Abbott, Grace. 1917. *The Immigrant and the Community.* New York: Century.

Ackelsberg, Martha A. 2010. *Resisting Citizenship: Feminist Essays on Politics, Community, and Democracy.* New York: Routledge.

Ackerman, Bruce. 1991. *We the People I: Foundations.* Cambridge, MA: Belknap Press of Harvard.

Addams, Jane. 1892. "Hull House, Chicago: An Effort toward Social Democracy." *Forum* 14: 226–241.

———. (1893a) 1970. "The Objective Value of a Social Settlement." In *Philanthropy and Social Progress*, edited by Henry C. Adams, 27–56. New York: Crowell.

———. (1893b) 1970. "The Subjective Necessity for Social Settlements." In *Philanthropy and Social Progress*, edited by Henry C. Adams, 1–26. New York: Crowell.

———. 1894. "Domestic Service and the Family Claim." In *The World's Congress of Representative Women*, vol. 2, edited by May Wright Sewall, 626–631. Chicago, IL: Rand McNally.

———. (1894) 1982. "A Modern Lear." In *The Social Thought of Jane Addams*, edited by Christopher Lasch, 105–123. New York: Irvington Publishers.

———. 1895. "The Settlement as a Factor in the Labor Movement." In *Hull-House Maps and Papers*, 183–204. New York: Thomas Y. Crowell.

———. 1896. "A Belated Industry." *American Journal of Sociology* 1 (5): 536–550.

———. (1899) 2003. "Democracy or Militarism." In *Jane Addams's Writings on Peace*, edited by Marilyn Fischer and Judy D. Whipps, 1–4. Bristol, UK: Thoemmes Press.

———. (1900) 1976. "Commercialism Disguised as Patriotism and Duty." In *Jane Addams on Peace, War, and International Understanding 1899–1932*, edited by Allen Davis, 15–18. New York: Garland Publishing.

———. (1901) 1977. "Respect for Law." In *Lynching and Rape: An Exchange of Views*, edited by Bettina Aptheker, 22–27. New York: American Institute for Marxist Studies.

———. (1901) 2003. "One Menace to the Century's Progress." In *Jane Addams's Writings on Peace*, edited by Marilyn Fischer and Judy D. Whipps, 9–12. Bristol, UK: Thoemmes Press.

———. (1902) 1976. "The Newer Ideals of Peace." In *Jane Addams on Peace, War, and International Understanding 1899–1932*, edited by Allen Davis, 19–25. New York: Garland Publishing.

———. (1902) 2002. *Democracy and Social Ethics*. Urbana: University of Illinois Press.

———. 1903. "The Servant Problem." *Good Housekeeping* 37 (3): 233–240.

———. (1904a) 1976. "Address of Miss Jane Addams." In *Jane Addams on Peace, War, and International Understanding 1899–1932*, edited by Allen Davis, 44–46. New York: Garland Publishing.

———. (1904b) 1976. "Address of Miss Jane Addams." In *Jane Addams on Peace, War, and International Understanding 1899–1932*, edited by Allen Davis, 47–48. New York: Garland Publishing.

———. (1904c) 1976. "Address of Miss Jane Addams." In *Jane Addams on Peace, War, and International Understanding 1899–1932*, edited by Allen Davis, 49–50. New York: Garland Publishing.

———. (1906) 2007. *Newer Ideals of Peace*. Urbana: University of Illinois Press.

———. (1907a) 1976. "New Ideals of Peace." In *Jane Addams on Peace, War, and International Understanding 1899–1932*, edited by Allen Davis, 51–55. New York: Garland Publishing.

———. (1907b) 1976. "The New Internationalism." In *Jane Addams on Peace, War, and International Understanding 1899–1932*, edited by Allen Davis, 56–59. New York: Garland Publishing.

———. (1910) 1961. *Twenty Years at Hull-House*. New York: New American Library.

———. 1911. "Social Control." *The Crisis* 1 (3): 22–23.

———. 1912. "My Experiences as a Progressive Delegate." *McClure's Magazine* 40:12–14.

———. (1912) 1982. "The Progressive Party and the Negro." In *The Social Thought of Jane Addams*, edited by Christopher Lasch, 169–174. New York: Irvington Publishers.

———. 1913a. "Has the Emancipation Act Been Nullified by National Indifference." *Survey* 29 (13): 566–567.

———. 1913b. "Miss Addams." *Ladies' Home Journal* 30 (1): 25.

———. 1913c. *A New Conscience and an Ancient Evil*. New York: Macmillan.

———. 1914. "The Larger Aspects of the Woman's Movement." *Annals of the American Academy of Political and Social Science* 56:1–8.

———. (1916) 2002. *The Long Road of Woman's Memory*. Urbana: University of Illinois Press.

———. (1917) 2003. "Labor as a Factor in the Newer Conception of International Relationships." In *Jane Addams's Writings on Peace*, edited by Marilyn Fischer and Judy D. Whipps, 165–170. Bristol, UK: Thoemmes Press.

———. (1918) 1976. "The Corn Mothers." In *Jane Addams on Peace, War, and International Understanding*, edited by Allen Davis, 155–164. New York: Garland Publishing.

———. (1919) 2003. "Addresses at the 1919 International Congress of Women, Zurich, 12–19 May." In *Jane Addams's Writings on Peace*, edited by Marilyn Fischer and Judy D. Whipps, 197–202. Bristol, UK: Thoemmes Press.

———. (1922) 2002. *Peace and Bread in Time of War*. Urbana: University of Illinois Press.

———. (1924) 1976. "Opening Address by Jane Addams." In *Jane Addams on Peace, War, and International Understanding*, edited by Allen Davis, 184–187. New York: Garland Publishing.

———. 1930. *The Second Twenty Years at Hull-House*. New York: MacMillan.

———. (1932) 1976. "How to Build a Peace Program? William Hard Asks—Jane Addams Answers." In *Jane Addams on Peace, War, and International Understanding*, edited by Allen Davis, 213–227. New York: Garland Publishing.

Addams, Jane, Emily Balch, and Alice Hamilton. (1915) 2003. *Women at The Hague: The International Congress of Women and Its Results*. Urbana: University of Illinois Press.

Alexander, Elizabeth. 1995. "'We Must Be About Our Father's Business': Anna Julia Cooper and the Incorporation of the Nineteenth-Century African-American Woman Intellectual." *Signs* 20 (2): 336–356.

Allen, Judith A. 2009. *The Feminism of Charlotte Perkins Gilman: Sexualities, Histories, Progressivism*. Chicago, IL: University of Chicago Press.

Allen, Polly. 1988. *Building Domestic Liberty: Charlotte Perkins Gilman's Architectural Feminism*. Amherst: University of Massachusetts Press.

Alonso, Harriet Hyman. 1993. *Peace as a Women's Issue: A History of the U.S. Movement for World Peace and Women's Rights*. Syracuse, NY: Syracuse University Press.

Alvarez, Sonia. 1990. *Engendering Democracy in Brazil: Women's Movements in Transition Politics*. Princeton, NJ: Princeton University Press.

Amalgamated Clothing Workers of America Research Department. 1922. "The Strike of 1910." In *The Clothing Workers of Chicago: 1910–1922*, 17–48. Chicago, IL: Chicago Joint Board, Amalgamated Clothing Workers of America.

Andersen, Kristi. 1996. *After Suffrage: Women in Partisan and Electoral Politics before the New Deal*. Chicago, IL: University of Chicago Press.

Andrias, Kate. 2016. "The New Labor Law." *Yale Law Journal* 126 (1): 2–100.

Ansell-Pearson, Keith. 1999. *An Introduction to Nietzsche as Political Thinker*. Cambridge: Cambridge University Press.

Anthony, Katharine. 1915. *Feminism in Germany and Scandinavia*. New York: Henry Holt.

Antin, Mary. (1912) 1969. *The Promised Land*. Boston: Houghton Mifflin.

Aptheker, Bettina. 1982. *Women's Legacy: Essays on Race, Sex, and Class in American History*. Amherst: University of Massachusetts Press.

Archibugi, Daniele. 1998. "Principles of Cosmopolitan Democracy." In *Re-imagining Political Community: Studies in Cosmopolitan Democracy*, edited by Daniele Archibugi, David Held, and Martin Kohler, 198–228. Stanford, CA: Stanford University Press.

Arendt, Hannah. 1965. *On Revolution*. London: Penguin Books.

———. 1989. *The Human Condition*. Chicago, IL: University of Chicago Press.

Aristotle. 1967. *The Politics of Aristotle*, edited and translated by Ernest Barker. New York: Oxford University Press.

Baer, Judith A. 1978. *The Chains of Protection: The Judicial Response to Women's Labor Legislation*. Westport, CT: Greenwood Press.

Balch, Emily Greene. 1927. *Occupied Haiti*. New York: Writers Publishing.

Balfour, Lawrie. 2005. "Representative Women: Slavery, Citizenship, and Feminist Theory in Du Bois's 'Damnation of Women.'" *Hypatia* 20 (3): 127–148.

———. 2010. "Darkwater's Democratic Vision." *Political Theory* 38 (4): 537–563.

Banks, Olive. 1986. *Faces of Feminism: A Study of Feminism as a Social Movement*. New York: Basil Blackwell.

Barber, Lucy G. 2004. *Marching on Washington: The Forging of an American Political Tradition.* Berkeley: University of California Press.

Barrett, James R., and David Roediger. 1997. "Inbetween Peoples: Race, Nationality and the 'New Immigrant' Working Class." *Journal of American Ethnic History* 16 (3): 3–44.

Bederman, Gail. 1995. *Manliness and Civilization: A Cultural History of Gender and Race in the United States, 1880–1917.* Chicago, IL: University of Chicago Press.

Benhabib, Seyla. 1995. "The Pariah and Her Shadow: Hannah Arendt's Biography of Rahel Varnhagen." In *Feminist Interpretations of Hannah Arendt,* edited by Bonnie Honig, 83–104. University Park: Pennsylvania State University Press.

———. 1996. "Toward a Deliberative Model of Democratic Legitimacy." In *Democracy and Difference: Contesting the Boundaries of the Political,* edited by Seyla Benhabib, 67–94. Princeton, NJ: Princeton University Press.

Berman, Sheri. 2009. "The Primacy of Economics versus the Primacy of Politics: Understanding the Ideological Dynamics of the Twentieth Century." *Perspectives on Politics* 7 (3): 561–578.

Bernal, Angelica Maria. 2017. *Beyond Origins: Rethinking Founding in a Time of Constitutional Democracy.* New York: Oxford University Press.

Bickford, Susan. 1996. *The Dissonance of Democracy.* Ithaca, NY: Cornell University Press.

Blackwell, Joyce. 2004. *No Peace without Freedom: Race and the Women's International League for Peace and Freedom, 1915–1975.* Carbondale: Southern Illinois University Press.

Blatch, Harriot Stanton. 1918. *Mobilizing Woman-Power.* New York: Womans Press.

———. 1920. *A Woman's Point of View.* New York: Womans Press.

Blatch, Harriot Stanton, and Alma Lutz. 1940. *Challenging Years: The Memoirs of Harriot Stanton Blatch.* New York: G. P. Putnam's Sons.

Boris, Eileen. 1993. "The Power of Motherhood: Black and White Activist Women Redefine the 'Political.'" In *Mothers of a New World: Maternalist Politics and the Origins of Welfare States,* edited by Seth Koven and Sonya Michel, 213–245. New York: Routledge.

———. 2019. *Making the Woman Worker: Precarious Labor and the Fight for Global Standards, 1919–2019.* New York: Oxford University Press.

Bosch, Mineke, with Annemarie Kloosterman, eds. 1990. *Politics and Friendship: Letters from the International Woman Suffrage Alliance, 1902–1942.* Columbus: Ohio State University Press.

Bosniak, Linda. 2001. "Denationalizing Citizenship." In *Citizenship Today: Global Perspectives and Practices,* edited by T. Alexander Aleinikoff and Douglas Klusmeyer, 237–251. Washington, D.C.: Carnegie Endowment for International Peace.

Brandeis, Louis D., and Josephine Goldmark. (1908) 1969. *Women in Industry.* New York: Arno and *New York Times.*

Breitzer, Susan Roth. 2010. "Uneasy Alliances: Hull House, the Garment Workers Strikes, and the Jews of Chicago." *Indiana Magazine of History* 106 (1): 40–70.

Brown, Elsa Barkley. 1997. "To Catch the Vision of Freedom: Reconstructing Southern Black Women's Political History, 1865–1880." In *African American Women and the Vote, 1837–1965,* edited by Ann D. Gordon with Bettye Collier-Thomas, John H. Bracey, Arlene Voski Avakian, and Joyce Avrech Berkman, 66–99. Amherst: University of Massachusetts Press.

Brown, Jennifer K. 1993. "The Nineteenth Amendment and Women's Equality." *Yale Law Journal* 102 (8): 2175–2204.

Brown, Victoria Bissell. 2010. "Sex and the City: Jane Addams Confronts Prostitution." In *Feminist Interpretations of Jane Addams*, edited by Maurice Hamington, 125–157. University Park: Pennsylvania State University Press.

Brown, Wendy. 1992. "Finding the Man in the State." *Feminist Studies* 18 (1): 7–34.

———. 2005. *Edgework: Critical Essays on Knowledge and Politics*. Princeton, NJ: Princeton University Press.

Buechler, Steven M. 1986. *The Transformation of the Woman Suffrage Movement: The Case of Illinois, 1850–1920*. New Brunswick, NJ: Rutgers University Press.

Buhle, Mari Jo. 1976. "Socialist Women and the 'Girl Strikers,' Chicago, 1910." *Signs* 1 (4): 1039–1051.

———. 1981. *Women and American Socialism, 1870–1920*. Urbana: University of Illinois Press.

Burroughs, Nannie Helen. 1902. "The Colored Woman and Her Relation to the Domestic Problem." In *The United Negro, His Problems and His Progress*, edited by John W. E. Bowen and I. Garland Penn, 324–329. Atlanta, GA: D. E. Luther Publishing.

———. 1915. "Black Women and Reform." *The Crisis* 10 (4): 10.

Bussey, Gertrude, and Margaret Tims. 1965. *Women's International League for Peace and Freedom 1915–1965*. London: George Allen & Unwin.

Carby, Hazel V. 1985. "'On the Threshold of Woman's Era': Lynching, Empire, and Sexuality in Black Feminist Theory." *Critical Inquiry* 12 (1): 262–277.

———. 1987. *Reconstructing Womanhood: The Emergence of the Afro-American Woman Novelist*. New York: Oxford University Press.

———. 2007. "The Souls of Black Men." In *Next to the Color Line: Gender, Sexuality, and W.E.B. Du Bois*, edited by Susan Gillman and Alys Eve Weinbaum, 234–268. Minneapolis: University of Minnesota Press.

Carroll, Susan J. 2006. "Moms Who Swing or Why the Promise of the Gender Gap Remains Unfulfilled." *Politics and Gender* 2 (3): 362–374.

———. 2018. "Voting Choices: The Significance of Women Voters and the Gender Gap." In *Gender and Elections: Shaping the Future of American Politics*, edited by Susan J. Carroll and Richard L. Fox, 116–143. New York: Cambridge University Press.

Carter, April. 2001. *The Political Theory of Global Citizenship*. New York: Routledge.

Chandler, Susan. 1995. "'That Biting, Stinging Thing Which Ever Shadows Us': African-American Social Workers in France during World War I." *Social Service Review* 69 (3): 498–514.

———. 2005. "Addie Hunton and the Construction of an African American Female Peace Perspective." *Affilia* 20 (3): 270–283.

Cho, Sumi, Kimberlé Williams Crenshaw, and Leslie McCall. 2013. "Toward a Field of Intersectionality Studies: Theory, Applications, and Praxis." *Signs* 38 (4): 785–810.

Cobble, Dorothy Sue. 2004. *The Other Women's Movement: Workplace Justice and Social Rights in Modern America*. Princeton, NJ: Princeton University Press.

———. 2014. "A Higher 'Standard of Life' for the World: U.S. Labor Women's Reform Internationalism and the Legacies of 1919." *Journal of American History* 100 (4): 1052–1085.

———. 2021. *For the Many: American Feminists and the Global Fight for Democratic Equality*. Princeton, NJ: Princeton University Press.

Cobble, Dorothy Sue, Linda Gordon, and Astrid Henry. 2014. *Feminism Unfinished: A Short Surprising History of American Women's Movements*. New York: Liveright Publishing.

Cochran, Molly. 2017. "The 'Newer Ideals' of Jane Addams's Progressivism: A Realistic Utopia of Cosmopolitan Justice." In *Progressivism and US Foreign Policy between the World Wars*, edited by Molly Cochran and Cornelia Navari, 143–165. New York: Palgrave MacMillan.

Cohen, Rose. (1918) 1995. *Out of the Shadow: A Russian Jewish Girlhood on the Lower East Side*. Ithaca, NY: Cornell University Press.

Collins, Patricia Hill. 1991. *Black Feminist Thought*. New York: Routledge.

———. 2011. "Piecing Together a Genealogical Puzzle: Intersectionality and American Pragmatism." *European Journal of Pragmatism and American Philosophy* 3 (2): 88–112.

Confortini, Catia Cecilia. 2012. *Intelligent Compassion: Feminist Critical Methodology in the Women's International League for Peace and Freedom*. New York: Oxford University Press.

Contee, Clarence G. 1972. "Du Bois, the NAACP, and the Pan-African Congress of 1919." *Journal of Negro History* 57 (1): 13–28.

Cook, Blanche Wiesen, ed. 1978. *Crystal Eastman on Women and Revolution*. New York: Oxford University Press.

Cooper, Anna J. (1892) 1988. *A View from the South*. New York: Oxford University Press.

———. 1894. "Discussion of the Same Subject." In *The World's Congress of Representative Women*, vol. 2, edited by May Wright Sewall, 711–715. Chicago, IL: Rand McNally.

———. 1913. *The Social Settlement: What It Is and What It Does*. Washington, D.C.: Murray Brothers Press.

Corder, J. Kevin, and Christina Wolbrecht. 2016. *Counting Women's Ballots: Female Voters from Suffrage through the New Deal*. New York: Cambridge University Press.

Costin, Lela B. 1982. "Feminism, Pacifism, Internationalism and the 1915 International Congress of Women." *Women's Studies International Forum* 5 (3/4): 301–315.

———. 1983. *Two Sisters for Social Justice: A Biography of Grace and Edith Abbott*. Urbana: University of Illinois Press.

Cott, Nancy F. 1987. *The Grounding of Modern Feminism*. New Haven, CT: Yale University Press.

———. 1989. "What's in a Name? The Limits of 'Social Feminism'; or, Expanding the Vocabulary of Women's History." *Journal of American History* 76 (3): 809–829.

———. 1990. "Across the Great Divide: Women in Politics before and after 1920." In *Women, Politics, and Change*, edited by Louise A. Tilly and Patricia Gurin, 153–176. New York: Russell Sage Foundation.

Crenshaw, Kimberlé. 1995. "Mapping the Margins: Intersectionality, Identity Politics, and Violence against Women of Color." In *Critical Race Theory: The Key Writings That Formed the Movement*, edited by Kimberlé Crenshaw, Neil Gotanda, Gary Peller, and Kendall Thomas, 357–383. New York: New Press.

Crenshaw, Kimberlé, Neil Gotanda, Gary Peller, and Kendall Thomas, eds. 1995. *Critical Race Theory: The Key Writings That Formed the Movement*. New York: New Press.

Daniels, Doris. 1979. "Building a Winning Coalition: The Suffrage Fight in New York State." *New York History* 60 (1): 58–80.

Davis, Allen F. 1964. "The Women's Trade Union League: Origins and Organization." *Labor History* 5 (1): 3–17.

———. 1973. *American Heroine: The Life and Legend of Jane Addams*. New York: Oxford University Press.

Dawley, Alan. 2003. *Changing the World: American Progressives in War and Revolution*. Princeton, NJ: Princeton University Press.

De Priest, Oscar. 1915. "Chicago and Woman's Suffrage." *The Crisis* 10 (4): 2.

Dewey, John. (1918) 1982. "What Are We Fighting For?" In *The Middle Works 1899–1924*, vol. 2, *1918–1919*, edited by Jo Ann Boydston, 98–106. Carbondale: Southern Illinois University Press.

———. 1945. "Democratic Versus Coercive International Organization: The Realism of Jane Addams." New introduction to *Peace and Bread in Time of War*, by Jane Addams, ix–xx. New York: King's Cross Press.

Douglas, Dorothy W. 1919. "American Minimum Wage Laws at Work." *American Economic Review* 9 (4): 701–738.

Douglass, Frederick. 1892. "Lynch Law in the South." *North American Review* 155 (428): 17–24.

———. (1893) 1991. "The Reason Why: Introduction." In *Selected Works of Ida B. Wells-Barnett*, compiled with an introduction by Trudier Harris, 50–61. New York: Oxford University Press.

DuBois, Ellen Carol. 1987. "Outgrowing the Compact of the Fathers: Equal Rights, Woman Suffrage, and the United States Constitution, 1820–1878." *Journal of American History* 74 (3): 836–862.

———. 1989. *Feminism and Suffrage: The Emergence of an Independent Women's Movement in America 1848–1869*. Ithaca, NY: Cornell University Press.

———. 1991. "Woman Suffrage and the Left: An International Socialist-Feminist Perspective." *New Left Review* 186:20–45.

———. 1994. "Woman Suffrage around the World: Three Phases of Suffragist Internationalism." In *Suffrage and Beyond: International Feminist Perspectives*, edited by Caroline Daley and Melanie Nolan, 252–274. New York: New York University Press.

———. 1997. *Harriot Stanton Blatch and the Winning of Woman Suffrage*. New Haven, CT: Yale University Press.

Du Bois, W.E.B. (1903) 1989. *The Souls of Black Folk*. New York: Bantam Books.

———. (1912) 1970. "Disfranchisement." In *W.E.B. Du Bois Speaks: Speeches and Addresses 1890–1919*, edited by Philip S. Foner, 230–238. New York: Pathfinder Press.

———. (1912) 1995. "The Black Mother." In *W.E.B. Du Bois: A Reader*, edited by David Levering Lewis, 294. New York: Henry Holt.

———. 1914. "Votes for Women." *The Crisis* 8:179–180.

———. 1915. "Woman Suffrage." *The Crisis* 11:29–30.

———. (1920) 2004. *Darkwater: Voices from within the Veil*. New York: Washington Square Press.

Durst, Anne. 2005. "'Of Women, by Women, and for Women': The Day Nursery Movement in the Progressive-Era United States." *Journal of Social History* 39 (1): 141–159.

Duster, Alfreda M., ed. 1970. *Crusade for Justice: The Autobiography of Ida B. Wells*. Chicago, IL: University of Chicago Press.

Dye, Nancy Schrom. 1975. "Creating a Feminist Alliance: Sisterhood and Class Conflict in the New York Women's Trade Union League, 1903–1914." *Feminist Studies* 2 (2/3): 24–38.

———. 1980. *As Equals and As Sisters: Feminism, the Labor Movement, and the Women's Trade Union League of New York*. Columbia: University of Missouri Press.

Edwards, Louise. 2008. *Gender, Politics, and Democracy: Women's Suffrage in China*. Stanford, CA: Stanford University Press.

Elshtain, Jean Bethke. 1987. *Women and War*. New York: Basic Books.

———. 2002. *Jane Addams and the Dream of American Democracy*. New York: Basic Books.

Engels, Friedrich. 1978. "The Origin of the Family, Private Property, and the State." In *The Marx-Engels Reader*, edited by Robert C. Tucker, 734–759. New York: W. W. Norton.

Englander, Susan. 1992. *Class Coalition and Class Conflict in the California Woman Suffrage Movement, 1907–1912*. San Francisco, CA: Mellen Research University Press.

Erickson, Nancy S. 1989. "Muller v. Oregon Reconsidered: The Origins of a Sex-Based Doctrine of Liberty of Contract." *Labor History* 30 (2): 228–250.

Esping-Andersen, Gosta. 1990. *The Three Worlds of Welfare Capitalism*. Princeton, NJ: Princeton University Press.

Ewen, Elizabeth. 1985. *Immigrant Women in the Land of Dollars: Life and Culture on the Lower East Side 1890–1925*. New York: Monthly Review Press.

Feimster, Crystal N. 2009. *Southern Horrors: Women and the Politics of Rape and Lynching*. Cambridge, MA: Harvard University Press.

Fischer, Marilyn. 2007. "Caring Globally: Jane Addams, World War One, and International Hunger." In *Global Feminist Ethics*, edited by Rebecca Whisnant and Peggy DesAutels, 61–79. New York: Rowman and Littlefield.

———. 2009. "The Conceptual Scaffolding of *Newer Ideals of Peace*." In *Jane Addams and the Practice of Democracy*, edited by Marilyn Fischer, Carol Nackenoff, and Wendy Chmielewski, 165–182. Urbana: University of Illinois Press.

———. 2010. "Trojan Women and Devil Baby Tales: Addams on Domestic Violence." In *Feminist Interpretations of Jane Addams*, edited by Maurice Hamington, 81–105. University Park: Pennsylvania State University Press.

———. 2019. *Jane Addams's Evolutionary Theorizing: Constructing Democracy and Social Ethics*. Chicago, IL: University of Chicago Press.

Foner, Eric. 2019. *The Second Founding: How the Civil War and Reconstruction Remade the Constitution*. New York: Norton.

Foucault, Michel. 1984. "Nietzsche, Genealogy, History." In *The Foucault Reader*, edited by Paul Rabinow, 76–100. New York: Pantheon Books.

Frankfurter, Felix. 1916. "Hours of Labor and Realism in Constitutional Law." *Harvard Law Review* 29 (4): 353–373.

Frankfurter, Felix, and Josephine Goldmark. 1917. *Oregon Minimum Wage Cases*. New York: National Consumers' League.

Fraser, Nancy. 1997. *Justice Interruptus: Critical Reflections on the "Postsocialist" Condition*. New York: Routledge.

———. 2009. "Feminism, Capitalism and the Cunning of History." *New Left Review* 56: 97–117.

Freedman, Estelle B. 2013. *Redefining Rape: Sexual Violence in the Era of Suffrage and Segregation*. Cambridge, MA: Harvard University Press.

Freeman, Jo. 2002. *A Room at a Time: How Women Entered Party Politics*. Lantham, MD: Rowman and Littlefield.

Ganobcsik-Williams, Lisa. 1999. "The Intellectualism of Charlotte Perkins Gilman: Evolutionary Perspectives on Race, Ethnicity, and Class." In *Charlotte Perkins Gilman: Optimist Reformer*, edited by Jill Rudd and Val Gough, 16–41. Iowa City: University of Iowa Press.

Giddings, Paula. 1985. *When and Where I Enter: The Impact of Black Women on Race and Sex in America*. New York: Bantam Books.

Gilkes, Cheryl Townsend. 1996. "The Margin as the Center of a Theory of History: African-American Women, Social Change, and the Sociology of W.E.B. Du Bois." In *W.E.B. Du Bois on Race and Culture*, edited by Bernard W. Bell, Emily Grosholz, and James B. Stewart, 111–139. New York: Routledge.

Gillman, Susan, and Alys Eve Weinbaum. 2007. *Next to the Color Line: Gender, Sexuality, and W.E.B. Du Bois*. Minneapolis: University of Minnesota Press.

Gilman, Charlotte Perkins. (1898) 1966. *Women and Economics: A Study of the Economic Relation between Men and Women as a Factor in Social Evolution*. New York: Harper & Row.

———. 1903. *The Home: Its Work and Influence*. New York: McClure, Phillips.

———. 1911a. *The Man-Made World or Our Androcentric Culture*. New York: Charlton.

———. 1911b. "Notice for *The Diary of a Shirtwaist* Striker." *The Forerunner* 2 (3): 86.

———. 1913a. "Education for Motherhood." *The Forerunner* 4 (10): 259–262.

———. 1913b. "Minimum Wage and Maximum Price." *The Forerunner* 4 (10): 269–270.

———. 1913c. "The New Mothers of a New World." *The Forerunner* 4 (6): 145–149.

———. 1913d. "On Ellen Key and the Woman Movement." *The Forerunner* 4 (2): 35–38.

———. 1914a. "Immigration, Importation, and Our Fathers." *The Forerunner* 5 (5): 117–119.

———. 1914b. "Pensions for 'Mothers' and 'Widows.'" *The Forerunner* 5 (1): 7–8.

———. (1915) 1979. *Herland*. New York: Pantheon Books.

———. 1916. "Maternity Benefits and Reformers." *The Forerunner* 7 (3): 65–66.

———. (1935) 1990. *The Living of Charlotte Perkins Gilman: An Autobiography*. Madison: University of Wisconsin Press.

Glendon, Mary Ann. 2001. *A World Made New: Eleanor Roosevelt and the Universal Declaration of Human Rights*. New York: Random House.

Glenn, Susan A. 1990. *Daughters of the Shtetl: Life and Labor in the Immigrant Generation*. Ithaca, NY: Cornell University Press.

Goldstein, Eric L. 2006. *The Price of Whiteness*. Princeton, NJ: Princeton University Press.

Gordon, Linda, ed. 1990. *Women, the State, and Welfare*. Madison: University of Wisconsin Press.

———. 1994. *Pitied but Not Entitled: Single Mothers and the History of Welfare, 1890–1935*. New York: Free Press.

Goss, Kristin A., and Michael T. Heaney. 2010. "Organizing Women *as Women*: Hybridity and Grassroots Collective Action in the 21st Century." *Perspectives on Politics* 8 (1): 27–52.

Gould, Carol C. 1993. "Feminism and Democratic Community Revisited." In *Democratic Community: NOMOS XXXV*, edited by John W. Chapman and Ian Shapiro, 396–413. New York: New York University Press.

Graham, Sara Hunter. 1996. *Woman Suffrage and the New Democracy*. New Haven, CT: Yale University Press.

Grant, Judith. 1993. *Fundamental Feminism: Contesting the Core Concepts of Feminist Theory*. New York: Routledge.

Greenberg, Anna. 2000. "Why Men Leave: Gender and Partisanship in the 1990s." Paper delivered at the Annual Meeting of the American Political Science Association, Washington, D.C., August 31–September 3, 2000.

Guinier, Lani, and Gerald Torres. 2014. "Changing the Wind: Notes toward a Demosprudence of Law and Social Movements." *Yale Law Journal* 123 (8): 2740–2804.

Gustafson, Melanie. 1997. "Partisan Women in the Progressive Era: The Struggle for Inclusion in American Political Parties." *Journal of Women's History* 9 (2): 8–30.

———. 2014. *Women in American History: Women and the Republican Party, 1854–1924*. Urbana: University of Illinois Press.

Gustafson, Melanie, Kristie Miller, and Elisabeth I. Perry, eds. 1999. *We Have Come to Stay: American Women and Political Parties 1880–1960*. Albuquerque: University of New Mexico Press.

Haley, Sarah. 2016. *No Mercy Here: Gender, Punishment, and the Making of Jim Crow Modernity*. Chapel Hill: University of North Carolina Press.

Hamilton, Alice. (1943) 1985. *Exploring the Dangerous Trades: The Autobiography of Alice Hamilton, M.D.* Boston: Northeastern University Press.

Hamington, Maurice. 2005. "Public Pragmatism: Jane Addams and Ida B. Wells on Lynching." *Journal of Speculative Philosophy* 19 (2): 167–174.

———. 2009. *The Social Philosophy of Jane Addams.* Urbana: University of Illinois Press.

Hansen, Jonathan. 2003. *The Lost Promise of Patriotism.* Chicago, IL: University of Chicago Press.

Harley, Sharon. 1982. "Beyond the Classroom: The Organizational Lives of Black Female Educators in the District of Columbia, 1890–1930." *Journal of Negro Education* 51 (3): 254–265.

Harper, Frances E. W. (1893) 1987. *Iola Leroy or Shadows Uplifted.* Boston, MA: Beacon Press.

———. 1894. "Woman's Political Future." In *World's Congress of Representative Women,* vol. 1, edited by May Wright Sewall, 433–437. Chicago, IL: Rand McNally.

Harper, Ida Husted, ed. (1922) 1969. *History of Woman Suffrage 1900–1920.* Vol. 5. New York: Arno Press.

Harrison, Cynthia. 1989. *On Account of Sex: The Politics of Women's Issues, 1945–1968.* Berkeley: University of California Press.

Hart, Vivien. 1992. "Feminism and Bureaucracy: The Minimum Wage Experiment in the District of Columbia." *Journal of American Studies* 26 (1): 1–22.

Hartsock, Nancy C. M. 1985. *Money, Sex, and Power: Toward a Feminist Historical Materialism.* Boston, MA: Northeastern University Press.

———. 1998. *The Feminist Standpoint Revisited and Other Essays.* Boulder, CO: Westview Press.

Harvey, David. 2007. *A Brief History of Neoliberalism.* New York: Oxford University Press.

Hasen, Richard L., and Leah M. Litman. 2020. "Thin and Thick Conceptions of the Nineteenth Amendment Right to Vote and Congress's Power to Enforce It." *Georgetown Law Journal* 108 (Nineteenth Amendment Edition): 27–72.

Hayden, Dolores. 1982. *The Grand Domestic Revolution: A History of Feminist Designs for American Homes, Neighborhoods, and Cities.* Cambridge, MA: MIT Press.

Heaney, Michael T. 2021. "Intersectionality at the Grassroots." *Politics, Groups, and Identities* 9 (3): 608–628.

Heater, Derek. 1990. *Citizenship: The Civic Ideal in World History.* London: Longman.

Held, David. 1995. *Democracy and the Global Order.* Stanford, CA: Stanford University Press.

———. 1998. "Democracy and Globalization." In *Re-imagining Political Community: Studies in Cosmopolitan Democracy,* edited by Daniele Archibugi, David Held, and Martin Kohler, 11–27. Stanford, CA: Stanford University Press.

Hendricks, Wanda A. 1995. "Ida B. Wells-Barnett and the Alpha Suffrage Club of Chicago." In *One Woman, One Vote: Rediscovering the Woman Suffrage Movement,* edited by Marjorie Spruill Wheeler, 263–275. Troutdale, OR: NewSage Press.

———. 1999. "African American Women as Political Constituents in Chicago, 1913–1915." In *We Have Come to Stay: American Women and Political Parties, 1880–1960,* edited by Melanie Gustafson, Kristie Miller, and Elisabeth Israels Perry, 55–64. Albuquerque: University of New Mexico Press.

Herman, Sondra. 1969. *Eleven against War: Studies in American Internationalist Thought, 1898–1921.* Stanford, CA: Hoover Institution Press.

Hernes, Helga Maria. 1987. *Welfare State and Woman Power: Essays in State Feminism.* Oslo: Norwegian University Press.

Higginbotham, Evelyn Brooks. 1993. *Righteous Discontent: The Women's Movement in the Black Baptist Church*. Cambridge, MA: Harvard University Press.

Hill, Mary A. 1980. *Charlotte Perkins Gilman: The Making of a Radical Feminist 1860–1896*. Philadelphia, PA: Temple University Press.

Hoffman, Beatrix. 2001. *The Wages of Sickness: The Politics of Health Insurance in Progressive America*. Chapel Hill: University of North Carolina Press.

Hoganson, Kristin. 1998. *Fighting for American Manhood: How Gender Politics Provoked the Spanish-American and Philippine-American Wars*. New Haven, CT: Yale University Press.

———. 2001. "'As Badly Off as the Filipinos': U.S. Women's Suffragists and the Imperial Issue at the Turn of the Twentieth Century." *Journal of Women's History* 13 (2): 9–33.

Hunton, Addie. 1904. "Negro Womanhood Defended." *Voice of the Negro* 1 (7): 280–282.

Hunton, Addie W., and Kathryn M. Johnson. (1920) 1971. *Two Colored Women with the American Expeditionary Forces*. New York: AMS Press.

Hutchings, Kimberly. 1999. "Feminist Politics and Cosmopolitan Citizenship." In *Cosmopolitan Citizenship*, edited by Kimberly Hutchings and Roland Dannreuther, 120–142. New York: St. Martin's Press.

Hutchings, Kimberly, and Roland Dannreuther, eds. 1999. *Cosmopolitan Citizenship*. New York: St. Martin's Press.

Hutchinson, Louise Daniel. 1981. *Anna J. Cooper, a Voice from the South*. Washington, D.C.: Smithsonian Institution Press.

Hyman, Colette A. 1985. "Labor Organizing and Female Institution-Building: The Chicago Women's Trade Union League, 1904–24." In *Women, Work and Protest: A Century of US Women's Labor History*, edited by Ruth Milkman, 22–41. Boston, MA: Routledge & Kegan Paul.

Hyman, Paula. 1980. "Immigrant Women and Consumer Protest: The New York City Kosher Meat Boycott of 1902." *American Jewish History* 70 (1): 91–105.

ICW (International Congress of Women). 1915. *Report of International Congress of Women, The Hague, April 28th–May 1st 1915*. Amsterdam: International Committee of Women for Permanent Peace.

Ishkanian, Armine, and Anita Pena Saavedra. 2019. "The Politics and Practices of Intersectional Prefiguration in Social Movements: The Case of Sisters Uncut." *Sociological Review* 67 (5): 985–1001.

IWSA (International Woman Suffrage Alliance). 1909. *Report of Fifth Congress, London, England*. London: Samuel Sidders.

———. 1913. *Report of the Seventh Congress, Budapest*. Manchester, UK: Percy Brothers, Hotspur Press.

Jackson, Shannon. 2001. *Lines of Activity: Performance, Historiography, Hull-House Domesticity*. Ann Arbor: University of Michigan Press.

———. 2009. "Toward a Queer Social Welfare Studies: Unsettling Jane Addams." In *Jane Addams and the Practice of Democracy*, edited by Marilyn Fischer, Carol Nackenoff, and Wendy Chmielewski, 143–162. Urbana: University of Illinois Press.

Jacobson, Matthew. 2000. *Barbarian Virtues: The United States Encounters Foreign Peoples at Home and Abroad, 1876–1917*. New York: Hill and Wang.

Jacoby, Robin Miller. 1975. "The Women's Trade Union League and American Feminism." *Feminist Studies* 3 (1/2): 126–140.

James, Joy. 1996. "The Profeminist Politics of W.E.B. Du Bois with Respects to Anna Julia Cooper and Ida B. Wells Barnett." In *W.E.B. Du Bois on Race and Culture*, edited by Bernard W. Bell, Emily Grosholz, and James B. Stewart, 141–160. New York: Routledge.

James, William. (1910) 1970. "The Moral Equivalent of War." In *War and Morality*, edited by Richard A. Wasserstrom, 4–14. Belmont, CA: Wadsworth.

Johnson, James Wilson. (1920a) 1995. "Self-Determining Haiti." In *The Selected Writings of James Weldon Johnson*, vol. 2, edited by Sondra Kathryn Wilson, 207–243. New York: Oxford University Press.

———. (1920b) 1995. "The Truth about Haiti." In *The Selected Writings of James Weldon Johnson*, vol. 2, edited by Sondra Kathryn Wilson, 244–252. New York: Oxford University Press.

———. (1924) 1995. "The Race Problem and Peace." In *The Selected Writings of James Weldon Johnson*, vol. 2, edited by Sondra Kathryn Wilson, 62–68. New York: Oxford University Press.

Jones, Martha S. 2021. *Vanguard: How Black Women Broke Barriers, Won the Vote, and Insisted on Equality for All*. New York: Basic Books.

Katz, Sherry J. 1995. "A Politics of Coalition: Socialist Women and the California Suffrage Movement, 1900–1911." In *One Woman, One Vote: Rediscovering the Woman Suffrage Movement*, edited by Marjorie Spruill Wheeler, 245–262. Troutdale, OR: NewSage Press.

Kazuko, Ono. 1978. *Chinese Women in a Century of Revolution, 1850–1950*. Edited by Joshua A. Fogel. Stanford, CA: Stanford University Press.

Keck, Margaret E., and Kathryn Sikkink. 1998. *Activists beyond Borders: Advocacy Networks in International Politics*. Ithaca, NY: Cornell University Press.

Kelley, Florence. (1894) 1998. "The Factory Laws in Illinois." In *Social Justice Feminists in the United States and Germany: A Dialogue in Documents, 1885–1933*, edited by Kathryn Kish Sklar, Anja Schuler, and Susan Strasser, 91–94. Ithaca, NY: Cornell University Press.

———. (1897) 1998. "Women Factory Inspectors in the United States." In *Social Justice Feminists in the United States and Germany: A Dialogue in Documents, 1885–1933*, edited by Kathryn Kish Sklar, Anja Schuler, and Susan Strasser, 96–104. Ithaca, NY: Cornell University Press.

———. 1898. "Hull House." *New England Magazine* 18 (5): 550–566.

———. 1911. "Minimum-Wage Boards." *American Journal of Sociology* 17 (3): 303–314.

———. 1912. "Minimum-Wage Laws." *Journal of Political Economy* 20 (10): 999–1010.

———. 1914. *Modern Industry in Relation to the Family, Health, Education, Morality*. New York: Longmans, Green.

———. 1915. "Votes and Mother's Pensions." *Woman Voter* 6 (3): 16.

Kenney, Mary. 1969. "Mary Kenny Is Invited In." In *Eighty Years at Hull-House*, edited by Allen F. Davis and Mary Lynn McCree, 34–35. Chicago, IL: Quadrangle Books.

Kessler, Carol Farley. 1995. *Charlotte Perkins Gilman: Her Progress toward Utopia with Selected Writings*. Syracuse, NY: Syracuse University Press.

Kessler-Harris, Alice. 1976. "Organizing the Unorganizable: Three Jewish Women and Their Union." *Labor History* 17 (1): 5–23.

———. 1982. *Out to Work: A History of Wage-Earning Women in the United States*. New York: Oxford University Press.

———. 1987. "Rose Schneiderman and the Limits of Women's Trade Unionism." In *Labor Leaders in America*, edited by Melvyn Dubofsky and Warren Van Tine, 160–184. Urbana: University of Illinois Press.

Key, Ellen. 1909. *Century of the Child*. New York: G. P. Putnam's Sons.

———. 1911. *Love and Marriage*. New York: G. P. Putnam's Sons.

———. 1913a. "Education for Motherhood." *Atlantic Monthly*, July 1913.

———. 1913b. "Education for Motherhood." *Atlantic Monthly*, August 1913.

———. (1914) 1970. *The Renaissance of Motherhood*. New York: Source Book Press.

———. 1916. *War, Peace, and the Future*. New York: G. P. Putnam's Sons.

Keyssar, Alexander. 2000. *The Right to Vote: The Contested History of Democracy in the United States*. New York: Basic Books.

Kimmel, Michael, and Amy Aronson. 1998. Introduction to *Women and Economics*, by Charlotte Perkins Gilman, vii–lxx. Berkeley: University of California Press.

Kingsbury, Celia Malone. 2010. *For Home and Country: World War I Propaganda on the Home Front*. Lincoln: University of Nebraska Press.

Kirkby, Diane. 1987. "'The Wage-Earning Woman and the State': The National Women's Trade Union League and Protective Labor Legislation, 1903–1923." *Labor History* 28 (1): 54–74.

Kloppenberg, James T. 1986. *Uncertain Victory: Social Democracy and Progressivism in European and American Thought, 1870–1920*. New York: Oxford University Press.

Knight, Louise W. 2005. *Citizen: Jane Addams and the Struggle for Democracy*. Chicago, IL: University of Chicago Press.

———. 2009. "Jane Addams's Theory of Cooperation." In *Jane Addams and the Practice of Democracy*, edited by Marilyn Fischer, Carol Nackenoff, and Wendy Chmielewski, 65–86. Urbana: University of Illinois Press.

Koven, Seth, and Sonya Michel. 1993. "Introduction: 'Mother Worlds.'" In *Mothers of a New World: Maternalist Politics and the Origins of Welfare States*, edited by Seth Koven and Sonya Michel, 1–42. New York: Routledge.

Kraditor, Aileen S. 1981. *The Ideas of the Woman Suffrage Movement, 1890–1920*. New York: W. W. Norton.

Kramer, Paul A. 2002. "Empires, Exceptions, and Anglo-Saxons: Race and Rule between the British and United States Empires, 1880–1910." *Journal of American History* 88 (4): 1315–1353.

Landes, Joan B. 1988. *Women and the Public Sphere in the Age of the French Revolution*. Ithaca, NY: Cornell University Press.

Lane, Ann J. 1979. Introduction to *Herland,* by Charlotte Perkins Gilman, v–xxiii. New York: Pantheon Books.

———. 1990. *To Herland and Beyond: The Life and Work of Charlotte Perkins Gilman*. New York: Pantheon Books.

Laughlin, Kathleen A., Julie Gallagher, Dorothy Sue Cobble, Eileen Boris, Premilla Nadasen, Stephanie Gilmore, and Leandra Zarnow. 2010. "Is It Time to Jump Ship? Historians Rethink the Waves Metaphor." *Feminist Formations* 22 (1): 76–135.

Lehrer, Susan. 1987. *Origins of Protective Labor Legislation for Women, 1905–1925*. Albany: State University of New York Press.

Lemlich, Clara. 1912. "The Inside of a Shirtwaist Factory: An Appeal to Women Who Wear Choice and Beautiful Clothing." *Good Housekeeping* 54 (3): 367–369.

Lemons, J. Stanley. 1973. *The Woman Citizen: Social Feminism in the 1920s*. Urbana: University of Illinois Press.

Lerner, Elinor. 1981. "Jewish Involvement in the New York City Woman Suffrage Movement." *American Jewish History* 50 (4): 442–461.

———. 1986. "Family Structure, Occupational Patterns and Support for Women's Suffrage." In *Women in Culture and Politics: A Century of Change*, edited by Judith Friedlander, Blanche Wiesen Cook, Alice Kessler-Harris, and Carroll Smith-Rosenberg, 223–236. Bloomington: Indiana University Press.

Levenstein, Harvey. 1980. "The England Kitchen and the Origins of Modern American Eating Habits." *American Quarterly* 32 (4): 369–386.

Levine, Susan. 2008. *School Lunch Politics: The Surprising History of America's Favorite Welfare Program*. Princeton, NJ: Princeton University Press.

Linklater, Andrew. 1998. "Citizenship and Sovereignty in the Post-Westphalian European State." In *Re-imagining Political Community: Studies in Cosmopolitan Democracy*, edited by Daniele Archibugi, David Held, and Martin Kohler, 113–137. Stanford, CA: Stanford University Press.

———. 1999. "Cosmopolitan Citizenship." In *Cosmopolitan Citizenship*, edited by Kimberly Hutchings and Roland Dannreuther, 35–59. New York: St. Martin's Press.

Lipschultz, Sybil. 1989. "Social Feminism and Legal Discourse: 1908–1923." *Yale Journal of Law and Feminism* 2:131–160.

———. 1996. "Hours and Wages: The Gendering of Labor Standards in America." *Journal of Women's History* 8 (1): 114–136.

Lubin, Carol Riegelman, and Anne Winslow. 1990. *Social Justice for Women: The International Labor Organization and Women*. Durham, NC: Duke University Press.

Machiavelli, Niccolò. 1979. "The Discourses." In *The Portable Machiavelli*, edited by Peter Bondanella and Mark Musa, 167–418. New York: Penguin Books.

MacMillan, Margaret. 2003. *Paris 1919*. New York: Random House.

MacMillan, Chrystal, Marie Stritt, and Maria Verone. 1913. *Woman Suffrage in Practice*. London: National Union of Women's Suffrage Societies.

Malkiel, Theresa Serber. (1910) 1990. *The Diary of a Shirtwaist Striker*. Ithaca, NY: ILR Press.

———. n.d. *Women and Freedom*. Milwaukee, WI: Co-operative Printery.

Mansbridge, Jane. 1993. "Feminism and Democratic Community." In *Democratic Community NOMOS XXXV*, edited by John W. Chapman and Ian Shapiro, 339–395. New York: New York University Press.

Marilley, Suzanne M. 1996. *Woman Suffrage and the Origins of Liberal Feminism in the United States, 1820–1920*. Cambridge, MA: Harvard University Press.

Marks, Milton B. 1901. "How the Jane Club Keeps House." *Good Housekeeping* 33 (6): 480–483.

Marshall, T. H. 1965. "Citizenship and Social Class." In *Class, Citizenship and Social Development: Essays by T. H. Marshall*, 65–122. New York: Doubleday.

Marx, Karl. 1978a. "The Civil War in France." In *The Marx-Engels Reader*, edited by Robert C. Tucker, 618–652. New York: W. W. Norton.

———. 1978b. "Marx on the History of His Opinions." In *The Marx-Engels Reader*, edited by Robert C. Tucker, 3–6. New York: W. W. Norton.

———. 1978c. "On the Realm of Necessity and the Realm of Freedom." In *The Marx-Engels Reader*, edited by Robert C. Tucker, 439–441. New York: W. W. Norton.

———. 1978d. "Wage Labor and Capital." In *The Marx-Engels Reader*, edited by Robert C. Tucker, 203–217. New York: W. W. Norton.

Materson, Lisa G. 2009a. "African American Women's Global Journeys and the Construction of Cross-Ethnic Racial Identity." *Women's Studies International Forum* 32 (1): 35–42.

———. 2009b. *For the Freedom of Her Race: Black Women and Electoral Politics in Illinois, 1877–1932*. Chapel Hill: University of North Carolina Press.

Mattis, Ann. 2010. "'Vulgar Strangers in the Home': Charlotte Perkins Gilman and Modern Servitude." *Women Studies* 39 (4): 283–303.

May, Vivian M. 2004. "Thinking from the Margins, Acting at the Intersections: Anna Julia Cooper's *A Voice from the South*." *Hypatia* 19 (2): 74–91.

McFeely, Mary Drake. 1988. *Lady Inspectors: The Campaign for a Better Workplace 1893–1921*. New York: Basil Blackwell.

McGuire, John Thomas. 2009. "From Socialism to Social Justice Feminism: Rose Schneiderman and the Quest for Urban Equity." *Journal of Urban History* 35 (7): 998–1019.

Mead, Rebecca J. 2004. *How the Vote Was Won: Woman Suffrage in the Western United States, 1868–1914*. New York: New York University Press.

Mettler, Suzanne. 1998. *Dividing Citizens: Gender and Federalism in New Deal Public Policy*. Ithaca, NY: Cornell University Press.

Michel, Sonya. 1993. "The Limits of Maternalist Policies toward American Wage-Earning Mothers during the Progressive Era." In *Mothers of a New World: Maternalist Politics and the Origins of Welfare States*, edited by Seth Koven and Sonya Michel, 277–320. New York: Routledge.

Mill, John Stuart. 1965. *Principles of Political Economy with Some of Their Applications to Social Philosophy*. In *Complete Works of John Stuart Mill*, vol. 3, edited by J. M. Robson. Toronto, ON: University of Toronto Press.

———. 1993. *On Liberty with The Subjection of Women and Chapters on Socialism*. New York: Cambridge University Press.

Miller, Sally M. 1978. "From Sweatshop Worker to Labor Leader: Theresa Malkiel A Case Study." *American Jewish History* 68 (2): 189–205.

Mink, Gwendolyn. 1995. *The Wages of Motherhood: Inequality in the Welfare State, 1917–1942*. Ithaca, NY: Cornell University Press.

Minow, Martha. 1990. *Making All the Difference: Inclusion, Exclusion, and American Law*. Ithaca, NY: Cornell University Press.

Moore, Dorothea. 1897. "A Day at Hull House." *American Journal of Sociology* 2 (5): 629–642.

Muller v. Oregon. (1908) 1969. In *Women in Industry*, by Louis D. Brandeis and Josephine Goldmark, 1–8. New York: Arno and *New York Times*.

Muncy, Robyn. 1991. *Creating a Female Dominion in American Reform 1890–1935*. New York: Oxford University Press.

Murib, Zein, and Liza Taylor. 2018. "Feminism in Coalition: Rethinking Strategies for Progressive Politics Across Differences." *New Political Science* 40 (1): 113–118.

Nackenoff, Carol. 1999. "Gendered Citizenship: Alternative Narratives of Political Incorporation in the United States, 1875–1925." In *The Liberal Tradition in America*, edited by David F. Ericson and Louisa Bertch Green, 137–167. New York: Routledge.

———. 2009. "New Politics for New Selves: Jane Addams's Legacy for Democratic Citizenship in the Twenty-First Century." In *Jane Addams and the Practice of Democracy*, edited by Marilyn Fischer, Carol Nackenoff, and Wendy Chmielewski, 119–142. Urbana: University of Illinois Press.

———. 2014. "The Private Roots of American Political Development: The Immigrants' Protective League's 'Friendly and Sympathetic Touch,' 1908–1924." *Studies in American Development* 28 (2): 129–160.

Naples, Nancy A. 1998. "Toward a Multiracial, Feminist Social-Democratic Praxis: Lessons from Grassroots Warriors in the U.S. War on Poverty." *Social Politics* 5 (3): 286–313.

Narayan, Uma. 1995. "Colonialism and Its Others: Considerations on Rights and Care Discourses." *Hypatia* 10 (2): 133–140.

Nedelsky, Jennifer. 2001. "Citizenship and Relational Feminism." In *Canadian Political Philosophy*, edited by Ronald Beiner and Wayne Norman, 131–146. Don Mills, ON: Oxford University Press.

Nelson, Keith L. 1970. "The 'Black Horror on the Rhine': Race as a Factor in Post-World War I Diplomacy." *Journal of Modern History* 42 (4): 606–627.

Neverdon-Morton, Cynthia. 1989. *Afro-American Women of the South and the Advancement of the Race, 1895–1925*. Knoxville: University of Tennessee Press.

Newman, Pauline. 1911. "From the Battlefield: Some Phases of the Cloak-Makers' Strike of Cleveland." *Life and Labor* 1 (October): 292–297.

———. 1914a. "Tenth Celebration of the Women's Trade Union League." *The Call*, May 3, 1914.

———. 1914b. "Woman Suffrage. A Means to an End." *The Call*, May 2, 1914.

———. 1917. "What Will Health Insurance Mean to the Insured?" *American Journal of Nursing* 17 (10): 942–945.

New York Times. 1915. "Mrs. Blatch Pours Out Wrath on Root." November 4, 1915.

———. 1919. "Call World Congress of Women Workers." August 18, 1919.

Nietzsche, Fredrich. 1956. *The Birth of Tragedy and The Genealogy of Morals*. New York: Doubleday.

Novkov, Julie. 2001. *Constituting Workers, Protecting Women: Gender, Law and Labor in the Progressive Era and New Deal Years*. Ann Arbor: University of Michigan Press.

Nutter, Kathleen Banks. 2000. *The Necessity of Organization: Mary Kenney O'Sullivan and Trade Unionism for Women, 1892–1912*. New York: Garland Publishing.

Oliver, Lawrence. 2015. "W.E.B. Du Bois, Charlotte Perkins Gilman, and 'A Suggestion on the Negro Problem.'" *American Literary Realism* 48 (1): 25–39.

Orleck, Annelise. 1995. *Common Sense and a Little Fire: Women and Working-Class Politics in the United States, 1900–1965*. Chapel Hill: University of North Carolina Press.

Orloff, Ann Shola. 1993. "Gender and the Social Rights of Citizenship: The Comparative Analysis of Gender Relations and Welfare States." *American Sociological Review* 58 (3): 303–328.

O'Sullivan, Mary K. 1912. "The Labor War at Lawrence." *The Survey* 28:72–74.

Ovington, Mary White. (1911) 1969. *Half a Man: The Status of the Negro in New York*. New York: Schocken Books.

———. 1914. "Socialism and the Feminist Movement." *New Review* 2 (3): 143–147.

———. 1924. "The National Association for the Advancement of Colored People." *Journal of Negro History* 9 (2): 107–116.

———. (1947) 1970. *The Walls Came Tumbling Down*. New York: Schocken Books.

Pastorello, Karen. 2008. *A Power among Them: Bessie Abramowitz Hillman and the Making of the Amalgamated Clothing Workers of America*. Urbana: University of Illinois Press.

———. 2009. "The Transfigured Few." In *Jane Addams and the Practice of Democracy*, edited by Marilyn Fischer, Carol Nackenoff, and Wendy Chmielewski, 98–118. Urbana: University of Illinois Press.

Pateman, Carole. 1970. *Participation and Democratic Theory*. Cambridge: Cambridge University Press.

———. 1989. *The Disorder of Women*. Stanford, CA: Stanford University Press.

———. 1994. "Three Questions about Womanhood Suffrage." In *Suffrage and Beyond: International Feminist Perspectives*, edited by Caroline Daley and Melanie Nolan, 331–348. New York: New York University Press.

Phillips, Anne. 1991. *Engendering Democracy*. University Park: Pennsylvania State University Press.

———. 1998. *The Politics of Presence*. New York: Oxford University Press.

Pitkin, Hanna Fenichel. 1981. "Justice: On Relating Private and Public." *Political Theory* 9 (3): 327–352.

———. 1987. *Fortune Is a Woman: Gender and Politics in the Thought of Niccolò Machia-velli*. Berkeley: University of California Press.

———. 1998. *The Attack of the Blob: Hannah Arendt's Concept of the Social*. Chicago, IL: University of Chicago Press.

Plastas, Melinda. 2011. *A Band of Noble Women: Racial Politics in the Women's Peace Movement*. Syracuse, NY: Syracuse University Press.

Plato. 1967. *The Republic of Plato*. Translated with introduction and notes by Francis MacDonald Cornford. New York: Oxford University Press.

Pleck, Elizabeth H. 1990. "A Mother's Wages: Income Earning among Married Italian and Black Women, 1896–1911." In *Black Women in American History: The 20th Century*, vol. 4, edited by Darlene Clark Hine, 367–392. Brooklyn, NY: Carlson Publishing.

Polacheck, Hilda Satt. 1989. *I Came a Stranger: The Story of a Hull-House Girl*. Urbana: University of Illinois Press.

Polanyi, Karl. 1957. *The Great Transformation*. Boston, MA: Beacon Press.

Prinz, Jesse. 2016. "Genealogies of Morals: Nietzsche's Method Compared." *Journal of Nietzsche Studies* 47 (2): 180–201.

Quataert, Jean H. 1983. "A Source Analysis in German Women's History: Factory Inspectors' Reports and the Shaping of Working-Class Lives, 1878–1914." *Central European History* 16 (2): 99–121.

———. 1993. "Woman's Work and the Early Welfare State in Germany: Legislators, Bureaucrats, and Clients before the First World War." In *Mothers of a New World: Maternalist Politics and the Origins of Welfare States*, edited by Seth Koven and Sonya Michel, 159–187. New York: Routledge.

Rabaka, Reiland. 2003. "W.E.B. Du Bois and 'The Damnation of Women': An Essay on Africana Anti-Sexist Critical Social Theory." *Journal of African American Studies* 7 (2): 37–60.

Rawls, John. 1971. *A Theory of Justice*. Cambridge, MA: Belknap Press of Harvard University Press.

Renda, Mary A. 2001. *Taking Haiti: Military Occupation and the Culture of U.S. Imperialism*. Chapel Hill: University of North Carolina Press.

Residents of Hull-House. 1895. *Hull-House Maps and Papers*. New York: Thomas Y. Crowell.

Richards, Ellen H. 1904. *The Rumford Kitchen Leaflets*. Boston, MA: Whitcomb and Barrows.

Rief, Michelle. 2004. "Thinking Locally, Acting Globally: The International Agenda of African American Clubwomen, 1880–1940." *Journal of African American History* 89 (3): 203–222.

Ritter, Gretchen. 2000. "Gender and Citizenship after the Nineteenth Amendment." *Polity* 32 (3): 345–375.

———. 2006. *The Constitution as Social Design*. Stanford, CA: Stanford University Press.

Robertson, Campbell, and Robert Gebeloff. 2020. "When It Comes to 'Essential,' It's a Woman's World Today." *New York Times*, April 19, 2020.

Rodgers, Daniel. T. 1998. *Atlantic Crossings: Social Politics in a Progressive Age*. Cambridge, MA: Belknap Press of Harvard University Press.

Roth, Benita. 2004. *Separate Roads to Feminism: Black, Chicana, and White Feminist Movements in America's Second Wave*. New York: Cambridge University Press.

Roth, Silke. 2021. "Intersectionality and Coalitions in Social Movement Research—A Survey and Outlook." *Social Compass* 15 (7): 1–16.

Rouse, Jacqueline Anne. 1989. *Lugenia Burns Hope: Black Southern Reformer*. Athens: University of Georgia Press.

———. 1991. "Atlanta's African-American Women's Attack on Segregation, 1900–1920." In *Gender, Class, Race, and Reform in the Progressive Era*, edited by Noralee Frankel and Nancy S. Dye, 10–23. Lexington: University Press of Kentucky.

Rousseau, Jean-Jacques. 1992. *The Social Contract and Discourses*. London: J. M. Dent.

Rupp, Leila J. 1997. *Worlds of Women: The Making of an International Women's Movement*. Princeton, NJ: Princeton University Press.

Salem, Dorothy. 1990. *To Better Our World: Black Women in Organized Reform, 1890–1920*. Brooklyn, NY: Carlson Publishing.

Sarvasy, Wendy. 1985. "A Reconsideration of the Development and Structure of John Stuart Mill's Socialism." *Western Political Science Quarterly* 38 (2): 312–333.

———. 1988. "Reagan and Low-Income Mothers: A Feminist Recasting of the Debate." In *Remaking the Welfare State: Retrenchment and Social Policy in America and Europe*, edited by Michael K. Brown, 253–276. Philadelphia, PA: Temple University Press.

———. 1991. "Subjection of Women, The." In *Women's Studies Encyclopedia*, vol. 3, edited by Helen Tierney, 429–431. New York: Greenwood Press.

———. 1992. "Beyond the Difference versus Equality Policy Debate: Postsuffrage Feminism, Citizenship, and the Quest for a Feminist Welfare State." *Signs* 17 (2): 329–362.

———. 1997. "Social Citizenship from a Feminist Perspective." *Hypatia* 12 (4): 54–73.

———. 2000. "Why We Need a Theory of Social Democracy." Paper delivered at the Annual Meeting of the American Political Science Association, Washington, D.C., August 31–September 3, 2000.

———. 2009. "A Global 'Common Table': Jane Addams's Theory of Democratic Cosmopolitanism and World Social Citizenship." In *Jane Addams and the Practice of Democracy*, edited by Marilyn Fischer, Carol Nackenoff, and Wendy Chmielewski, 183–202. Urbana: University of Illinois Press.

———. 2010. "Engendering Democracy by Socializing It: Jane Addams's Contribution to Feminist Political Theorizing." In *Feminist Interpretations of Jane Addams*, edited by Maurice Hamington, 293–310. University Park: Pennsylvania State University Press.

———. 2015. "Militarized Occupations: Evolution of Women's International League for Peace and Freedom's 1920s Intersectional Conversation." *New Political Science* 37 (4): 476–493.

———. 2022. "Dobbs and Religious Liberty." *New Political Science* 44 (3): 489–492.

———. forthcoming. "Essential Citizenship: Theorizing Practices of Women Agrifood Workers." In *Palgrave Handbook on Gender and Citizenship: Intersectional and Transnational Perspectives*, edited by Birte Siim and Pauline Stoltz. New York: Palgrave MacMillan.

Sarvasy, Wendy, and Patrizia Longo. 2004. "The Globalization of Care: Kant's World Citizenship and Filipina Migrant Domestic Workers." *International Feminist Journal of Politics* 6 (3): 392–415.

Sarvasy, Wendy, and Judith Van Allen. 1984. "Fighting the Feminization of Poverty: Socialist-Feminist Analysis and Strategy." *Review of Radical Political Economics* 16 (4): 89–110.

Schechter, Patricia A. 2001. *Ida B. Wells-Barnett and American Reform, 1880–1930*. Chapel Hill: University of North Carolina Press.

Scheiber, Jane Lang, and Harry N. Scheiber. 1969. "The Wilson Administration and the Wartime Mobilization of Black Americans, 1917–18." *Labor History* 10 (3): 433–458.

Schepps, Mollie. (1912) 1976. "Senators vs Working Women." In *American Working Women*, compiled and edited by Rosalyn Baxandall, Linda Gordon, and Susan Reverby, 216–218. New York: Vintage Books.

Schneider, Elizabeth M. 2000. *Battered Women and Feminist Lawmaking*. New Haven, CT: Yale University Press.

Schneiderman, Rose. 1905. "A Cap Maker's Story: Rose Schneiderman." *The Independent* 58 (2943): 935–938.

———. (1912) 1998. "Miss Rose Schneiderman, Cap Maker, Replies to New York Senator on Delicacy and Charm of Women." New York: Wage Earners' Suffrage League. Microfilm, History of Women, reel 951, #9222. Document 28 in Thomas Dublin and Kerri Harney, "How Did Immigrant Textile Workers Struggle to Achieve an American Standard of Living: The 1912 Strike in Lawrence, Massachusetts," *Women and Social Movements in the United States* 2:1–5.

———. 1913. "The White Goods Workers of New York: Their Struggle for Human Conditions." *Life and Labor* 3 (May): 132–136.

Schneiderman, Rose, with Lucy Goldthwaite. 1967. *All for One*. New York: Paul S. Eriksson.

Schofield, Ann. 1997. *"To Do and to Be": Portraits of Four Women Activists, 1893–1986*. Boston, MA: Northeastern University Press.

Schott, Linda K. 1997. *Reconstructing Women's Thoughts: The Women's International League for Peace and Freedom Before World War II*. Stanford, CA: Stanford University Press.

Seigfried, Charlene Haddock. 1996. *Pragmatism and Feminism: Reweaving the Social Fabric*. Chicago, IL: University of Chicago Press.

———. 2002a. Introduction to *Democracy and Social Ethics*, by Jane Addams, ix–xxxviii. Urbana: University of Illinois Press.

———. 2002b. Introduction to *The Long Road of Woman's Memory*, by Jane Addams, ix–xxxiv. Urbana: University of Illinois Press.

Shklar, Judith. 1991. *American Citizenship: The Quest for Community*. Cambridge, MA: Harvard University Press.

Siegel, Reva B. 2002. "She the People: The Nineteenth Amendment, Sex Equality, Federalism, and the Family." *Harvard Law Review* 115 (4): 947–1046.

———. 2019. "The Nineteenth Amendment and the Democratization of the Family." *Yale Law Journal Forum* 129:450–495.

Silliman, Jael, Marlene Gerber Fried, Loretta Ross, and Elena R. Gutierrez. 2004. *Undivided Rights: Women of Color Organize for Reproductive Justice*. Cambridge, MA: South End Press.

Sklar, Kathryn Kish. 1985. "Hull House in the 1890s: A Community of Women Reformers." *Signs* 10 (4): 658–677.

———. 1990. "Who Funded Hull House." In *Lady Bountiful Revisited: Women, Philanthropy, and Power*, edited by Kathleen D. McCarthy, 94–115. New Brunswick, NJ: Rutgers University Press.

———. 1993. "The Historical Foundations of Women's Power in the Creation of the American Welfare State, 1830–1930." In *Mothers of a New World: Maternalist Politics and the Origins of Welfare States*, edited by Seth Koven and Sonya Michel, 43–93. New York: Routledge.

———. 1995. *Florence Kelley and the Nation's Work*. New Haven, CT: Yale University Press.

Sklar, Kathryn Kish, Anja Schuler, and Susan Strasser, eds. 1998. *Social Justice Feminists in the United States and Germany: A Dialogue in Documents, 1885–1933*. Ithaca, NY: Cornell University Press.

Skocpol, Theda. 1992. *Protecting Soldiers and Mothers: The Political Origins of Social Policy in the United States*. Cambridge, MA: Belnap Press of Harvard University Press.

Smooth, Wendy. 2006. "Intersectionality in Electoral Politics: A Mess Worth Making." *Politics and Gender* 2 (3): 400–414.

Sparks, Holloway. 1997. "Dissident Citizenship: Democratic Theory, Political Courage, and Activist Women." *Hypatia* 12 (4): 74–110.

Steinson, Barbara J. 1980. "'The Mother Half of Humanity': American Women in the Peace and Preparedness Movements in W.W.I." In *Women, War, and Revolution*, edited by Carol R. Berkin and Clara M. Lovett, 259–281. New York: Holmes & Meier Publishing.

Stevens, Alzina Parsons. 1899. "Life in a Social Settlement—Hull-House, Chicago." *Self Culture* 9 (1): 42–51.

Stivers, Camilla. 2009. "A Civic Machinery for Democratic Expression: Jane Addams on Public Administration." In *Jane Addams and the Practice of Democracy*, edited by Marilyn Fischer, Carol Nackenoff, and Wendy Chmielewski, 87–97. Urbana: University of Illinois Press.

Stoler, Ann Laura. 2002. *Carnal Knowledge and Imperial Power: Race and the Intimate in Colonial Rule*. Berkeley: University of California Press.

Swartz, Marvin. 1971. *The Union of Democratic Control in British Politics during the First World War*. Oxford, UK: Clarendon Press.

Tax, Meredith. 1980. *The Rising of the Women: Feminist Solidarity and Class Conflict, 1880–1917*. New York: Monthly Review Press.

Taylor, Liza. 2022. *Feminism in Coalition: Thinking with US Women of Color Feminism*. Durham, NC: Duke University Press.

Terborg-Penn, Rosalyn. 1983. "Discontented Black Feminists: Prelude and Postscript to the Passage of the Nineteenth Amendment." In *Decades of Discontent: The Women's Movement 1920–1940*, edited by Lois Scharf and Joan M. Jensen, 261–278. Westport, CT: Greenwood Press.

———. 1998. *African American Women in the Struggle for the Vote, 1850–1920*. Bloomington: Indiana University Press.

Terrell, Mary Church. 1902. "What Role Is the Educated Negro Woman to Play in the Uplifting of Her Race?" In *Twentieth Century Negro Literature*, edited by D. W. Culp, 172–176. Naperville, IL: JL Nichols.

———. 1904. "Lynching from a Negro's Point of View." *North American Review* 178 (571): 853–868.

———. 1905. "Purity and the Negro." *The Light* 41:19–25.

———. 1907. "Peonage in the United States: The Convict Lease System and the Chain Gangs." *Nineteenth Century* 62 (August): 306–322.

———. (1912) 1995. "The Justice of Woman Suffrage." In *Votes for Women: The Woman Suffrage Movement in Tennessee, the South, and the Nation*, edited by Marjorie Spruill Wheeler, 152–155. Knoxville: University of Tennessee Press.

———. 1915. "Woman Suffrage and the 15th Amendment." *The Crisis* 10 (4): 14.

———. 1940. *A Colored Woman in a White World*. New York: Arno Press.

Thompson, Janna. 1998. "Community Identity and World Citizenship." In *Re-imagining Political Community: Studies in Cosmopolitan Democracy*, edited by Daniele Archibugi, David Held, and Martin Kohler, 179–197. Stanford, CA: Stanford University Press.

Thompson, Mildred I. 1990. *Ida B. Wells-Barnett: An Exploration of An American Black Woman, 1893–1930*. Brooklyn, NY: Carlson Publishing.

Tronto, Joan C. 1987. "Beyond Gender Difference to a Theory of Care." *Signs* 12 (4): 644–663.

———. 1993. *Moral Boundaries: A Political Argument for an Ethic of Care*. New York: Routledge.

———. 2013. *Caring Democracy: Markets, Equality, and Justice*. New York: New York University Press.

Unger, Roberto Mangabeira. 1983. *The Critical Legal Studies Movement*. Cambridge, MA: Harvard University Press.

Van Wienen, Mark W. 2003. "A Rose by Any Other Name: Charlotte Perkins Stetson (Gilman) and the Case for American Reform Socialism." *American Quarterly* 55 (4): 603–634.

Vapnek, Lara. 2009. *Breadwinners: Working Women and Economic Independence, 1865–1920*. Urbana: University of Illinois Press.

———. 2014. "The 1919 International Congress of Working Women: Transnational Debates on the 'Woman Worker.'" *Journal of Women's History* 26 (1): 160–184.

Veit, Helen Zoe. 2013. *Modern Food, Moral Food: Self-Control, Science, and the Rise of Modern American Eating in the Early Twentieth Century*. Chapel Hill: University of North Carolina Press.

Vellacott, Jo. 1993. "A Place for Pacifism and Transnationalism in Feminist Theory: The Early Work of the Women's International League for Peace and Freedom." *Women's History Review* 2 (1): 23–56.

Vetter, Lisa Pace. 2017. *The Political Thought of America's Founding Feminists*. New York: New York University Press.

Wald, Lillian D. 1915a. *The House on Henry Street*. New York: Henry Holt.

———. 1915b. "Suffragists Got Their Best Support from the Foreign Born." *New York Times*, November 6, 1915.

Walker-McWilliams, Marcia. 2016. *Reverend Addie Wyatt: Faith and the Fight for Labor, Gender, and Racial Equality*. Urbana: University of Illinois Press.

Walzer, Michael. 1990. "The Communitarian Critique of Liberalism." *Political Theory* 18 (1): 6–23.

Washington, Mary Helen. 1988. Introduction to *A Voice from the South*, by Anna Julia Cooper, xxvii–liv. New York: Oxford University Press.

Weiler, N. Sue. 1979–1980. "Walkout: The Chicago Men's Garment Workers' Strike, 1910–1911." *Chicago History* 8 (4): 238–249.

Weinbaum, Alys Eve. 2001. "Writing Feminist Genealogy: Charlotte Perkins Gilman, Racial Nationalism, and the Reproduction of Maternalist Feminism." *Feminist Studies* 27 (2): 271–302.

Wells-Barnett, Ida B. (1895) 1991. *A Red Record*. In *Selected Works of Ida B. Wells-Barnett*, compiled with an introduction by Trudier Harris, 138–252. New York: Oxford University Press.

———. (1900) 1990. "The Negro's Case in Equity." In *Ida B. Wells-Barnett: An Exploratory Study of an American Black Woman, 1893–1930*, by Mildred I. Thompson, 245–248. Brooklyn, NY: Carlson Publishing.

———. (1901) 1977. "Lynching and the Excuse for It." In *Lynching and Rape: An Exchange of Views*, edited by Bettina Aptheker, 28–34. New York: American Institute for Marxist Studies.

——. (1909) 1990. "Lynching: Our National Crime." In *Ida B. Wells-Barnett: An Exploratory Study of an American Black Woman, 1893–1930*, by Mildred I. Thompson, 261–265. Brooklyn, NY: Carlson Publishing.

——. (1910) 1990. "How Enfranchisement Stops Lynching." In *Ida B. Wells-Barnett: An Exploratory Study of an American Black Woman, 1893–1930*, by Mildred I. Thompson, 267–276. Brooklyn, NY: Carlson Publishing.

Wheeler, Marjorie Spruill, 1995. "The Woman Suffrage Movement in the Inhospitable South." In *Votes for Women: The Woman Suffrage Movement in Tennessee, the South, and the Nation*, edited by Marjorie Spruill Wheeler, 25–52. Knoxville: University of Tennessee Press.

Whitaker, Lois Duke, ed. 2008. *Voting the Gender Gap.* Urbana: University of Illinois Press.

White, Deborah Gray. 1993. "The Cost of Club Work, the Price of Black Feminism." In *Visible Women: New Essays on American Activism*, edited by Nancy A. Hewitt and Suzanne Lebsock, 247–269. Urbana: University of Illinois Press.

White, Julie Anne. 2000. *Democracy, Justice, and the Welfare State: Reconstructing Public Care.* University Park: Pennsylvania State University Press.

Whittick, Arnold. 1979. *Woman into Citizen.* Santa Barbara, CA: ABC-Clio.

Wikander, Ulla. 1995. "Some 'Kept the Flag of Feminist Demands Waving': Debates at International Congresses on Protecting Women Workers." In *Protecting Women: Labor Legislation in Europe, the United States, and Australia, 1880–1920*, edited by Ulla Wikander, Alice Kessler-Harris, and Jane Lewis, 29–62. Urbana: University of Illinois Press.

Williams, Fannie Barrier. 1914. "Colored Women of Chicago." *Southern Workman* 43: 564–566.

Williams, Patricia. 1987. "Alchemical Notes: Reconstructing Ideals from Deconstructed Rights." *Harvard Civil Rights-Civil Liberties Law Review* 22 (2): 401–433.

WILPF (Women's International League for Peace and Freedom). 1919. *Report of the International Congress of Women, May 12–17, Zurich.* Geneva, Switzerland: WILPF.

——. 1921. *Report of the Third International Congress of Women, July 10–17, Vienna.* Geneva, Switzerland: WILPF.

——. 1924. *Report of the Fourth Congress of the Women's International League for Peace and Freedom, May 1–7, Washington.* Geneva, Switzerland: WILPF.

"With the First International Congress of Working Women." 1919. *Life and Labor* 9 (12): 308–315.

Wolcott, Victoria W. 1997. "'Bible, Bath, and Broom': Nannie Helen Burroughs's National Training School and African-American Racial Uplift." *Journal of Women's History* 9 (1): 88–110.

Wolin, Sheldon. 1989. *The Presence of the Past: Essays on the State and the Constitution.* Baltimore, MD: Johns Hopkins University Press.

——. 1996. "Fugitive Democracy." In *Democracy and Difference: Contesting the Boundaries of the Political*, edited by Seyla Benhabib, 67–94. Princeton, NJ: Princeton University Press.

Wollstonecraft, Mary. (1792) 1992. *A Vindication of the Rights of Woman.* New York: Penguin Books.

Young, Iris Marion. 1997. *Intersecting Voices: Dilemmas of Gender, Political Philosophy, and Policy.* Princeton, NJ: Princeton University Press.

Yuval-Davis, Nira. 1999. "The 'Multi-Layered Citizen': Citizenship in the Age of 'Globalization.'" *International Feminist Journal of Politics* 1 (1): 119–136.

Zeiger, Susan. 1996. "She Didn't Raise Her Boy to Be a Slacker: Motherhood, Conscription, and the Culture of the First World War." *Feminist Studies* 22 (1): 7–39.

Zimmerman, Elaine. 1984. "California Hearings on the Feminization of Poverty." *Signs* 10 (2): 394–410.

Zimmerman, Joan G. 1991. "The Jurisprudence of Equality: The Women's Minimum Wage, the First Equal Rights Amendment, and *Adkins v. Children's Hospital*, 1905–1923." *Journal of American History* 78 (1): 188–225.

Index

Wendy Sarvasy is Lecturer Emerita of Political Science at California State University, East Bay, and an intersectional activist.

www.ingramcontent.com/pod-product-compliance
Lightning Source LLC
Chambersburg PA
CBHW031403270326
41929CB00010BA/1303